# A FOREST IN THE DESERT
## THE LIFE OF SAINT JOHN THE SHORT

A GRAPHIC NOVEL BY CREATIVE ORTHODOX

A FOREST IN THE DESERT: THE LIFE OF SAINT JOHN THE SHORT

ISBN 978-0-9959930-2-0 (PAPERBACK)
ISBN 978-0-9959930-3-7 (E-BOOK)



WWW.CREATIVEORTHODOX.COM

In memory of my grandfather, Moheb, who taught me all about the Church Fathers.

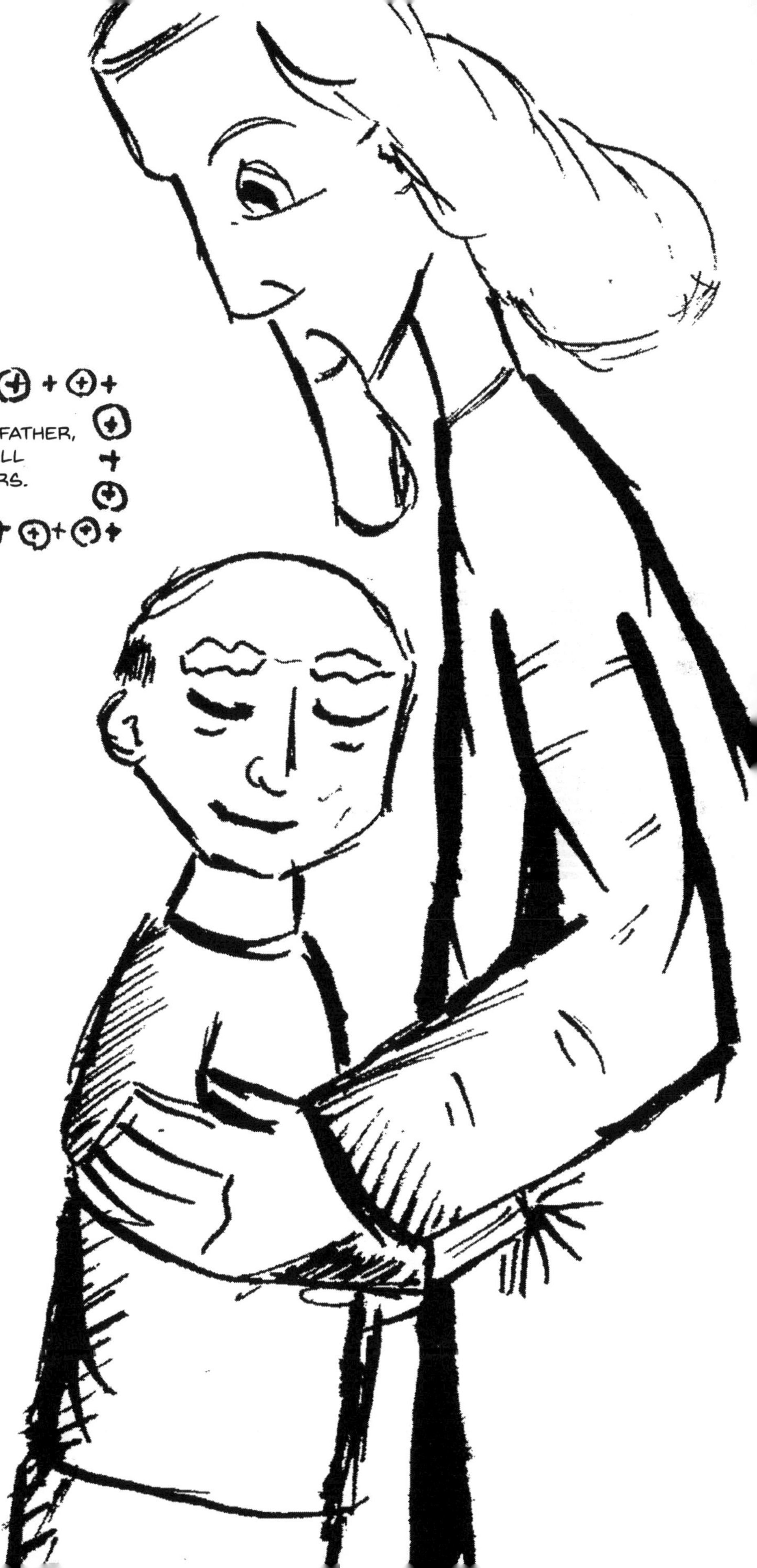

# PREFACE

### WHAT I'M ABOUT TO TELL YOU MAY OR MAY NOT HAVE HAPPENED, BUT IT IS THE TRUTH.

THE SAINTS OFFER TO US THEIR FRIENDSHIP WHEN WE NEED IT MOST. I STARTED THIS GRAPHIC NOVEL IN 2013 WHEN I WAS LET GO AND WASN'T ABLE TO FIND A JOB FOR ABOUT A YEAR AFTERWARDS. I NEEDED AN OUTLET TO STRUCTURE MY DAYS AND FEEL PRODUCTIVE. SKETCHES TURNED TO PANELS AND PANELS TURNED TO PAGES, A JOURNEY THAT OCCUPIED MUCH OF THE LAST 6 YEARS OF MY LIFE.

ILLUSTRATING THE LIFE OF A FOURTH CENTURY SAINT IS NO EASY TASK. THE BULK OF WHAT WE KNOW OF SAINT JOHN'S LIFE COMES FROM THE WRITING OF A 9TH CENTURY BISHOP BY THE NAME ZACHARIAS FROM A CITY CALLED SAKHA. I SPENT A GREAT DEAL OF TIME UNDERSTANDING THE CHARACTER OF ABBA JOHN: ASKING WHY HE MADE THE CHOICES HE MADE AND HOW HE FELT WHEN MAKING THEM. THIS RISKS THE HISTORICAL ACCURACY OF THE BOOK, BUT SEEING THAT I'M RETELLING THE RETELLING OF A 6TH CENTURY RETELLING OF A 4TH CENTURY LIFE, HISTORICAL ACCURACY MAY NOT BE A REALISTIC PRIORITY. I HAVE A HUNCH THAT IT WASN'T BISHOP ZACHARIAS' PRIORITY EITHER.

I REACHED OUT TO PROF. TIM VIVIAN, A RENOWNED PROFESSOR OF RELIGIOUS STUDIES, TO ASK ABOUT SOME OF THE HARDER-TO-BELIEVE PARTS IN ABBA JOHN'S LIFE. PROF. TIM HAD TRANSLATED THE WORK INTO ENGLISH ALONG WITH DEACON SEVERUS MIKHAIL. PROFESSOR TIM REPLIED WITH THE QUOTE ABOVE: "WHAT I AM ABOUT TO TELL YOU MAY OR MAY NOT HAVE HAPPENED, BUT IT IS THE TRUTH".

WHEN IT COMES TO THE LIVES OF THE FATHERS, IT'S NOT THE EXACT DATES OR DETAILS THAT BENEFIT US MOST, IT'S THEIR CHARACTER AND VIRTUES THAT GIVE US AN EXAMPLE TO FOLLOW IN OUR OWN LIVES.

SAINT JOHN THE SHORT IS A PRIME EXAMPLE IN OBEDIENCE, AS HE'S WIDELY KNOWN HIGH AND LOW FOR THE TREE OF OBEDIENCE. TO ME, HOWEVER, THAT'S NOT EVEN HIS DEFINING CHARACTERISTIC! IT'S HIS COMPASSION AND LOVE FOR CHRIST AND GOD'S CREATION THAT NEVER CEASE TO AMAZE ME. HE SERVED HIS COMMUNITY, LOVED EVERYONE UNCONDITIONALLY AND TOOK GOOD CARE OF HIS SPIRITUAL CHILDREN.

ALL I CAN HOPE FOR IS THAT THIS GRAPHIC NOVEL TELLS THE LIFE OF A HOLY MAN AND GIVES US AN EXAMPLE TO LEAD SIMILARLY VIRTUE-FILLED CHRIST-CENTERED LIVES.

MICHAEL ELGAMAL
FEBRUARY 28, 2018

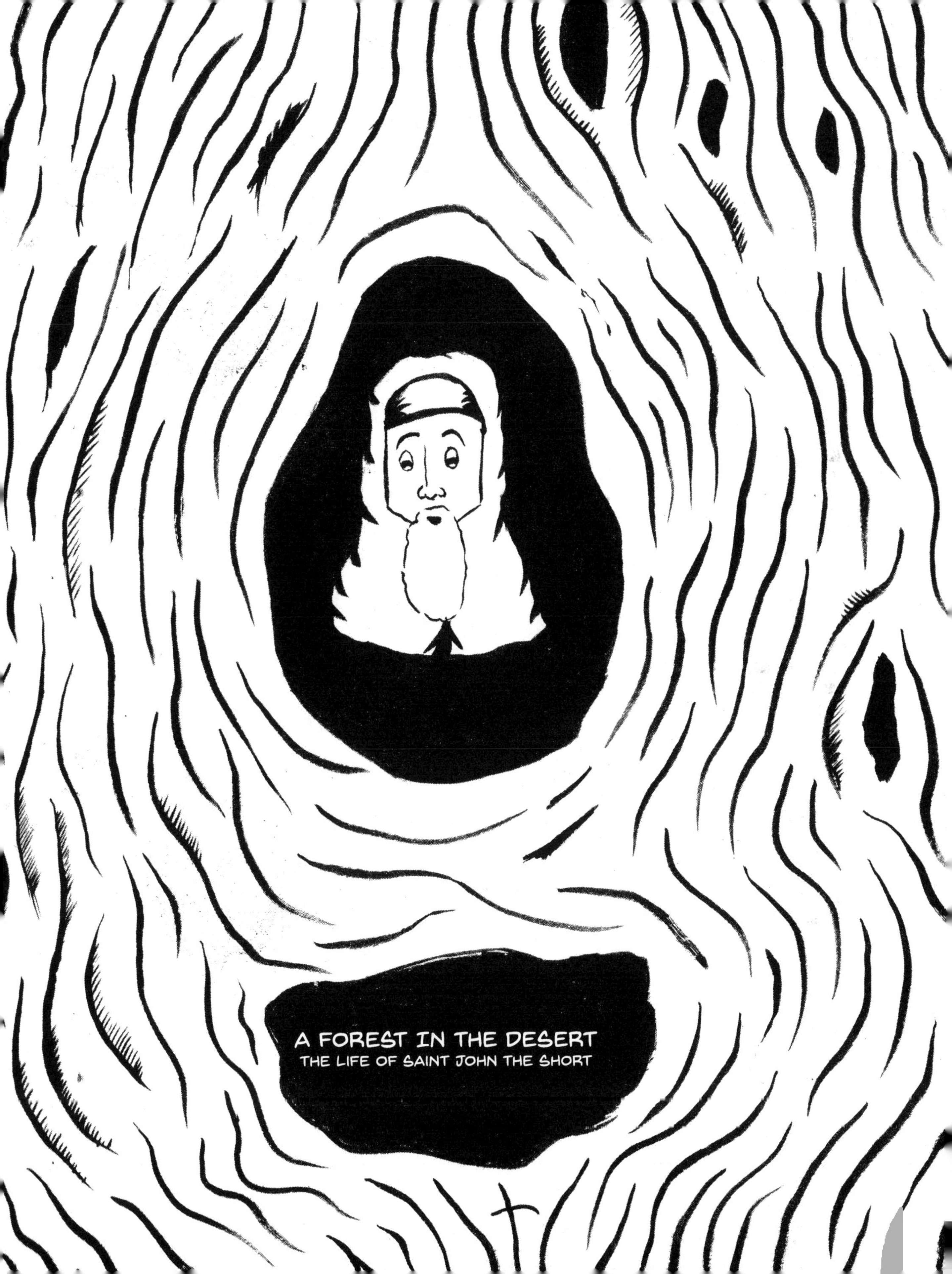
A FOREST IN THE DESERT
THE LIFE OF SAINT JOHN THE SHORT

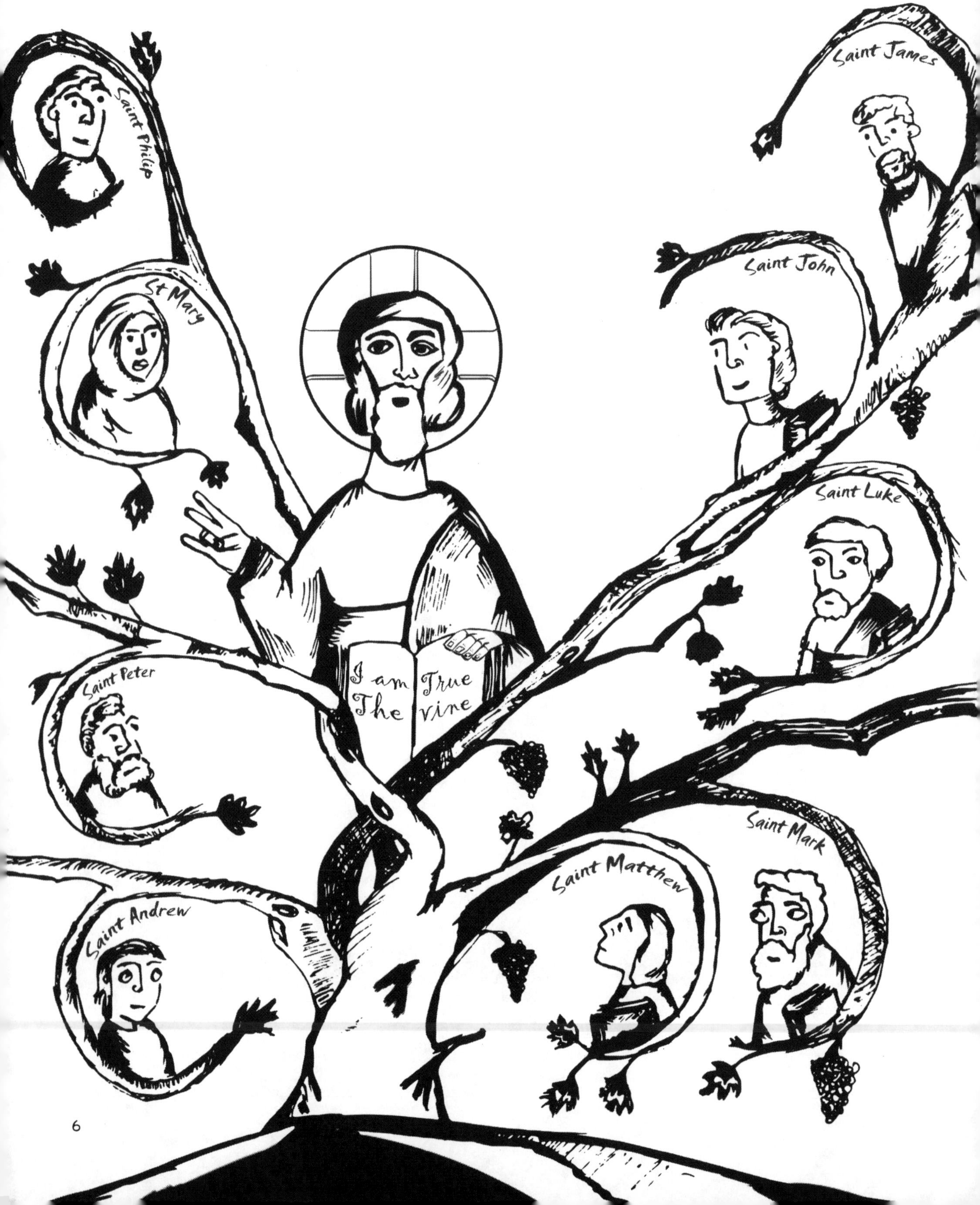
Saint Philip
Saint James
St Mary
Saint John
Saint Luke
I am The True vine
Saint Peter
Saint Mark
Saint Matthew
Saint Andrew

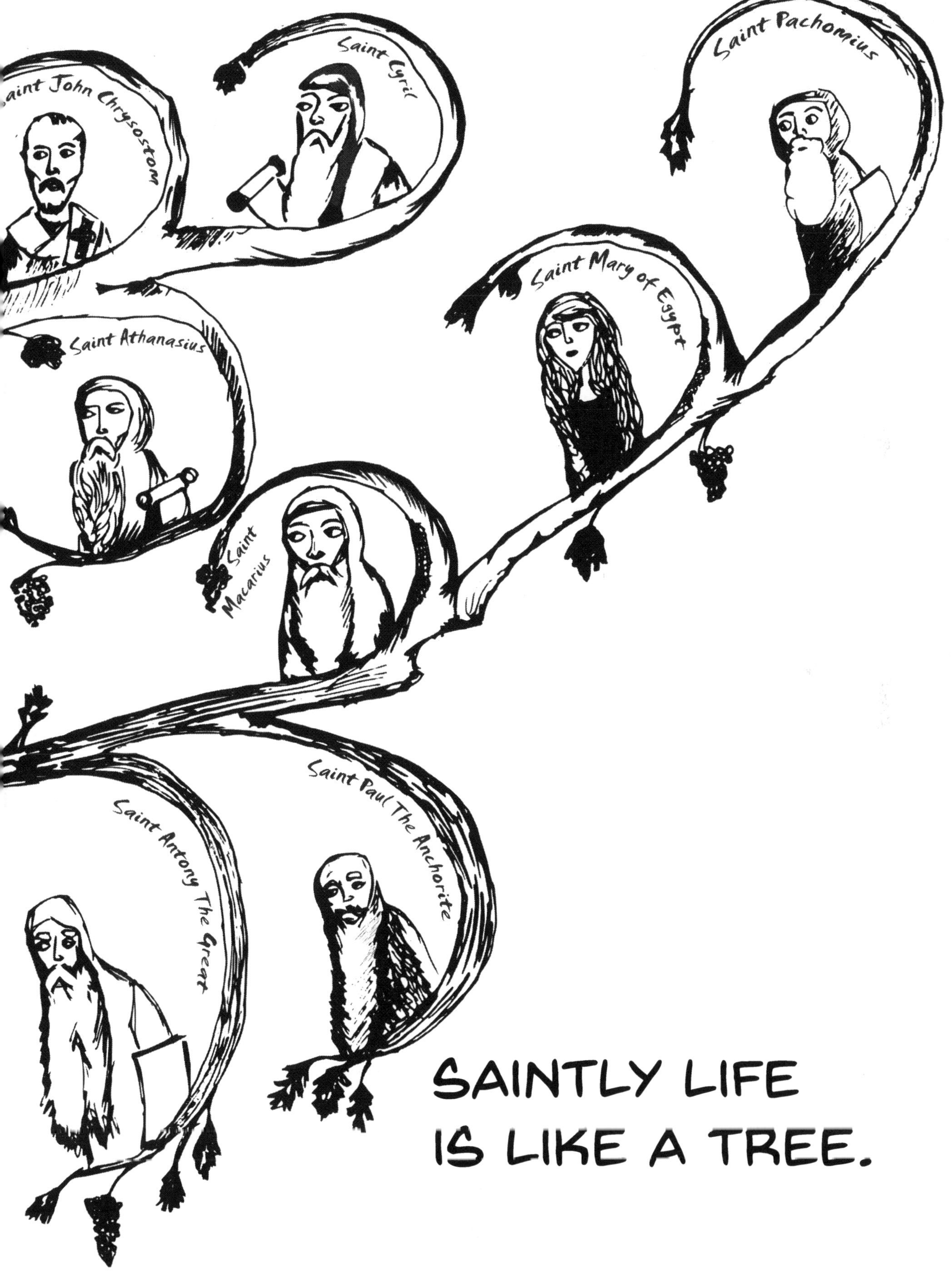
Saint John Chrysostom
Saint Cyril
Saint Pachomius
Saint Mary of Egypt
Saint Athanasius
Saint Macarius
Saint Paul The Anchorite
Saint Antony The Great

SAINTLY LIFE
IS LIKE A TREE.

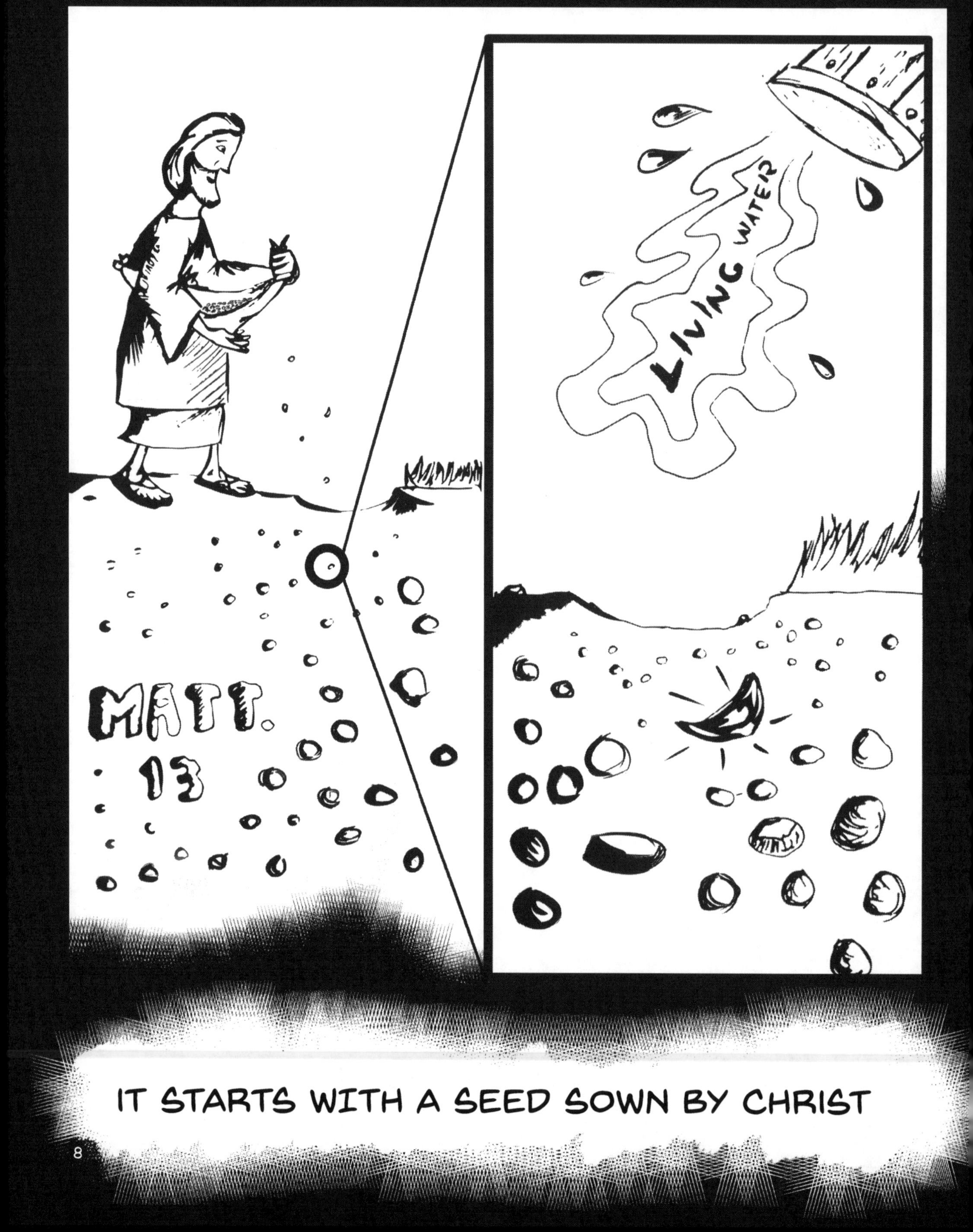
MATT. 13
LIVING WATER

IT STARTS WITH A SEED SOWN BY CHRIST

THAT GROWS THROUGH ATTENTION & CARE TO SPIRITUAL LIFE

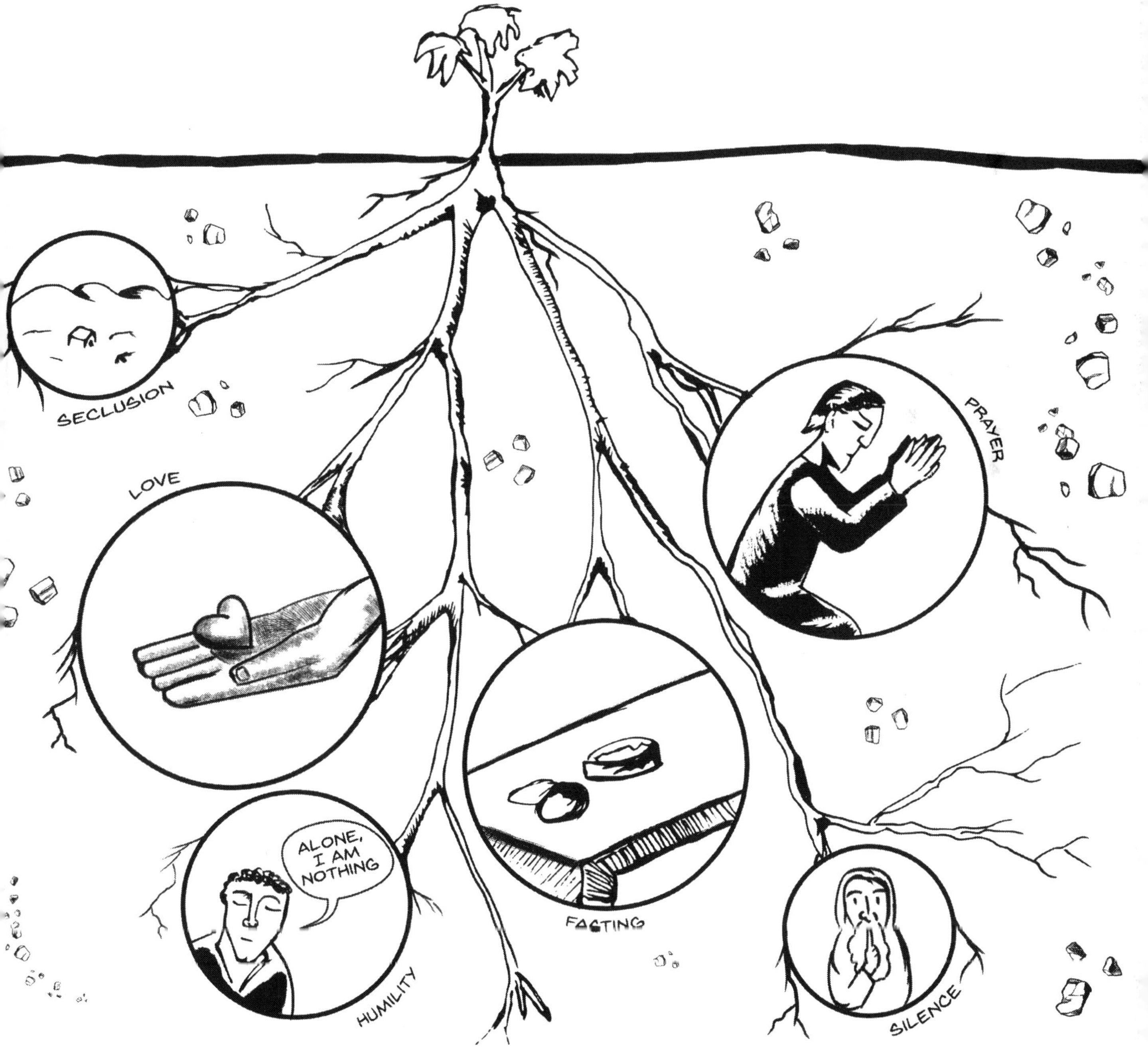

SECLUSION
LOVE
PRAYER
ALONE, I AM NOTHING
FASTING
HUMILITY
SILENCE

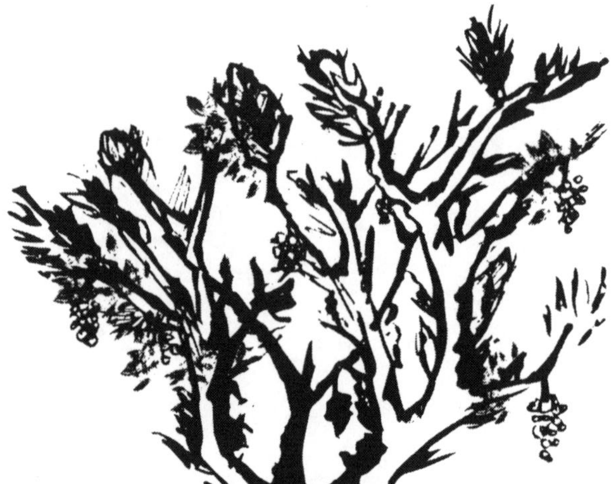

INTO A FRUITFUL TREE.
NOT ONLY STRENGTHENING
AND NURTURING ITSELF,
BUT ALSO GIVING RISE TO
COUNTLESS OTHER TREES.

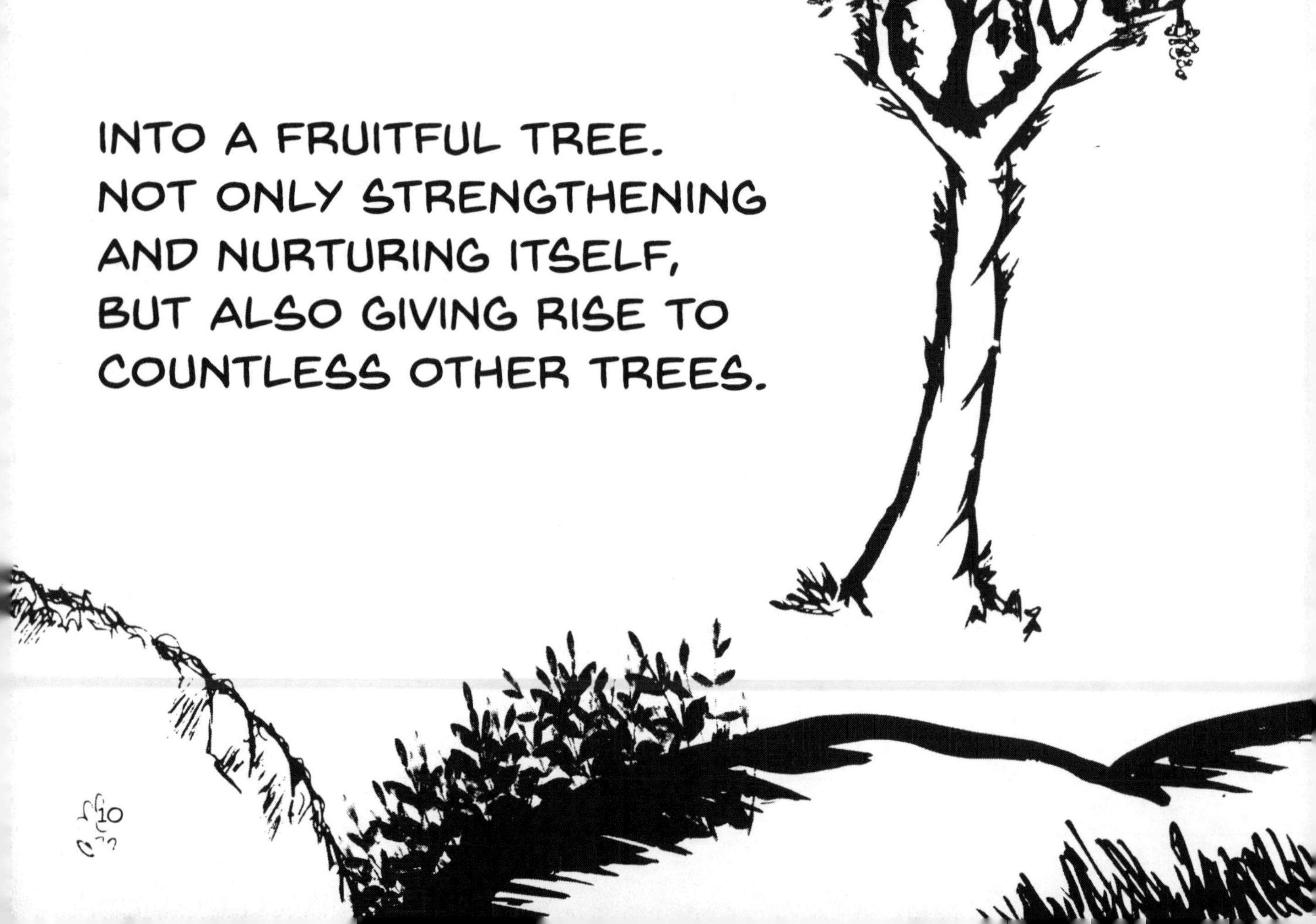

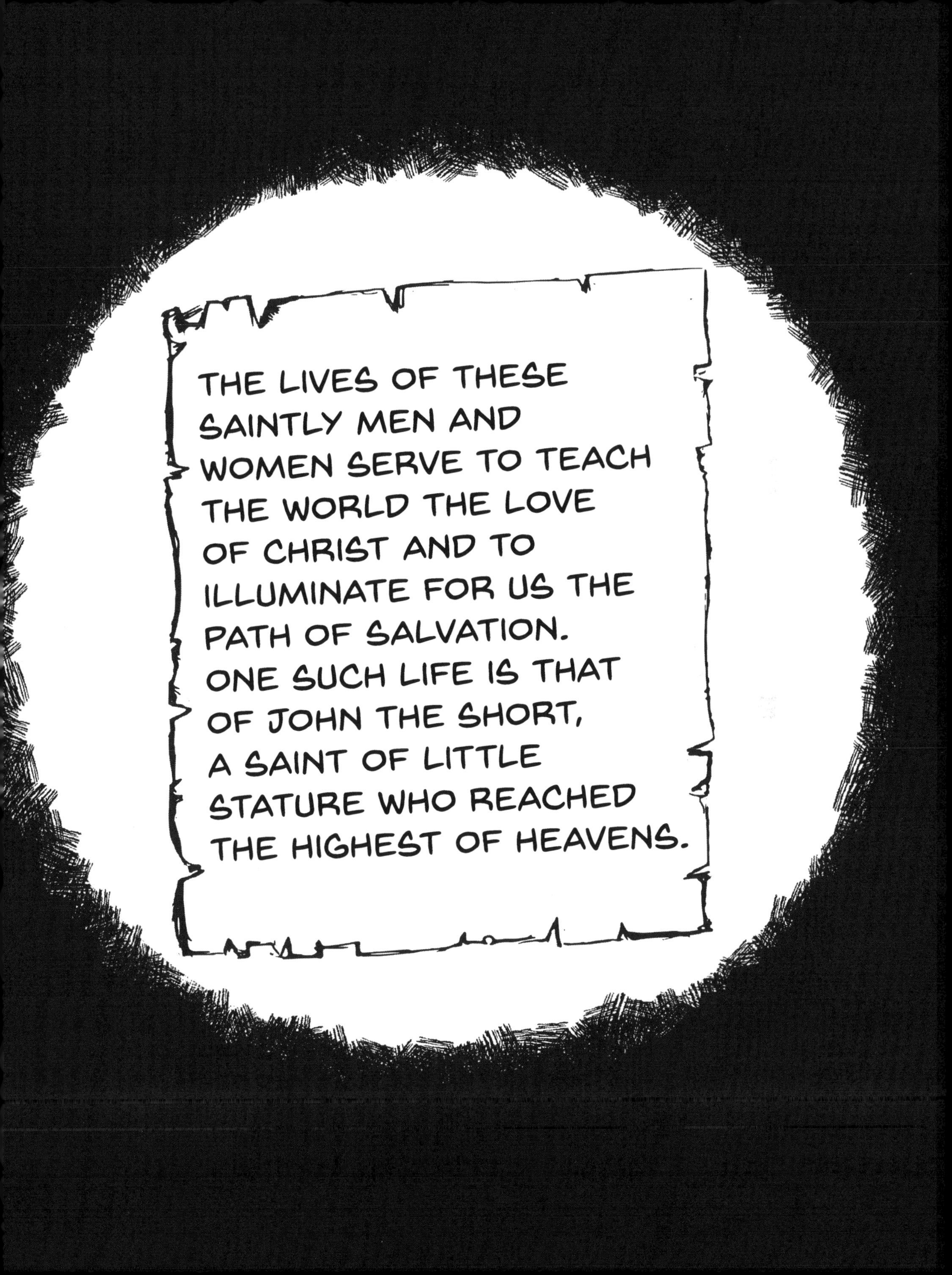
THE LIVES OF THESE SAINTLY MEN AND WOMEN SERVE TO TEACH THE WORLD THE LOVE OF CHRIST AND TO ILLUMINATE FOR US THE PATH OF SALVATION. ONE SUCH LIFE IS THAT OF JOHN THE SHORT, A SAINT OF LITTLE STATURE WHO REACHED THE HIGHEST OF HEAVENS.

# Chapter One
## Seeds

THIS IS THE STORY OF SAINT JOHN.  JOHN WHO?

THE BAPTIST?

THE EVANGELIST?

THIS IS THE STORY
OF JOHN THE SHORT.

NOT AS IN SHORT-TEMPERED, BECAUSE HE WAS
LONG-SUFFERING. MAYBE SHORT SIGHTED,  BUT
THAT WAS JUST SHORT-TERM. JOHN WAS
JUST SHORT.

HE WAS BORN IN THE YEAR 339 IN A CITY IN UPPER
EGYPT CALLED "EL BAHNASA."

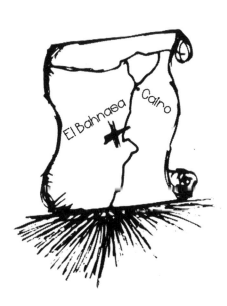

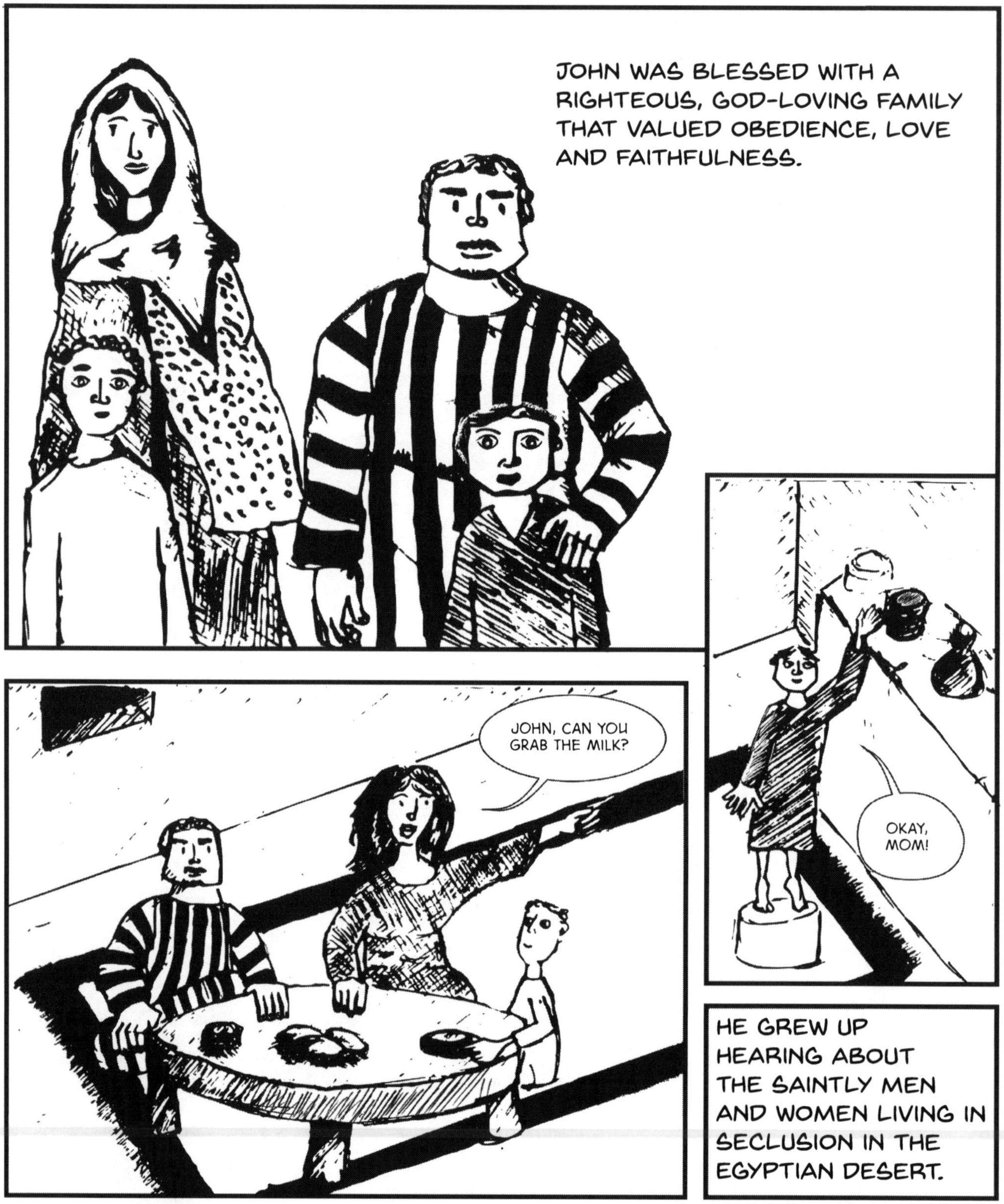
JOHN WAS BLESSED WITH A RIGHTEOUS, GOD-LOVING FAMILY THAT VALUED OBEDIENCE, LOVE AND FAITHFULNESS.
JOHN, CAN YOU GRAB THE MILK?
OKAY, MOM!
HE GREW UP HEARING ABOUT THE SAINTLY MEN AND WOMEN LIVING IN SECLUSION IN THE EGYPTIAN DESERT.

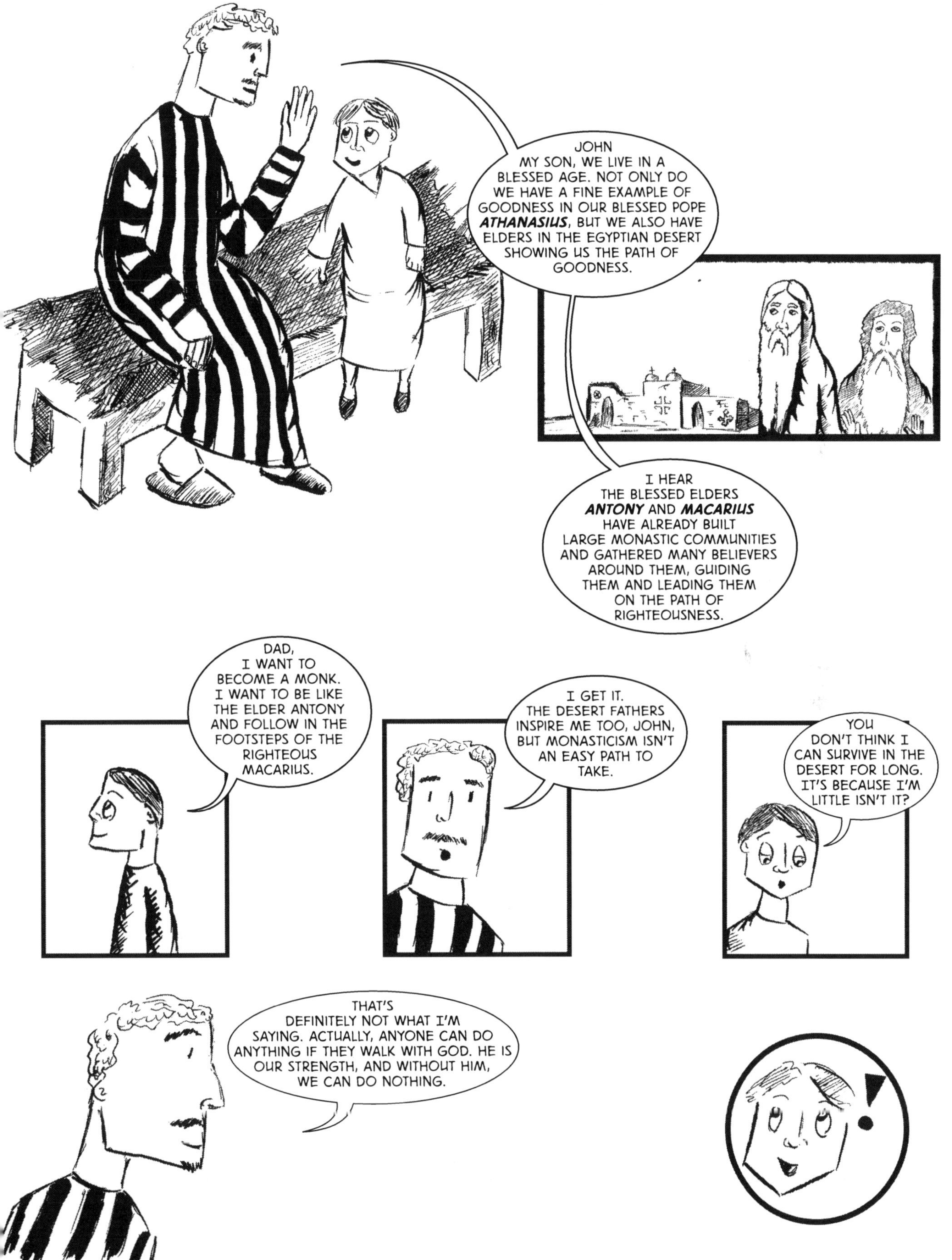
JOHN
MY SON, WE LIVE IN A BLESSED AGE. NOT ONLY DO WE HAVE A FINE EXAMPLE OF GOODNESS IN OUR BLESSED POPE ***ATHANASIUS***, BUT WE ALSO HAVE ELDERS IN THE EGYPTIAN DESERT SHOWING US THE PATH OF GOODNESS.
I HEAR THE BLESSED ELDERS ***ANTONY*** AND ***MACARIUS*** HAVE ALREADY BUILT LARGE MONASTIC COMMUNITIES AND GATHERED MANY BELIEVERS AROUND THEM, GUIDING THEM AND LEADING THEM ON THE PATH OF RIGHTEOUSNESS.
DAD, I WANT TO BECOME A MONK. I WANT TO BE LIKE THE ELDER ANTONY AND FOLLOW IN THE FOOTSTEPS OF THE RIGHTEOUS MACARIUS.
I GET IT. THE DESERT FATHERS INSPIRE ME TOO, JOHN, BUT MONASTICISM ISN'T AN EASY PATH TO TAKE.
YOU DON'T THINK I CAN SURVIVE IN THE DESERT FOR LONG. IT'S BECAUSE I'M LITTLE ISN'T IT?
THAT'S DEFINITELY NOT WHAT I'M SAYING. ACTUALLY, ANYONE CAN DO ANYTHING IF THEY WALK WITH GOD. HE IS OUR STRENGTH, AND WITHOUT HIM, WE CAN DO NOTHING.
!

IN EXCITEMENT, JOHN PACKED A BIBLE, A PRAYER BOOK AND VERY LITTLE FOOD. WITH A SET-GOAL AND A DRIVEN HEART, JOHN MADE HIS WAY TO THE DOOR - READY TO LEAVE HIS PAST LIFE AND FOLLOW IN THE FOOTSTEPS OF THE DESERT FATHERS.

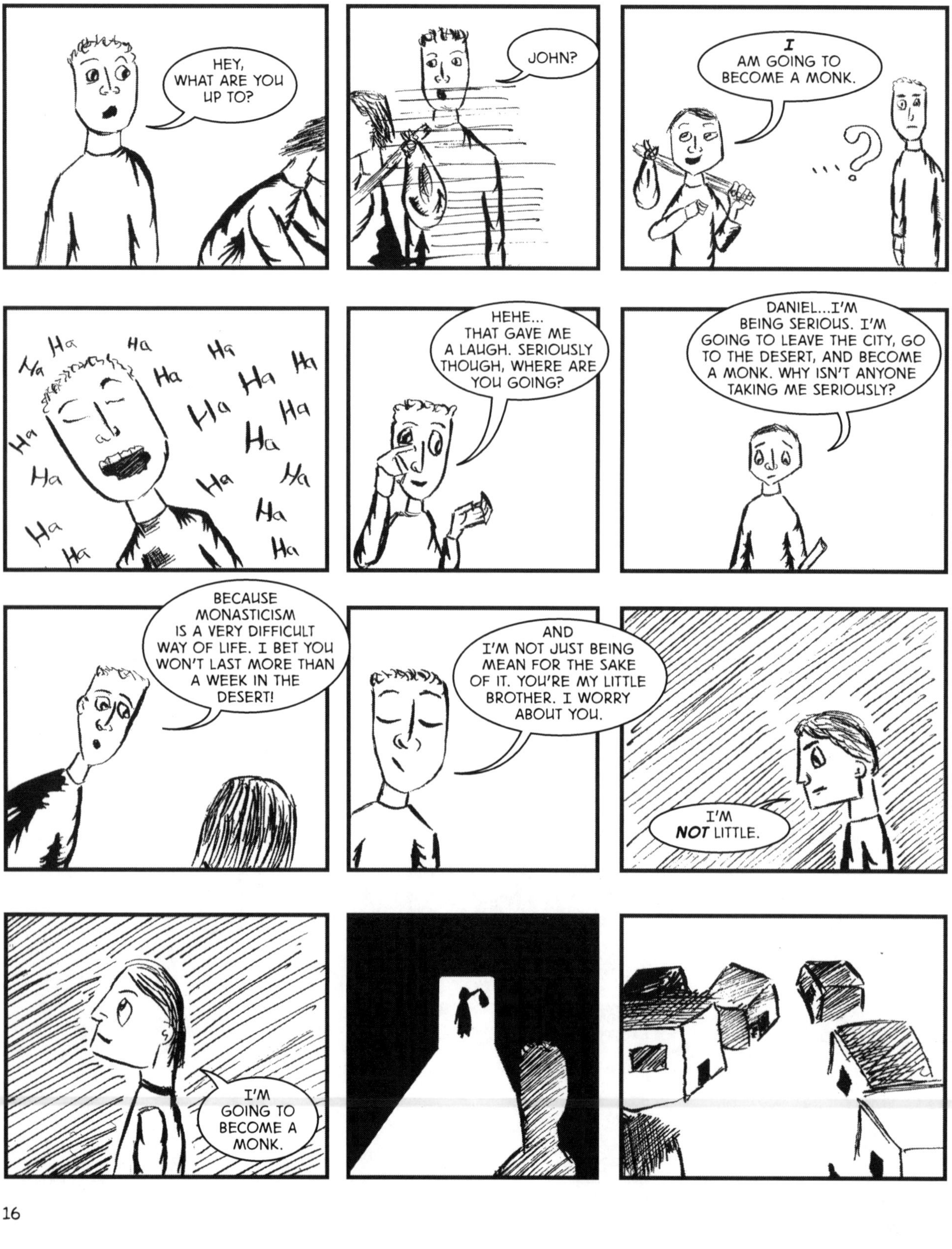
HEY, WHAT ARE YOU UP TO?
JOHN?
I AM GOING TO BECOME A MONK.
...?
Ha Ha Ha Ha Ha Ha Ha Ha Ha Ha Ha Ha Ha Ha Ha Ha Ha Ha
HEHE... THAT GAVE ME A LAUGH. SERIOUSLY THOUGH, WHERE ARE YOU GOING?
DANIEL...I'M BEING SERIOUS. I'M GOING TO LEAVE THE CITY, GO TO THE DESERT, AND BECOME A MONK. WHY ISN'T ANYONE TAKING ME SERIOUSLY?
BECAUSE MONASTICISM IS A VERY DIFFICULT WAY OF LIFE. I BET YOU WON'T LAST MORE THAN A WEEK IN THE DESERT!
AND I'M NOT JUST BEING MEAN FOR THE SAKE OF IT. YOU'RE MY LITTLE BROTHER. I WORRY ABOUT YOU.
I'M **NOT** LITTLE.
I'M GOING TO BECOME A MONK.

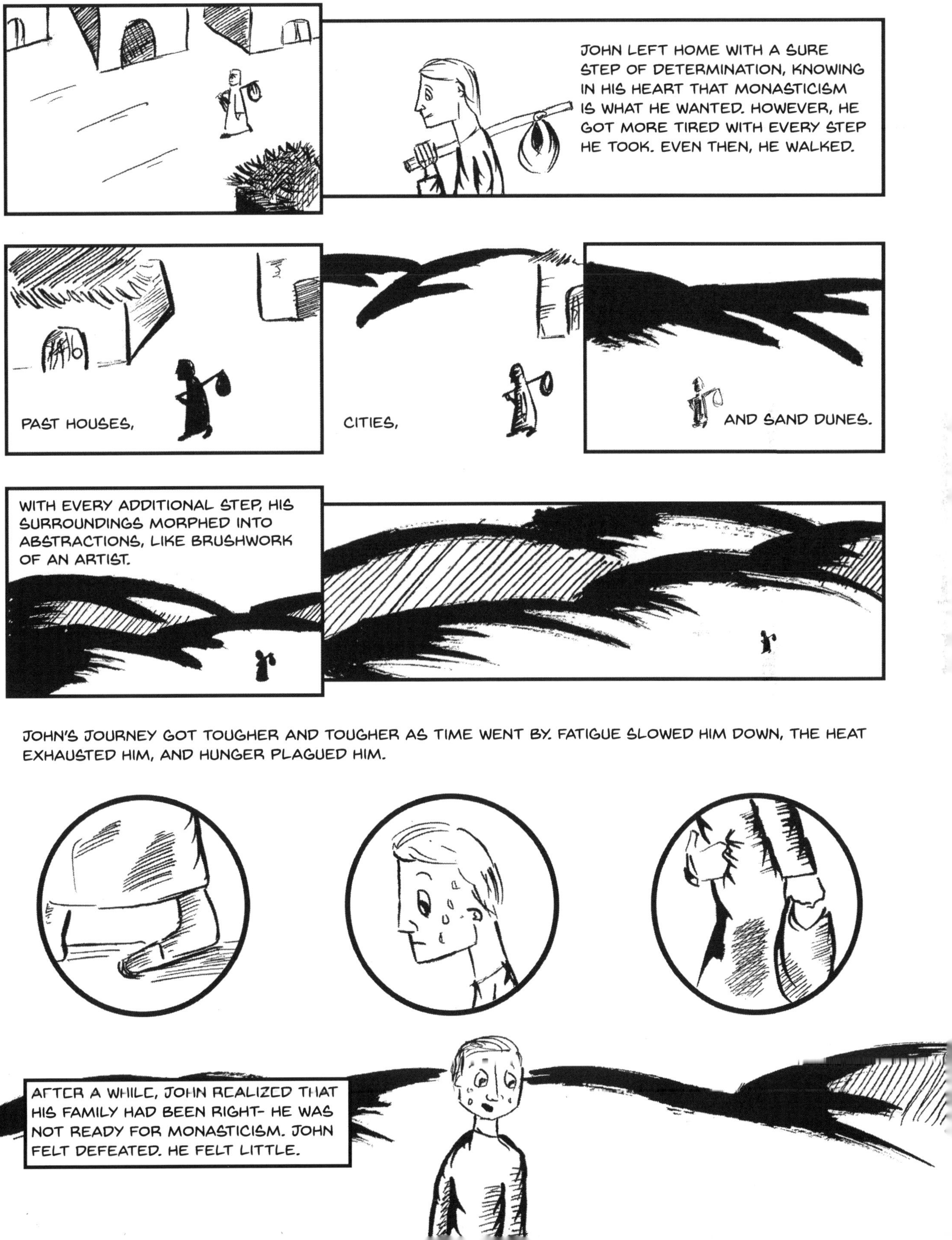
JOHN LEFT HOME WITH A SURE STEP OF DETERMINATION, KNOWING IN HIS HEART THAT MONASTICISM IS WHAT HE WANTED. HOWEVER, HE GOT MORE TIRED WITH EVERY STEP HE TOOK. EVEN THEN, HE WALKED.
PAST HOUSES,
CITIES,
AND SAND DUNES.
WITH EVERY ADDITIONAL STEP, HIS SURROUNDINGS MORPHED INTO ABSTRACTIONS, LIKE BRUSHWORK OF AN ARTIST.
JOHN'S JOURNEY GOT TOUGHER AND TOUGHER AS TIME WENT BY. FATIGUE SLOWED HIM DOWN, THE HEAT EXHAUSTED HIM, AND HUNGER PLAGUED HIM.
AFTER A WHILE, JOHN REALIZED THAT HIS FAMILY HAD BEEN RIGHT- HE WAS NOT READY FOR MONASTICISM. JOHN FELT DEFEATED. HE FELT LITTLE.

HE DIDN'T KNOW IF IT JUST WASN'T GOD'S WILL FOR HIM TO BE A MONK OR A SIMPLE LACK OF TRAINING. ONE THING HE DID KNOW WAS THAT HE WOULDN'T SURVIVE IN THE DESERT MUCH LONGER. WITH A HEAVY HEART, JOHN TURNED BACK AND HEADED HOME.

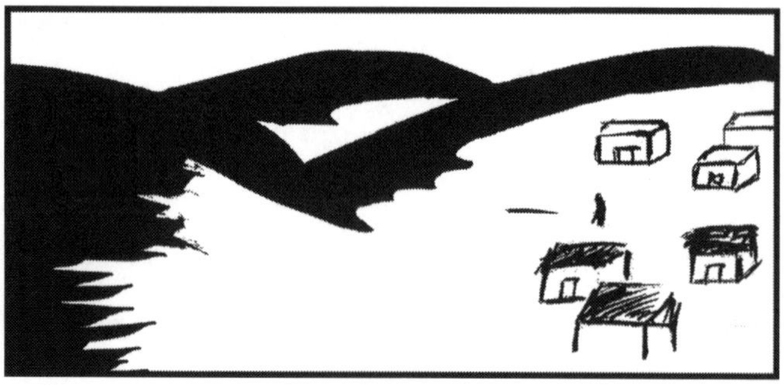

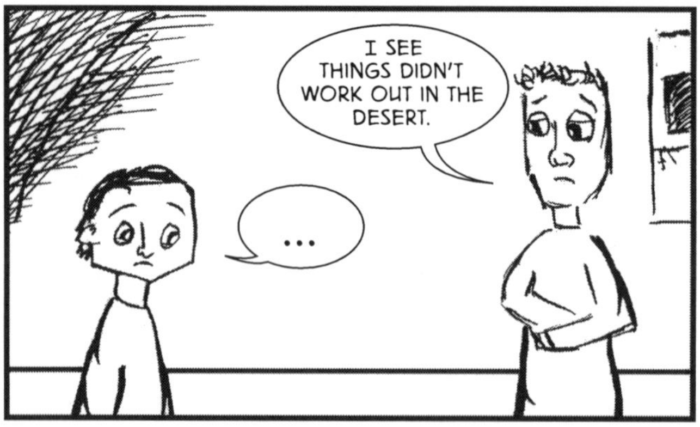
I SEE THINGS DIDN'T WORK OUT IN THE DESERT.
...

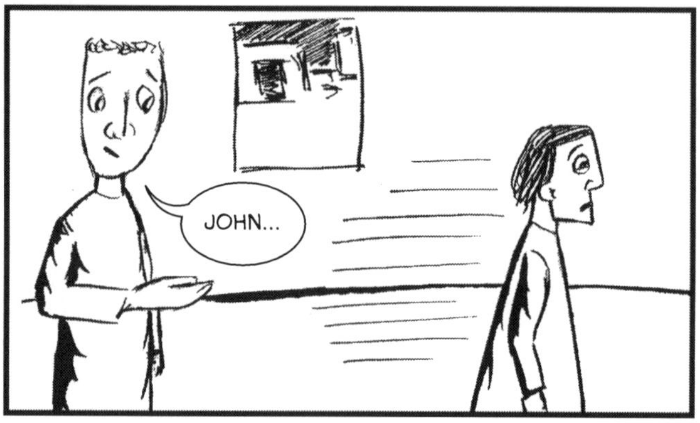
JOHN...

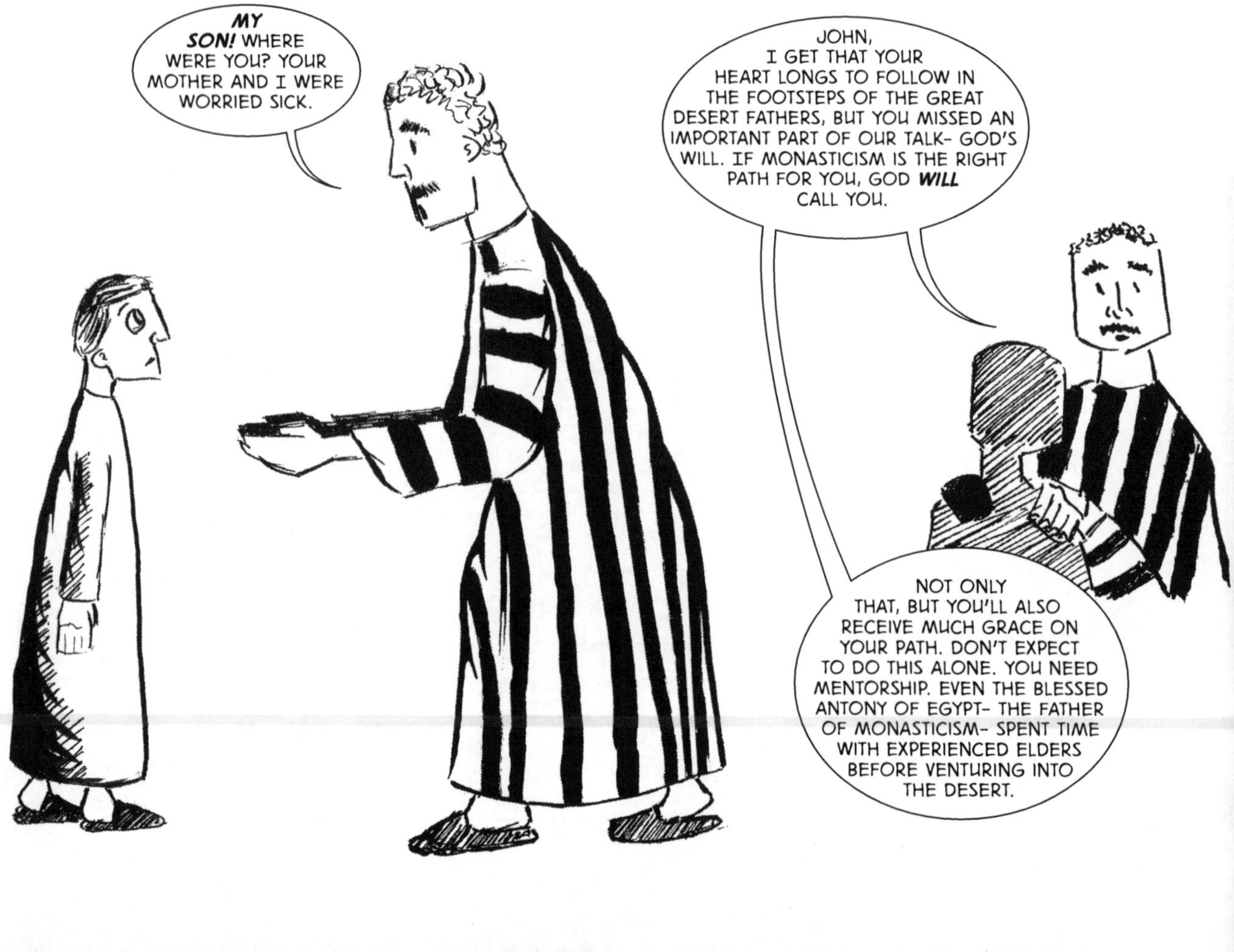
**MY SON!** WHERE WERE YOU? YOUR MOTHER AND I WERE WORRIED SICK.
JOHN, I GET THAT YOUR HEART LONGS TO FOLLOW IN THE FOOTSTEPS OF THE GREAT DESERT FATHERS, BUT YOU MISSED AN IMPORTANT PART OF OUR TALK- GOD'S WILL. IF MONASTICISM IS THE RIGHT PATH FOR YOU, GOD ***WILL*** CALL YOU.
NOT ONLY THAT, BUT YOU'LL ALSO RECEIVE MUCH GRACE ON YOUR PATH. DON'T EXPECT TO DO THIS ALONE. YOU NEED MENTORSHIP. EVEN THE BLESSED ANTONY OF EGYPT- THE FATHER OF MONASTICISM- SPENT TIME WITH EXPERIENCED ELDERS BEFORE VENTURING INTO THE DESERT.

AFTER SPEAKING WITH HIS FATHER, JOHN QUIETLY RETREATED INTO HIS ROOM AND BEGAN TO PRAY.

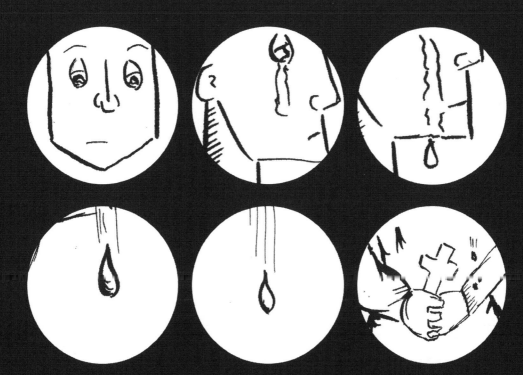

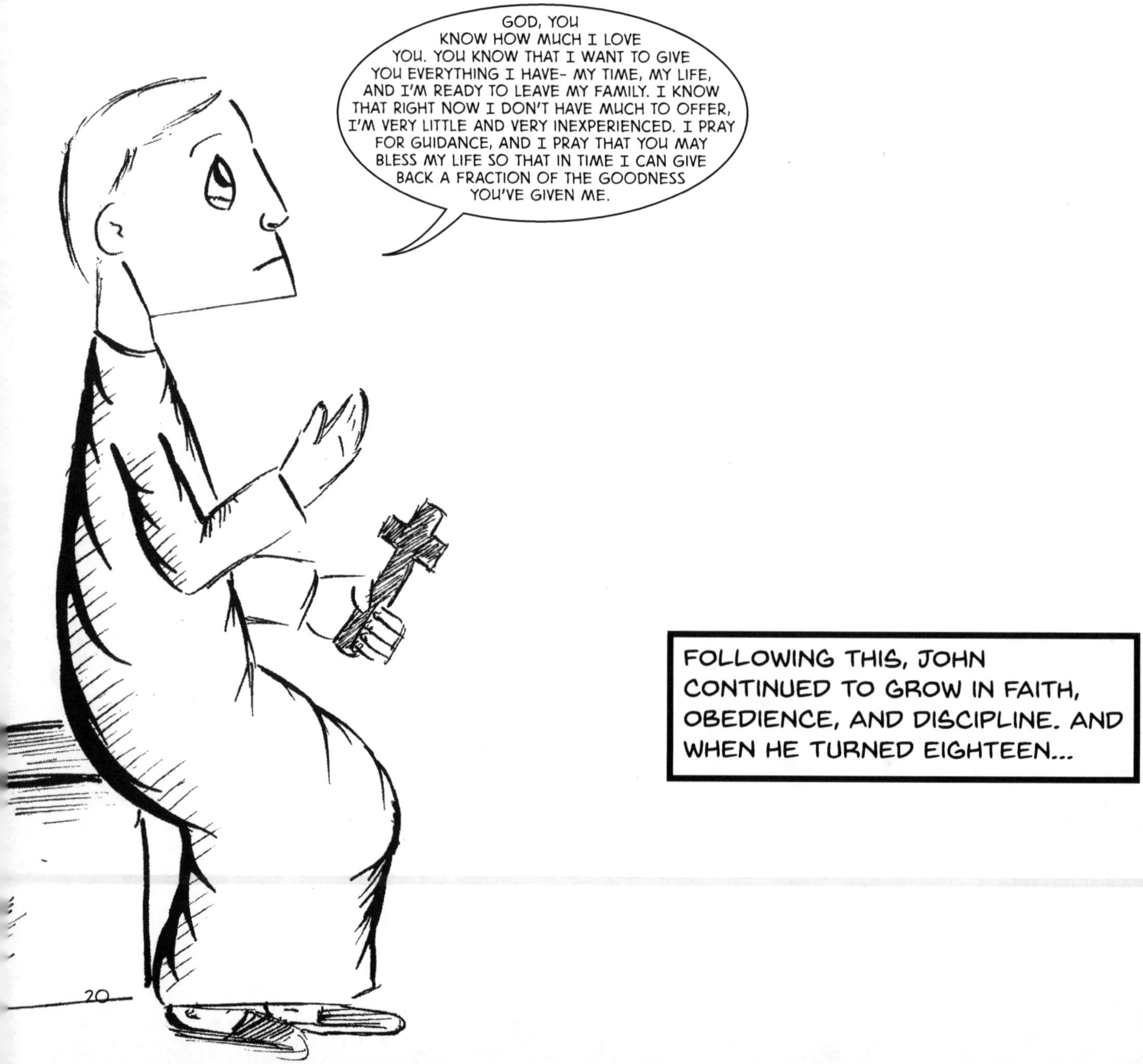
GOD, YOU KNOW HOW MUCH I LOVE YOU. YOU KNOW THAT I WANT TO GIVE YOU EVERYTHING I HAVE- MY TIME, MY LIFE, AND I'M READY TO LEAVE MY FAMILY. I KNOW THAT RIGHT NOW I DON'T HAVE MUCH TO OFFER, I'M VERY LITTLE AND VERY INEXPERIENCED. I PRAY FOR GUIDANCE, AND I PRAY THAT YOU MAY BLESS MY LIFE SO THAT IN TIME I CAN GIVE BACK A FRACTION OF THE GOODNESS YOU'VE GIVEN ME.
FOLLOWING THIS, JOHN CONTINUED TO GROW IN FAITH, OBEDIENCE, AND DISCIPLINE. AND WHEN HE TURNED EIGHTEEN...

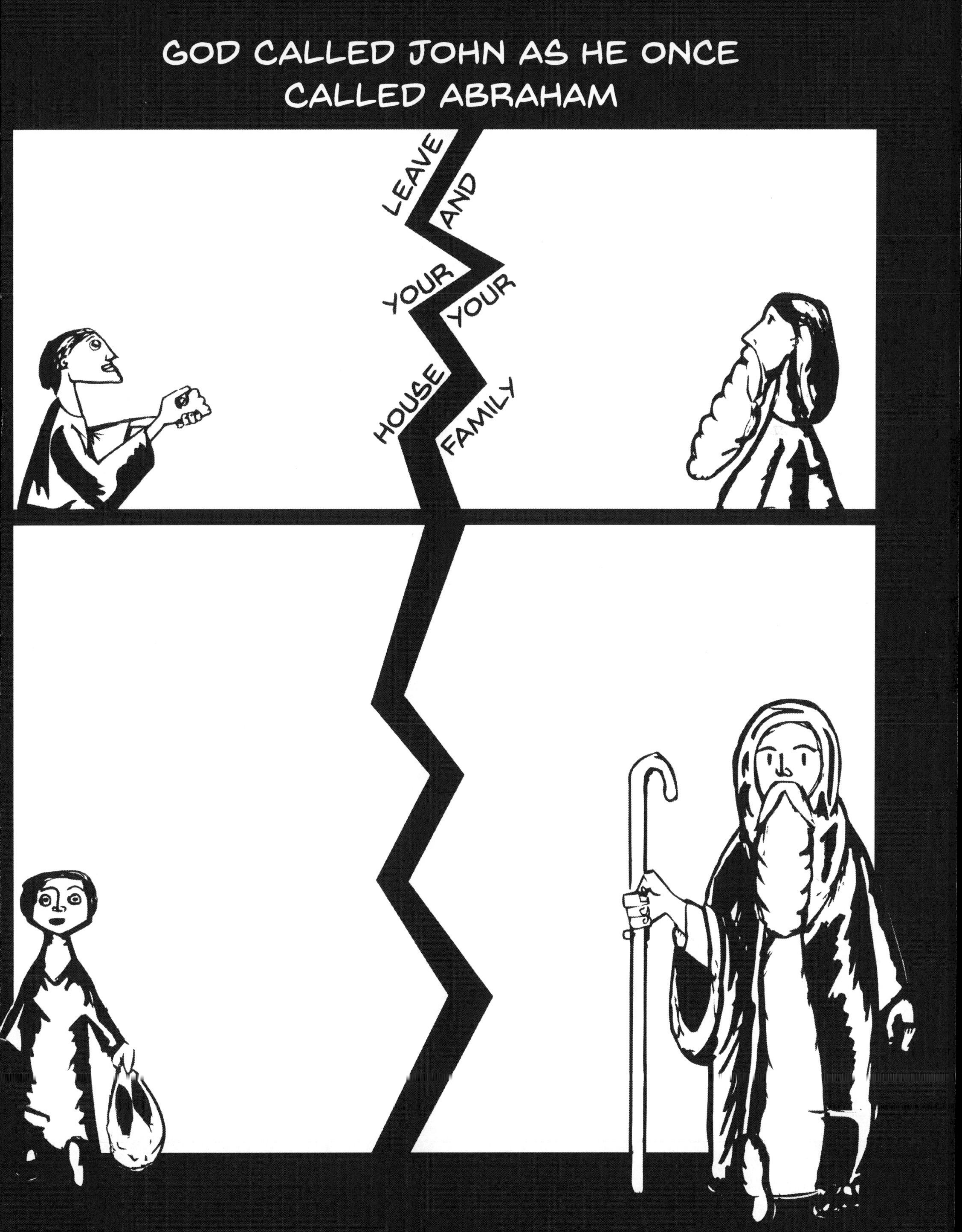
GOD CALLED JOHN AS HE ONCE CALLED ABRAHAM
LEAVE YOUR HOUSE
AND YOUR FAMILY

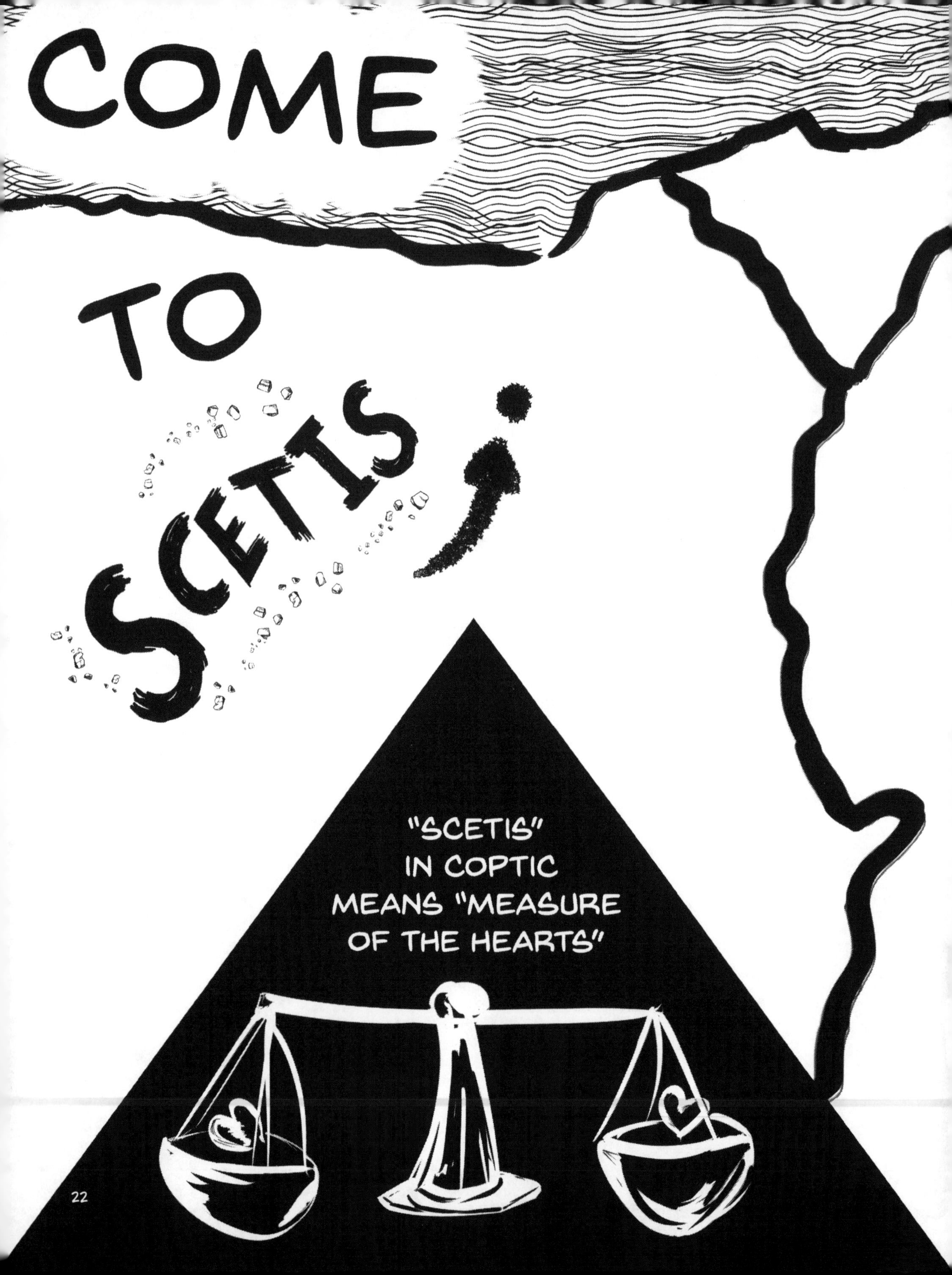
COME
TO
SCETIS;
"SCETIS" IN COPTIC MEANS "MEASURE OF THE HEARTS"

LIFE OF MONKS IN SCETIS WAS A LIFE OF SOLITUDE.
A MONK LIVED ALONE IN HIS CELL

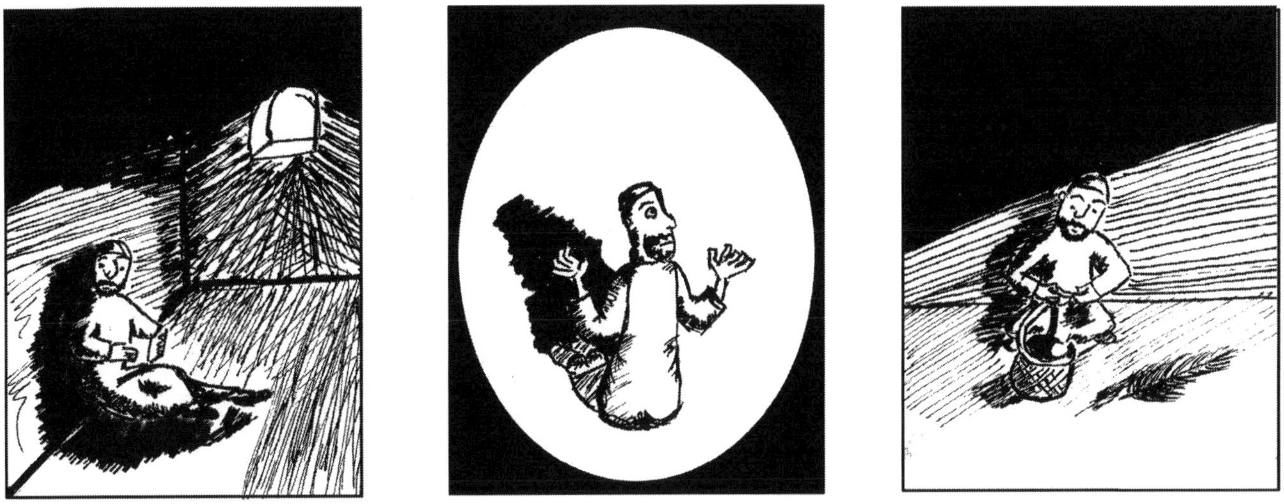

EXCEPT ON WEEKENDS

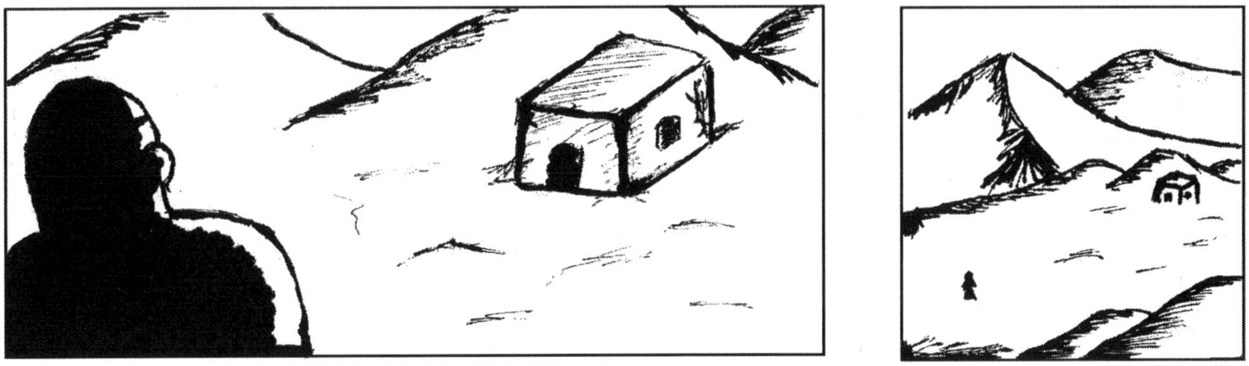

WHEN A NUMBER OF MONKS HELD THE DIVINE LITURGY.

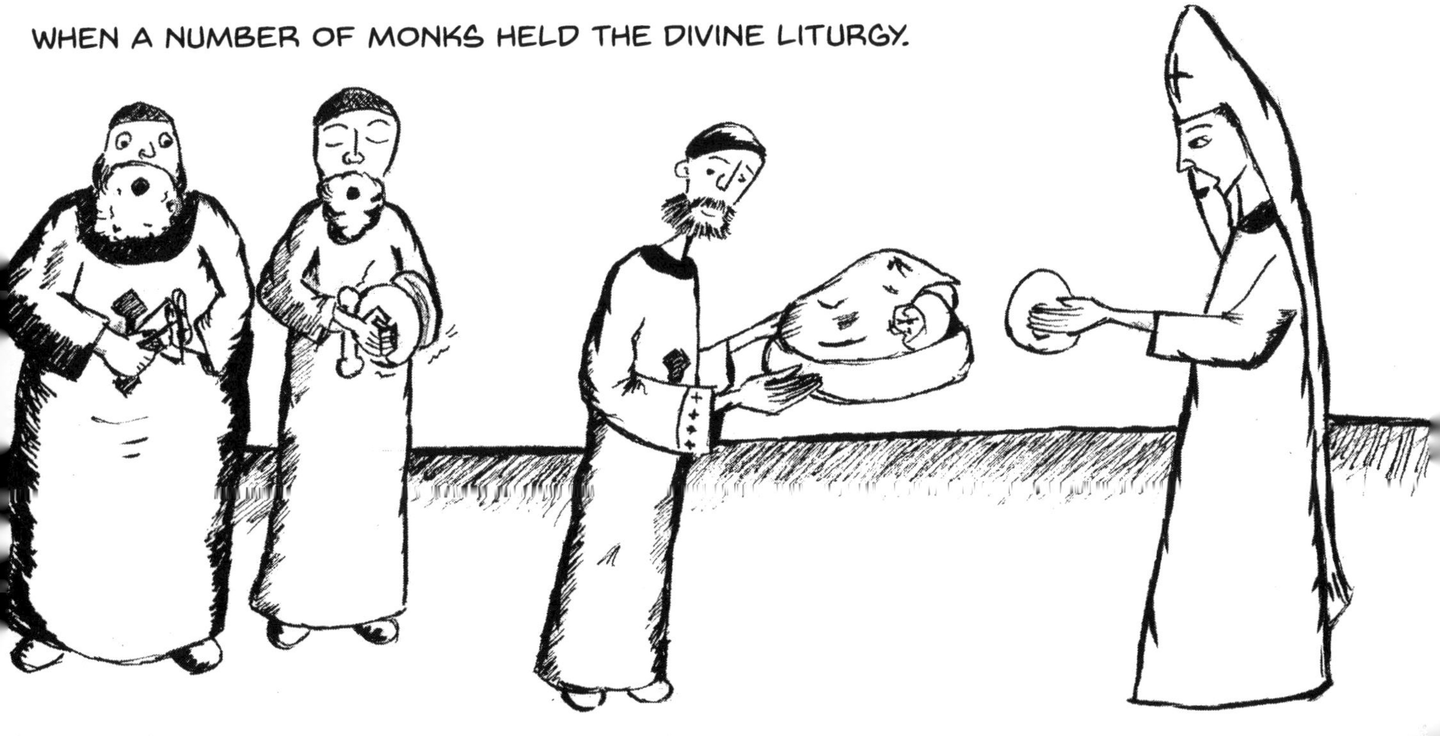

MONKS USUALLY STARTED THEIR DAY SHORTLY AFTER MIDNIGHT.

THEY WOULD GET UP AND PRAY UNTIL DAWN.

AT DAWN, THEY WOULD START WORK.

THIS WAS TO AVOID LAZINESS AND STAY FOCUSED ON GOD. MONKS TYPICALLY PLAIT BASKETS WHILE READING THE BIBLE OR PRAYING, MAKING SURE THEY'RE IN CONSTANT PRAYER AND NEVER DISTRACTED FROM GOD.

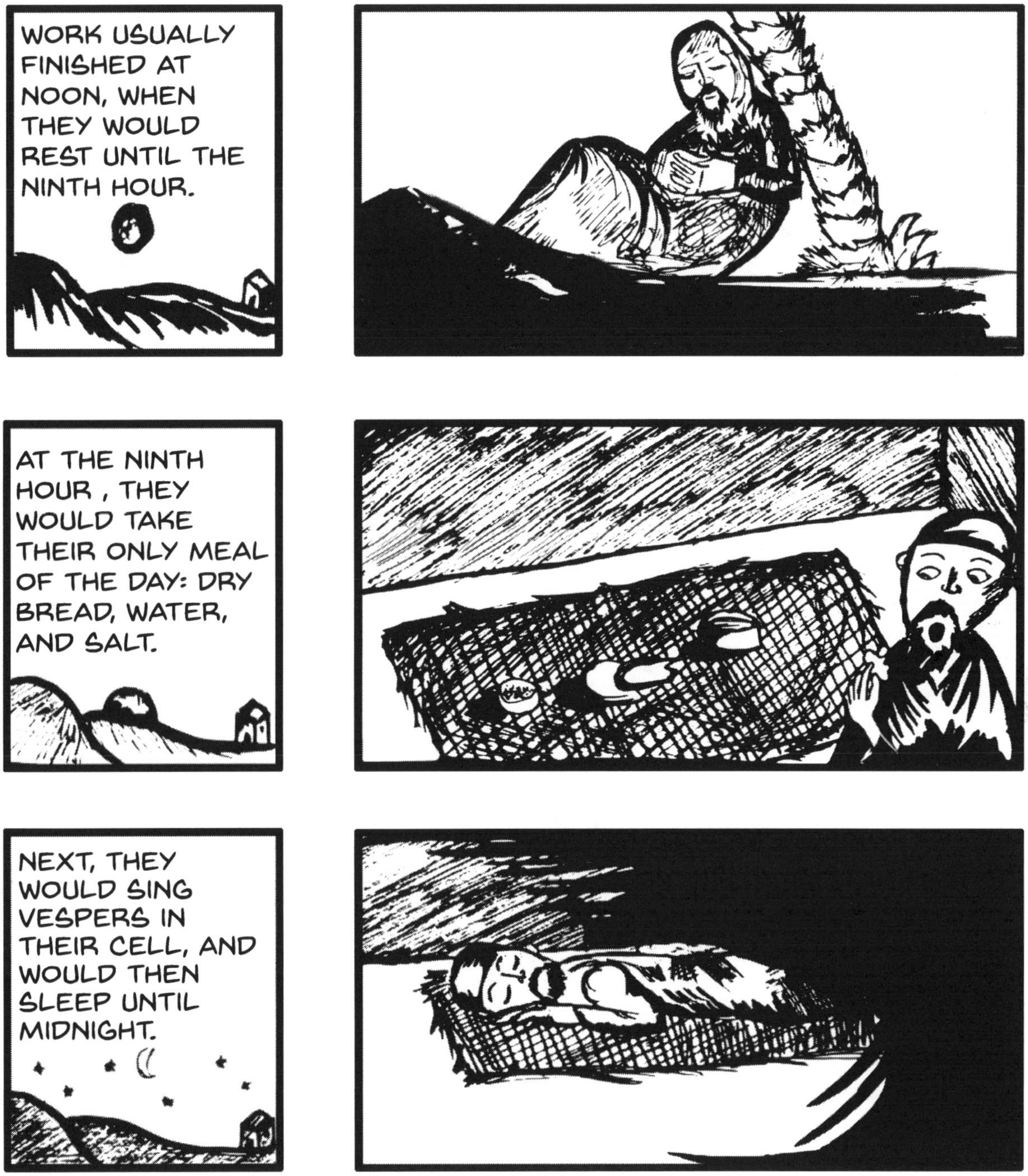
WORK USUALLY FINISHED AT NOON, WHEN THEY WOULD REST UNTIL THE NINTH HOUR.
AT THE NINTH HOUR , THEY WOULD TAKE THEIR ONLY MEAL OF THE DAY: DRY BREAD, WATER, AND SALT.
NEXT, THEY WOULD SING VESPERS IN THEIR CELL, AND WOULD THEN SLEEP UNTIL MIDNIGHT.

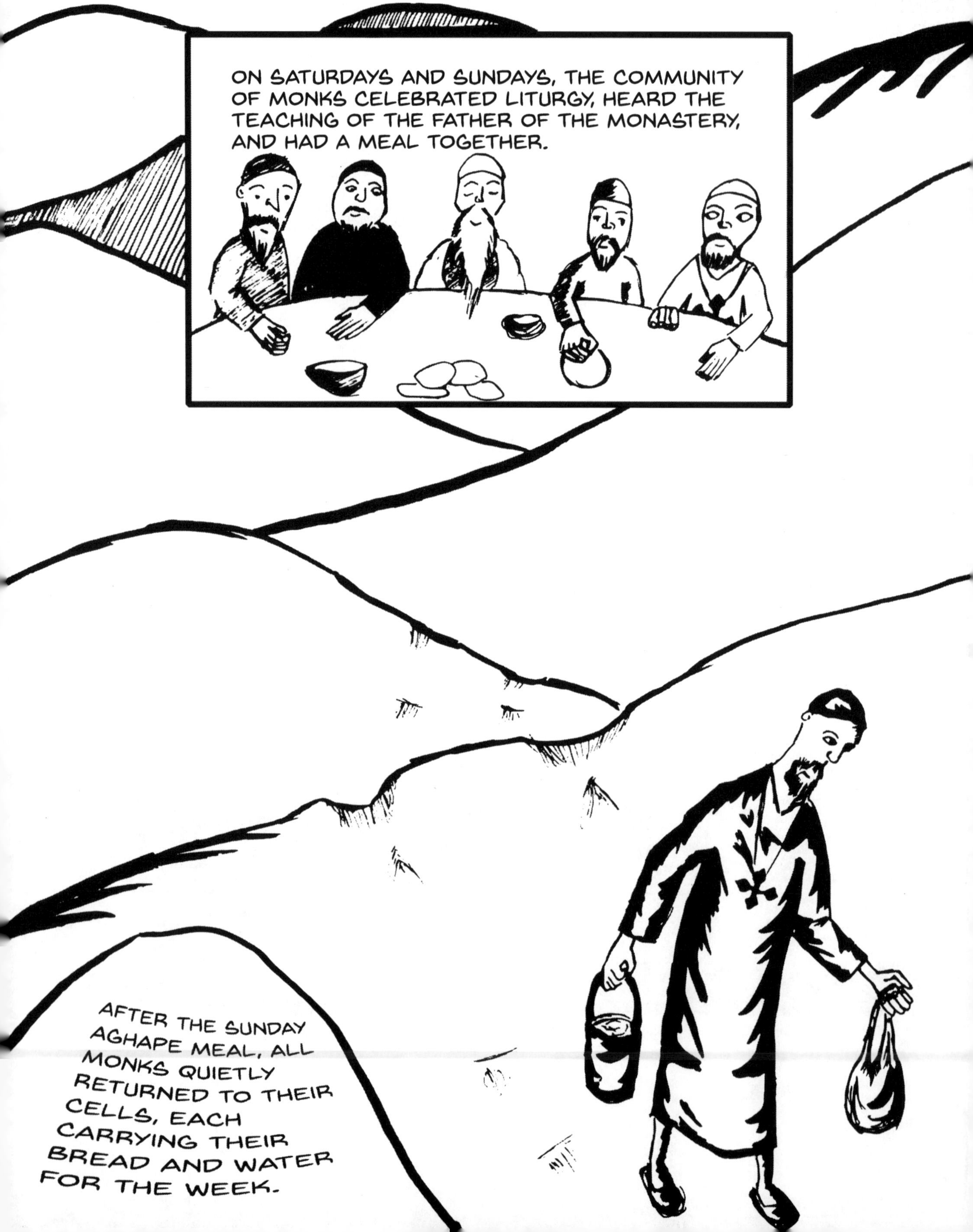
ON SATURDAYS AND SUNDAYS, THE COMMUNITY OF MONKS CELEBRATED LITURGY, HEARD THE TEACHING OF THE FATHER OF THE MONASTERY, AND HAD A MEAL TOGETHER.
AFTER THE SUNDAY AGHAPE MEAL, ALL MONKS QUIETLY RETURNED TO THEIR CELLS, EACH CARRYING THEIR BREAD AND WATER FOR THE WEEK.

JOHN LOVED LEARNING ABOUT THE MONKS OF SCETIS. HE
HAD ALWAYS WONDERED IF HE HAD THE DISCIPLINE TO LIVE A
MONASTIC LIFE, BUT THAT WAS THE LAST THING ON HIS MIND AT
THE TIME.

HIS JOURNEY GREW MORE DIFFICULT
THE DEEPER HE STEPPED INTO THE DESERT. THE
USUALLY SOFT SAND PARTICLES FELT LIKE A MILLION
LITTLE PUNCHES AS THEY GOT CARRIED WITH THE
WIND AND BRUSHED AGAINST HIS SKIN.

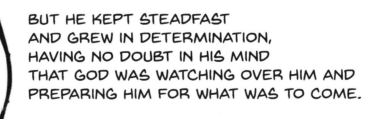

BUT HE KEPT STEADFAST
AND GREW IN DETERMINATION,
HAVING NO DOUBT IN HIS MIND
THAT GOD WAS WATCHING OVER HIM AND
PREPARING HIM FOR WHAT WAS TO COME.

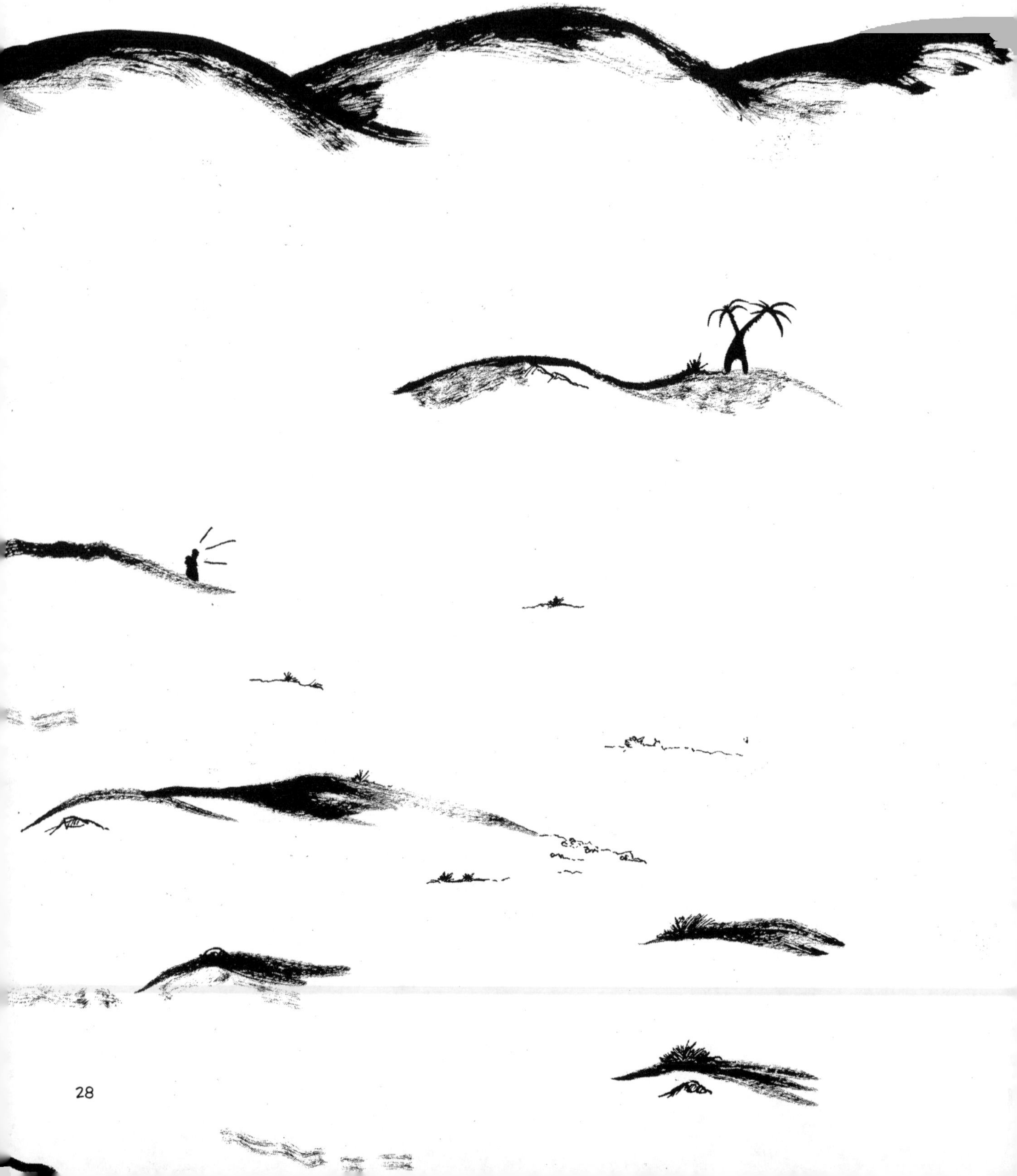

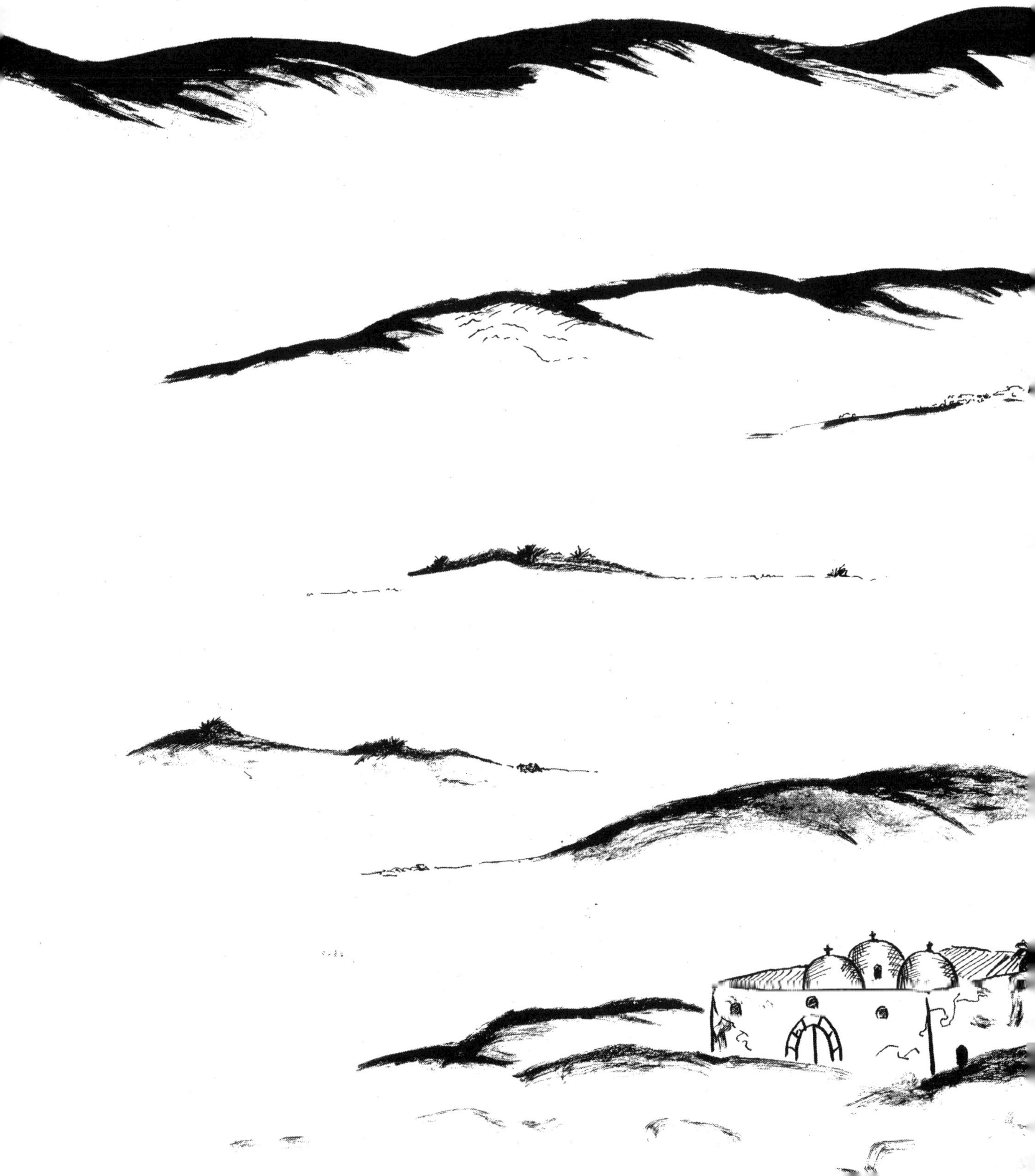

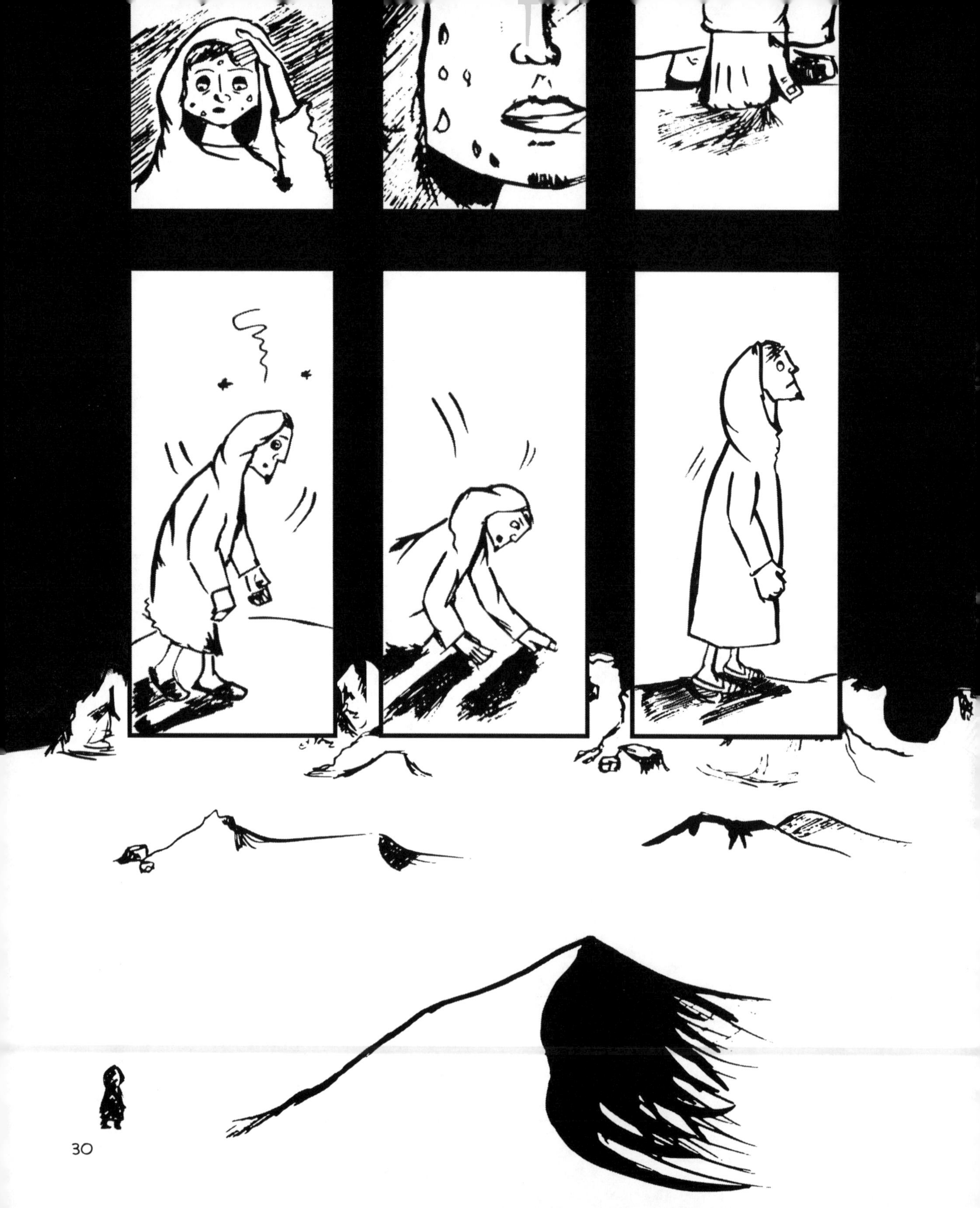

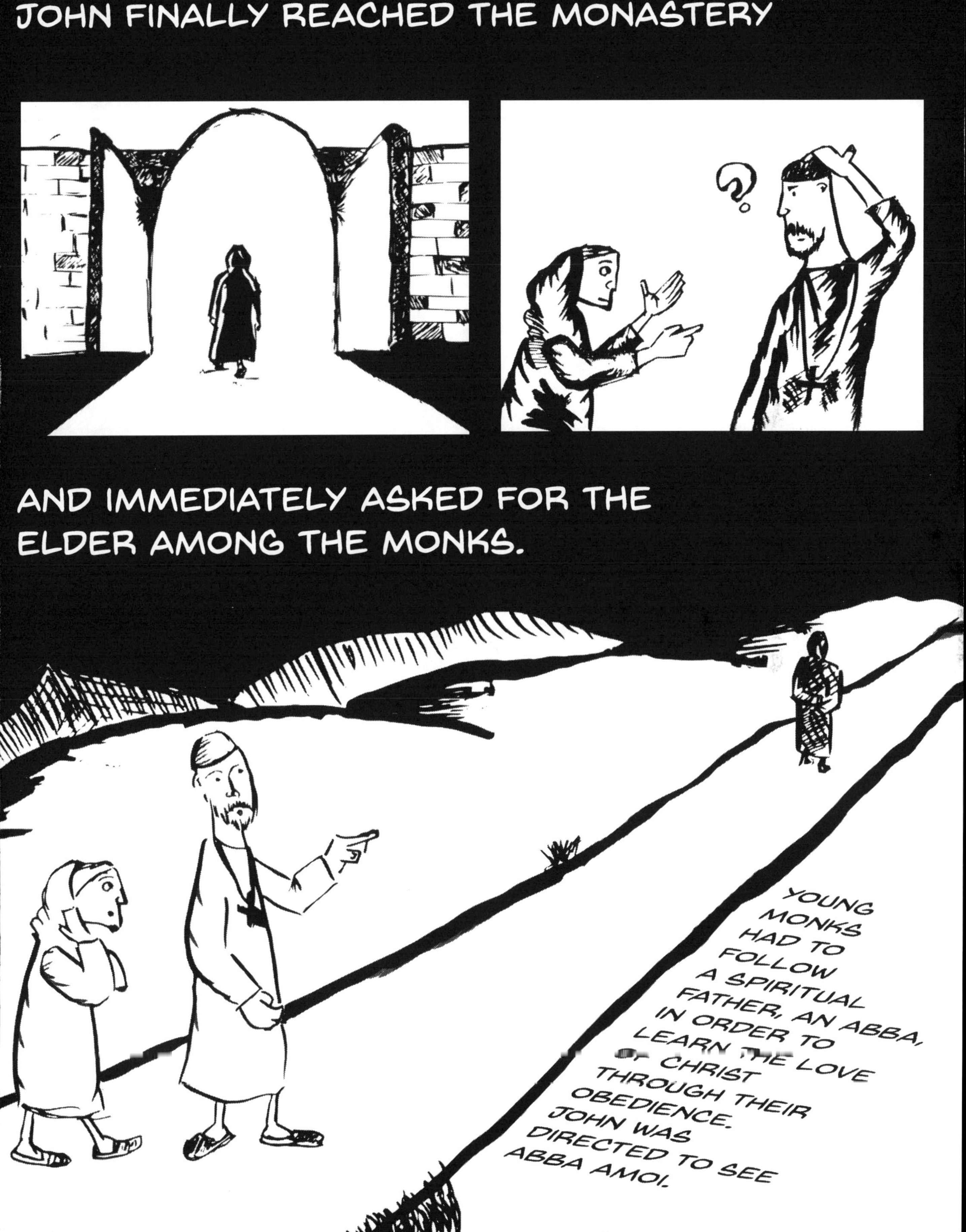
JOHN FINALLY REACHED THE MONASTERY
AND IMMEDIATELY ASKED FOR THE ELDER AMONG THE MONKS.
YOUNG MONKS HAD TO FOLLOW A SPIRITUAL FATHER, AN ABBA, IN ORDER TO LEARN THE LOVE OF CHRIST THROUGH THEIR OBEDIENCE. JOHN WAS DIRECTED TO SEE ABBA AMOI.

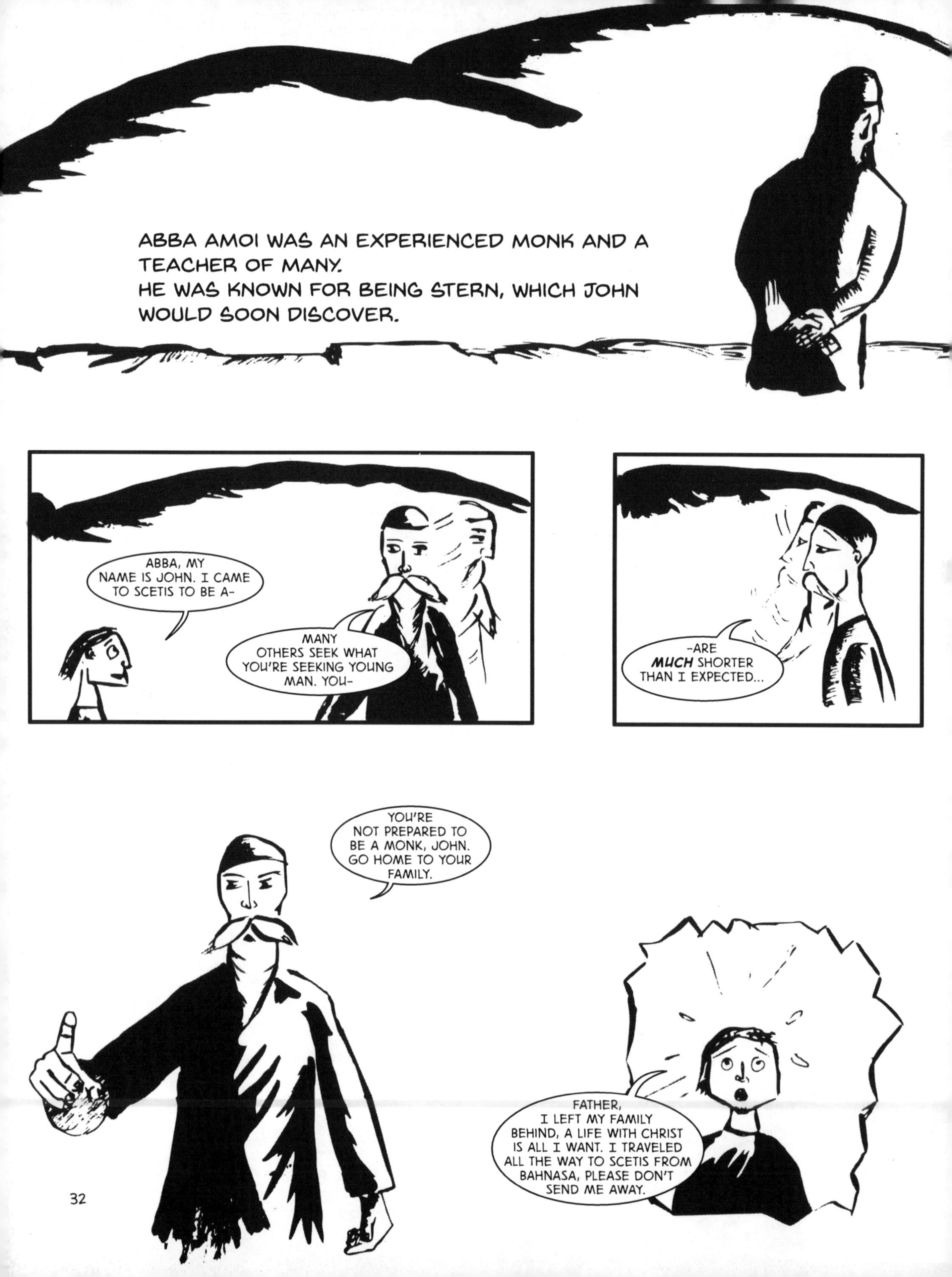
ABBA AMOI WAS AN EXPERIENCED MONK AND A TEACHER OF MANY.
HE WAS KNOWN FOR BEING STERN, WHICH JOHN WOULD SOON DISCOVER.
ABBA, MY NAME IS JOHN. I CAME TO SCETIS TO BE A-
MANY OTHERS SEEK WHAT YOU'RE SEEKING YOUNG MAN. YOU-
-ARE ***MUCH*** SHORTER THAN I EXPECTED...
YOU'RE NOT PREPARED TO BE A MONK, JOHN. GO HOME TO YOUR FAMILY.
FATHER, I LEFT MY FAMILY BEHIND, A LIFE WITH CHRIST IS ALL I WANT. I TRAVELED ALL THE WAY TO SCETIS FROM BAHNASA, PLEASE DON'T SEND ME AWAY.

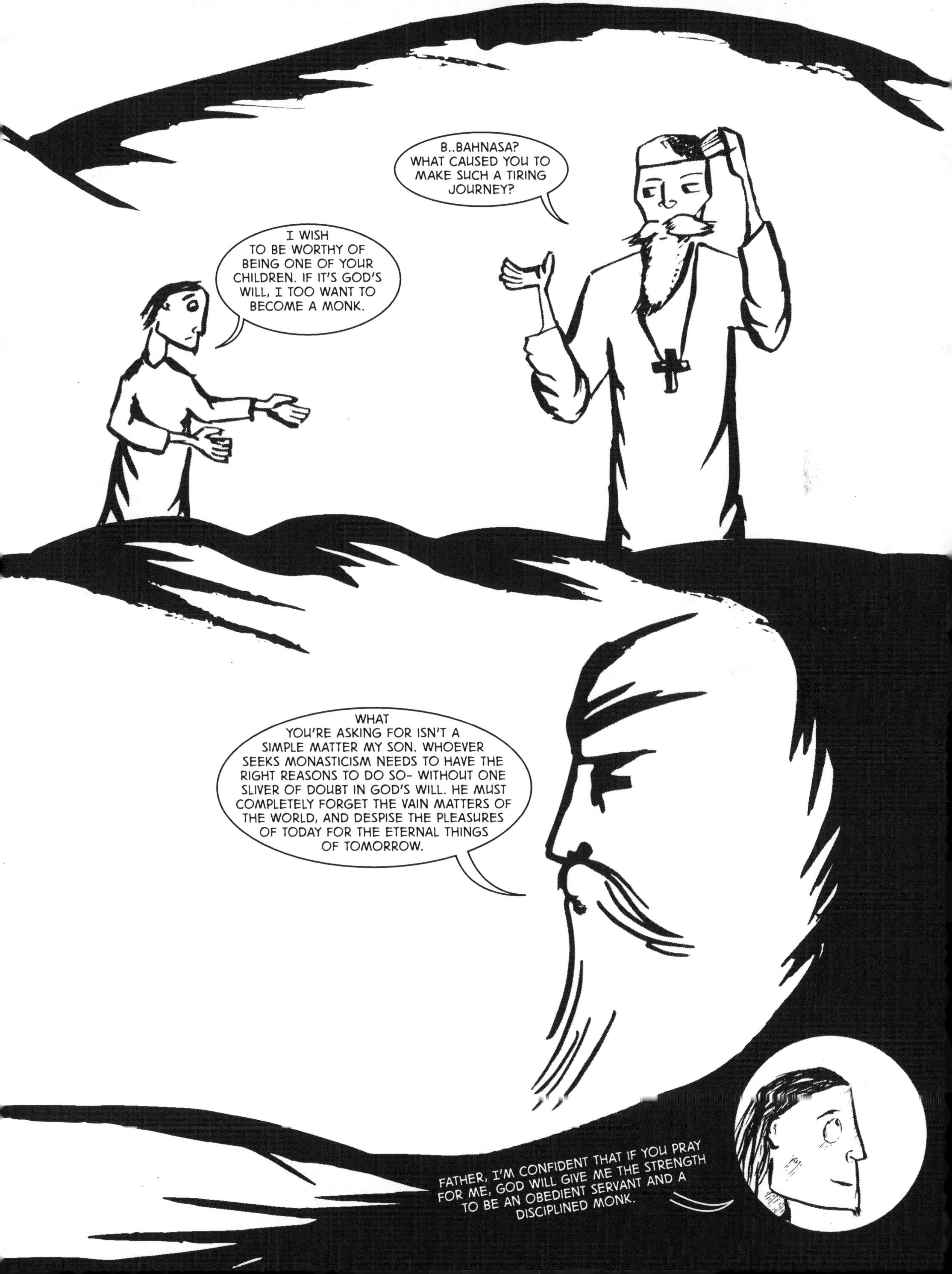
B..BAHNASA? WHAT CAUSED YOU TO MAKE SUCH A TIRING JOURNEY?
I WISH TO BE WORTHY OF BEING ONE OF YOUR CHILDREN. IF IT'S GOD'S WILL, I TOO WANT TO BECOME A MONK.
WHAT YOU'RE ASKING FOR ISN'T A SIMPLE MATTER MY SON. WHOEVER SEEKS MONASTICISM NEEDS TO HAVE THE RIGHT REASONS TO DO SO- WITHOUT ONE SLIVER OF DOUBT IN GOD'S WILL. HE MUST COMPLETELY FORGET THE VAIN MATTERS OF THE WORLD, AND DESPISE THE PLEASURES OF TODAY FOR THE ETERNAL THINGS OF TOMORROW.
FATHER, I'M CONFIDENT THAT IF YOU PRAY FOR ME, GOD WILL GIVE ME THE STRENGTH TO BE AN OBEDIENT SERVANT AND A DISCIPLINED MONK.

AFTER THEIR CONVERSATION, ABBA AMOI ASKED JOHN TO SIT DOWN AND WAIT FOR HIM WHILE HE WENT TO HIS CELL TO PRAY. IN TRUE CHRISTIAN FASHION, ABBA AMOI NEVER MADE ANY DECISION WITHOUT PRAYING TO GOD AND ASKING FOR HIS WILL.

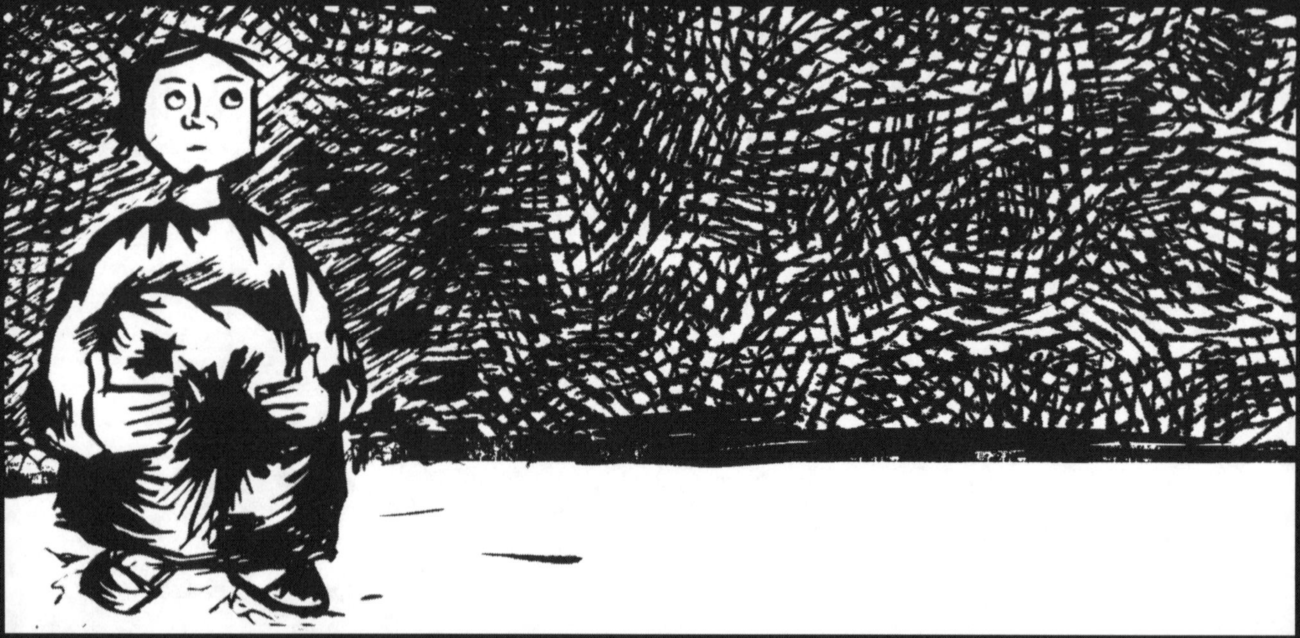

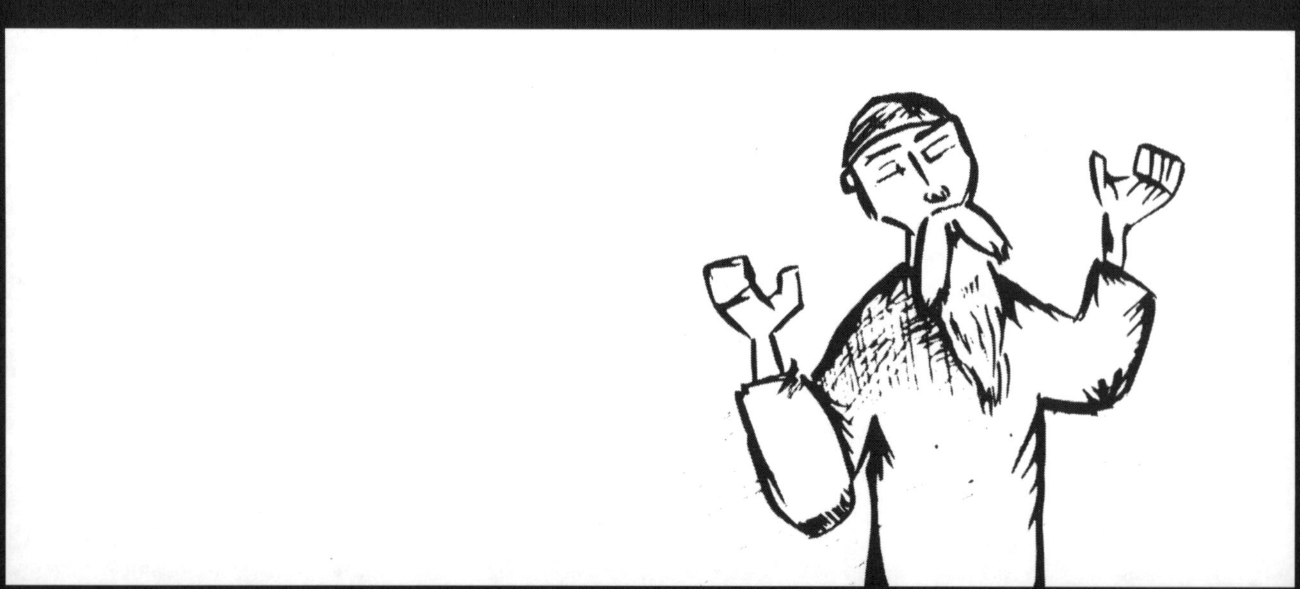

ABBA AMOI PRAYED THE NIGHT AWAY, PLEADING AND ASKING GOD TO REVEAL WHAT WAS PLEASING TO HIM CONCERNING JOHN. AS THE NIGHT PASSED, AN ANGEL OF THE LORD APPEARED TO ABBA AMOI AND SAID THE FOLLOWING:

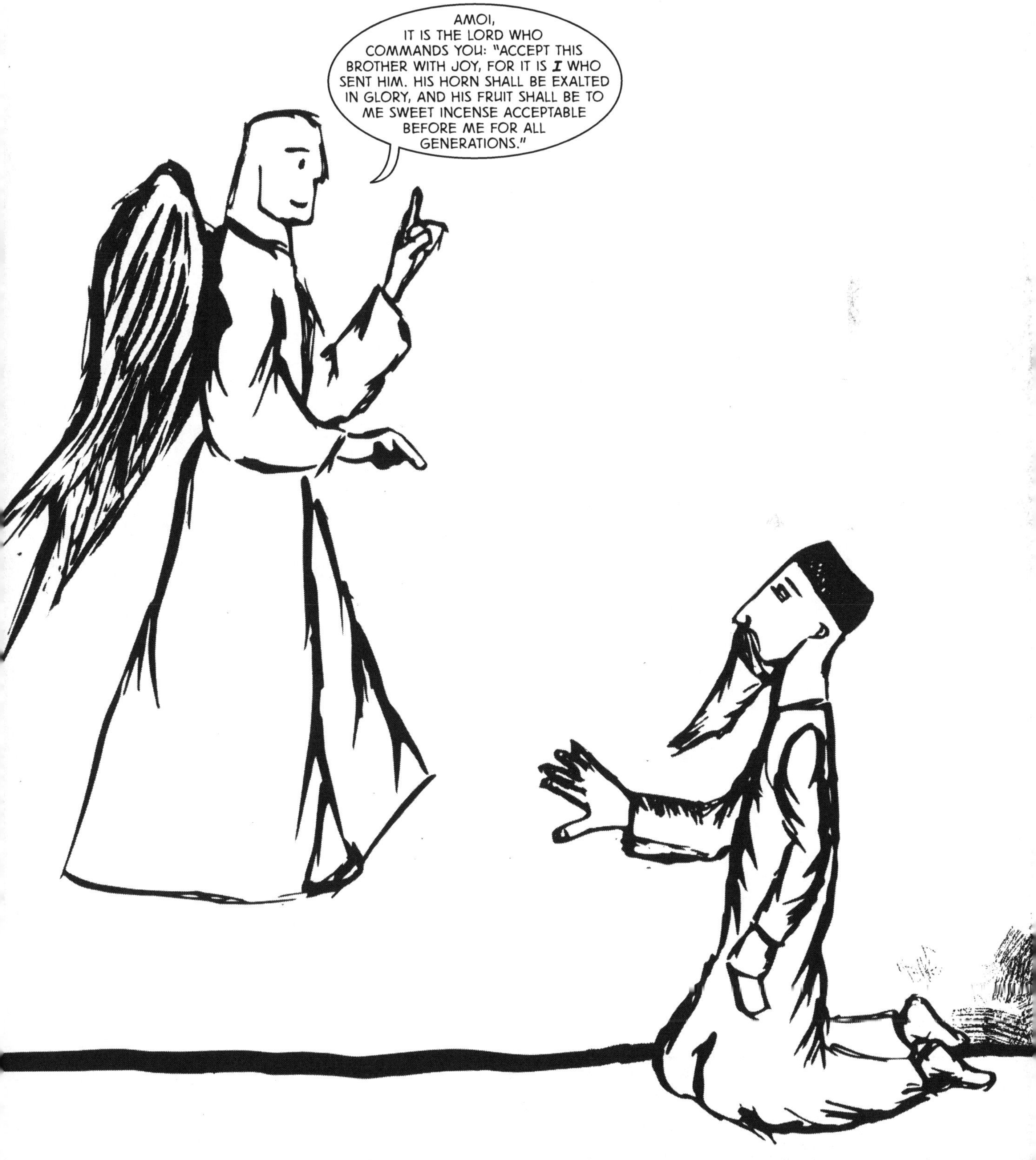
AMOI, IT IS THE LORD WHO COMMANDS YOU: "ACCEPT THIS BROTHER WITH JOY, FOR IT IS *I* WHO SENT HIM. HIS HORN SHALL BE EXALTED IN GLORY, AND HIS FRUIT SHALL BE TO ME SWEET INCENSE ACCEPTABLE BEFORE ME FOR ALL GENERATIONS."

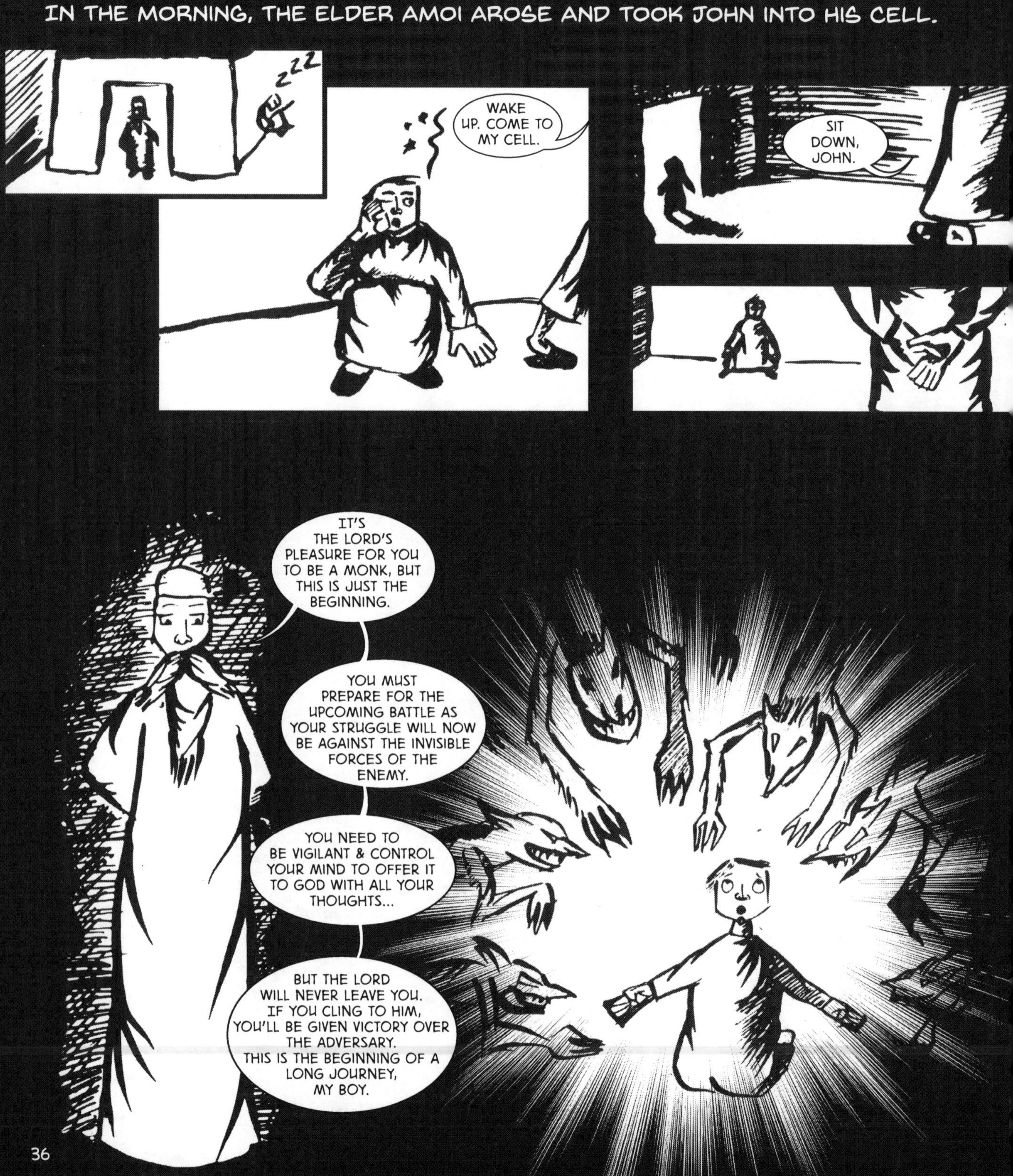
IN THE MORNING, THE ELDER AMOI AROSE AND TOOK JOHN INTO HIS CELL.
ZZZ
WAKE UP. COME TO MY CELL.
SIT DOWN, JOHN.
IT'S THE LORD'S PLEASURE FOR YOU TO BE A MONK, BUT THIS IS JUST THE BEGINNING.
YOU MUST PREPARE FOR THE UPCOMING BATTLE AS YOUR STRUGGLE WILL NOW BE AGAINST THE INVISIBLE FORCES OF THE ENEMY.
YOU NEED TO BE VIGILANT & CONTROL YOUR MIND TO OFFER IT TO GOD WITH ALL YOUR THOUGHTS...
BUT THE LORD WILL NEVER LEAVE YOU. IF YOU CLING TO HIM, YOU'LL BE GIVEN VICTORY OVER THE ADVERSARY. THIS IS THE BEGINNING OF A LONG JOURNEY, MY BOY.

AFTER PREPARING HIM, ABBA AMOI THEN CUT JOHN'S HAIR AS PART OF HIS ORDINATION. IT WAS TO SIGNIFY THAT AS A MONK, JOHN SHOULDN'T CARE ABOUT HIS APPEARANCE AND SHOULD ONLY FOCUS ON HEAVENLY MATTERS.

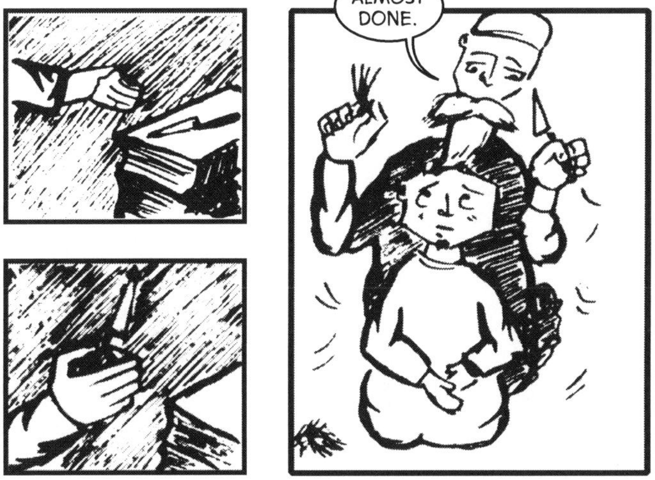
ALMOST DONE.

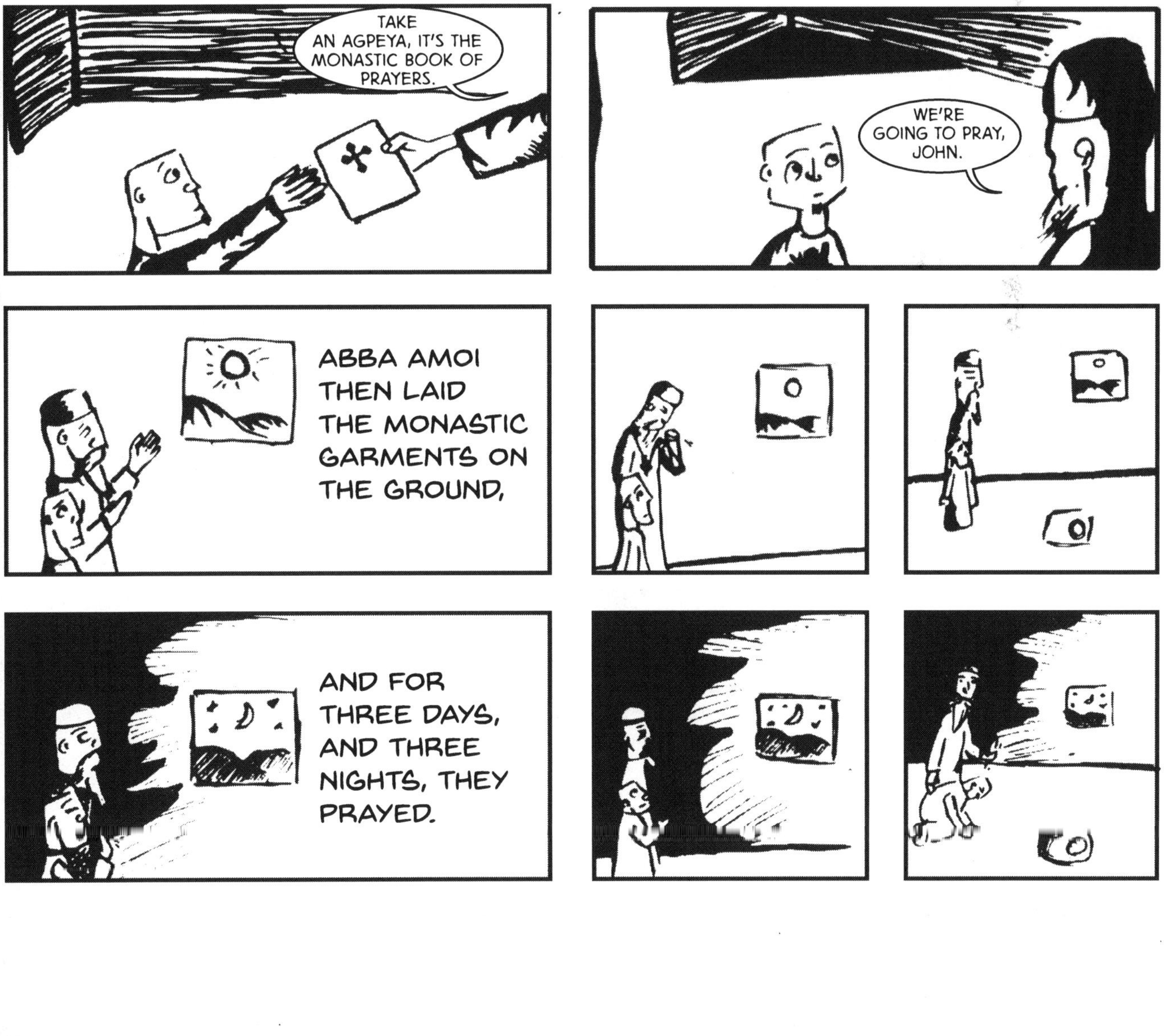
TAKE AN AGPEYA, IT'S THE MONASTIC BOOK OF PRAYERS.
WE'RE GOING TO PRAY, JOHN.
ABBA AMOI THEN LAID THE MONASTIC GARMENTS ON THE GROUND,
AND FOR THREE DAYS, AND THREE NIGHTS, THEY PRAYED.

AFTER THE THREE DAYS AND THREE NIGHTS, AN ANGEL OF THE LORD APPEARED BEFORE THEM AND SEALED THE GARMENTS THRICE WITH THE SIGN OF THE CROSS. ABBA AMOI FINALLY RECEIVED YOUNG JOHN AS A MONK AND A DISCIPLE.

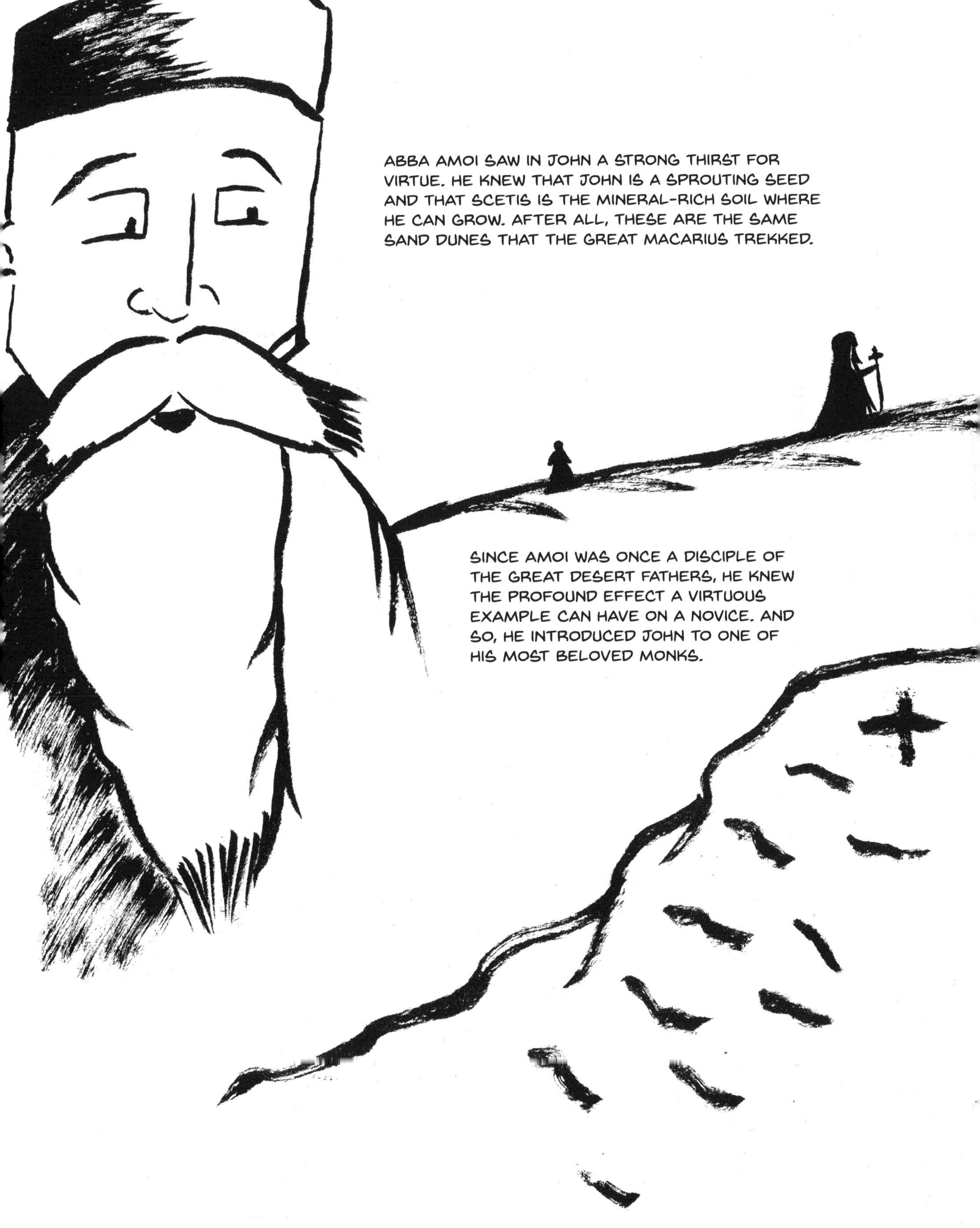
ABBA AMOI SAW IN JOHN A STRONG THIRST FOR VIRTUE. HE KNEW THAT JOHN IS A SPROUTING SEED AND THAT SCETIS IS THE MINERAL-RICH SOIL WHERE HE CAN GROW. AFTER ALL, THESE ARE THE SAME SAND DUNES THAT THE GREAT MACARIUS TREKKED.
SINCE AMOI WAS ONCE A DISCIPLE OF THE GREAT DESERT FATHERS, HE KNEW THE PROFOUND EFFECT A VIRTUOUS EXAMPLE CAN HAVE ON A NOVICE. AND SO, HE INTRODUCED JOHN TO ONE OF HIS MOST BELOVED MONKS.

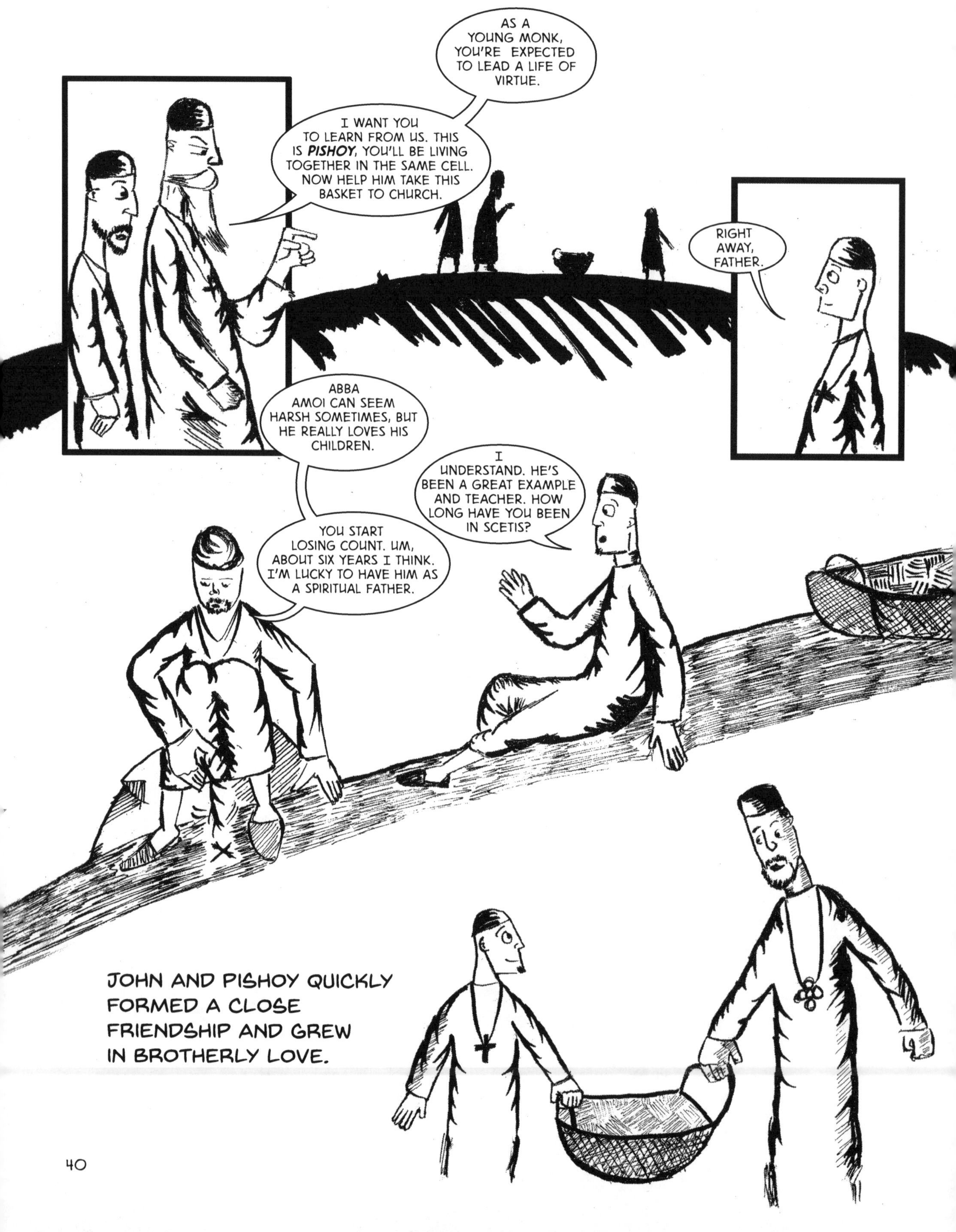
AS A YOUNG MONK, YOU'RE EXPECTED TO LEAD A LIFE OF VIRTUE.
I WANT YOU TO LEARN FROM US. THIS IS **PISHOY**, YOU'LL BE LIVING TOGETHER IN THE SAME CELL. NOW HELP HIM TAKE THIS BASKET TO CHURCH.
RIGHT AWAY, FATHER.
ABBA AMOI CAN SEEM HARSH SOMETIMES, BUT HE REALLY LOVES HIS CHILDREN.
I UNDERSTAND. HE'S BEEN A GREAT EXAMPLE AND TEACHER. HOW LONG HAVE YOU BEEN IN SCETIS?
YOU START LOSING COUNT. UM, ABOUT SIX YEARS I THINK. I'M LUCKY TO HAVE HIM AS A SPIRITUAL FATHER.
JOHN AND PISHOY QUICKLY FORMED A CLOSE FRIENDSHIP AND GREW IN BROTHERLY LOVE.

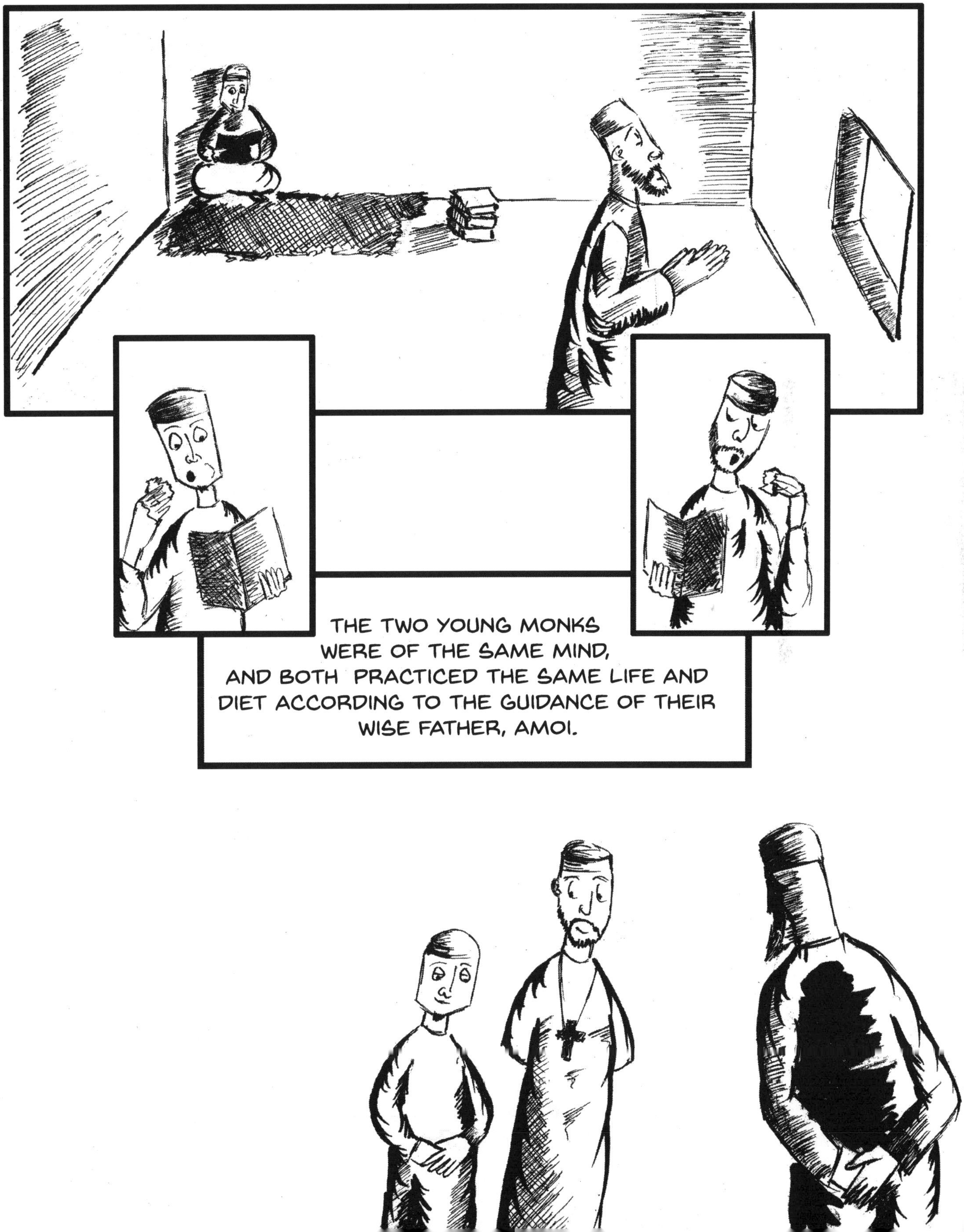
THE TWO YOUNG MONKS WERE OF THE SAME MIND, AND BOTH PRACTICED THE SAME LIFE AND DIET ACCORDING TO THE GUIDANCE OF THEIR WISE FATHER, AMOI.

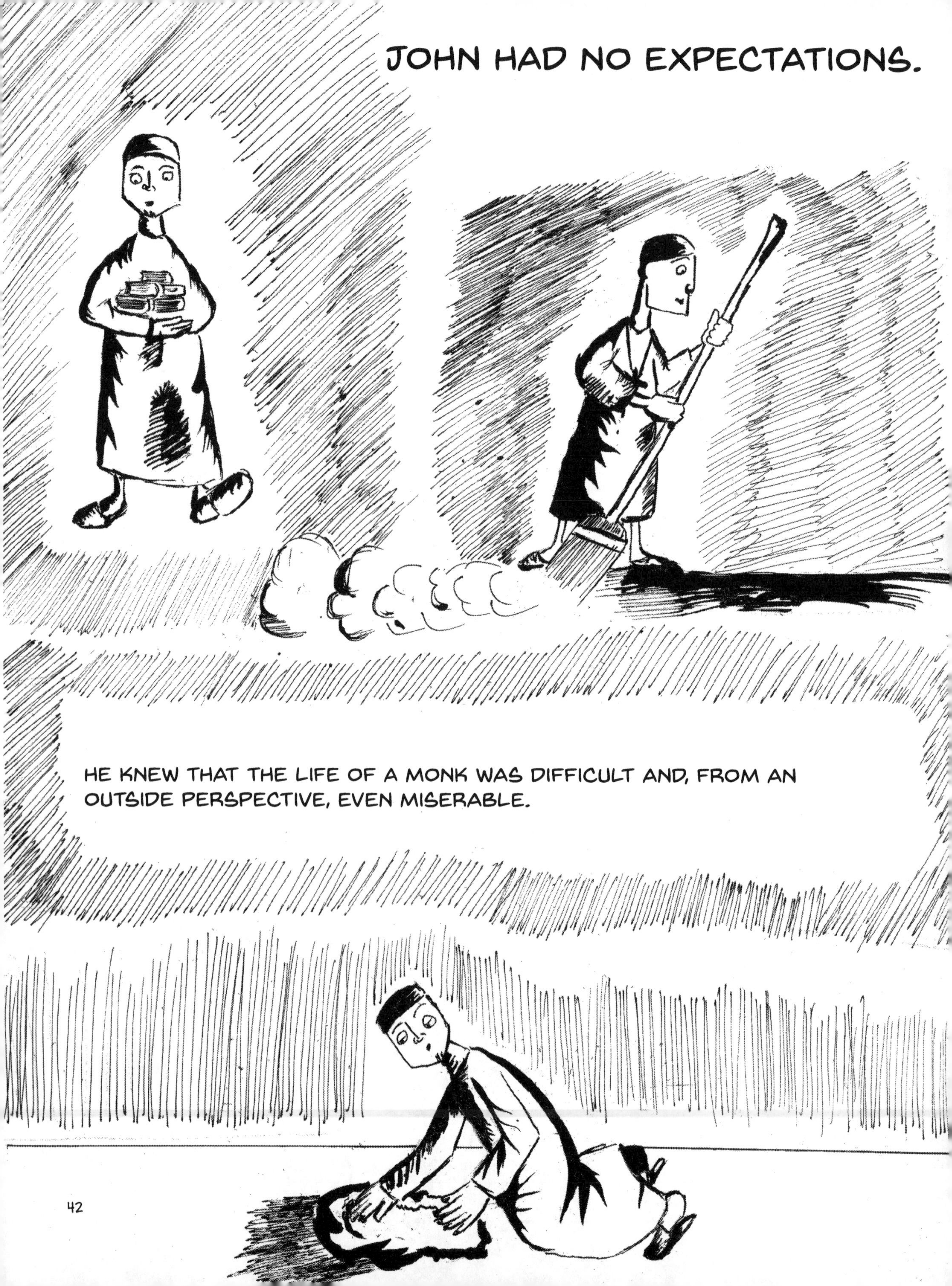
JOHN HAD NO EXPECTATIONS.
HE KNEW THAT THE LIFE OF A MONK WAS DIFFICULT AND, FROM AN OUTSIDE PERSPECTIVE, EVEN MISERABLE.

YOU'RE ABLE TO TELL THE SECOND YOU SET FOOT IN SCETIS

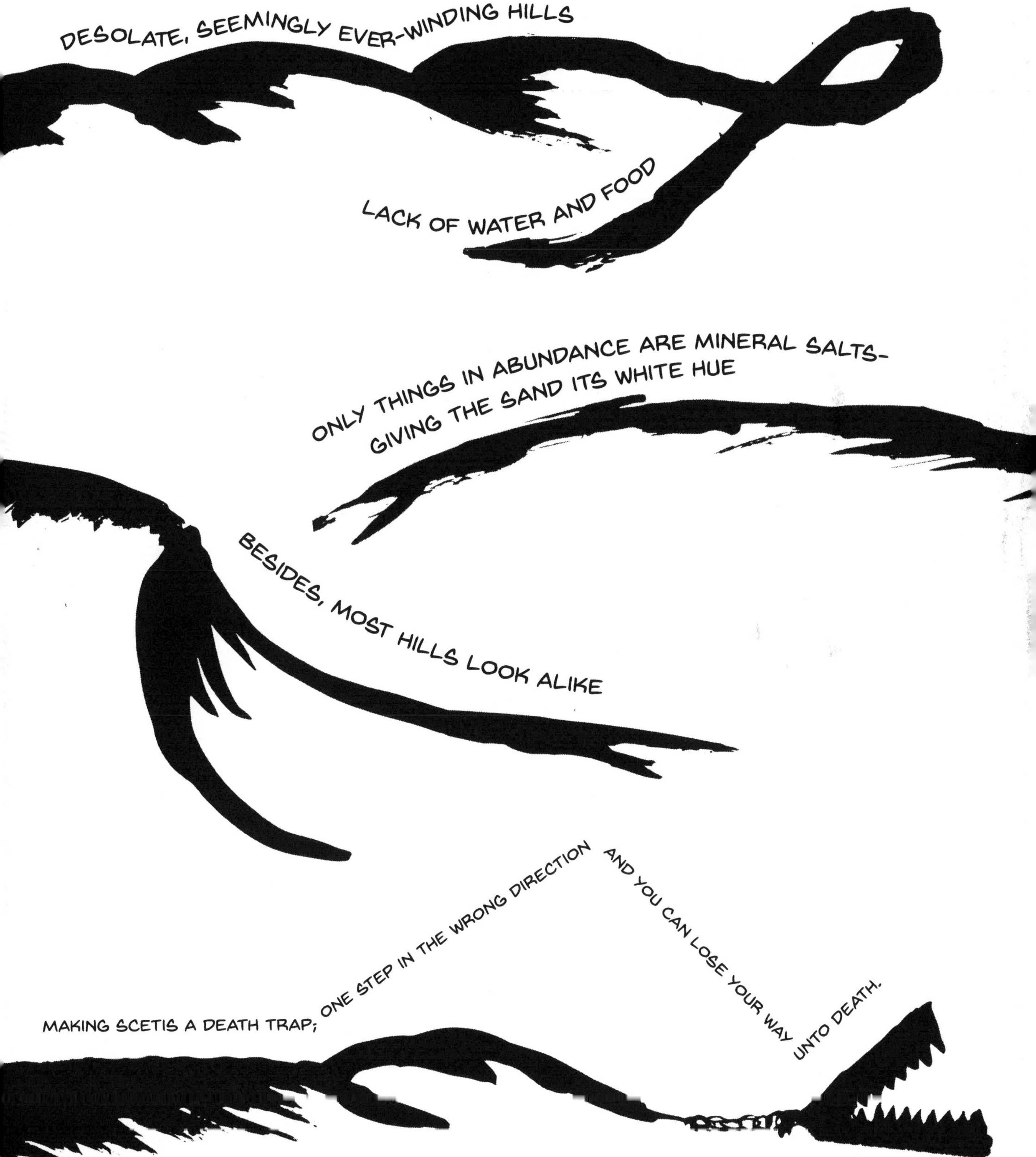
DESOLATE, SEEMINGLY EVER-WINDING HILLS
LACK OF WATER AND FOOD
ONLY THINGS IN ABUNDANCE ARE MINERAL SALTS-
GIVING THE SAND ITS WHITE HUE
BESIDES, MOST HILLS LOOK ALIKE
MAKING SCETIS A DEATH TRAP;
ONE STEP IN THE WRONG DIRECTION
AND YOU CAN LOSE YOUR WAY
UNTO DEATH.

THIS PLACE DOESN'T ONLY TEST A MAN'S HEART, IT PUSHES ONE'S BODY TO ITS LIMITS.

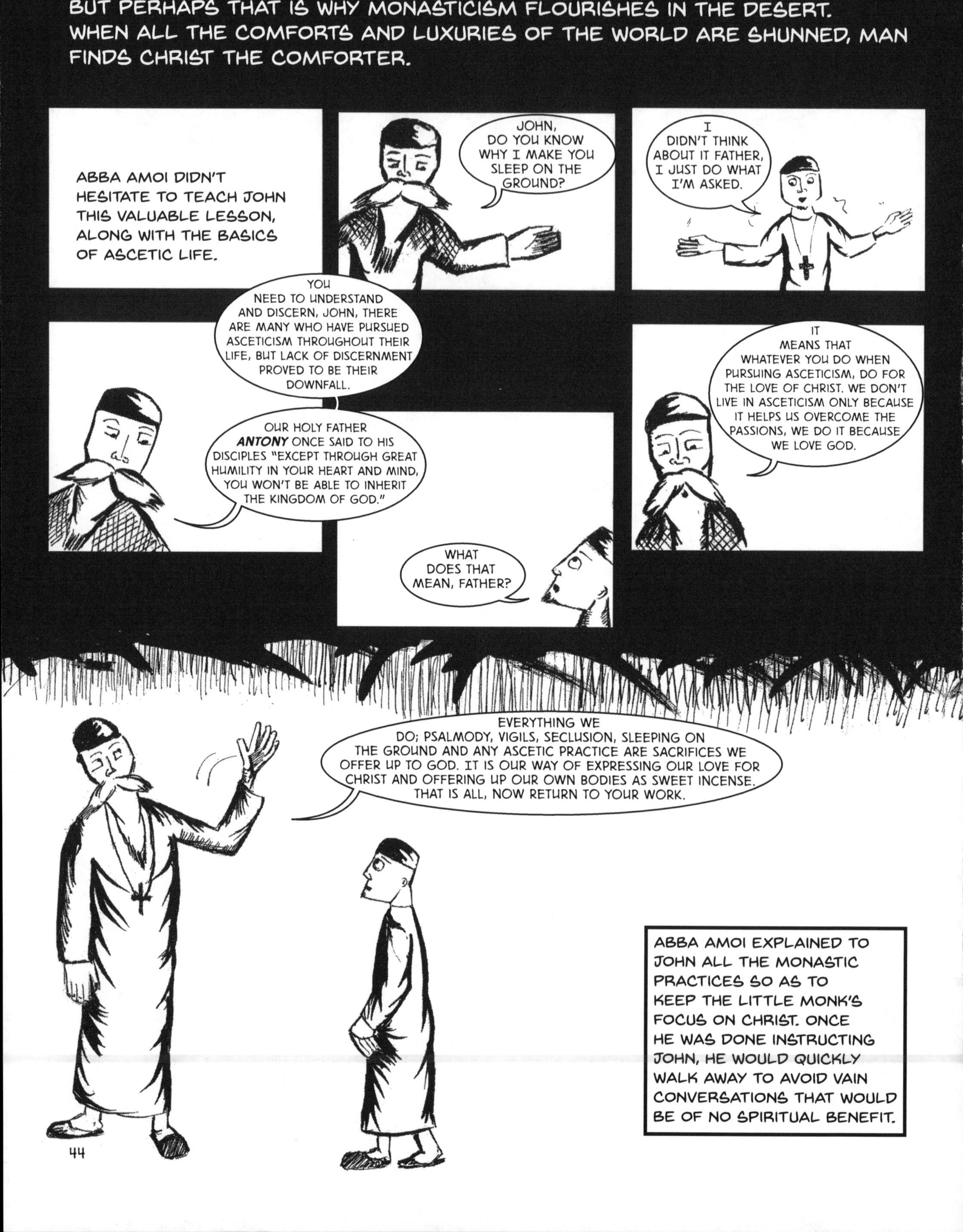
BUT PERHAPS THAT IS WHY MONASTICISM FLOURISHES IN THE DESERT. WHEN ALL THE COMFORTS AND LUXURIES OF THE WORLD ARE SHUNNED, MAN FINDS CHRIST THE COMFORTER.
ABBA AMOI DIDN'T HESITATE TO TEACH JOHN THIS VALUABLE LESSON, ALONG WITH THE BASICS OF ASCETIC LIFE.
JOHN, DO YOU KNOW WHY I MAKE YOU SLEEP ON THE GROUND?
I DIDN'T THINK ABOUT IT FATHER, I JUST DO WHAT I'M ASKED.
YOU NEED TO UNDERSTAND AND DISCERN, JOHN, THERE ARE MANY WHO HAVE PURSUED ASCETICISM THROUGHOUT THEIR LIFE, BUT LACK OF DISCERNMENT PROVED TO BE THEIR DOWNFALL.
OUR HOLY FATHER **ANTONY** ONCE SAID TO HIS DISCIPLES "EXCEPT THROUGH GREAT HUMILITY IN YOUR HEART AND MIND, YOU WON'T BE ABLE TO INHERIT THE KINGDOM OF GOD."
WHAT DOES THAT MEAN, FATHER?
IT MEANS THAT WHATEVER YOU DO WHEN PURSUING ASCETICISM, DO FOR THE LOVE OF CHRIST. WE DON'T LIVE IN ASCETICISM ONLY BECAUSE IT HELPS US OVERCOME THE PASSIONS, WE DO IT BECAUSE WE LOVE GOD.
EVERYTHING WE DO; PSALMODY, VIGILS, SECLUSION, SLEEPING ON THE GROUND AND ANY ASCETIC PRACTICE ARE SACRIFICES WE OFFER UP TO GOD. IT IS OUR WAY OF EXPRESSING OUR LOVE FOR CHRIST AND OFFERING UP OUR OWN BODIES AS SWEET INCENSE. THAT IS ALL, NOW RETURN TO YOUR WORK.
ABBA AMOI EXPLAINED TO JOHN ALL THE MONASTIC PRACTICES SO AS TO KEEP THE LITTLE MONK'S FOCUS ON CHRIST. ONCE HE WAS DONE INSTRUCTING JOHN, HE WOULD QUICKLY WALK AWAY TO AVOID VAIN CONVERSATIONS THAT WOULD BE OF NO SPIRITUAL BENEFIT.

LIKEWISE, JOHN LEARNED TO ALWAYS STRIVE TO KEEP HIS FOCUS ON WHAT IS HEAVENLY AND BENEFICIAL.

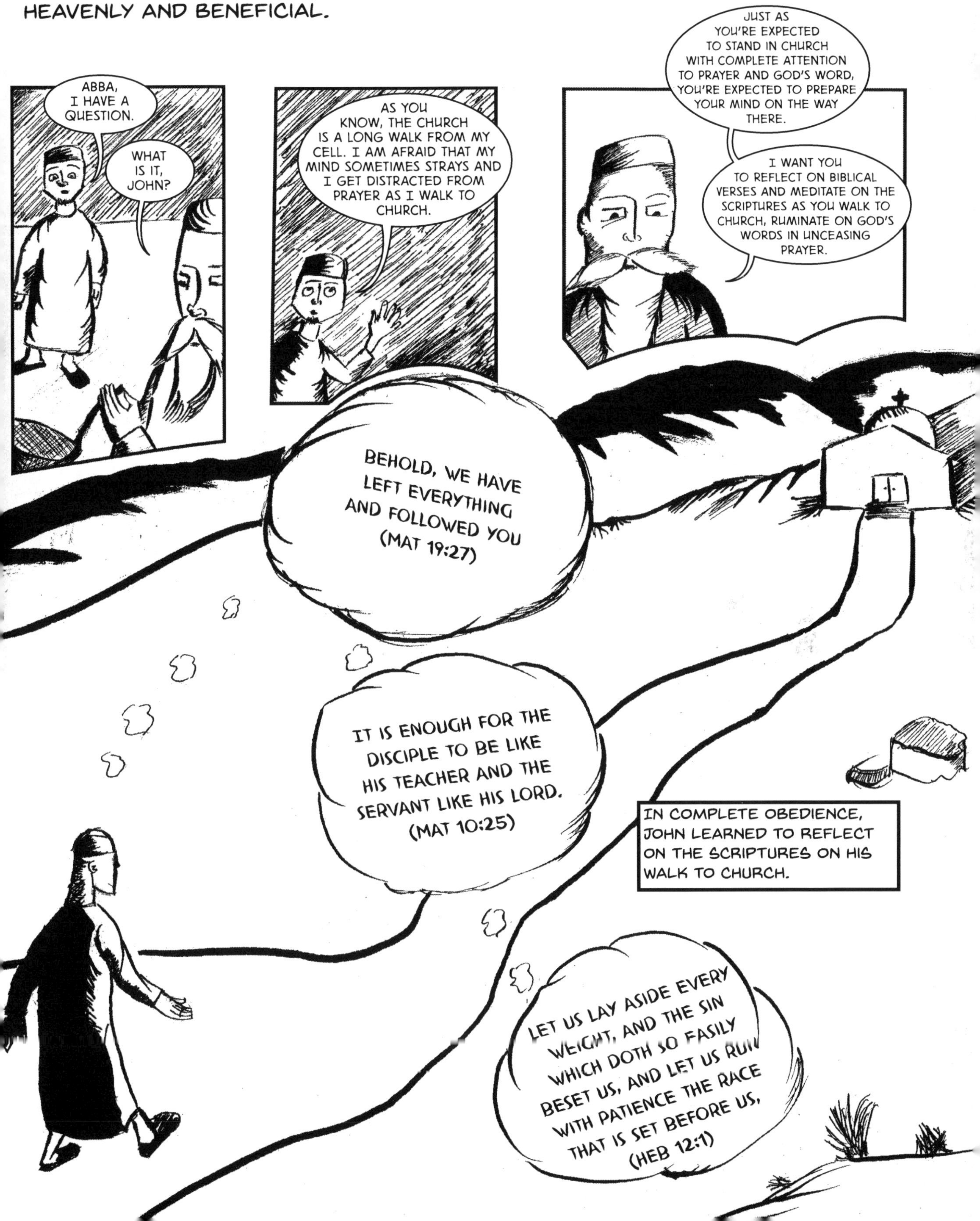
ABBA, I HAVE A QUESTION.
WHAT IS IT, JOHN?
AS YOU KNOW, THE CHURCH IS A LONG WALK FROM MY CELL. I AM AFRAID THAT MY MIND SOMETIMES STRAYS AND I GET DISTRACTED FROM PRAYER AS I WALK TO CHURCH.
JUST AS YOU'RE EXPECTED TO STAND IN CHURCH WITH COMPLETE ATTENTION TO PRAYER AND GOD'S WORD, YOU'RE EXPECTED TO PREPARE YOUR MIND ON THE WAY THERE.
I WANT YOU TO REFLECT ON BIBLICAL VERSES AND MEDITATE ON THE SCRIPTURES AS YOU WALK TO CHURCH, RUMINATE ON GOD'S WORDS IN UNCEASING PRAYER.
BEHOLD, WE HAVE LEFT EVERYTHING AND FOLLOWED YOU (MAT 19:27)
IT IS ENOUGH FOR THE DISCIPLE TO BE LIKE HIS TEACHER AND THE SERVANT LIKE HIS LORD. (MAT 10:25)
IN COMPLETE OBEDIENCE, JOHN LEARNED TO REFLECT ON THE SCRIPTURES ON HIS WALK TO CHURCH.
LET US LAY ASIDE EVERY WEIGHT, AND THE SIN WHICH DOTH SO EASILY BESET US, AND LET US RUN WITH PATIENCE THE RACE THAT IS SET BEFORE US, (HEB 12:1)

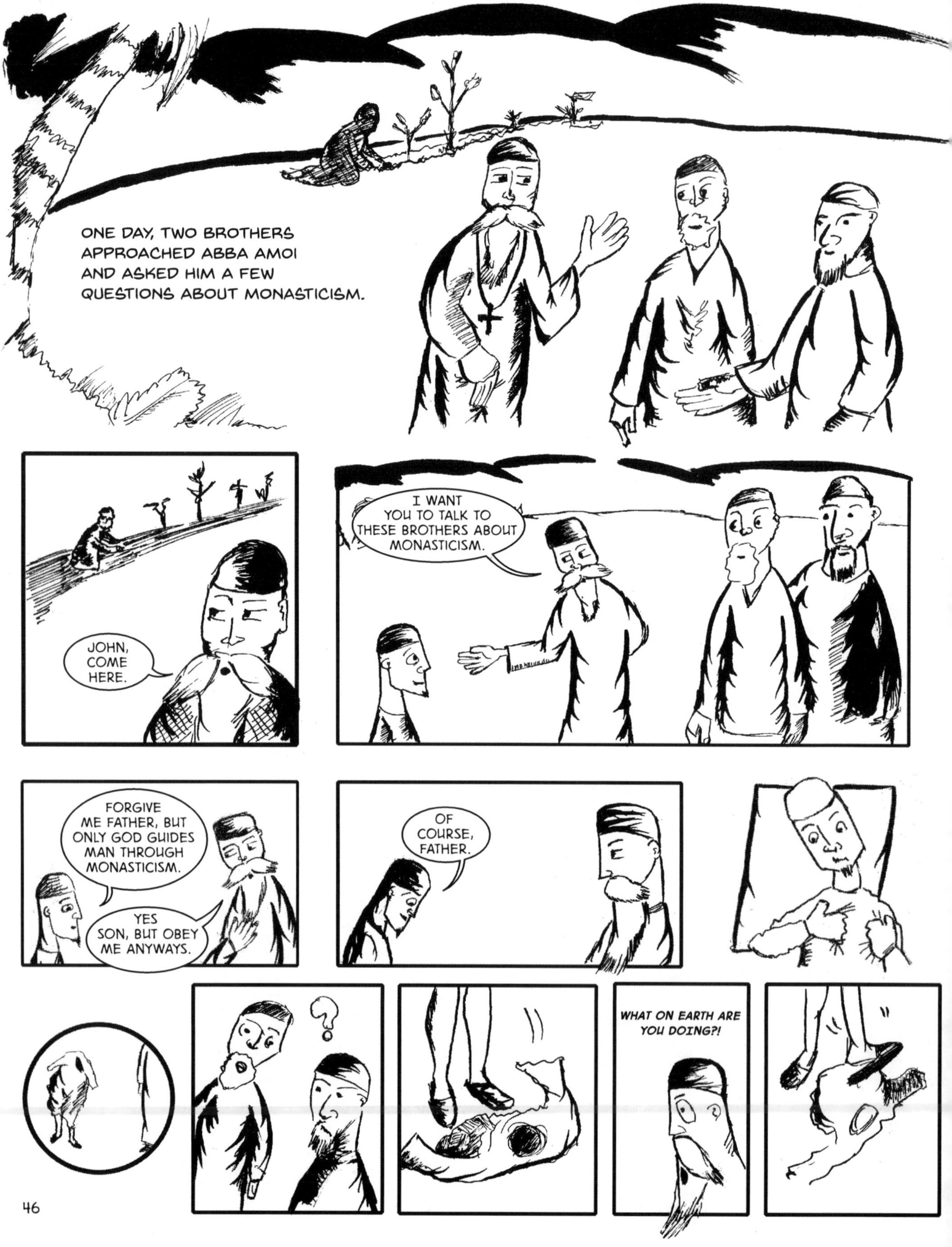
ONE DAY, TWO BROTHERS APPROACHED ABBA AMOI AND ASKED HIM A FEW QUESTIONS ABOUT MONASTICISM.
JOHN, COME HERE.
I WANT YOU TO TALK TO THESE BROTHERS ABOUT MONASTICISM.
FORGIVE ME FATHER, BUT ONLY GOD GUIDES MAN THROUGH MONASTICISM.
YES SON, BUT OBEY ME ANYWAYS.
OF COURSE, FATHER.
?
WHAT ON EARTH ARE YOU DOING?!

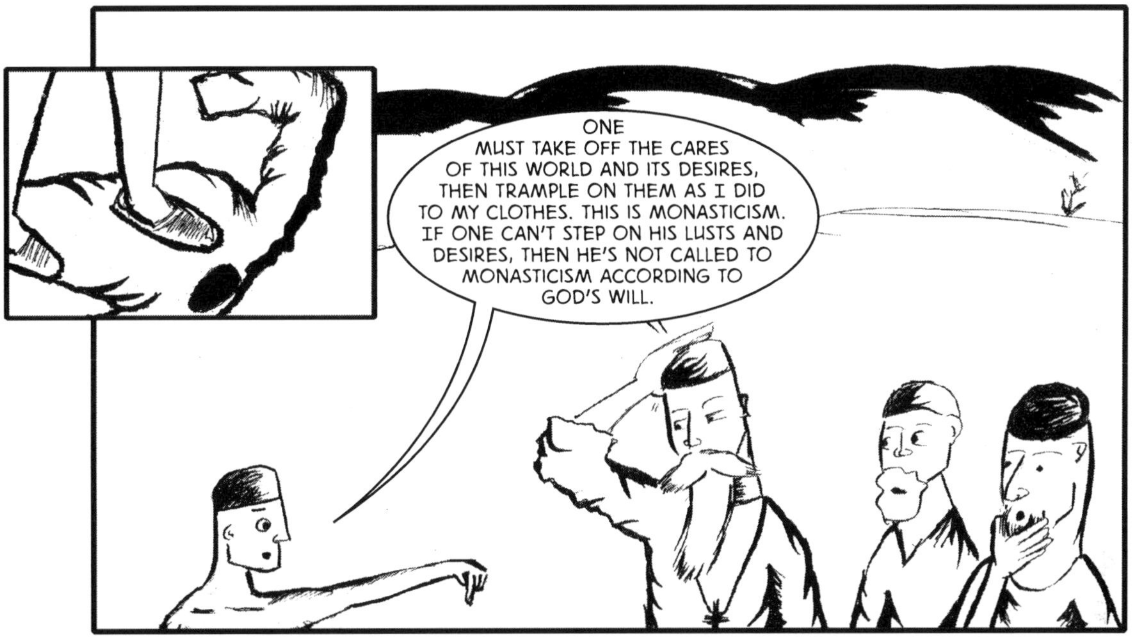
ONE MUST TAKE OFF THE CARES OF THIS WORLD AND ITS DESIRES, THEN TRAMPLE ON THEM AS I DID TO MY CLOTHES. THIS IS MONASTICISM. IF ONE CAN'T STEP ON HIS LUSTS AND DESIRES, THEN HE'S NOT CALLED TO MONASTICISM ACCORDING TO GOD'S WILL.

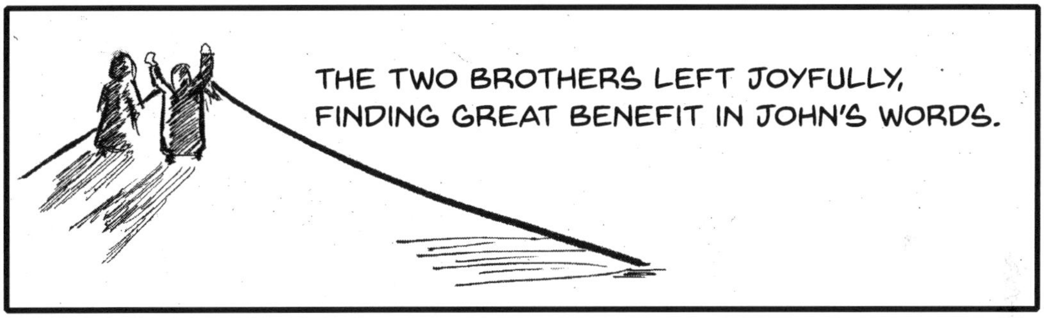
THE TWO BROTHERS LEFT JOYFULLY, FINDING GREAT BENEFIT IN JOHN'S WORDS.

JOHN'S ACTION SEEMED STRANGE TO SOME & ATTENTION SEEKING TO OTHERS- BUT NOT TO AMOI'S DISCERNING HEART.

ABBA AMOI LEARNED DISCERNMENT FROM THE DESERT FATHERS. HE SAW JOHN'S SOUL AS OTHERS DIDN'T.

HE SAW THAT JOHN WAS SPECIAL, A FRUIT THAT WAS QUICKLY GROWING TOWARDS PERFECTION.

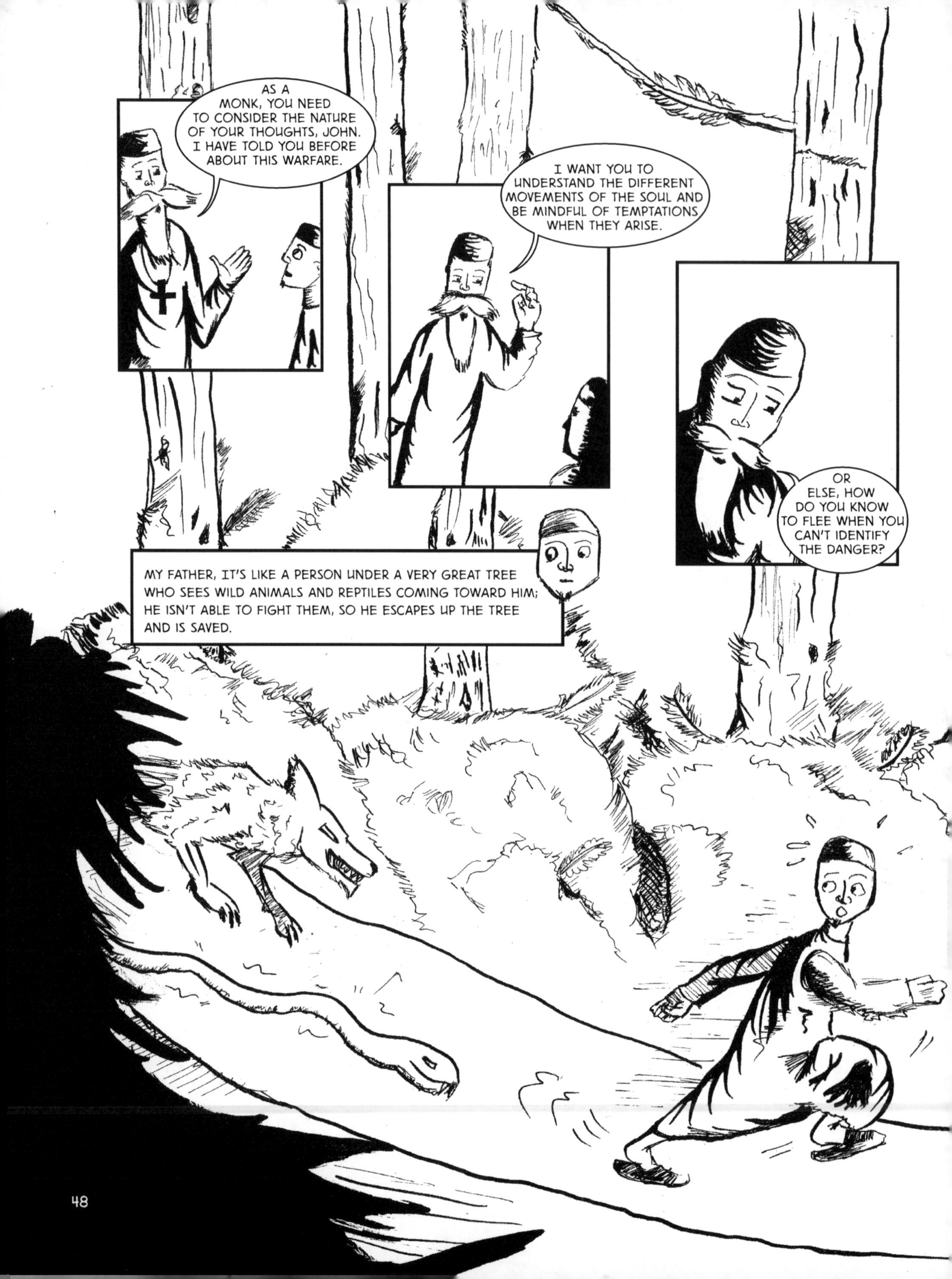

AS A MONK, YOU NEED TO CONSIDER THE NATURE OF YOUR THOUGHTS, JOHN. I HAVE TOLD YOU BEFORE ABOUT THIS WARFARE.
I WANT YOU TO UNDERSTAND THE DIFFERENT MOVEMENTS OF THE SOUL AND BE MINDFUL OF TEMPTATIONS WHEN THEY ARISE.
OR ELSE, HOW DO YOU KNOW TO FLEE WHEN YOU CAN'T IDENTIFY THE DANGER?
MY FATHER, IT'S LIKE A PERSON UNDER A VERY GREAT TREE WHO SEES WILD ANIMALS AND REPTILES COMING TOWARD HIM; HE ISN'T ABLE TO FIGHT THEM, SO HE ESCAPES UP THE TREE AND IS SAVED.

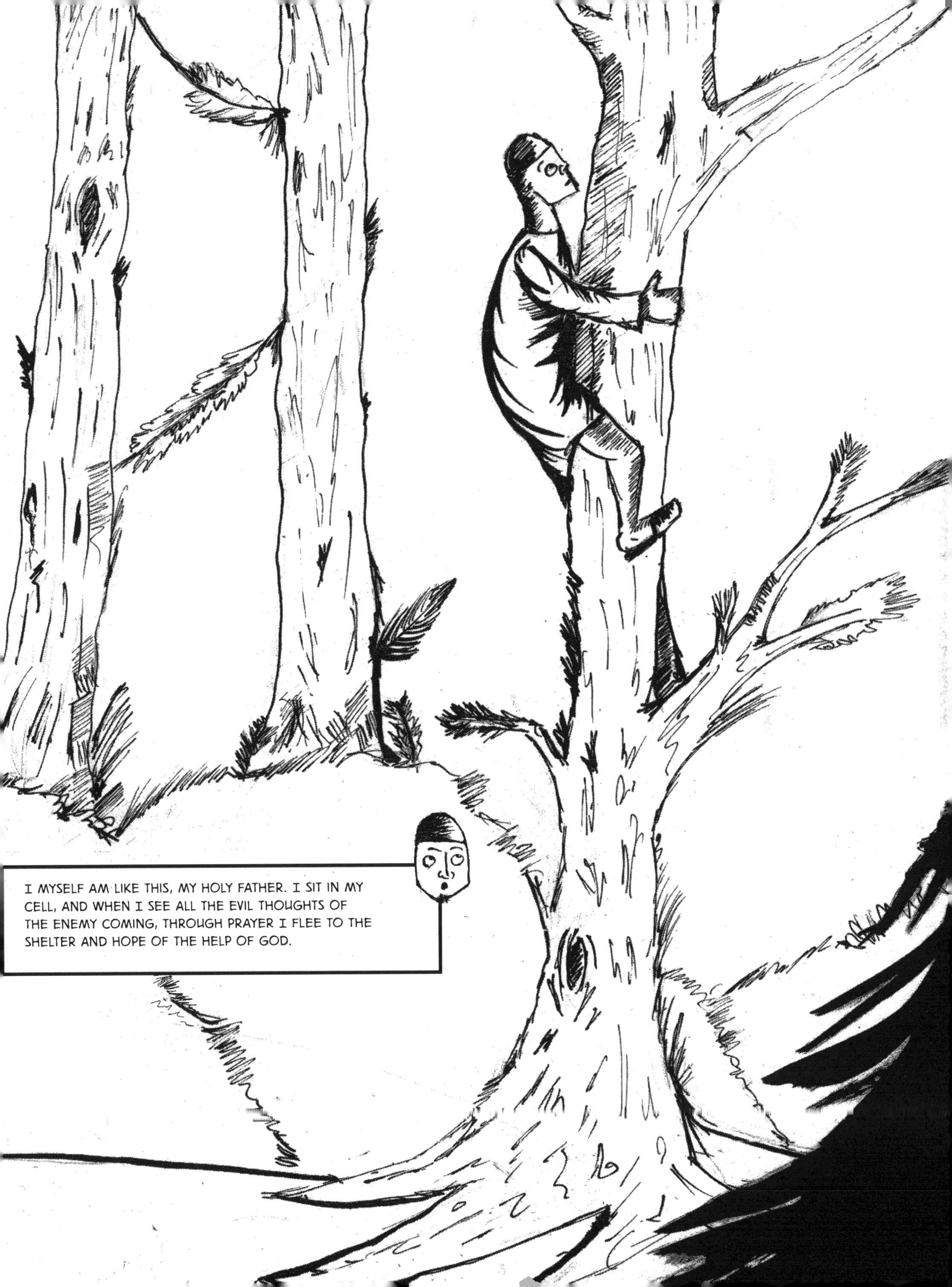
I MYSELF AM LIKE THIS, MY HOLY FATHER. I SIT IN MY CELL, AND WHEN I SEE ALL THE EVIL THOUGHTS OF THE ENEMY COMING, THROUGH PRAYER I FLEE TO THE SHELTER AND HOPE OF THE HELP OF GOD.

# Chapter Two
# Roots

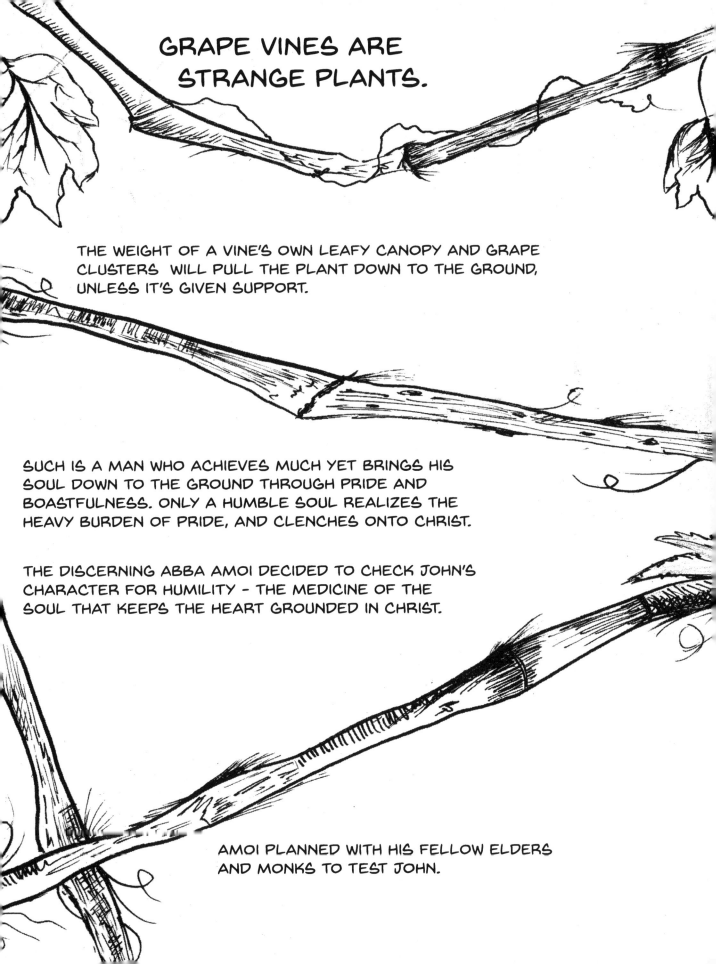

# GRAPE VINES ARE STRANGE PLANTS.

THE WEIGHT OF A VINE'S OWN LEAFY CANOPY AND GRAPE CLUSTERS WILL PULL THE PLANT DOWN TO THE GROUND, UNLESS IT'S GIVEN SUPPORT.

SUCH IS A MAN WHO ACHIEVES MUCH YET BRINGS HIS SOUL DOWN TO THE GROUND THROUGH PRIDE AND BOASTFULNESS. ONLY A HUMBLE SOUL REALIZES THE HEAVY BURDEN OF PRIDE, AND CLENCHES ONTO CHRIST.

THE DISCERNING ABBA AMOI DECIDED TO CHECK JOHN'S CHARACTER FOR HUMILITY - THE MEDICINE OF THE SOUL THAT KEEPS THE HEART GROUNDED IN CHRIST.

AMOI PLANNED WITH HIS FELLOW ELDERS AND MONKS TO TEST JOHN.

ONE EARLY MORNING, JOHN MADE HIS WAY JOYFULLY TO CHURCH ONLY TO BE GREETED BY AN ANGRY ELDER!

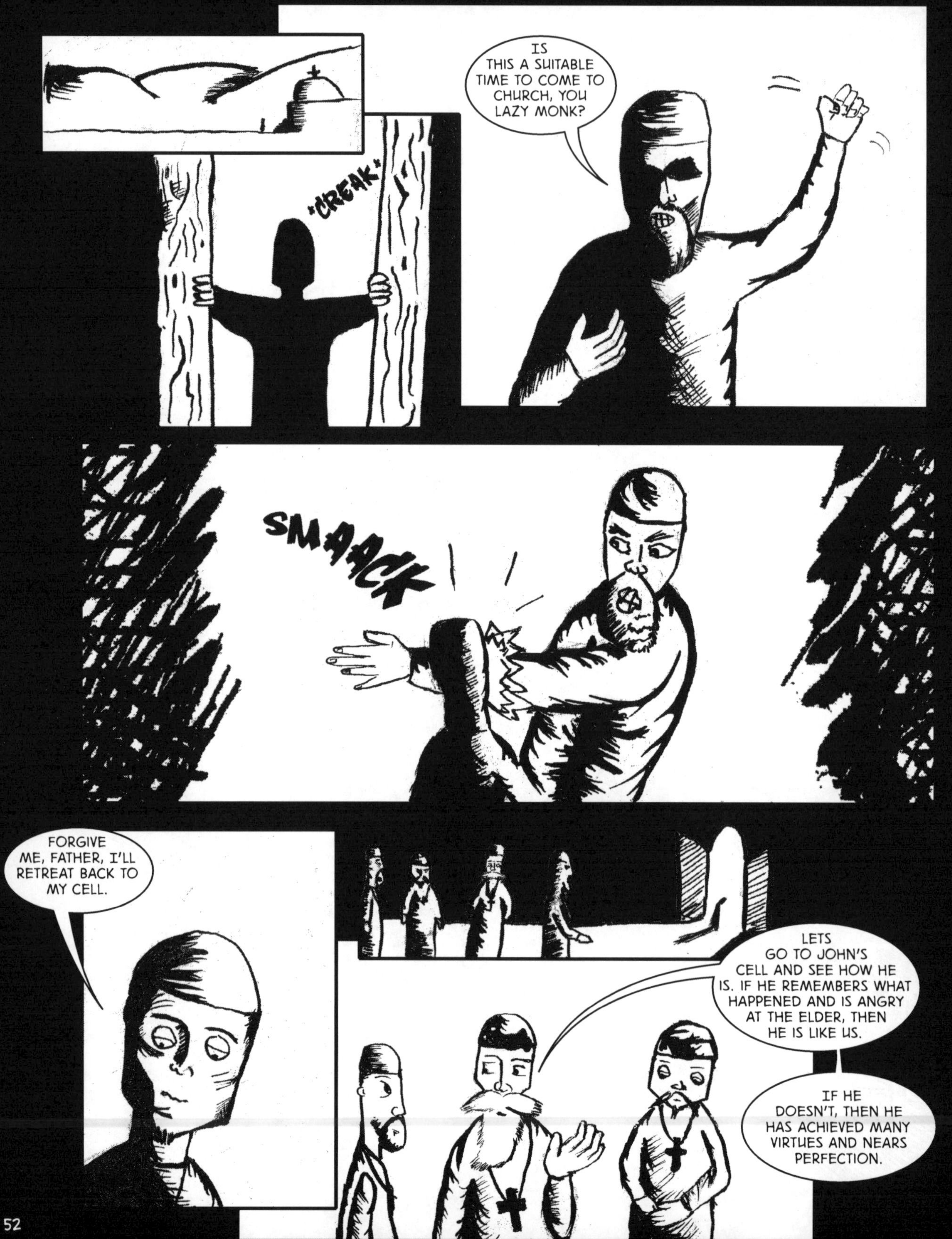
*CREAK*
IS THIS A SUITABLE TIME TO COME TO CHURCH, YOU LAZY MONK?
SMAACK
FORGIVE ME, FATHER, I'LL RETREAT BACK TO MY CELL.
LETS GO TO JOHN'S CELL AND SEE HOW HE IS. IF HE REMEMBERS WHAT HAPPENED AND IS ANGRY AT THE ELDER, THEN HE IS LIKE US.
IF HE DOESN'T, THEN HE HAS ACHIEVED MANY VIRTUES AND NEARS PERFECTION.

THE THREE MONKS HEADED TO JOHN'S CELL.

UPON ARRIVAL THEY HEARD JOHN'S VOICE, ALONG WITH OTHERS, SINGING VARIOUS HYMNS. STRUCK WITH CURIOSITY AND NOT WANTING TO INTERRUPT, THE THREE MONKS PEEKED THROUGH THE WINDOW.

THE MONKS SAW JOHN SITTING IN THE MIDDLE OF THE ROOM SURROUNDED BY ANGELS!

THEIR VOICES WERE AS CAPTIVATING AS THEY WERE HEAVENLY.

THE MONKS STOOD STILL AND MARVELED AT THIS SIGHT.

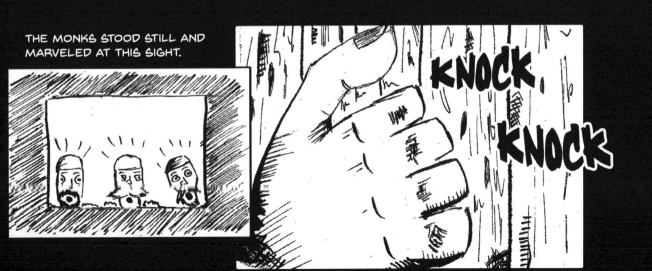

KNOCK. KNOCK

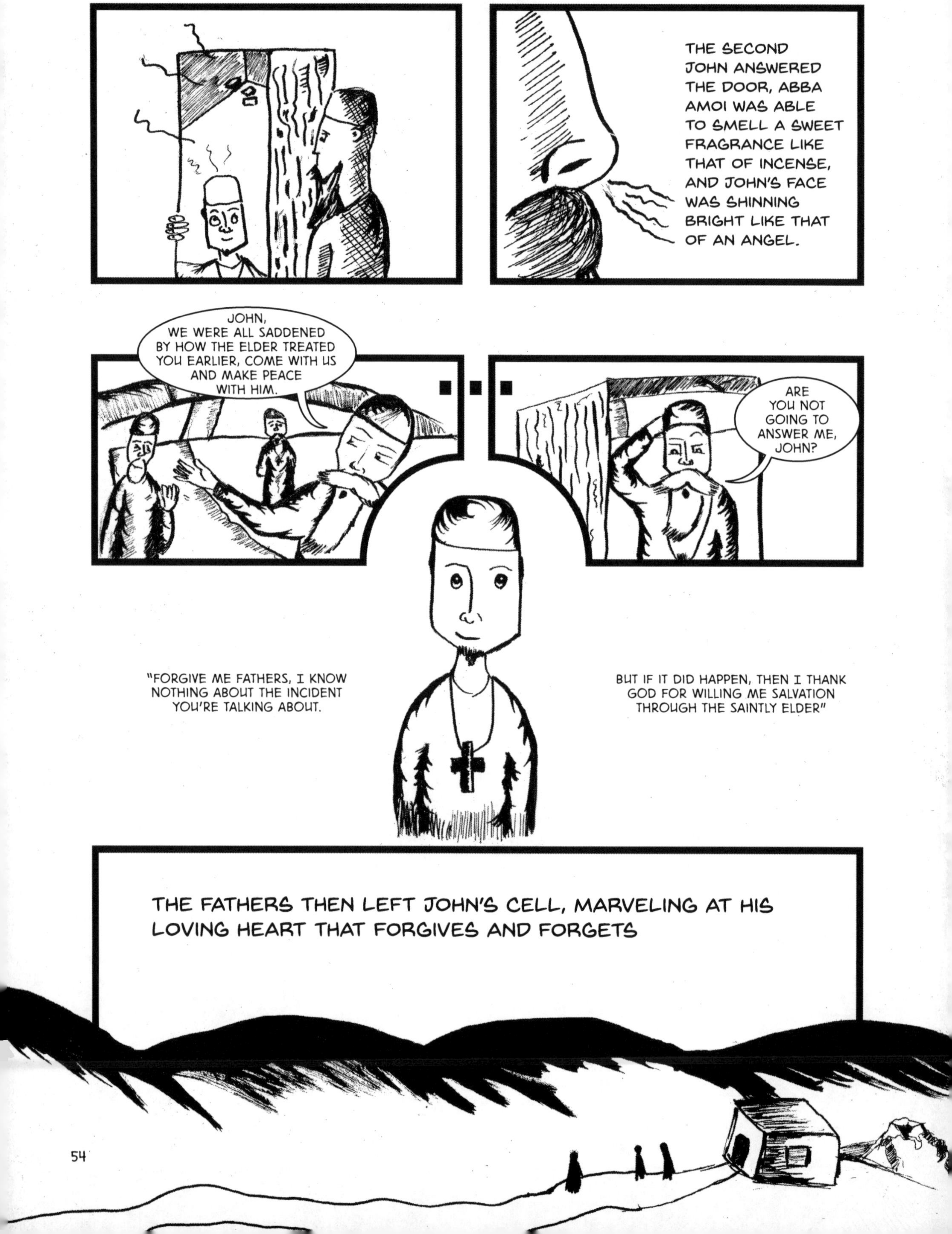
THE SECOND JOHN ANSWERED THE DOOR, ABBA AMOI WAS ABLE TO SMELL A SWEET FRAGRANCE LIKE THAT OF INCENSE, AND JOHN'S FACE WAS SHINNING BRIGHT LIKE THAT OF AN ANGEL.
JOHN, WE WERE ALL SADDENED BY HOW THE ELDER TREATED YOU EARLIER, COME WITH US AND MAKE PEACE WITH HIM.
ARE YOU NOT GOING TO ANSWER ME, JOHN?
"FORGIVE ME FATHERS, I KNOW NOTHING ABOUT THE INCIDENT YOU'RE TALKING ABOUT.
BUT IF IT DID HAPPEN, THEN I THANK GOD FOR WILLING ME SALVATION THROUGH THE SAINTLY ELDER"
THE FATHERS THEN LEFT JOHN'S CELL, MARVELING AT HIS LOVING HEART THAT FORGIVES AND FORGETS

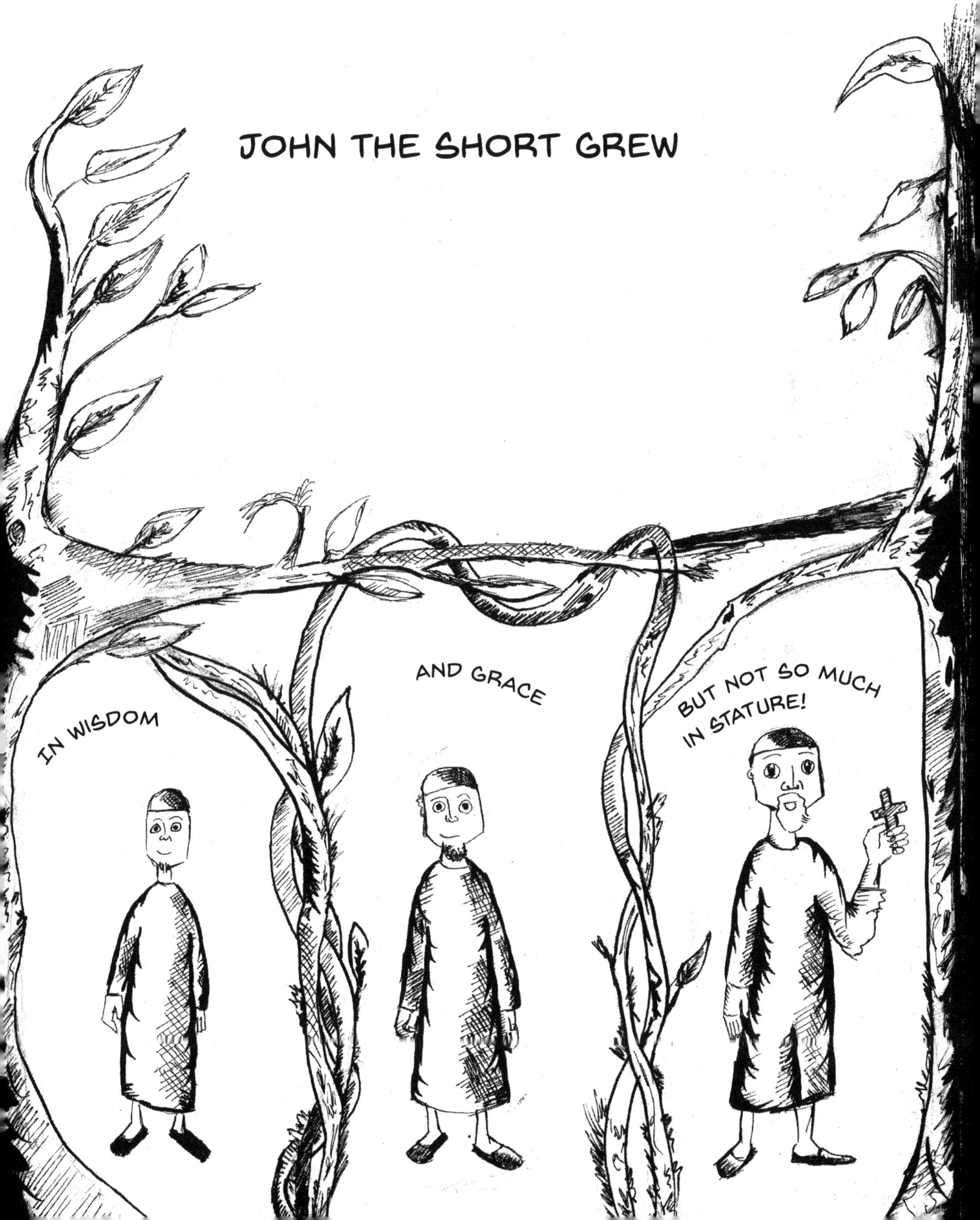
JOHN THE SHORT GREW
IN WISDOM
AND GRACE
BUT NOT SO MUCH IN STATURE!

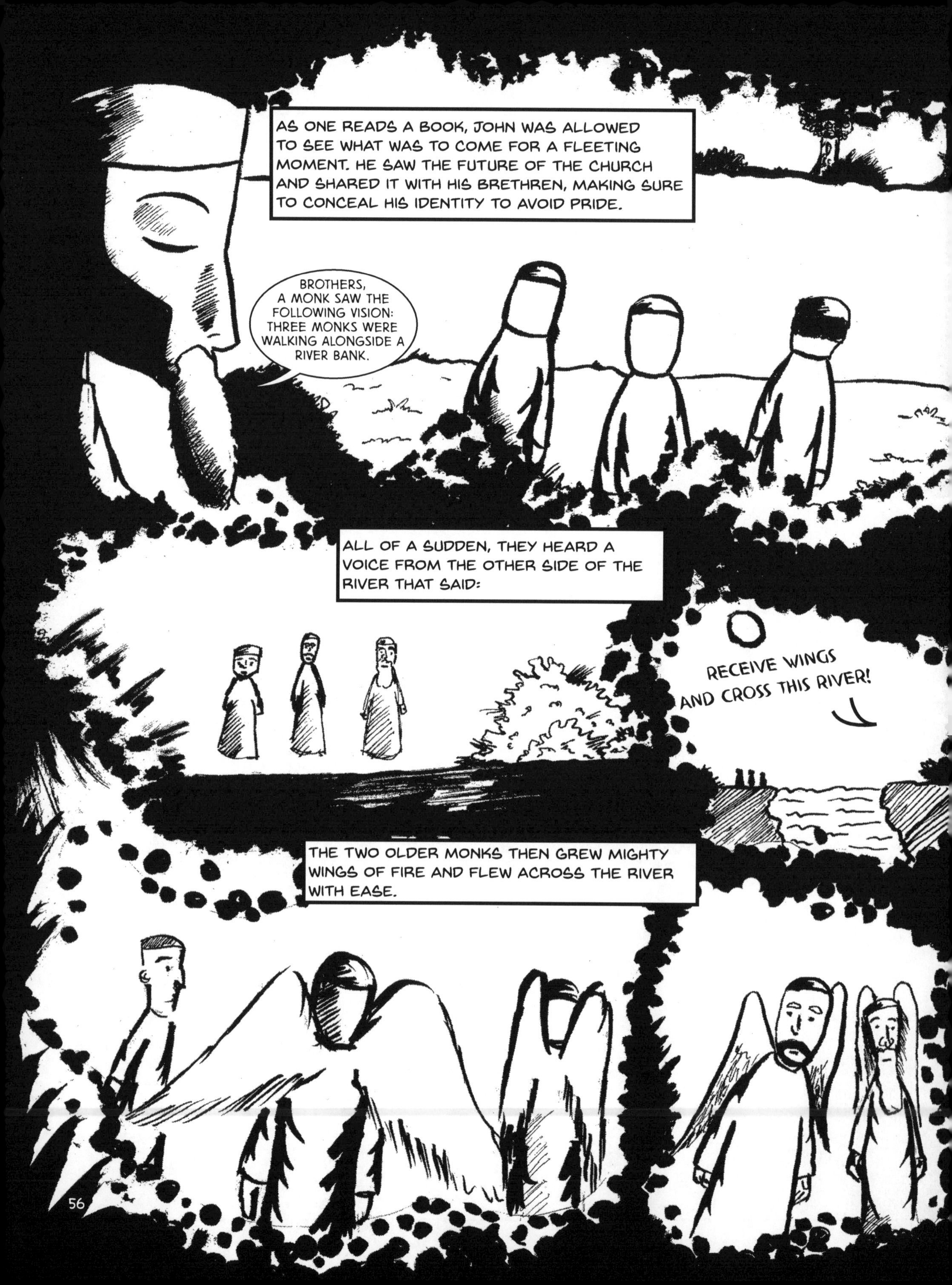

AS ONE READS A BOOK, JOHN WAS ALLOWED TO SEE WHAT WAS TO COME FOR A FLEETING MOMENT. HE SAW THE FUTURE OF THE CHURCH AND SHARED IT WITH HIS BRETHREN, MAKING SURE TO CONCEAL HIS IDENTITY TO AVOID PRIDE.
BROTHERS, A MONK SAW THE FOLLOWING VISION: THREE MONKS WERE WALKING ALONGSIDE A RIVER BANK.
ALL OF A SUDDEN, THEY HEARD A VOICE FROM THE OTHER SIDE OF THE RIVER THAT SAID:
RECEIVE WINGS AND CROSS THIS RIVER!
THE TWO OLDER MONKS THEN GREW MIGHTY WINGS OF FIRE AND FLEW ACROSS THE RIVER WITH EASE.

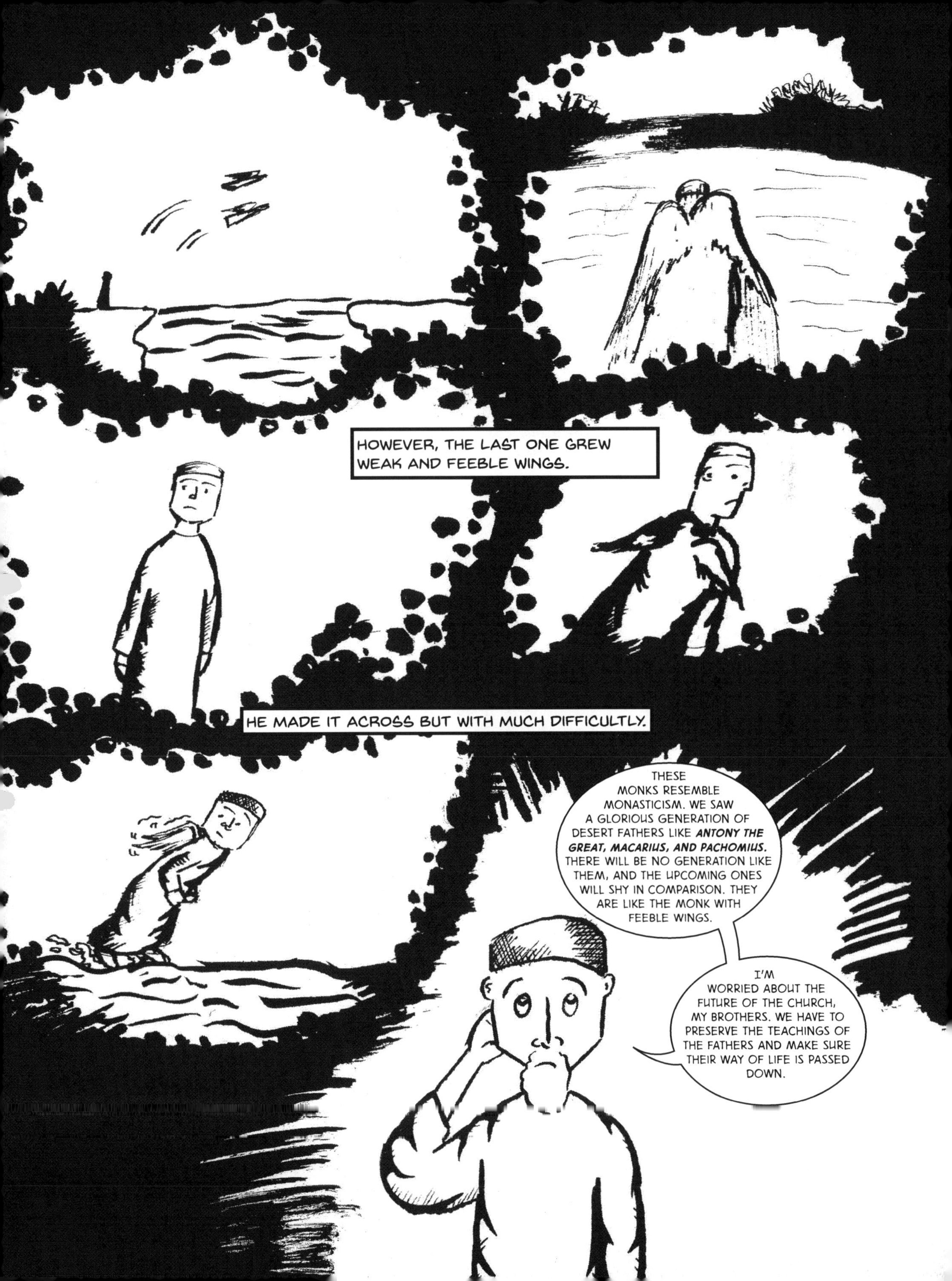
HOWEVER, THE LAST ONE GREW WEAK AND FEEBLE WINGS.
HE MADE IT ACROSS BUT WITH MUCH DIFFICULTLY.
THESE MONKS RESEMBLE MONASTICISM. WE SAW A GLORIOUS GENERATION OF DESERT FATHERS LIKE ***ANTONY THE GREAT, MACARIUS, AND PACHOMIUS.*** THERE WILL BE NO GENERATION LIKE THEM, AND THE UPCOMING ONES WILL SHY IN COMPARISON. THEY ARE LIKE THE MONK WITH FEEBLE WINGS.
I'M WORRIED ABOUT THE FUTURE OF THE CHURCH, MY BROTHERS. WE HAVE TO PRESERVE THE TEACHINGS OF THE FATHERS AND MAKE SURE THEIR WAY OF LIFE IS PASSED DOWN.

THIS VISION MOTIVATED JOHN TO BE MORE OBEDIENT TO HIS FATHER, AMOI, AND WORK HARDER TO LIVE A LIFE OF PRAYER AND ASCETICISM.

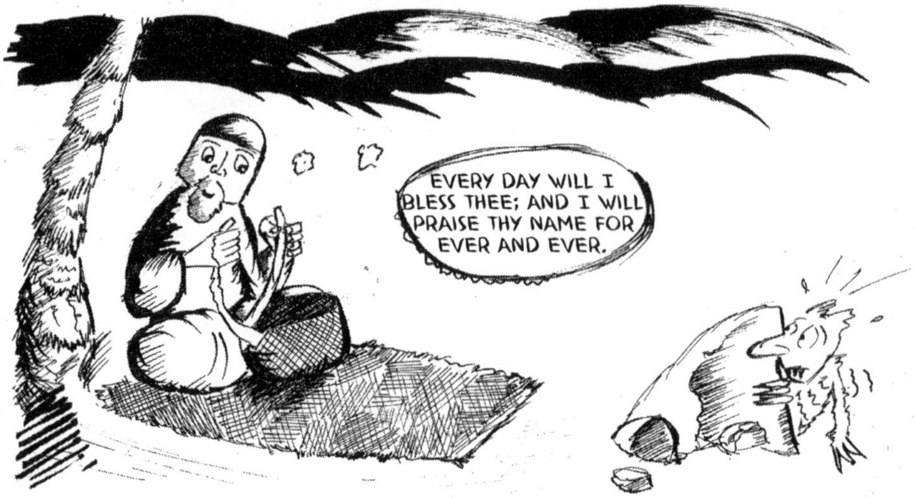
EVERY DAY WILL I BLESS THEE; AND I WILL PRAISE THY NAME FOR EVER AND EVER.

## HE PROGRESSED IN VIRTUE

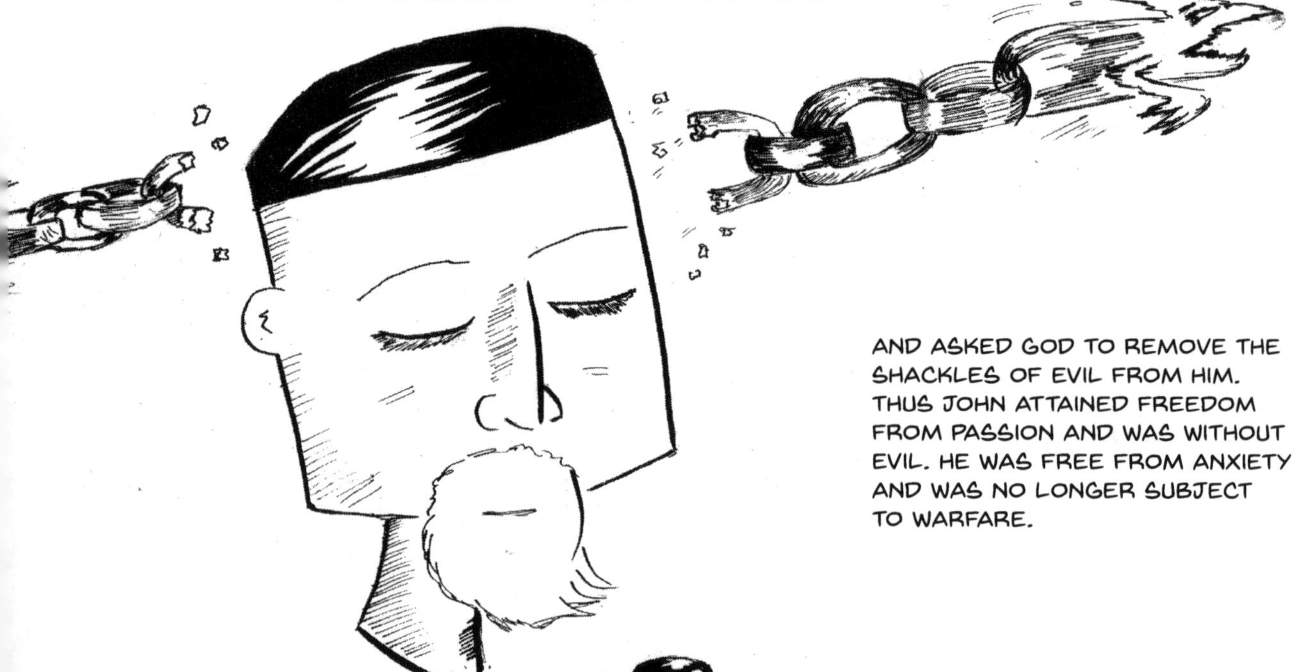

AND ASKED GOD TO REMOVE THE SHACKLES OF EVIL FROM HIM. THUS JOHN ATTAINED FREEDOM FROM PASSION AND WAS WITHOUT EVIL. HE WAS FREE FROM ANXIETY AND WAS NO LONGER SUBJECT TO WARFARE.

HOWEVER, HE SOON REALIZED THE DANGER OF SUCH A REQUEST AND QUICKLY WENT TO ABBA AMOI FOR GUIDANCE.

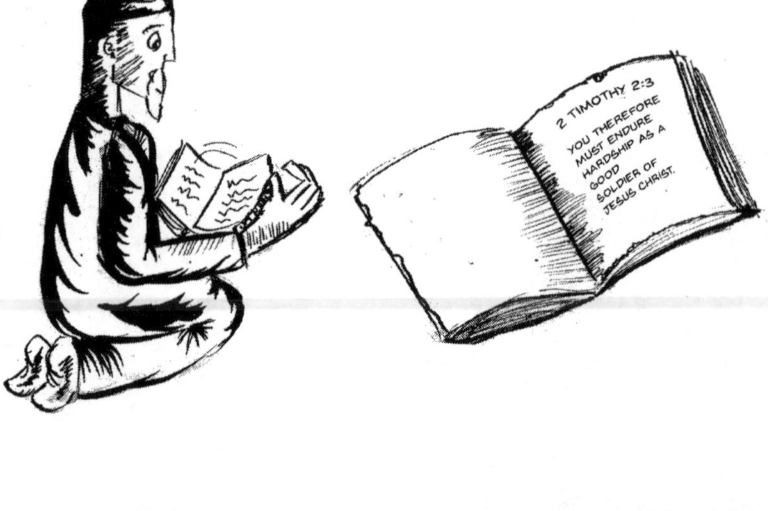
2 TIMOTHY 2:3
YOU THEREFORE MUST ENDURE HARDSHIP AS A GOOD SOLDIER OF JESUS CHRIST.

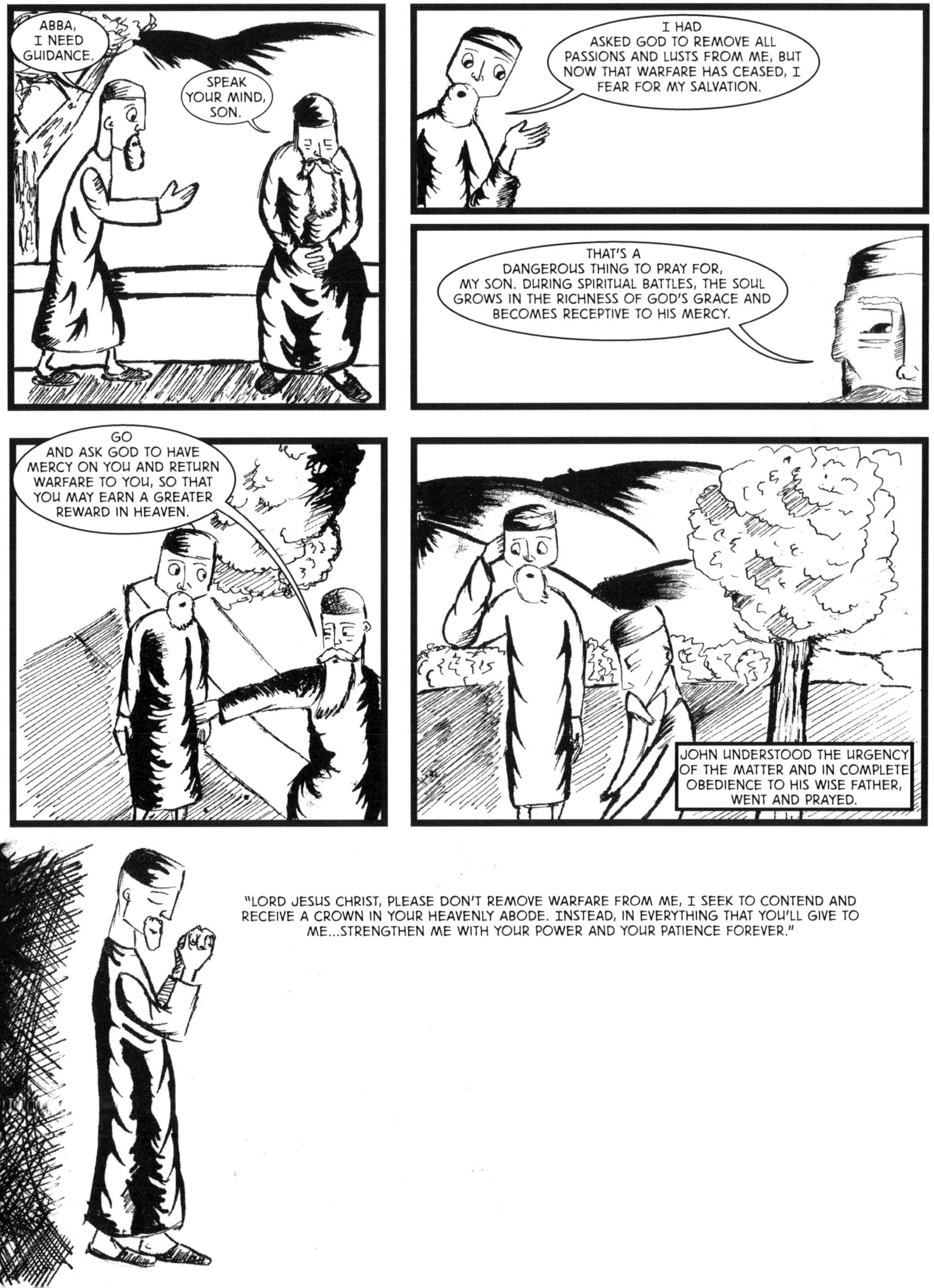
ABBA, I NEED GUIDANCE.
SPEAK YOUR MIND, SON.
I HAD ASKED GOD TO REMOVE ALL PASSIONS AND LUSTS FROM ME, BUT NOW THAT WARFARE HAS CEASED, I FEAR FOR MY SALVATION.
THAT'S A DANGEROUS THING TO PRAY FOR, MY SON. DURING SPIRITUAL BATTLES, THE SOUL GROWS IN THE RICHNESS OF GOD'S GRACE AND BECOMES RECEPTIVE TO HIS MERCY.
GO AND ASK GOD TO HAVE MERCY ON YOU AND RETURN WARFARE TO YOU, SO THAT YOU MAY EARN A GREATER REWARD IN HEAVEN.
JOHN UNDERSTOOD THE URGENCY OF THE MATTER AND IN COMPLETE OBEDIENCE TO HIS WISE FATHER, WENT AND PRAYED.
"LORD JESUS CHRIST, PLEASE DON'T REMOVE WARFARE FROM ME, I SEEK TO CONTEND AND RECEIVE A CROWN IN YOUR HEAVENLY ABODE. INSTEAD, IN EVERYTHING THAT YOU'LL GIVE TO ME...STRENGTHEN ME WITH YOUR POWER AND YOUR PATIENCE FOREVER."

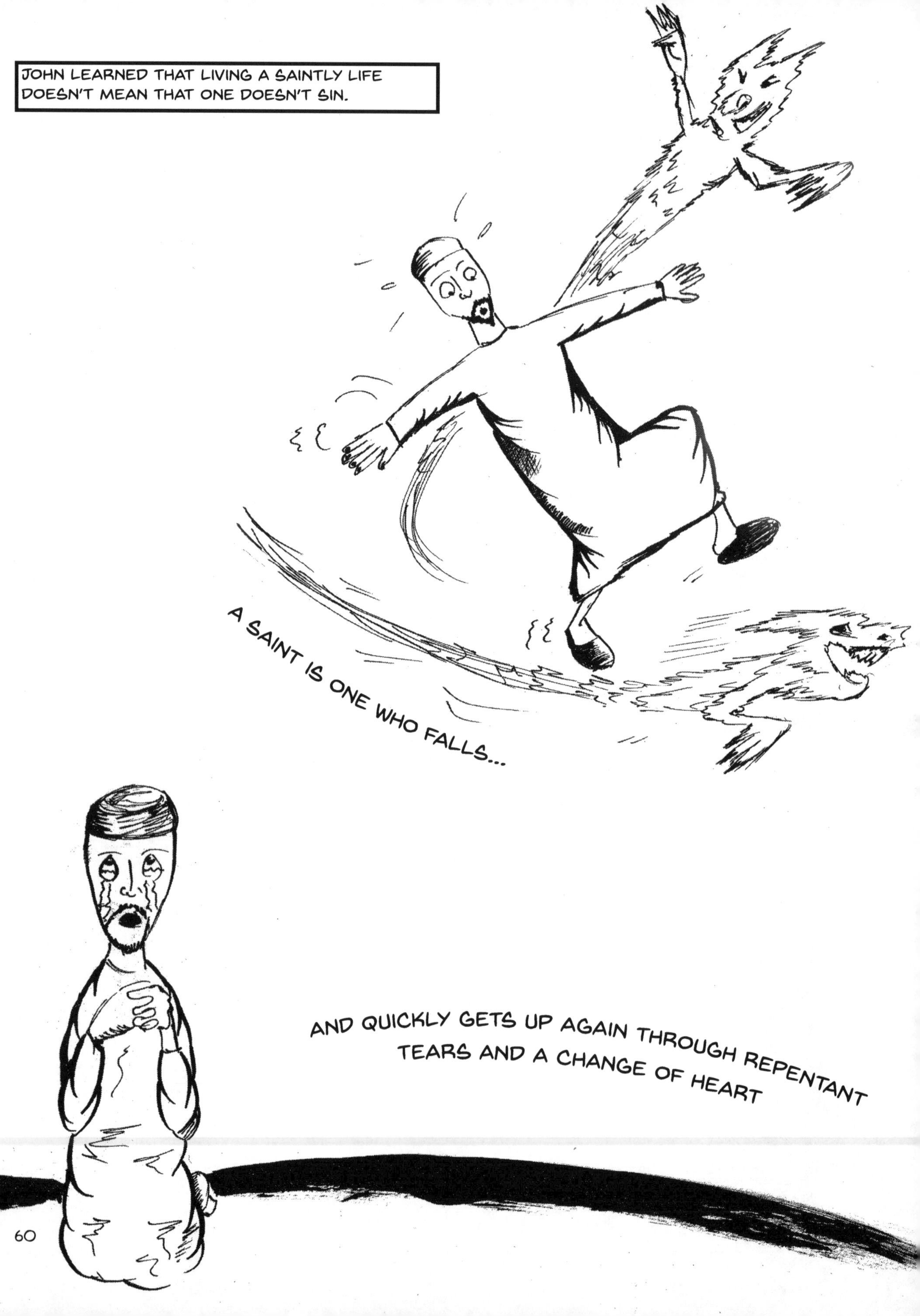
JOHN LEARNED THAT LIVING A SAINTLY LIFE DOESN'T MEAN THAT ONE DOESN'T SIN.
A SAINT IS ONE WHO FALLS...
AND QUICKLY GETS UP AGAIN THROUGH REPENTANT TEARS AND A CHANGE OF HEART

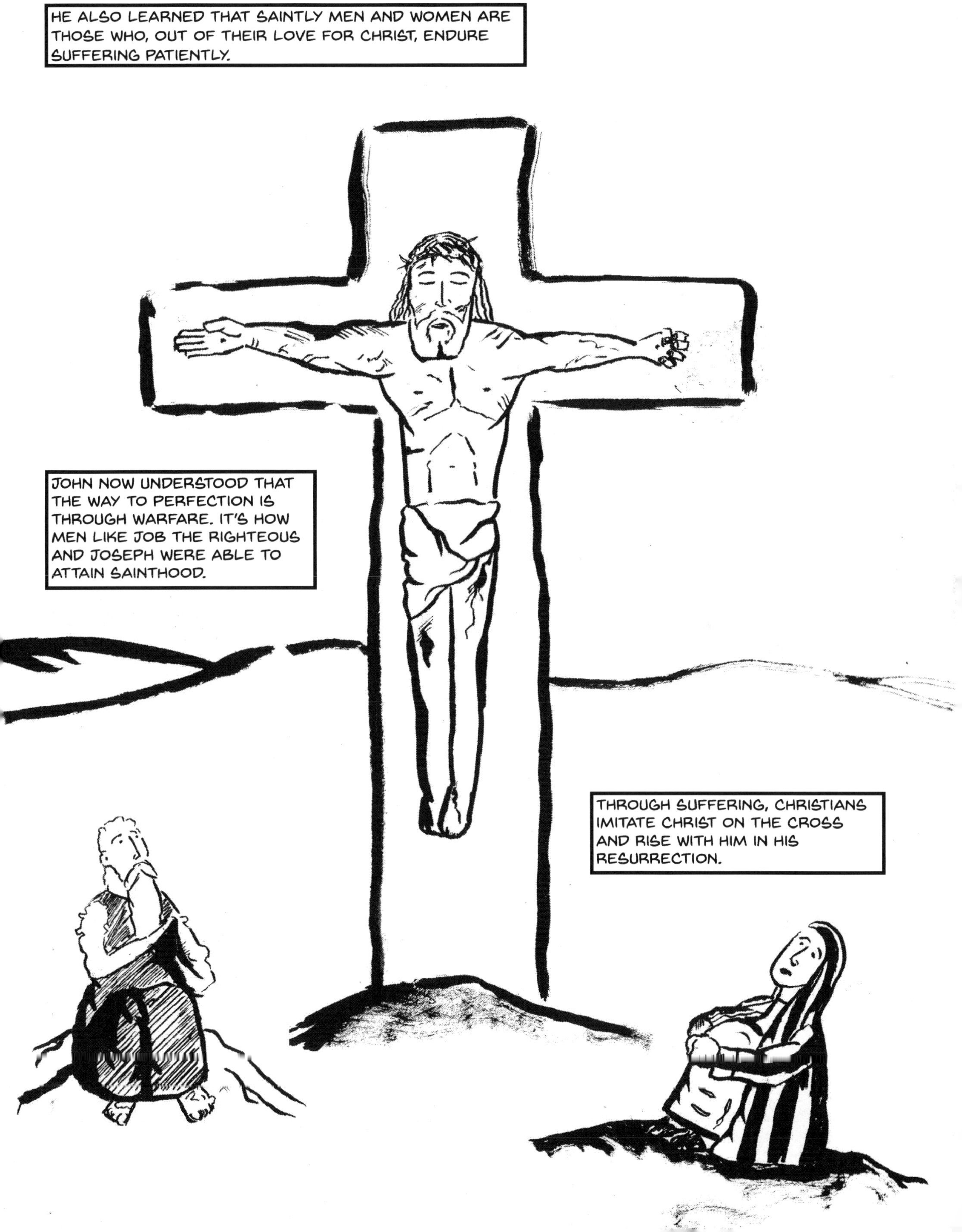
HE ALSO LEARNED THAT SAINTLY MEN AND WOMEN ARE THOSE WHO, OUT OF THEIR LOVE FOR CHRIST, ENDURE SUFFERING PATIENTLY.
JOHN NOW UNDERSTOOD THAT THE WAY TO PERFECTION IS THROUGH WARFARE. IT'S HOW MEN LIKE JOB THE RIGHTEOUS AND JOSEPH WERE ABLE TO ATTAIN SAINTHOOD.
THROUGH SUFFERING, CHRISTIANS IMITATE CHRIST ON THE CROSS AND RISE WITH HIM IN HIS RESURRECTION.

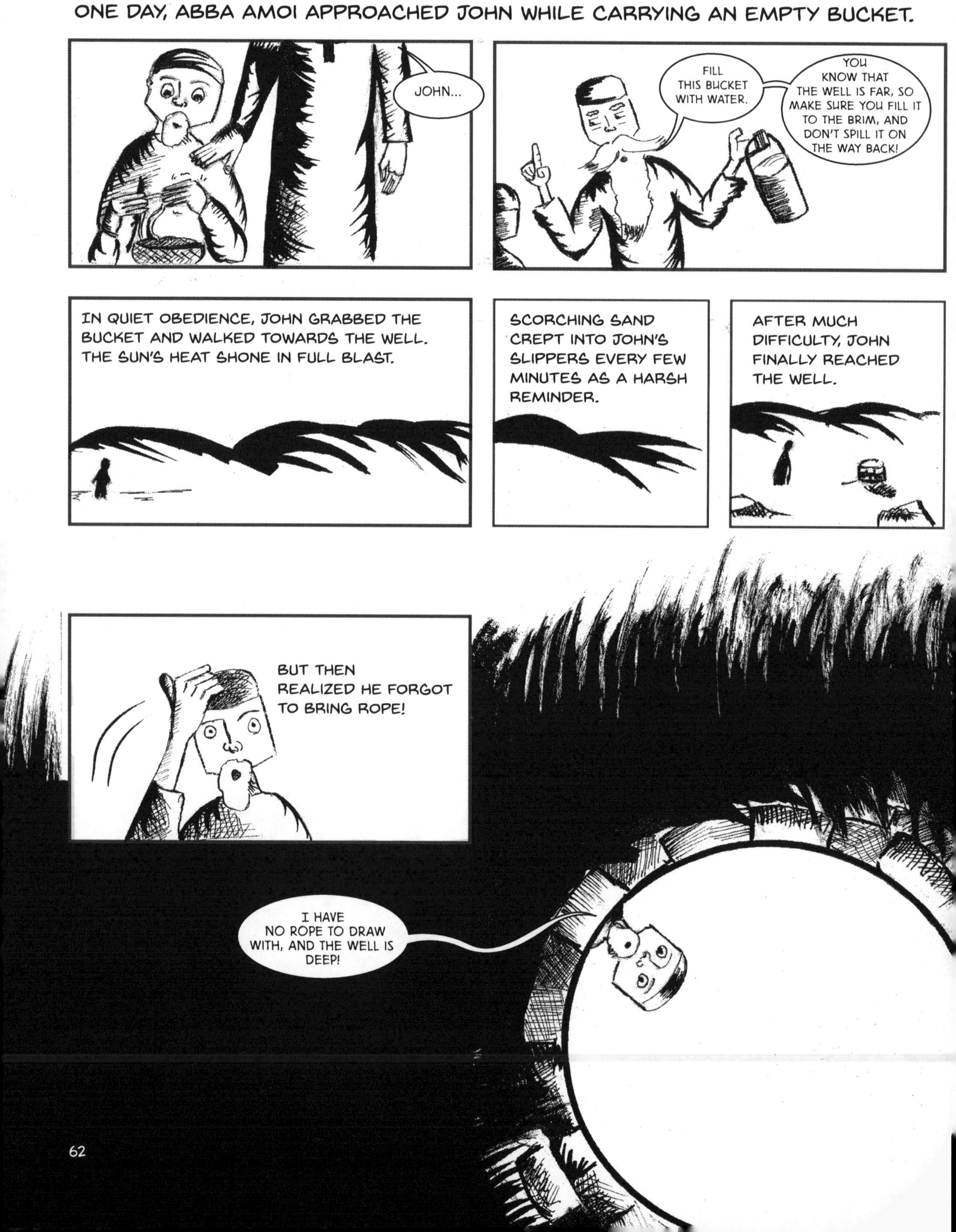
ONE DAY, ABBA AMOI APPROACHED JOHN WHILE CARRYING AN EMPTY BUCKET.
JOHN...
FILL THIS BUCKET WITH WATER.
YOU KNOW THAT THE WELL IS FAR, SO MAKE SURE YOU FILL IT TO THE BRIM, AND DON'T SPILL IT ON THE WAY BACK!
IN QUIET OBEDIENCE, JOHN GRABBED THE BUCKET AND WALKED TOWARDS THE WELL. THE SUN'S HEAT SHONE IN FULL BLAST.
SCORCHING SAND CREPT INTO JOHN'S SLIPPERS EVERY FEW MINUTES AS A HARSH REMINDER.
AFTER MUCH DIFFICULTY, JOHN FINALLY REACHED THE WELL.
BUT THEN REALIZED HE FORGOT TO BRING ROPE!
I HAVE NO ROPE TO DRAW WITH, AND THE WELL IS DEEP!

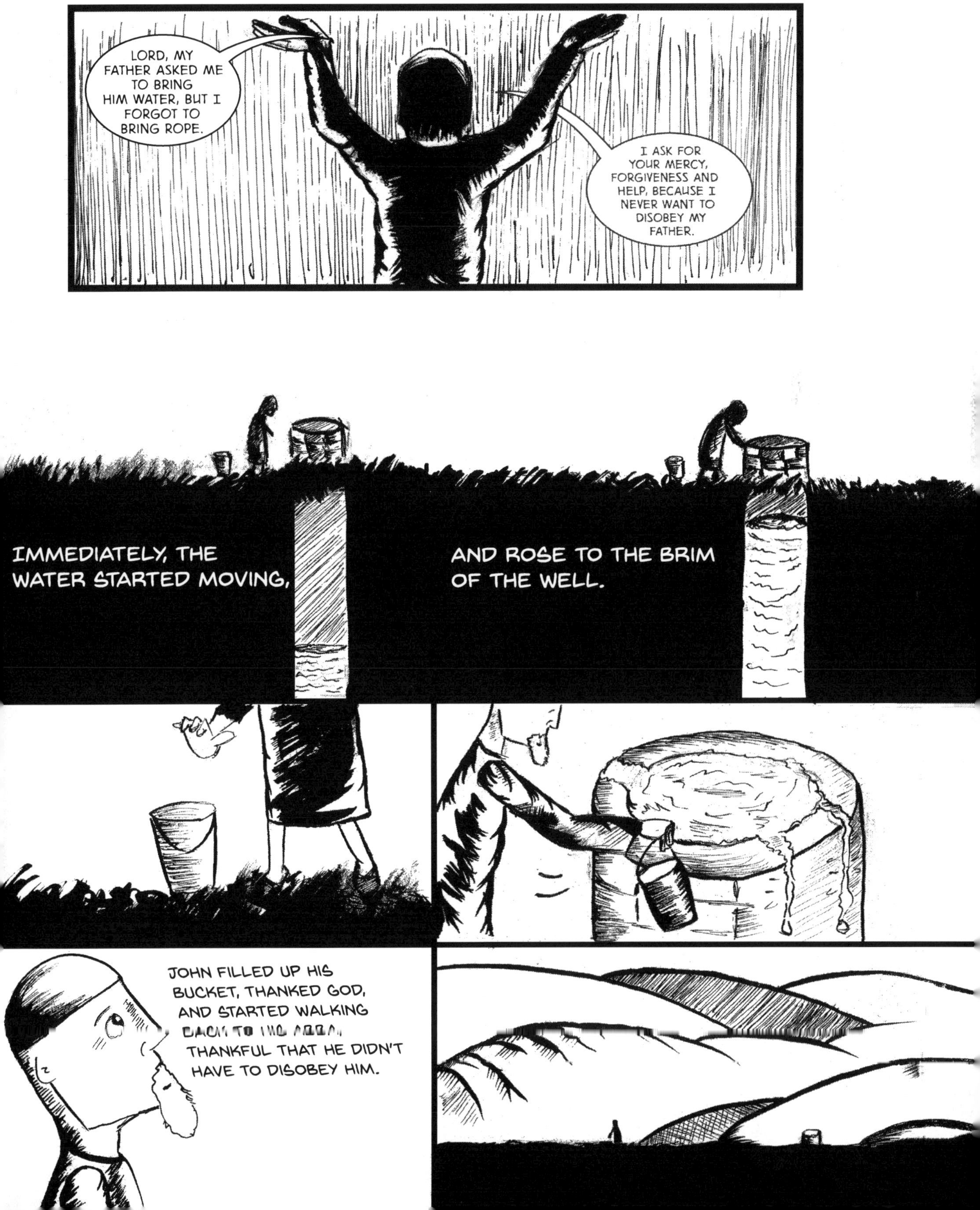
LORD, MY FATHER ASKED ME TO BRING HIM WATER, BUT I FORGOT TO BRING ROPE.
I ASK FOR YOUR MERCY, FORGIVENESS AND HELP, BECAUSE I NEVER WANT TO DISOBEY MY FATHER.
IMMEDIATELY, THE WATER STARTED MOVING,
AND ROSE TO THE BRIM OF THE WELL.
JOHN FILLED UP HIS BUCKET, THANKED GOD, AND STARTED WALKING
THANKFUL THAT HE DIDN'T HAVE TO DISOBEY HIM.

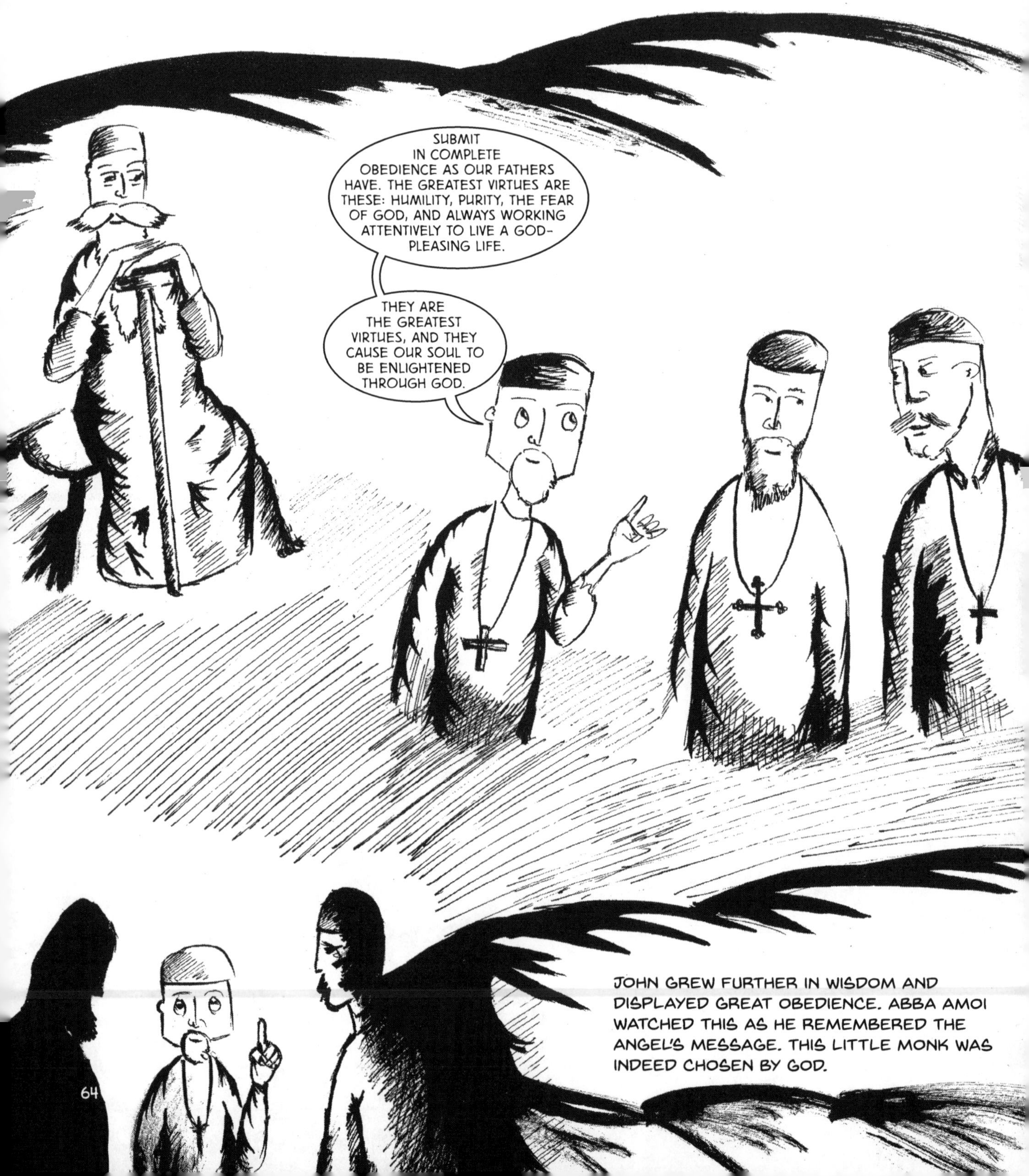
SUBMIT IN COMPLETE OBEDIENCE AS OUR FATHERS HAVE. THE GREATEST VIRTUES ARE THESE: HUMILITY, PURITY, THE FEAR OF GOD, AND ALWAYS WORKING ATTENTIVELY TO LIVE A GOD-PLEASING LIFE.
THEY ARE THE GREATEST VIRTUES, AND THEY CAUSE OUR SOUL TO BE ENLIGHTENED THROUGH GOD.
JOHN GREW FURTHER IN WISDOM AND DISPLAYED GREAT OBEDIENCE. ABBA AMOI WATCHED THIS AS HE REMEMBERED THE ANGEL'S MESSAGE. THIS LITTLE MONK WAS INDEED CHOSEN BY GOD.

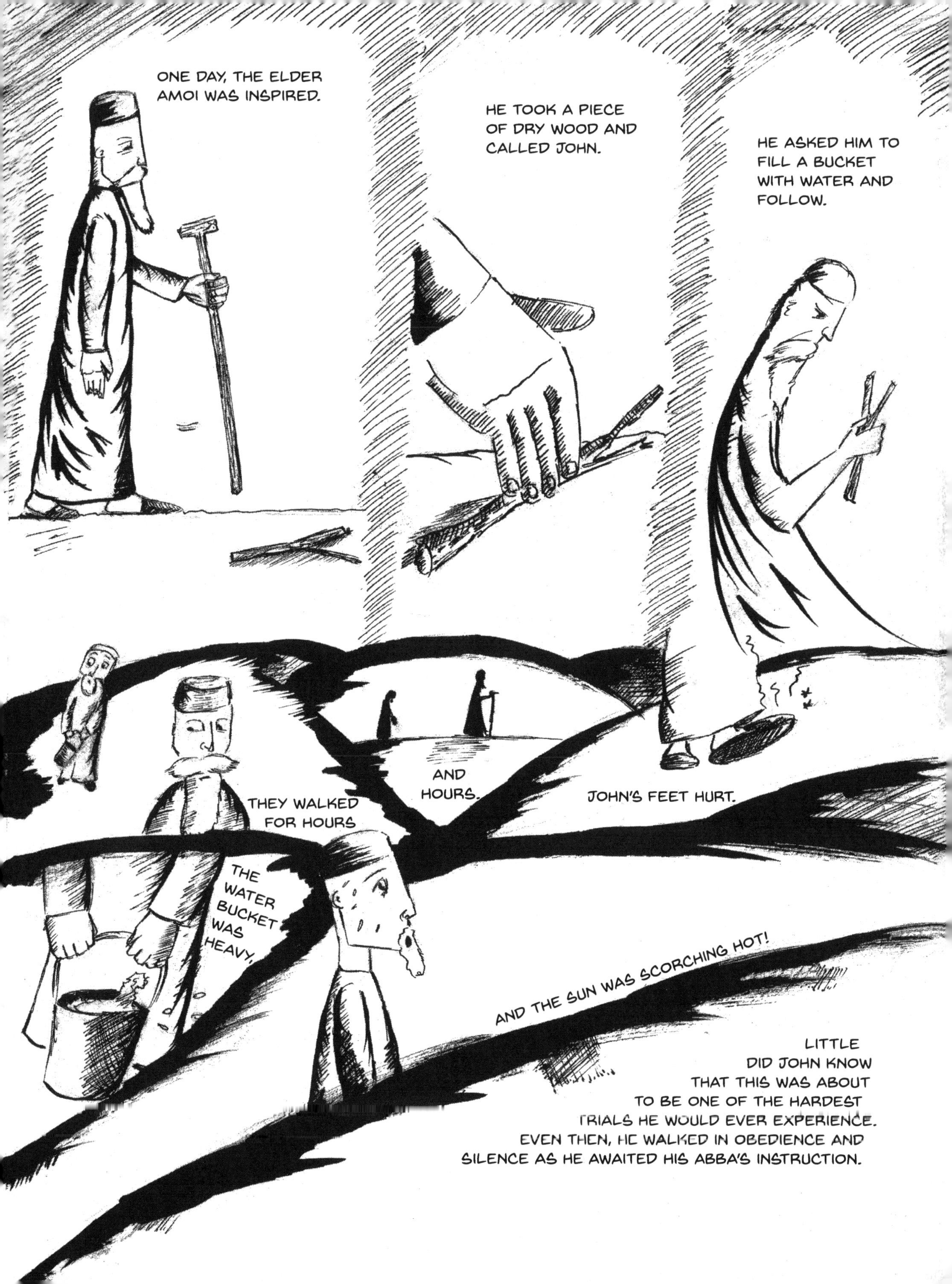
ONE DAY, THE ELDER AMOI WAS INSPIRED.
HE TOOK A PIECE OF DRY WOOD AND CALLED JOHN.
HE ASKED HIM TO FILL A BUCKET WITH WATER AND FOLLOW.
THEY WALKED FOR HOURS
AND HOURS.
JOHN'S FEET HURT.
THE WATER BUCKET WAS HEAVY,
AND THE SUN WAS SCORCHING HOT!
LITTLE DID JOHN KNOW THAT THIS WAS ABOUT TO BE ONE OF THE HARDEST TRIALS HE WOULD EVER EXPERIENCE. EVEN THEN, HE WALKED IN OBEDIENCE AND SILENCE AS HE AWAITED HIS ABBA'S INSTRUCTION.

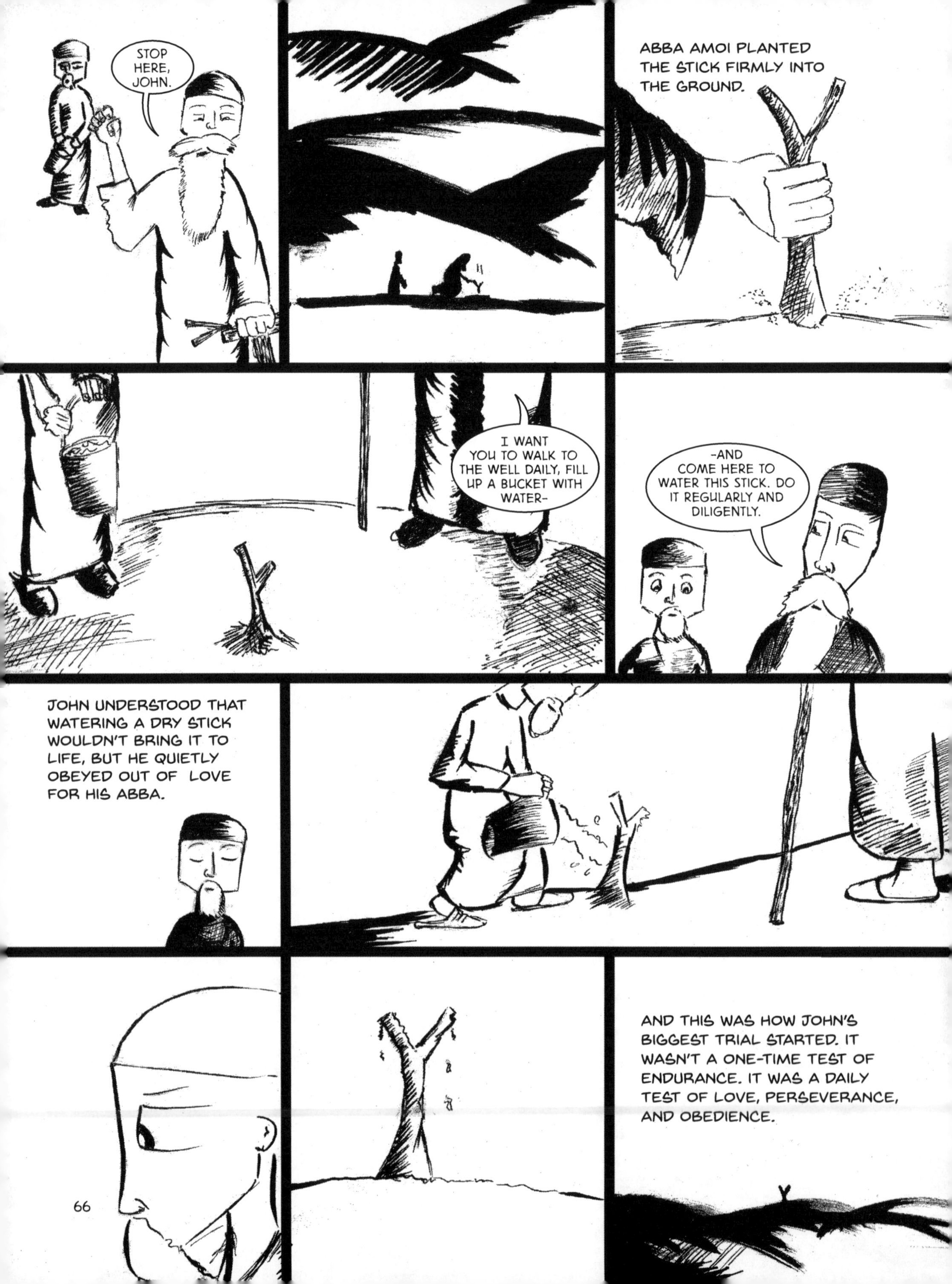
STOP HERE, JOHN.
ABBA AMOI PLANTED THE STICK FIRMLY INTO THE GROUND.
I WANT YOU TO WALK TO THE WELL DAILY, FILL UP A BUCKET WITH WATER-
-AND COME HERE TO WATER THIS STICK. DO IT REGULARLY AND DILIGENTLY.
JOHN UNDERSTOOD THAT WATERING A DRY STICK WOULDN'T BRING IT TO LIFE, BUT HE QUIETLY OBEYED OUT OF LOVE FOR HIS ABBA.
AND THIS WAS HOW JOHN'S BIGGEST TRIAL STARTED. IT WASN'T A ONE-TIME TEST OF ENDURANCE. IT WAS A DAILY TEST OF LOVE, PERSEVERANCE, AND OBEDIENCE.

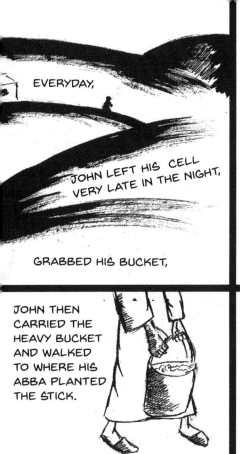

EVERYDAY,

JOHN LEFT HIS CELL VERY LATE IN THE NIGHT,

GRABBED HIS BUCKET,

AND WALKED TO THE WELL AS HE RECITED THE PSALMS.

WHEN HE REACHED THE WELL, HE WOULD FILL UP HIS BUCKET WITH WATER.

JOHN THEN CARRIED THE HEAVY BUCKET AND WALKED TO WHERE HIS ABBA PLANTED THE STICK.

HE WATERED IT AND ALWAYS MADE SURE IT WAS WATERED SUFFICIENTLY.

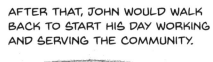

AFTER THAT, JOHN WOULD WALK BACK TO START HIS DAY WORKING AND SERVING THE COMMUNITY.

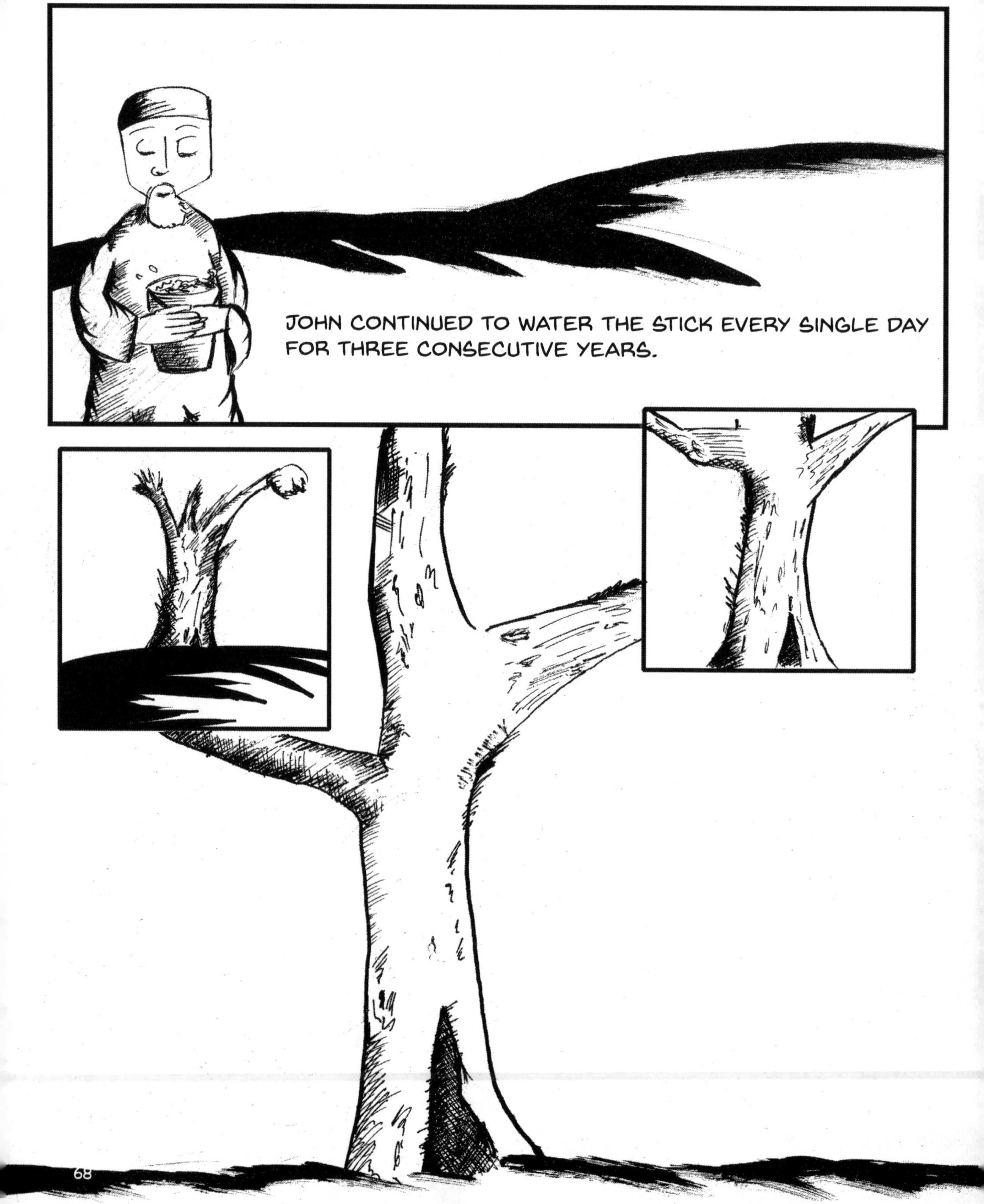
JOHN CONTINUED TO WATER THE STICK EVERY SINGLE DAY FOR THREE CONSECUTIVE YEARS.

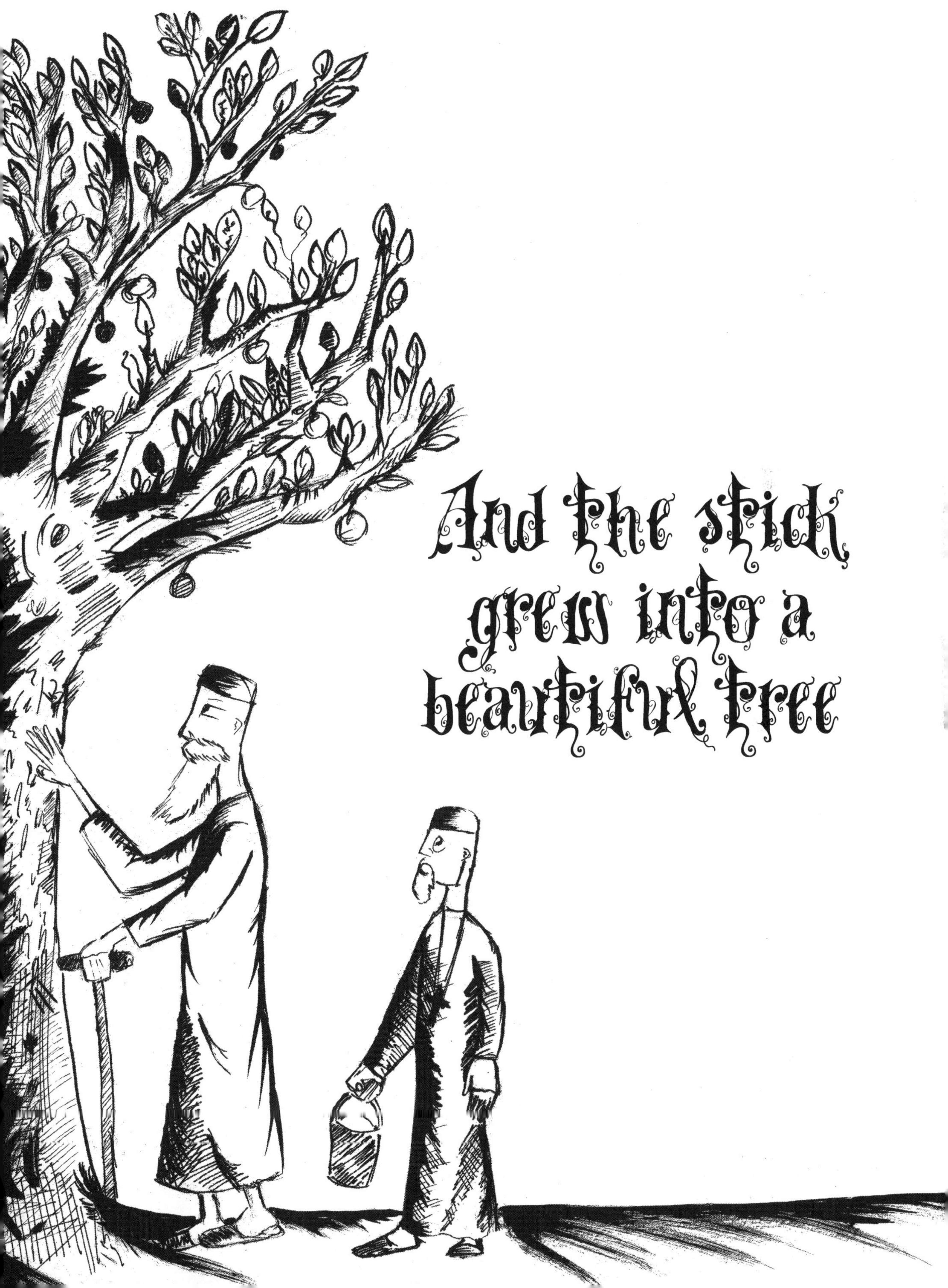

And the stick grew into a beautiful tree

ABBA AMOI TOOK THE FRUIT OF THE TREE, GATHERED THE MONKS, AND GAVE IT TO THE ELDERS, SAYING, ***"TAKE, EAT FROM THE FRUIT OF OBEDIENCE."*** THE YOUNGER MONKS BEGAN SEEING JOHN AS AN ABBA AND A TEACHER - LOOKING TO LEARN FROM HIM WHAT HE LEARNED FROM ABBA AMOI.

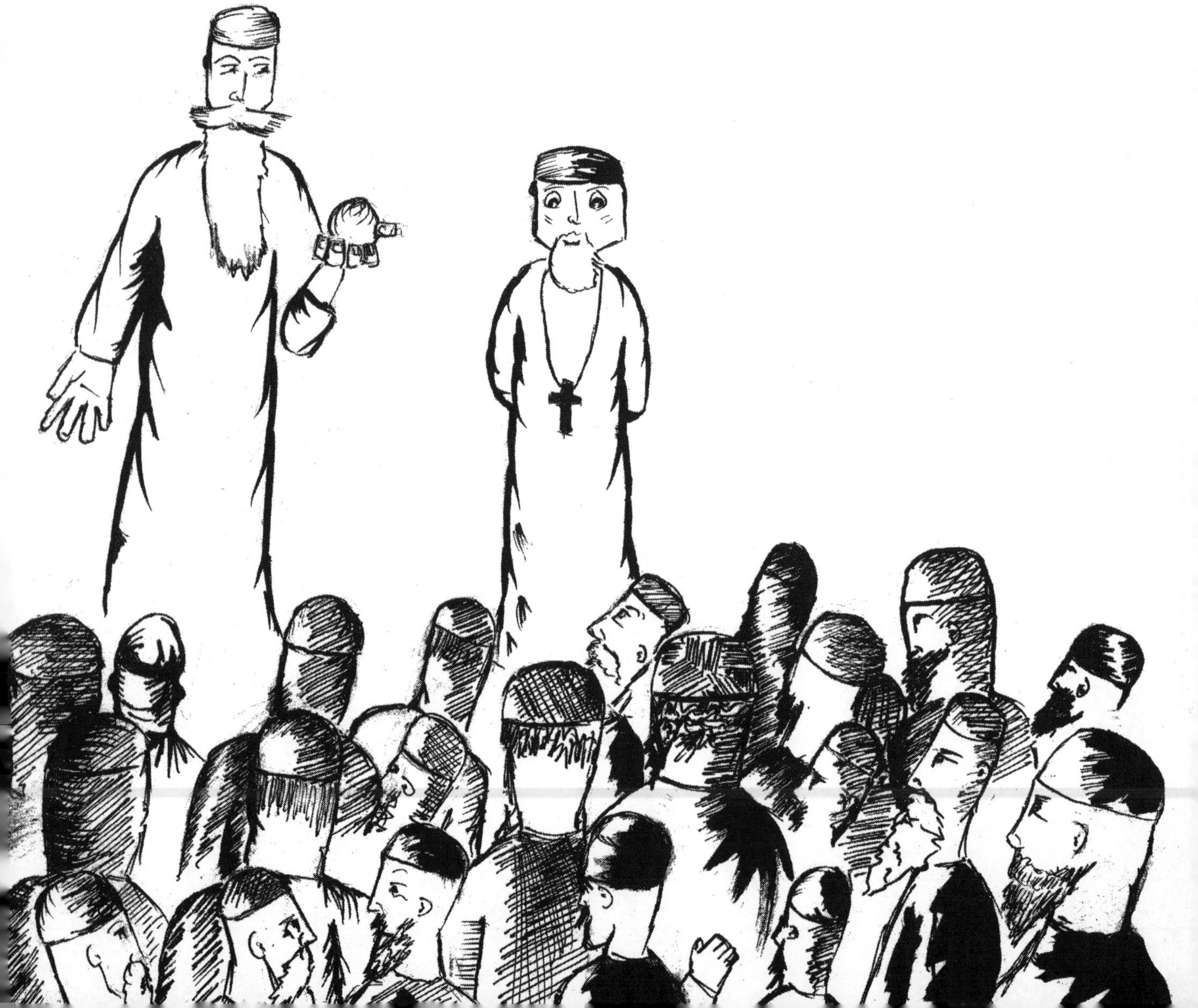

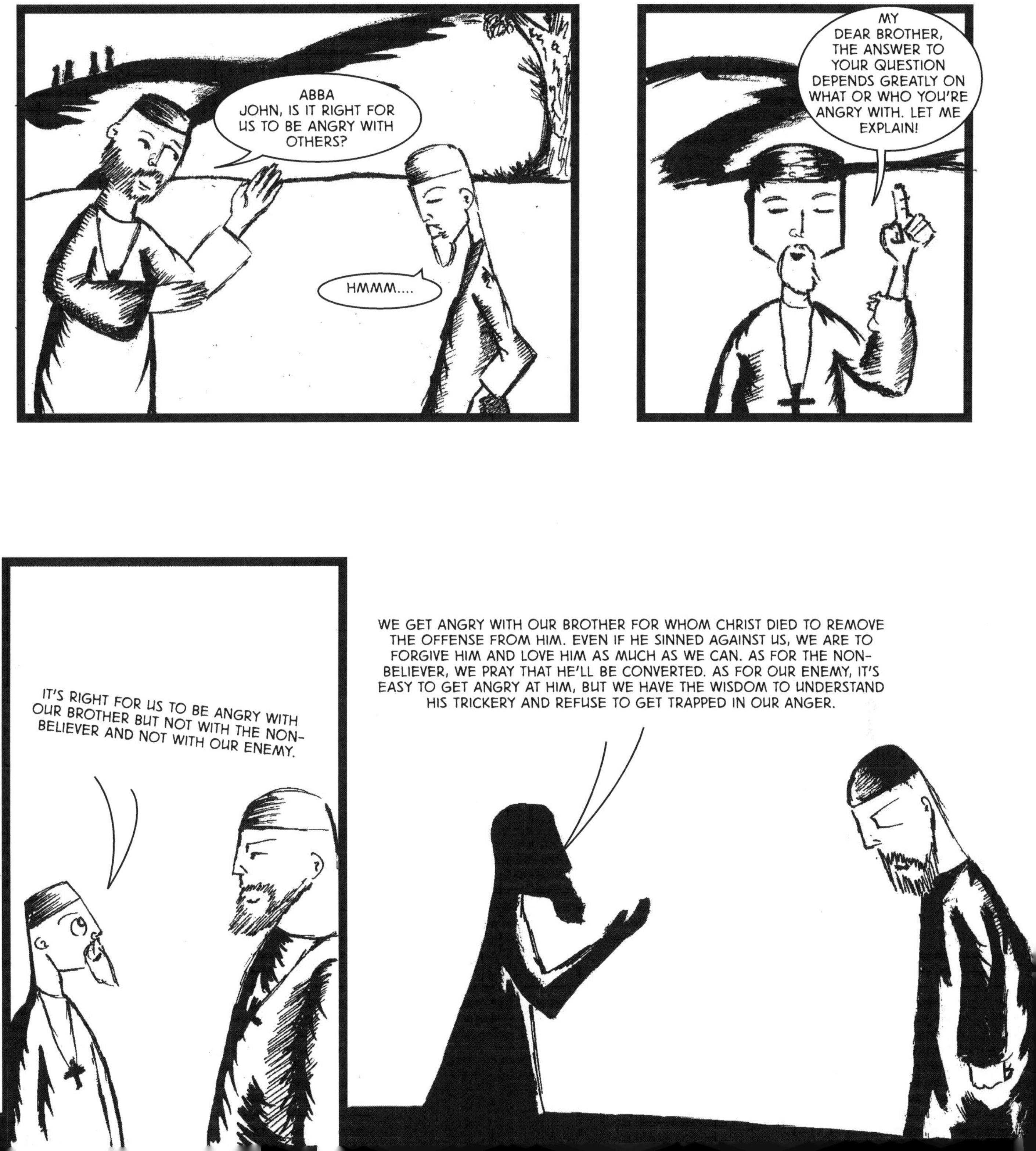
ABBA JOHN, IS IT RIGHT FOR US TO BE ANGRY WITH OTHERS?
HMMM....
MY DEAR BROTHER, THE ANSWER TO YOUR QUESTION DEPENDS GREATLY ON WHAT OR WHO YOU'RE ANGRY WITH. LET ME EXPLAIN!
IT'S RIGHT FOR US TO BE ANGRY WITH OUR BROTHER BUT NOT WITH THE NON-BELIEVER AND NOT WITH OUR ENEMY.
WE GET ANGRY WITH OUR BROTHER FOR WHOM CHRIST DIED TO REMOVE THE OFFENSE FROM HIM. EVEN IF HE SINNED AGAINST US, WE ARE TO FORGIVE HIM AND LOVE HIM AS MUCH AS WE CAN. AS FOR THE NON-BELIEVER, WE PRAY THAT HE'LL BE CONVERTED. AS FOR OUR ENEMY, IT'S EASY TO GET ANGRY AT HIM, BUT WE HAVE THE WISDOM TO UNDERSTAND HIS TRICKERY AND REFUSE TO GET TRAPPED IN OUR ANGER.

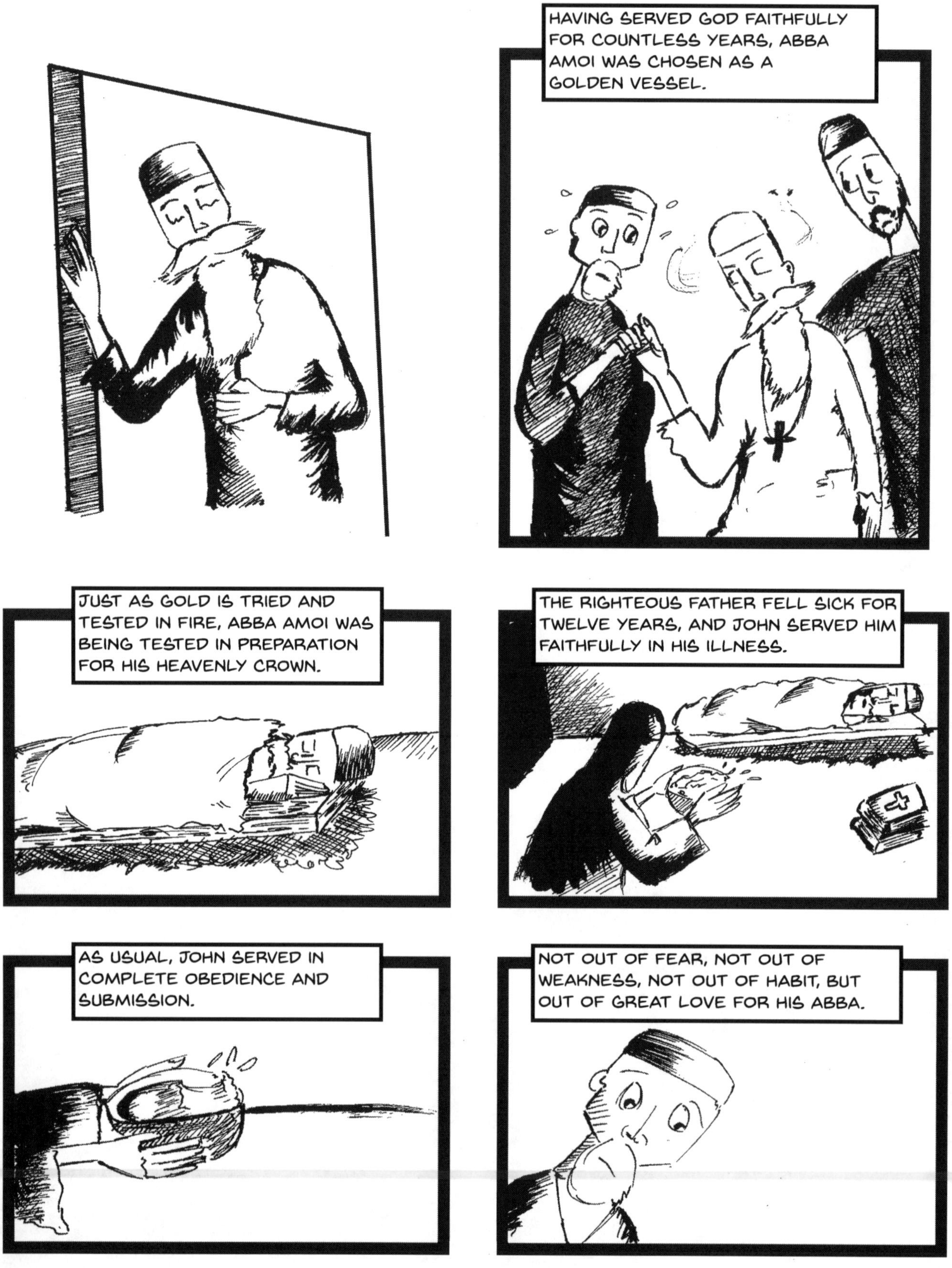
HAVING SERVED GOD FAITHFULLY FOR COUNTLESS YEARS, ABBA AMOI WAS CHOSEN AS A GOLDEN VESSEL.
JUST AS GOLD IS TRIED AND TESTED IN FIRE, ABBA AMOI WAS BEING TESTED IN PREPARATION FOR HIS HEAVENLY CROWN.
THE RIGHTEOUS FATHER FELL SICK FOR TWELVE YEARS, AND JOHN SERVED HIM FAITHFULLY IN HIS ILLNESS.
AS USUAL, JOHN SERVED IN COMPLETE OBEDIENCE AND SUBMISSION.
NOT OUT OF FEAR, NOT OUT OF WEAKNESS, NOT OUT OF HABIT, BUT OUT OF GREAT LOVE FOR HIS ABBA.

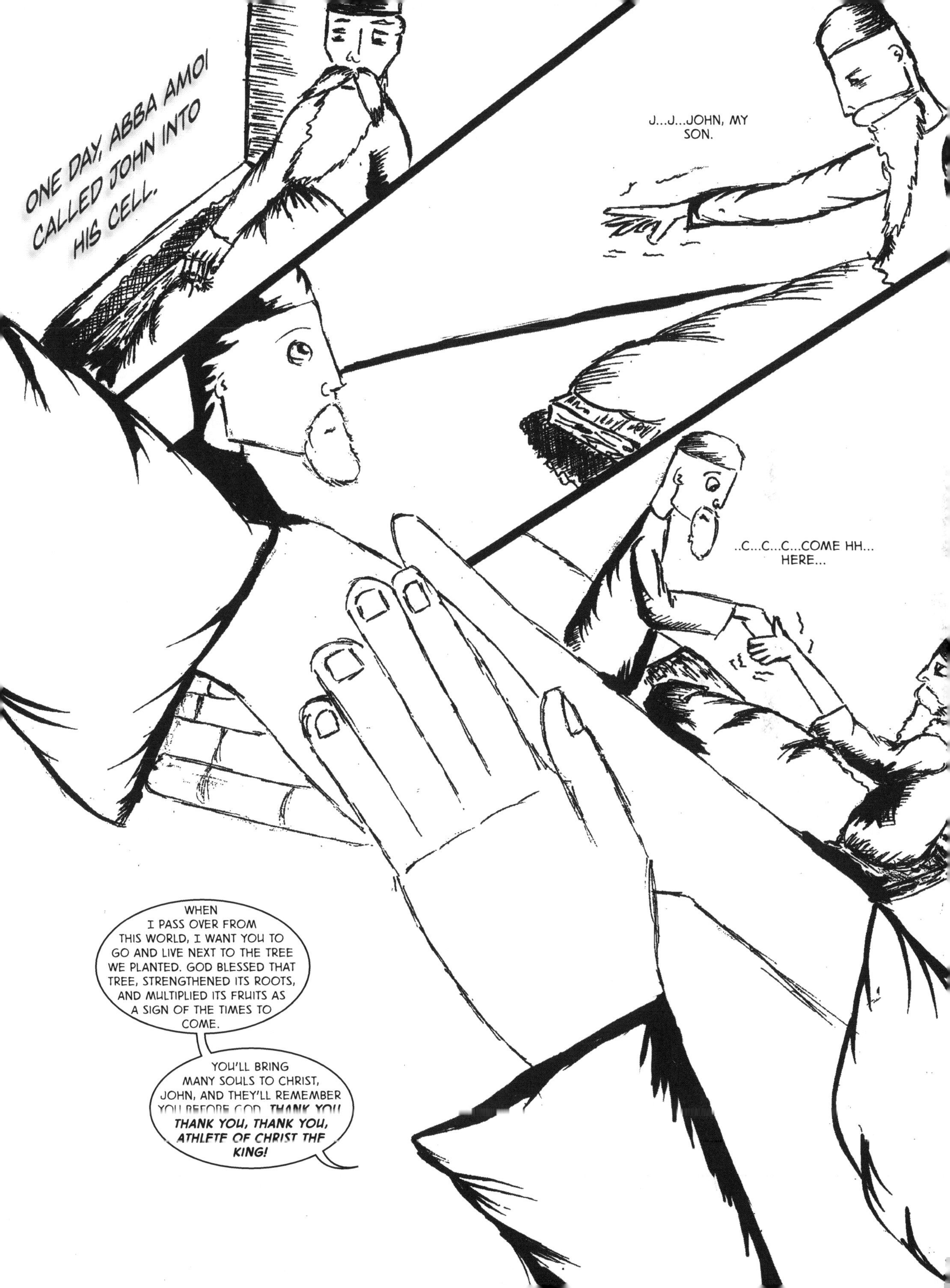
ONE DAY, ABBA AMOI CALLED JOHN INTO HIS CELL.
J...J...JOHN, MY SON.
..C...C...C...COME HH... HERE...
WHEN I PASS OVER FROM THIS WORLD, I WANT YOU TO GO AND LIVE NEXT TO THE TREE WE PLANTED. GOD BLESSED THAT TREE, STRENGTHENED ITS ROOTS, AND MULTIPLIED ITS FRUITS AS A SIGN OF THE TIMES TO COME.
YOU'LL BRING MANY SOULS TO CHRIST, JOHN, AND THEY'LL REMEMBER YOU BEFORE GOD. THANK YOU THANK YOU, THANK YOU, ATHLETE OF CHRIST THE KING!

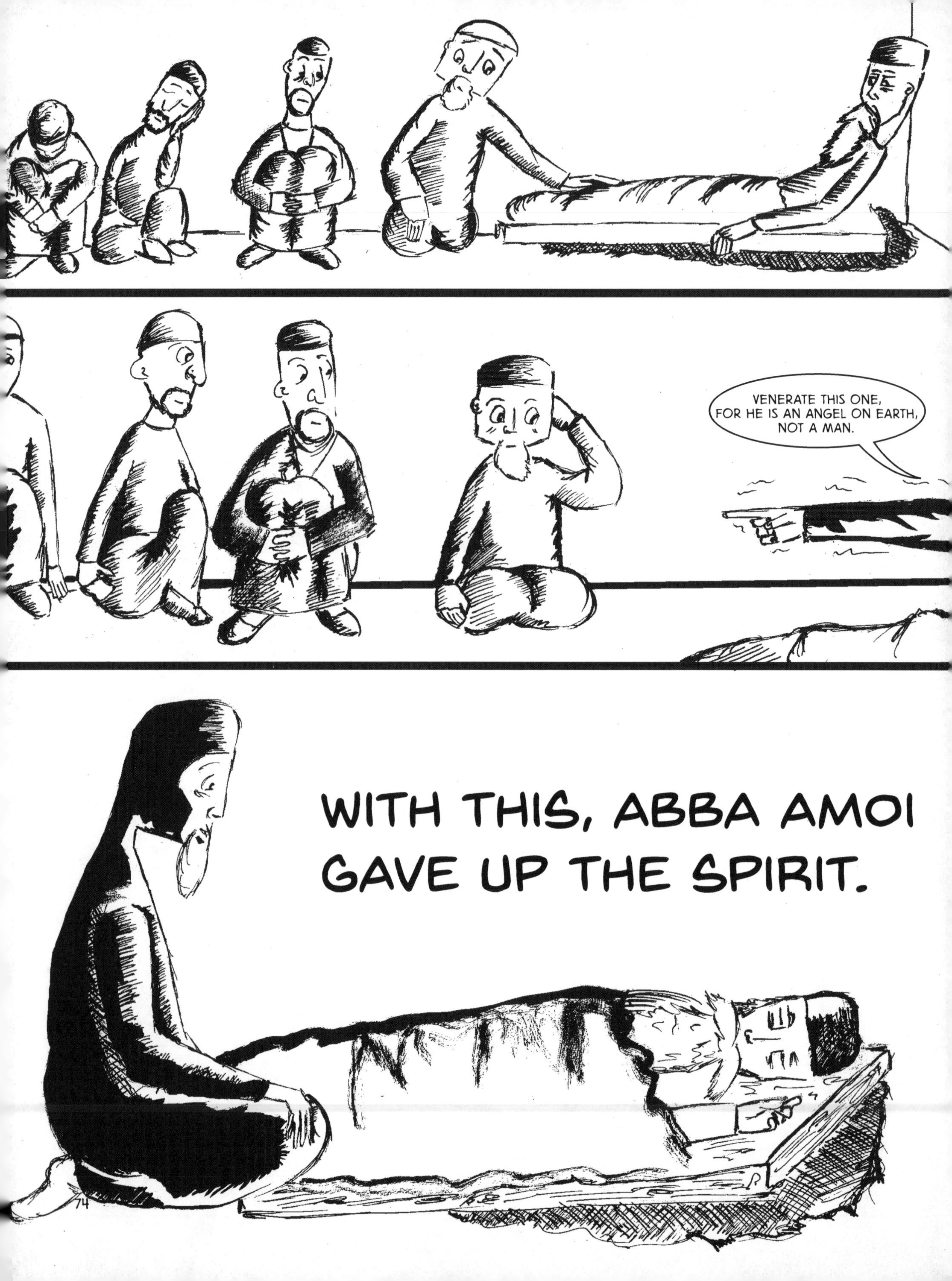
VENERATE THIS ONE, FOR HE IS AN ANGEL ON EARTH, NOT A MAN.
WITH THIS, ABBA AMOI GAVE UP THE SPIRIT.

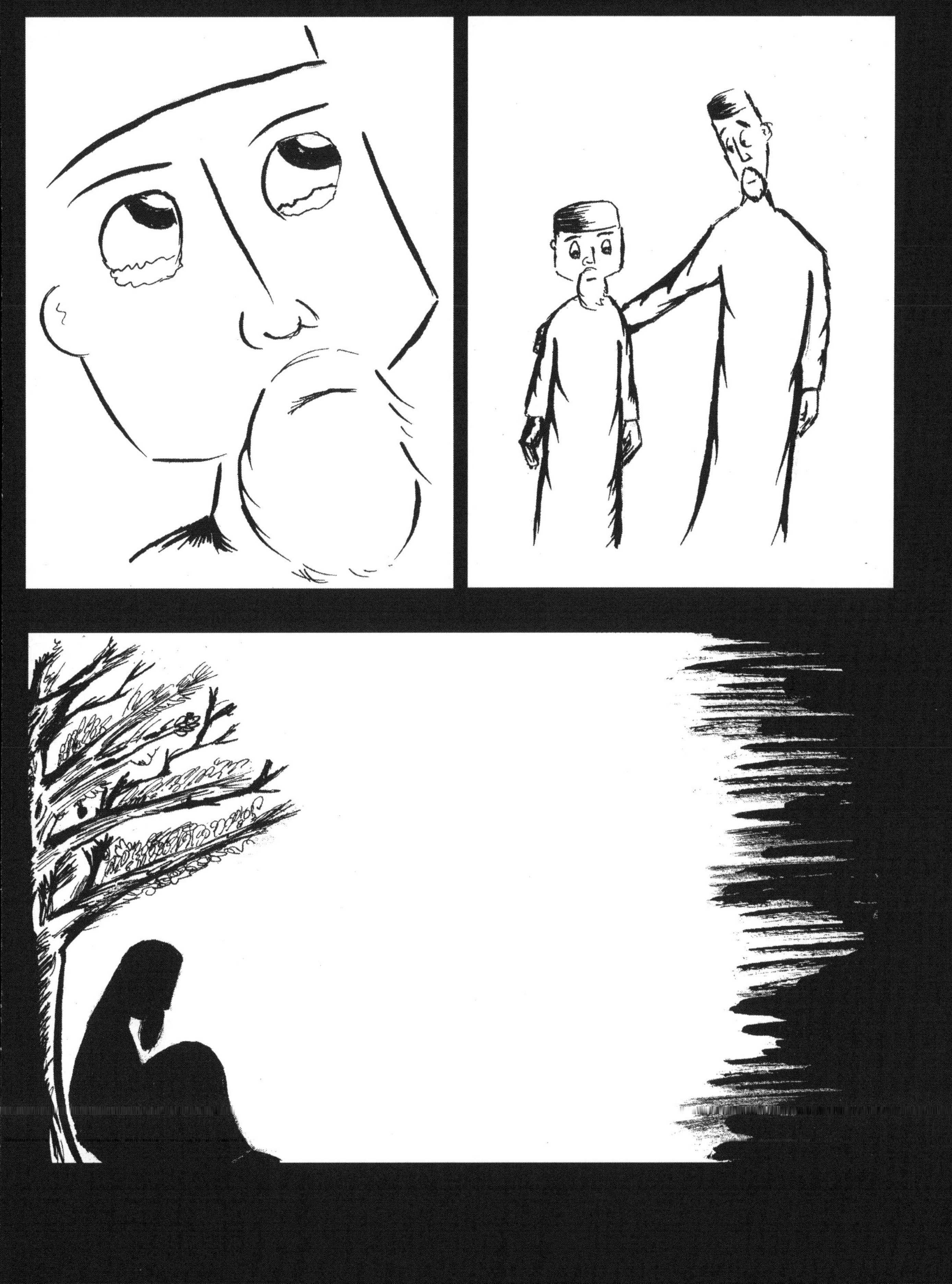

# Chapter Three
# Branches

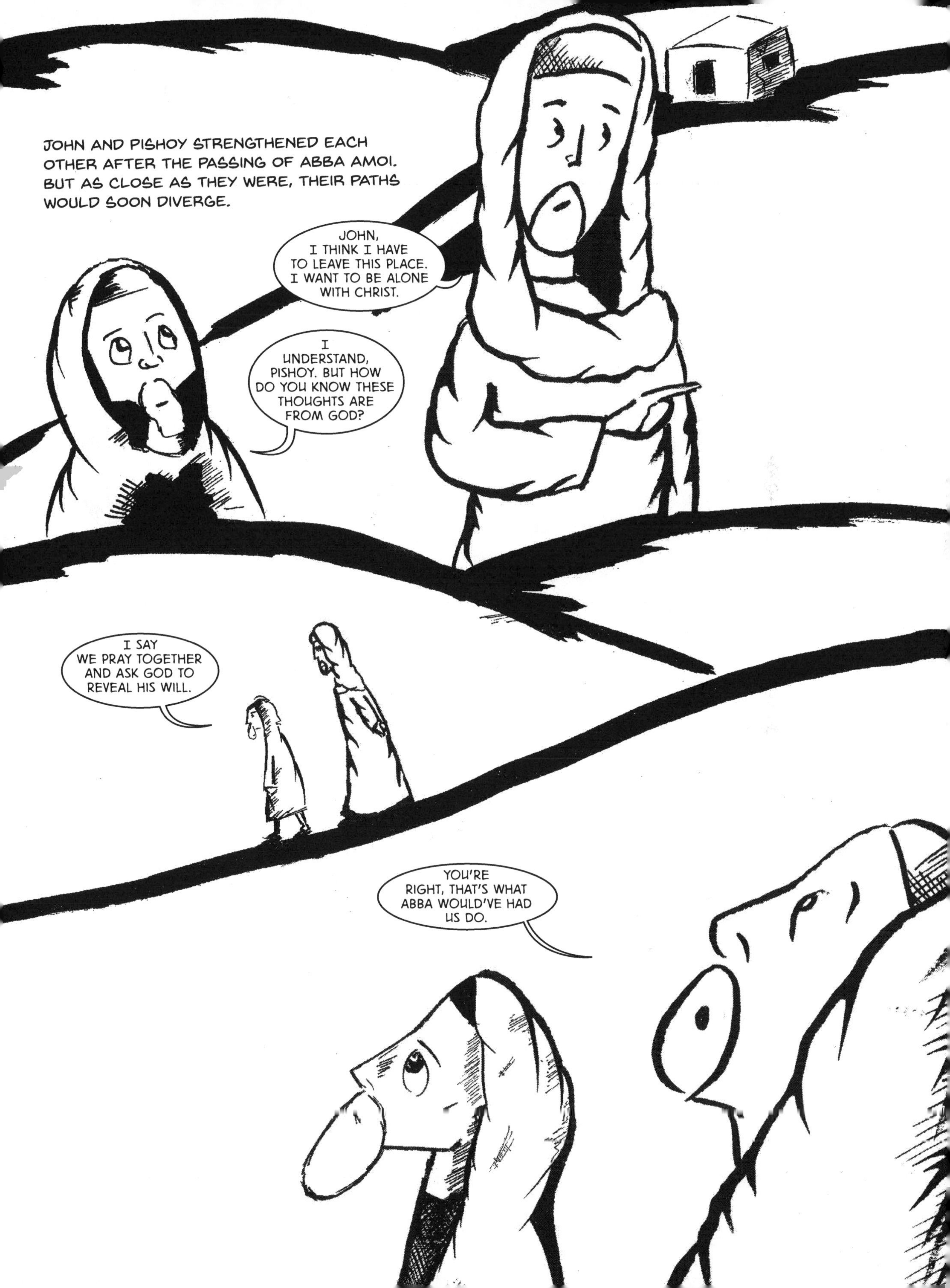
JOHN AND PISHOY STRENGTHENED EACH OTHER AFTER THE PASSING OF ABBA AMOI. BUT AS CLOSE AS THEY WERE, THEIR PATHS WOULD SOON DIVERGE.
JOHN, I THINK I HAVE TO LEAVE THIS PLACE. I WANT TO BE ALONE WITH CHRIST.
I UNDERSTAND, PISHOY. BUT HOW DO YOU KNOW THESE THOUGHTS ARE FROM GOD?
I SAY WE PRAY TOGETHER AND ASK GOD TO REVEAL HIS WILL.
YOU'RE RIGHT, THAT'S WHAT ABBA WOULD'VE HAD US DO.

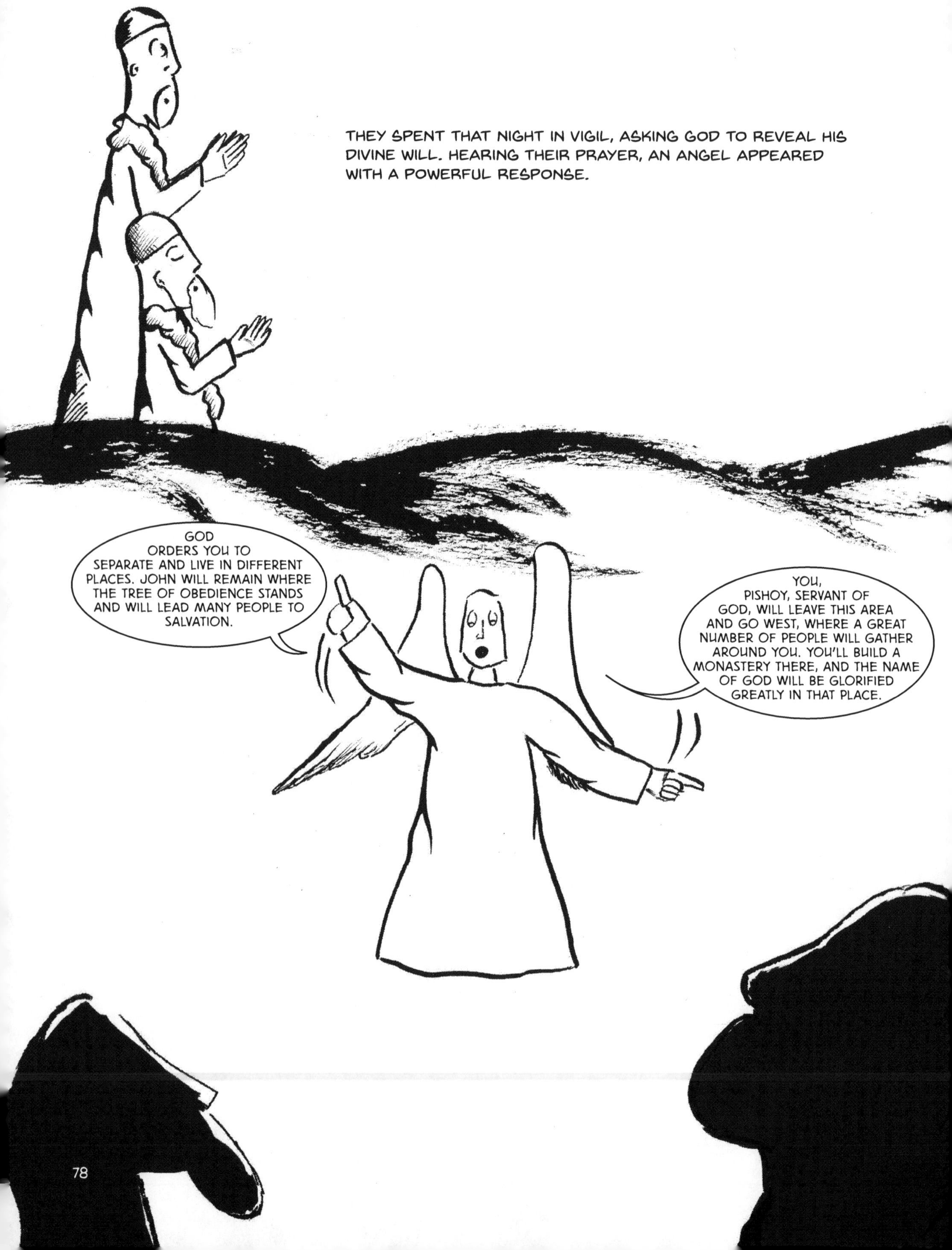
THEY SPENT THAT NIGHT IN VIGIL, ASKING GOD TO REVEAL HIS DIVINE WILL. HEARING THEIR PRAYER, AN ANGEL APPEARED WITH A POWERFUL RESPONSE.
GOD ORDERS YOU TO SEPARATE AND LIVE IN DIFFERENT PLACES. JOHN WILL REMAIN WHERE THE TREE OF OBEDIENCE STANDS AND WILL LEAD MANY PEOPLE TO SALVATION.
YOU, PISHOY, SERVANT OF GOD, WILL LEAVE THIS AREA AND GO WEST, WHERE A GREAT NUMBER OF PEOPLE WILL GATHER AROUND YOU. YOU'LL BUILD A MONASTERY THERE, AND THE NAME OF GOD WILL BE GLORIFIED GREATLY IN THAT PLACE.

AFTER THE ANGEL DISAPPEARED, THE TWO MONKS PARTED WAYS. THEY WERE SADDENED TO LEAVE EACH OTHER, BUT EAGER TO OBEY GOD'S COMMAND AND SPEND TIME PRAYING IN SECLUSION.

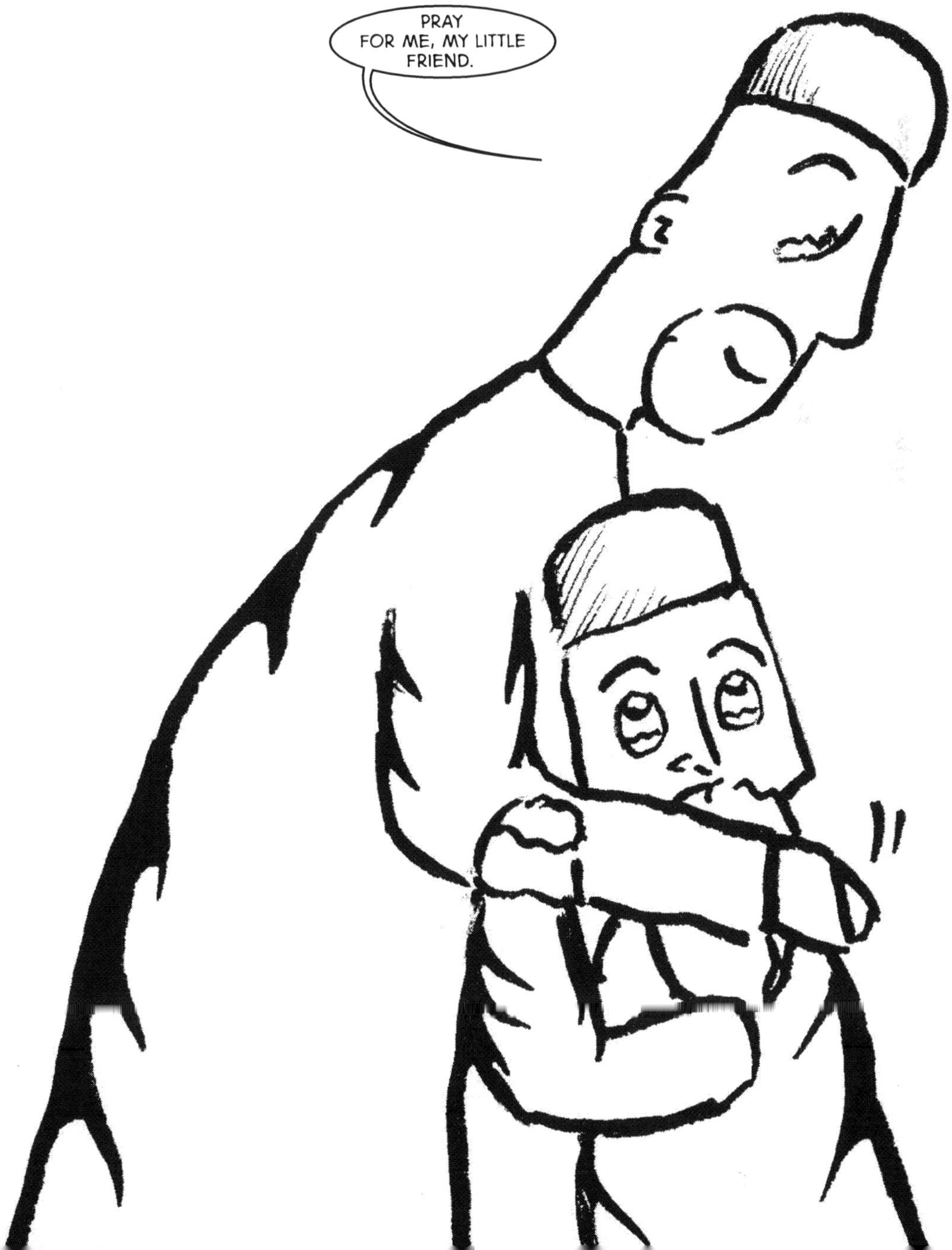
PRAY FOR ME, MY LITTLE FRIEND.

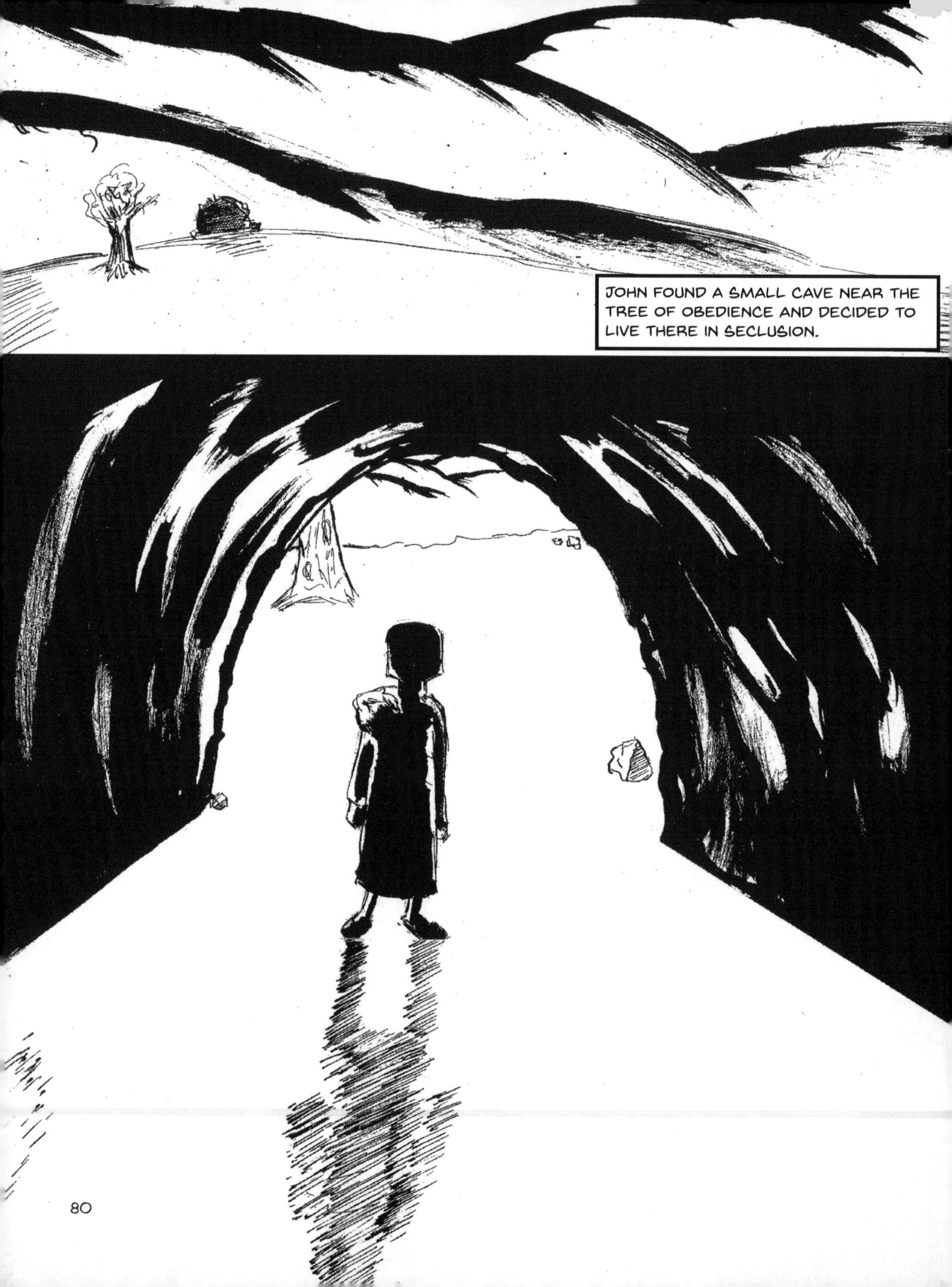
JOHN FOUND A SMALL CAVE NEAR THE TREE OF OBEDIENCE AND DECIDED TO LIVE THERE IN SECLUSION.

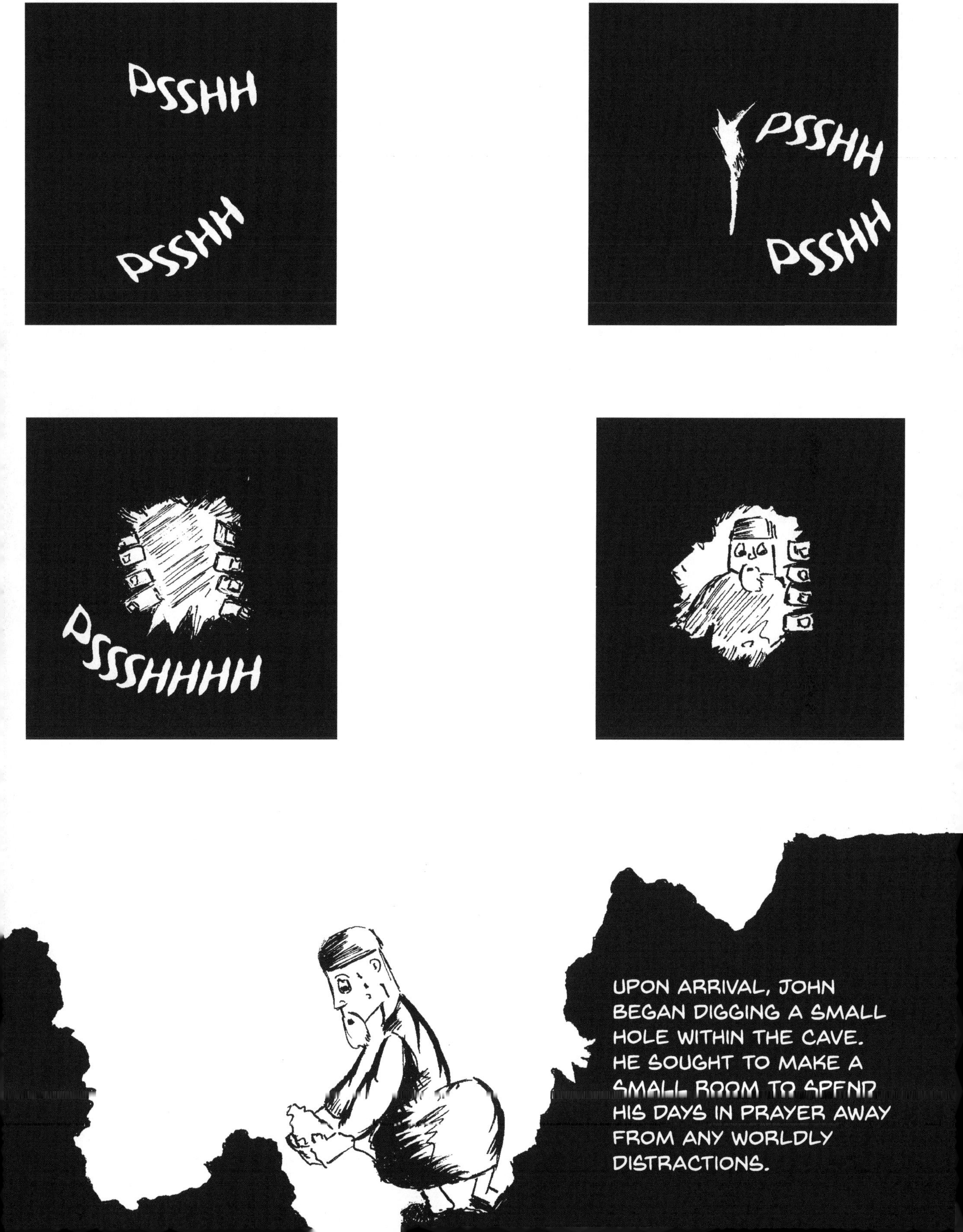
PSSHH
PSSHH
PSSHH
PSSHH
PSSSHHHH
UPON ARRIVAL, JOHN BEGAN DIGGING A SMALL HOLE WITHIN THE CAVE. HE SOUGHT TO MAKE A SMALL ROOM TO SPEND HIS DAYS IN PRAYER AWAY FROM ANY WORLDLY DISTRACTIONS.

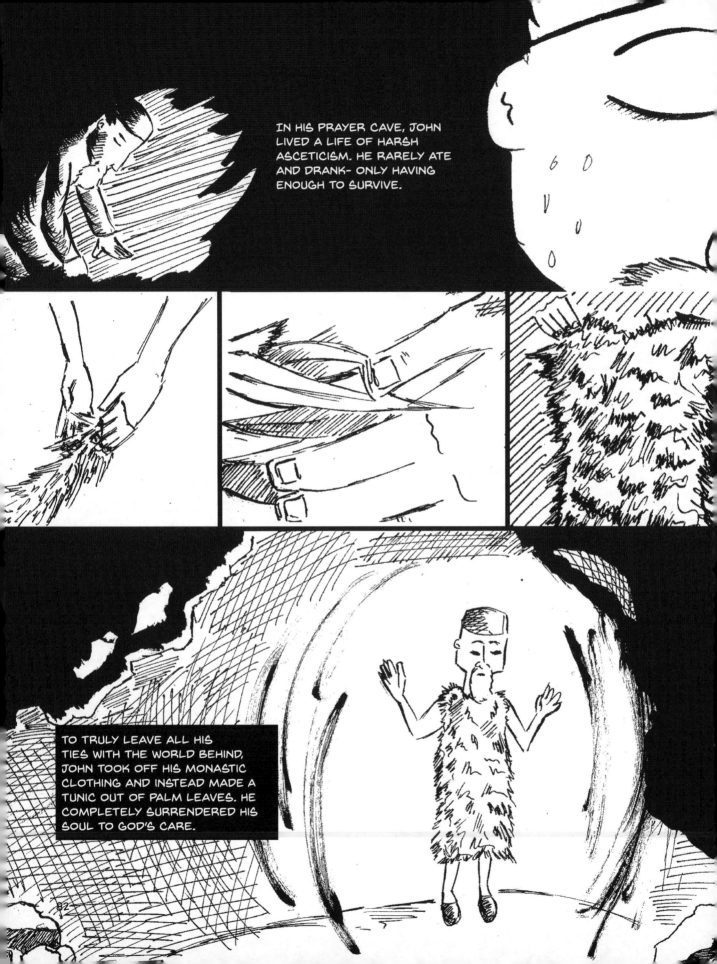

IN HIS PRAYER CAVE, JOHN LIVED A LIFE OF HARSH ASCETICISM. HE RARELY ATE AND DRANK— ONLY HAVING ENOUGH TO SURVIVE.

TO TRULY LEAVE ALL HIS TIES WITH THE WORLD BEHIND, JOHN TOOK OFF HIS MONASTIC CLOTHING AND INSTEAD MADE A TUNIC OUT OF PALM LEAVES. HE COMPLETELY SURRENDERED HIS SOUL TO GOD'S CARE.

AFTER SOME TIME, WORD SPREAD OF ABBA JOHN'S LOCATION, SO A FEW YOUNG MONKS VISITED JOHN'S CAVE

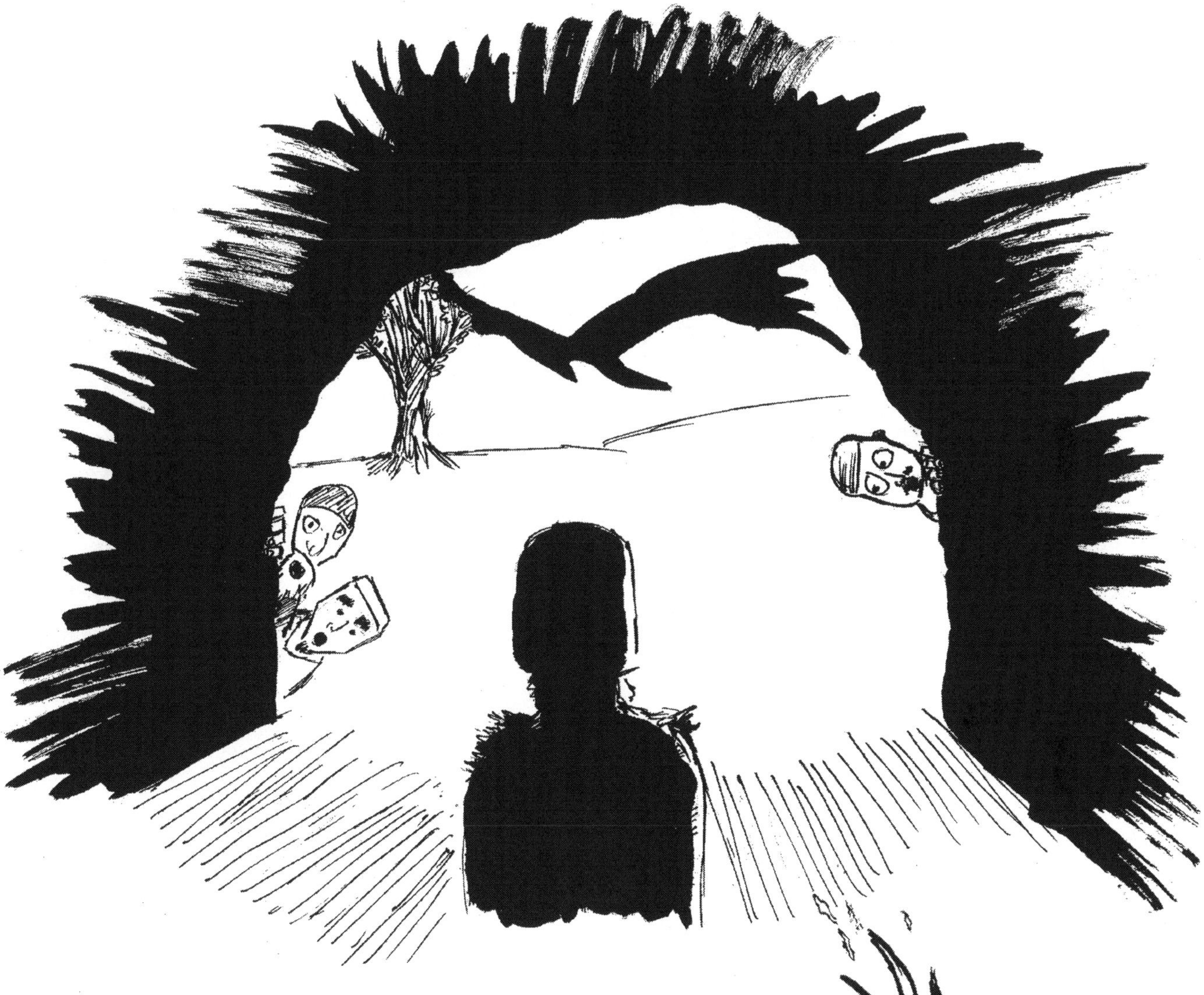

WHEN THEY FIRST LAID EYES ON HIM, THE NOVICE MONKS SAW JOHN'S FACE SHINING LIKE A BURNING FLAME AS PIETY AND HOLINESS REFLECTED IN HIS DEMEANOR.

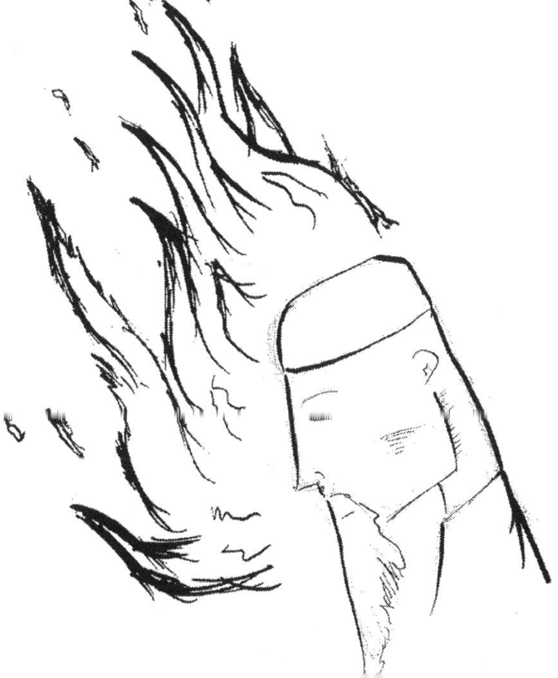

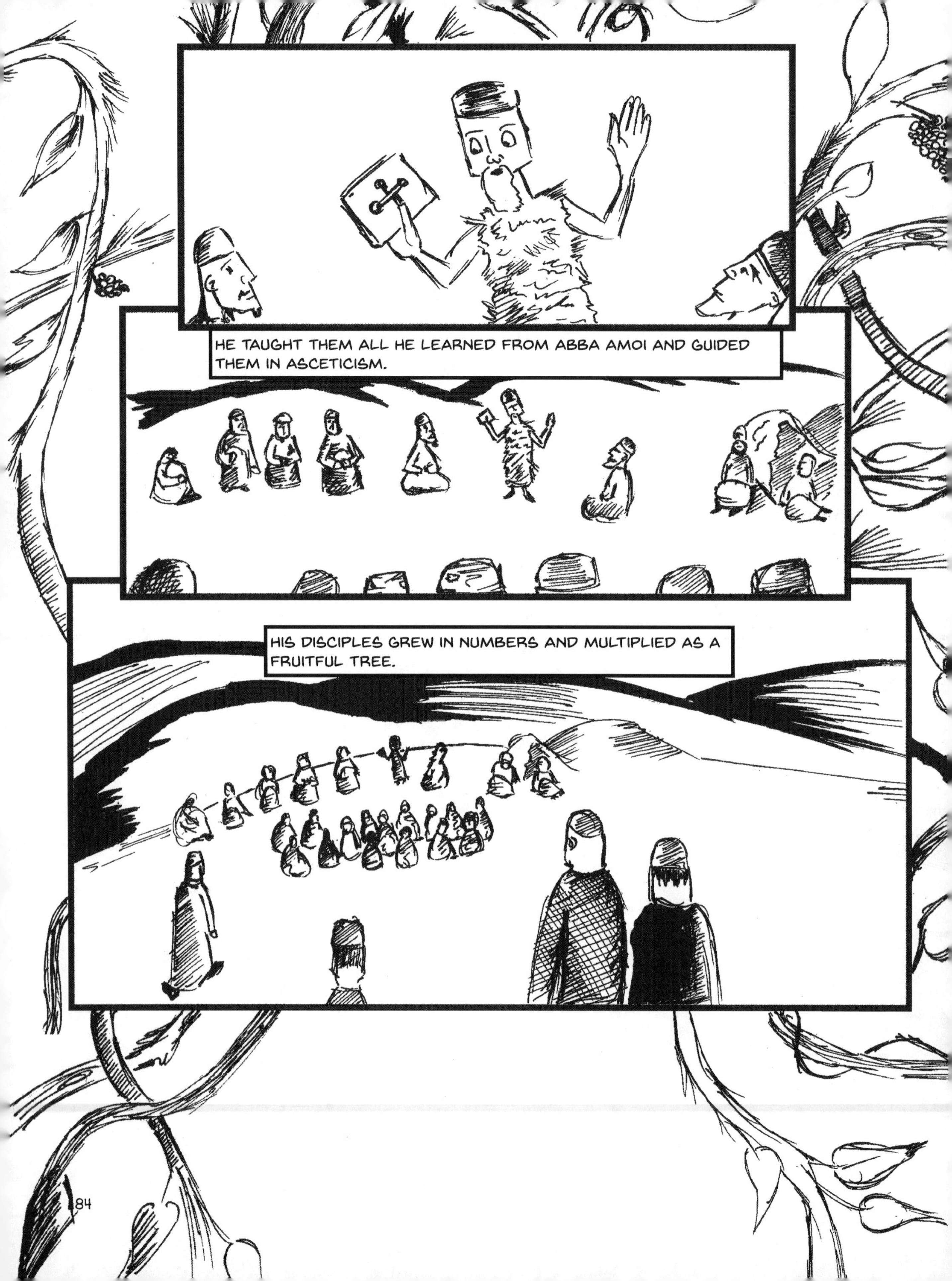
HE TAUGHT THEM ALL HE LEARNED FROM ABBA AMOI AND GUIDED THEM IN ASCETICISM.
HIS DISCIPLES GREW IN NUMBERS AND MULTIPLIED AS A FRUITFUL TREE.

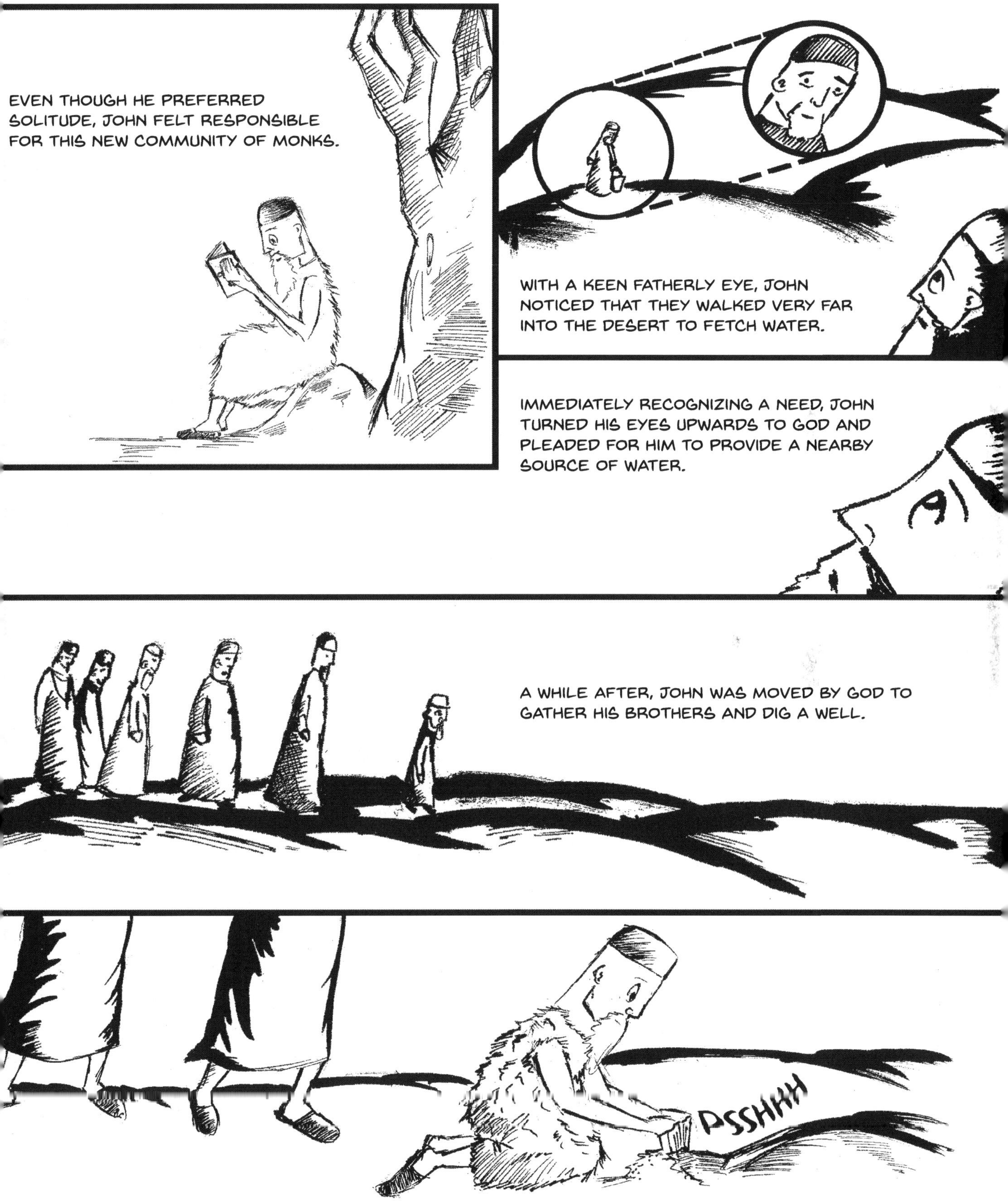
EVEN THOUGH HE PREFERRED SOLITUDE, JOHN FELT RESPONSIBLE FOR THIS NEW COMMUNITY OF MONKS.
WITH A KEEN FATHERLY EYE, JOHN NOTICED THAT THEY WALKED VERY FAR INTO THE DESERT TO FETCH WATER.
IMMEDIATELY RECOGNIZING A NEED, JOHN TURNED HIS EYES UPWARDS TO GOD AND PLEADED FOR HIM TO PROVIDE A NEARBY SOURCE OF WATER.
A WHILE AFTER, JOHN WAS MOVED BY GOD TO GATHER HIS BROTHERS AND DIG A WELL.
PSSHHH

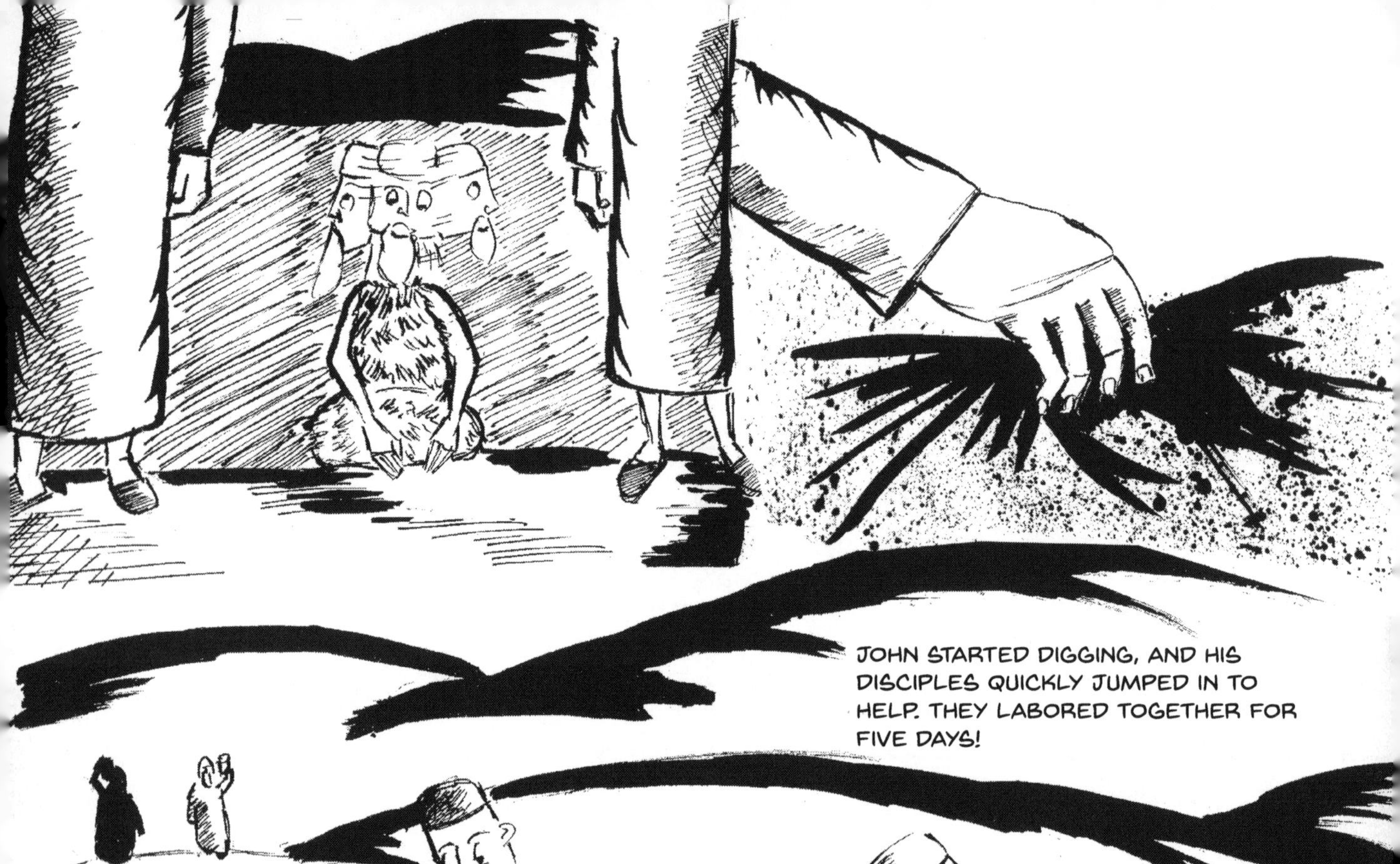
JOHN STARTED DIGGING, AND HIS DISCIPLES QUICKLY JUMPED IN TO HELP. THEY LABORED TOGETHER FOR FIVE DAYS!

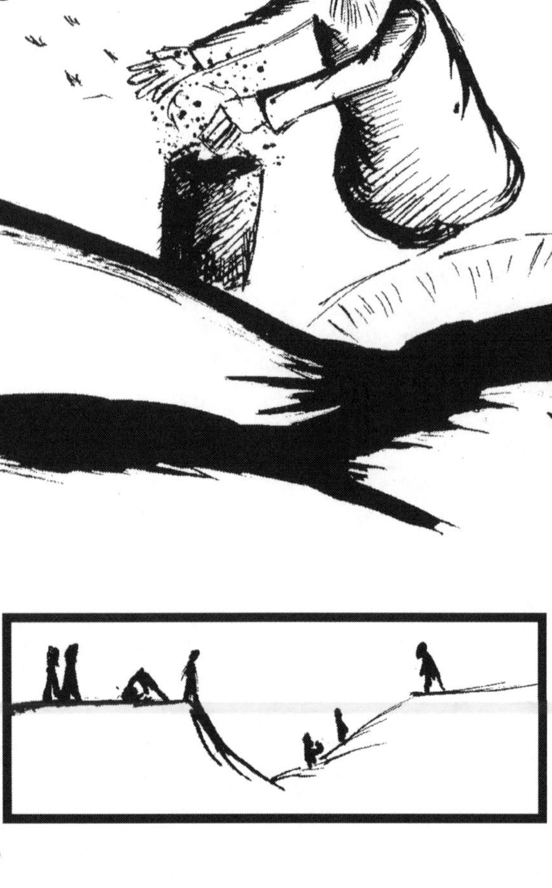

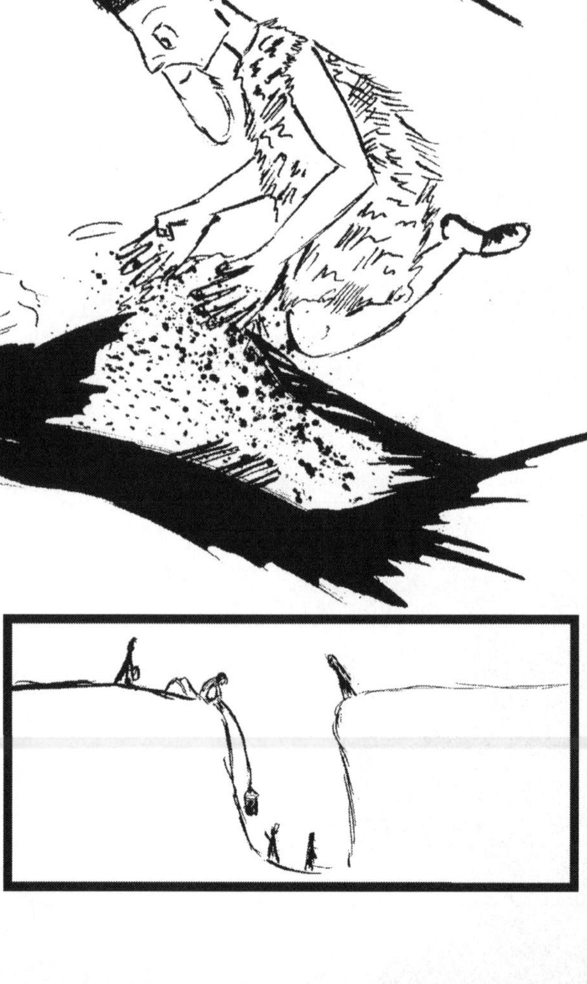

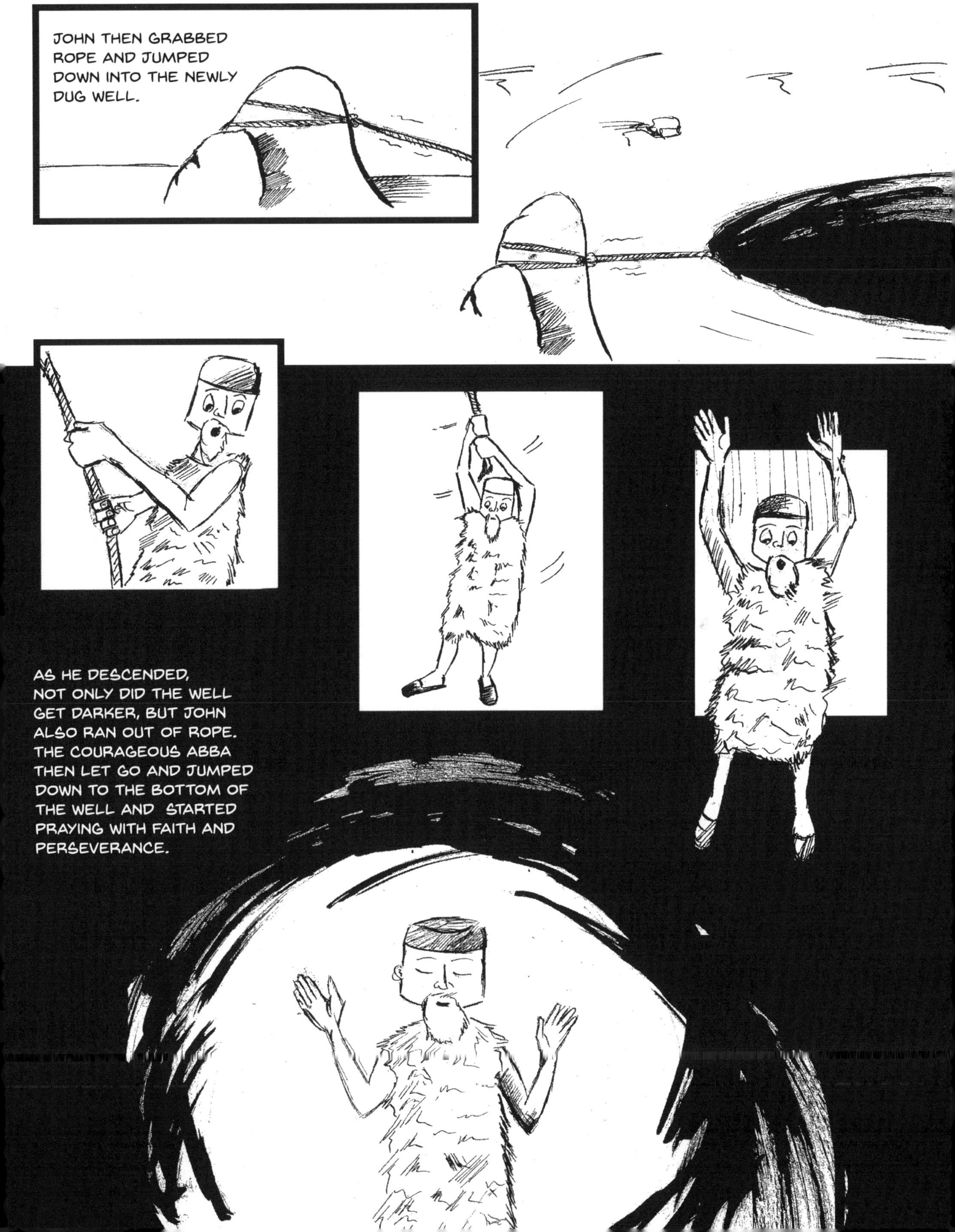
JOHN THEN GRABBED ROPE AND JUMPED DOWN INTO THE NEWLY DUG WELL.
AS HE DESCENDED, NOT ONLY DID THE WELL GET DARKER, BUT JOHN ALSO RAN OUT OF ROPE. THE COURAGEOUS ABBA THEN LET GO AND JUMPED DOWN TO THE BOTTOM OF THE WELL AND STARTED PRAYING WITH FAITH AND PERSEVERANCE.

JOHN SPENT THE ENTIRE NIGHT PRAYING.
GOD ANSWERED HIS PRAYERS, AND WATER
FLOWED ABUNDANTLY AS A SWEET WELL
SPRANG UP.

THE WATER GUSHED INTO THE WELL AND FILLED QUITE RAPIDLY, REACHING JOHN'S WAIST IN NO TIME. HE THEN USED THE RISING WATER LEVEL TO SHOOT UP AND REACH THE ROPE, RACING THE WATER TO THE TOP OF THE WELL.

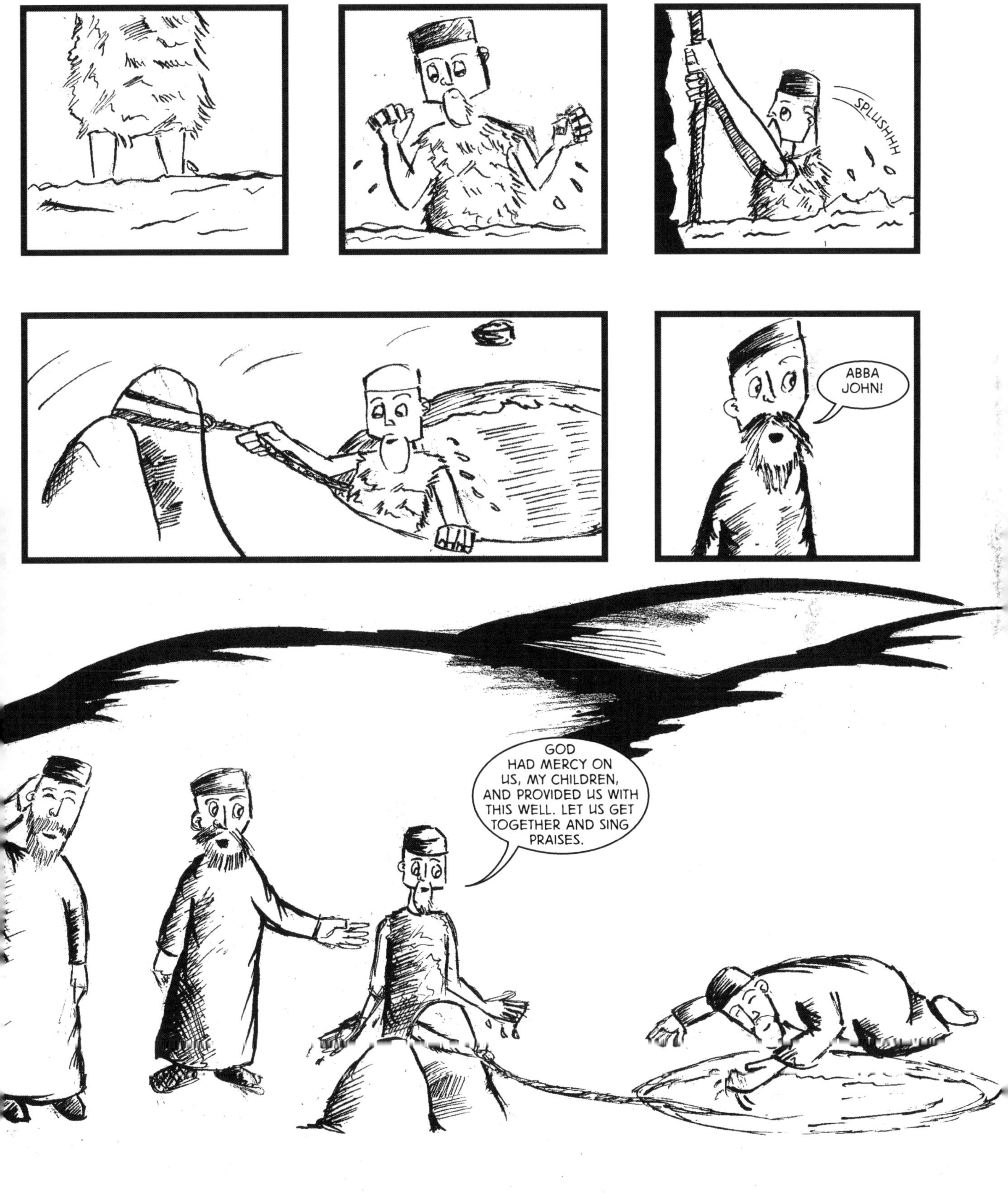
SPLUSHHH
ABBA JOHN!
GOD HAD MERCY ON US, MY CHILDREN, AND PROVIDED US WITH THIS WELL. LET US GET TOGETHER AND SING PRAISES.

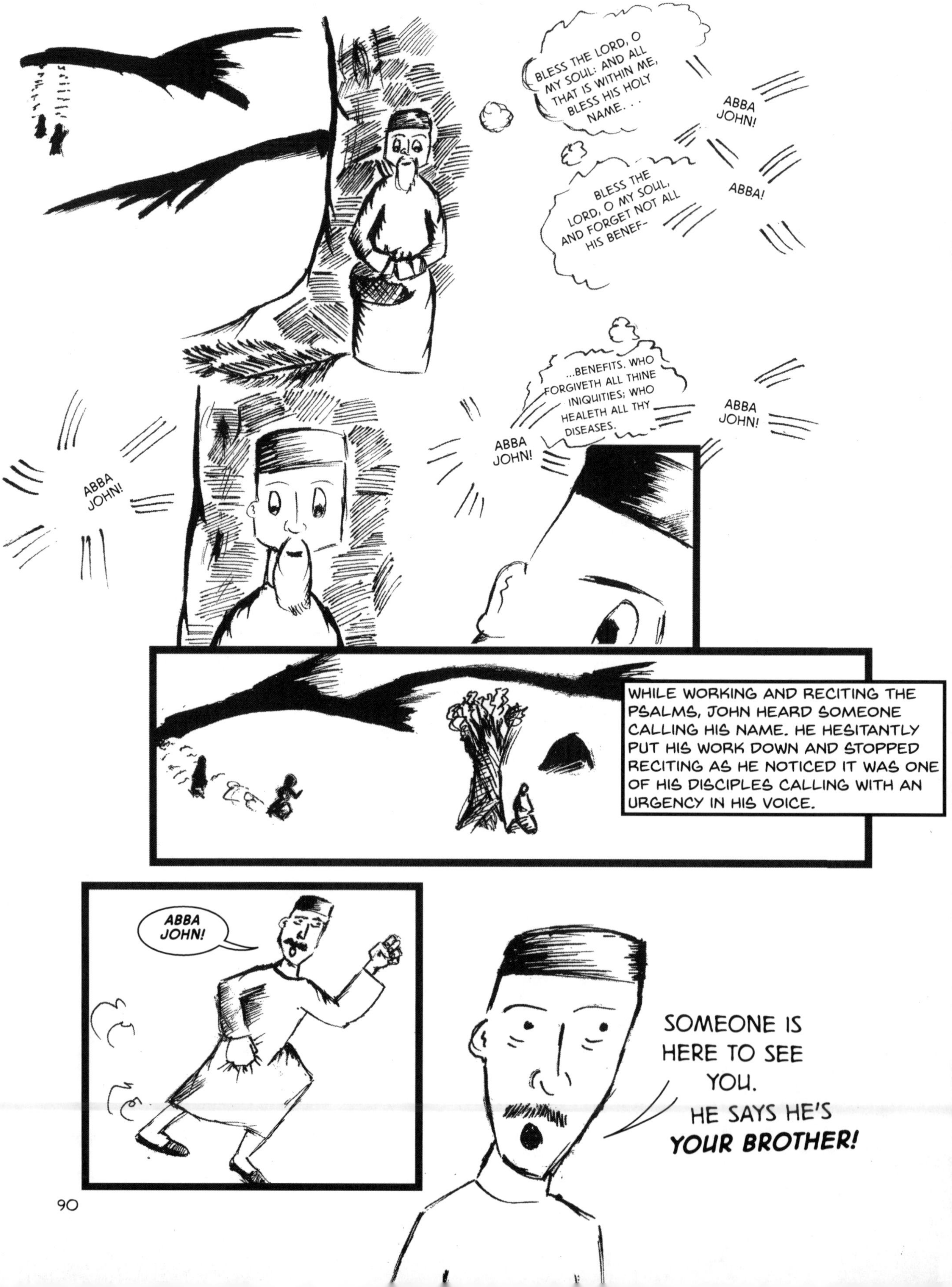

BLESS THE LORD, O MY SOUL: AND ALL THAT IS WITHIN ME, BLESS HIS HOLY NAME. . .
ABBA JOHN!
BLESS THE LORD, O MY SOUL, AND FORGET NOT ALL HIS BENEF-
ABBA!
...BENEFITS. WHO FORGIVETH ALL THINE INIQUITIES; WHO HEALETH ALL THY DISEASES.
ABBA JOHN!
ABBA JOHN!
ABBA JOHN!
WHILE WORKING AND RECITING THE PSALMS, JOHN HEARD SOMEONE CALLING HIS NAME. HE HESITANTLY PUT HIS WORK DOWN AND STOPPED RECITING AS HE NOTICED IT WAS ONE OF HIS DISCIPLES CALLING WITH AN URGENCY IN HIS VOICE.
ABBA JOHN!
SOMEONE IS HERE TO SEE YOU.
HE SAYS HE'S *YOUR BROTHER!*

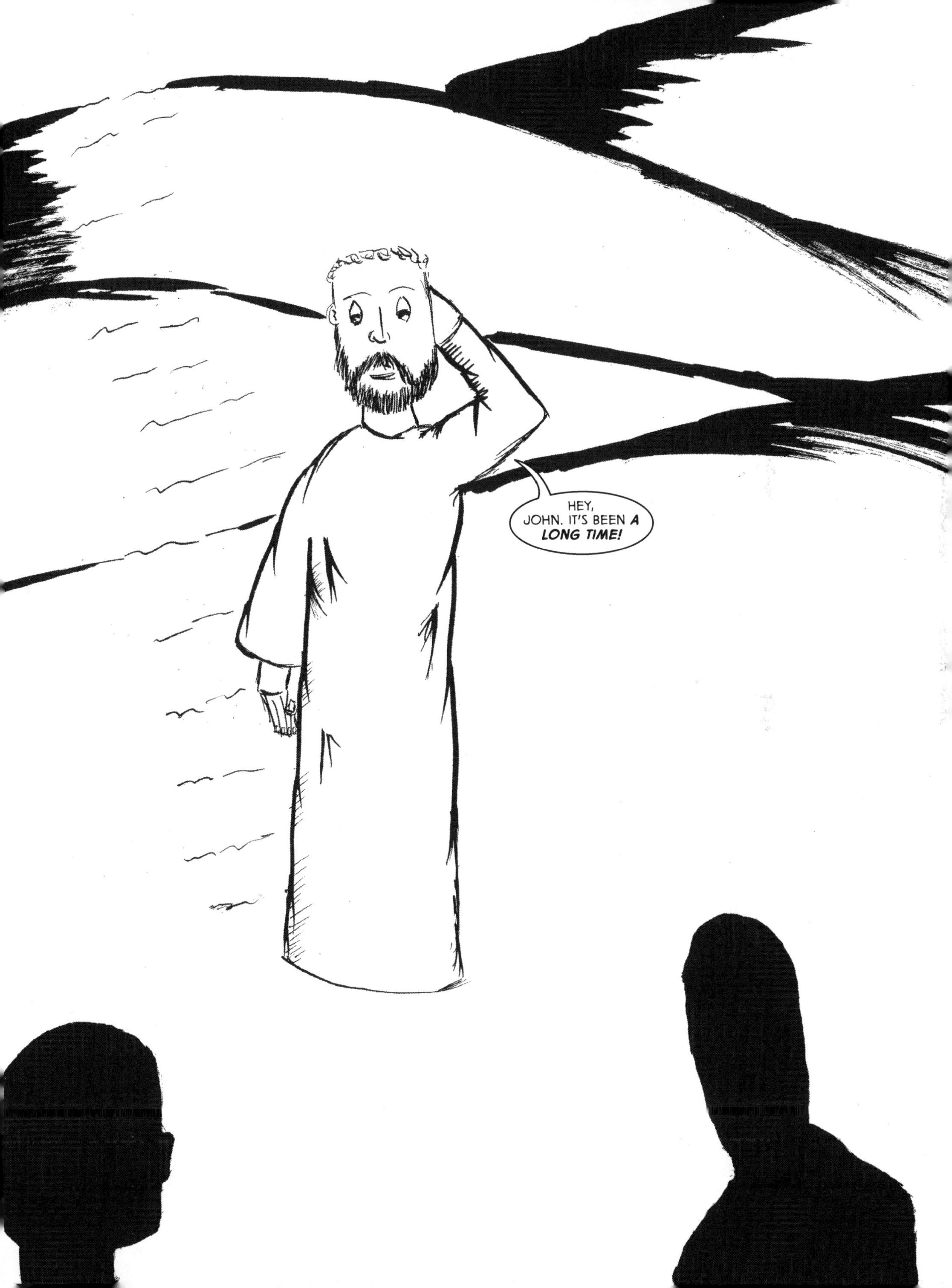
HEY, JOHN. IT'S BEEN *A LONG TIME!*

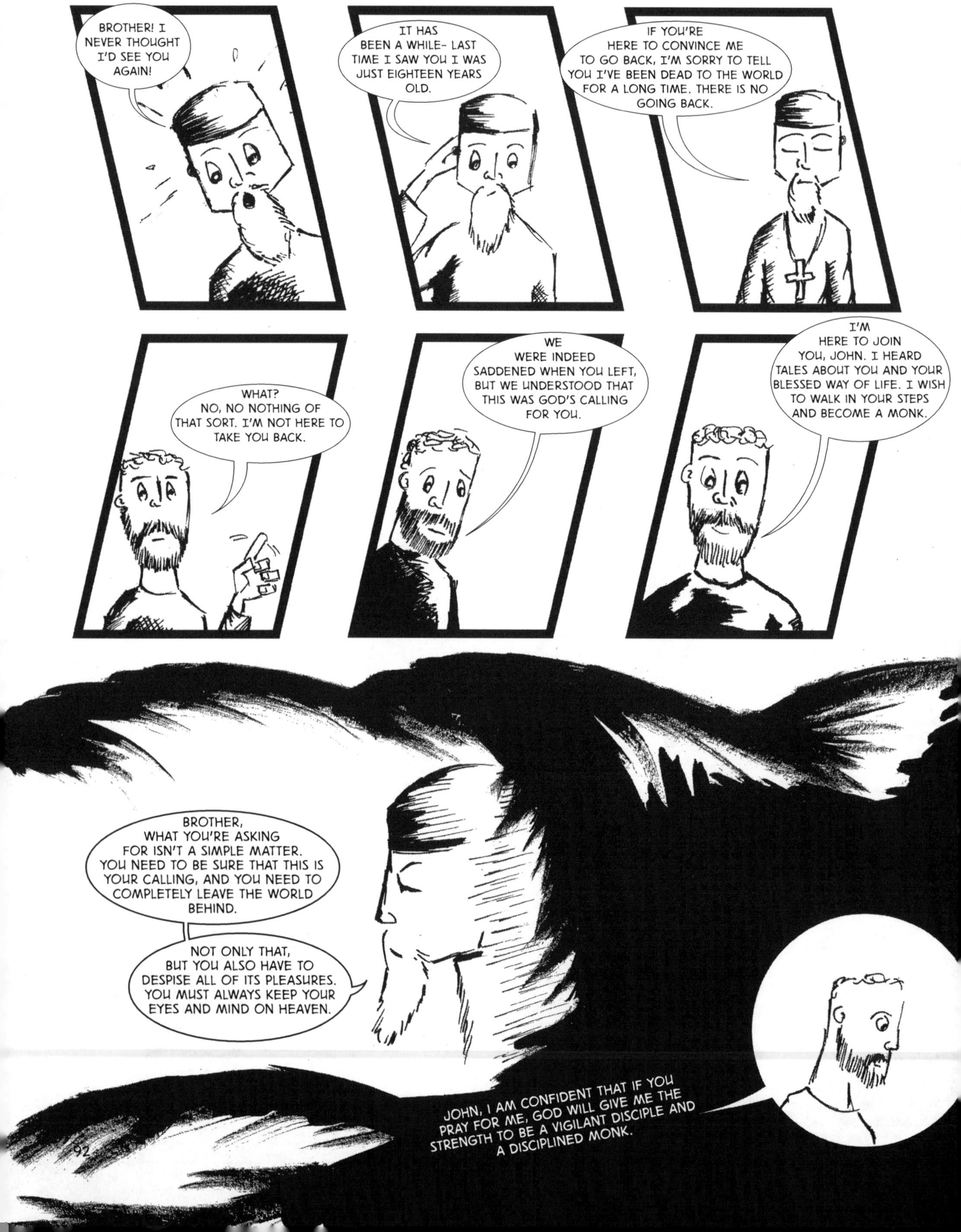

BROTHER! I NEVER THOUGHT I'D SEE YOU AGAIN!
IT HAS BEEN A WHILE- LAST TIME I SAW YOU I WAS JUST EIGHTEEN YEARS OLD.
IF YOU'RE HERE TO CONVINCE ME TO GO BACK, I'M SORRY TO TELL YOU I'VE BEEN DEAD TO THE WORLD FOR A LONG TIME. THERE IS NO GOING BACK.
WHAT? NO, NO NOTHING OF THAT SORT. I'M NOT HERE TO TAKE YOU BACK.
WE WERE INDEED SADDENED WHEN YOU LEFT, BUT WE UNDERSTOOD THAT THIS WAS GOD'S CALLING FOR YOU.
I'M HERE TO JOIN YOU, JOHN. I HEARD TALES ABOUT YOU AND YOUR BLESSED WAY OF LIFE. I WISH TO WALK IN YOUR STEPS AND BECOME A MONK.
BROTHER, WHAT YOU'RE ASKING FOR ISN'T A SIMPLE MATTER. YOU NEED TO BE SURE THAT THIS IS YOUR CALLING, AND YOU NEED TO COMPLETELY LEAVE THE WORLD BEHIND.
NOT ONLY THAT, BUT YOU ALSO HAVE TO DESPISE ALL OF ITS PLEASURES. YOU MUST ALWAYS KEEP YOUR EYES AND MIND ON HEAVEN.
JOHN, I AM CONFIDENT THAT IF YOU PRAY FOR ME, GOD WILL GIVE ME THE STRENGTH TO BE A VIGILANT DISCIPLE AND A DISCIPLINED MONK.

IT WAS STRANGE FOR JOHN TO SEE HIS OLDER BROTHER ONCE AGAIN, BUT HE UNDERSTOOD THAT GOD ALLOWED THIS TO HAPPEN FOR THEIR BENEFIT. LITTLE DID HE KNOW THAT HIS BROTHER'S ARRIVAL WOULD HELP JOHN UNDERSTAND MANY LESSONS AND GROW IN THE FAITH.

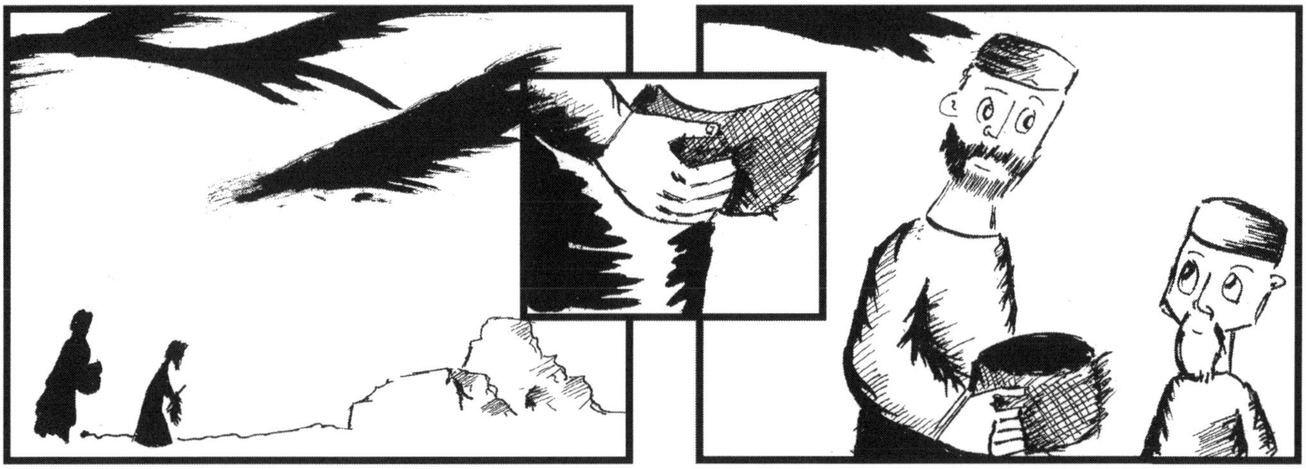

JOHN IMMEDIATELY STARTED TEACHING HIS BROTHER THE MANY FACETS OF A MONK'S LIFE.

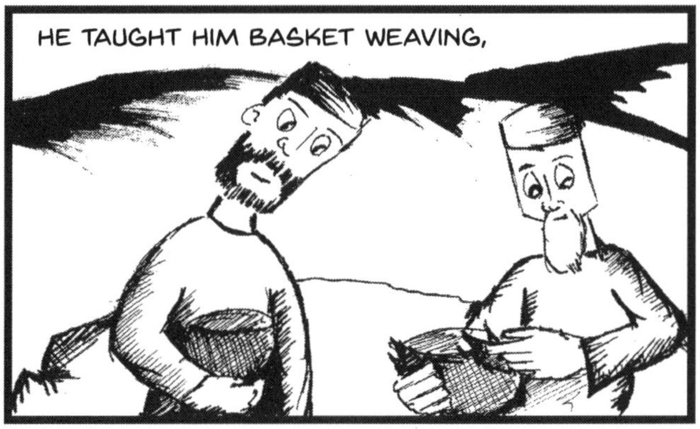
HE TAUGHT HIM BASKET WEAVING,

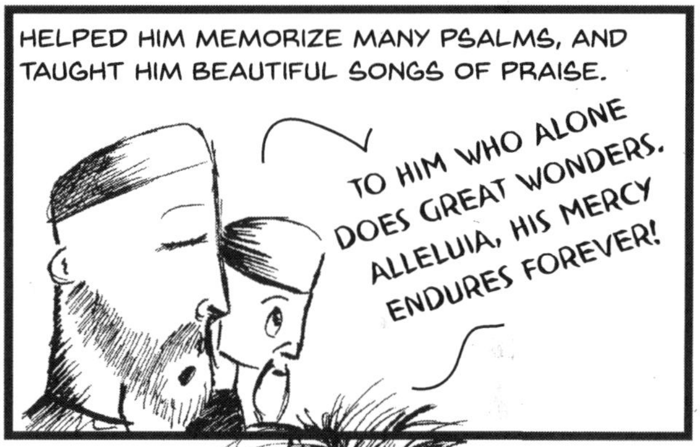
HELPED HIM MEMORIZE MANY PSALMS, AND TAUGHT HIM BEAUTIFUL SONGS OF PRAISE.
TO HIM WHO ALONE DOES GREAT WONDERS. ALLELUIA, HIS MERCY ENDURES FOREVER!

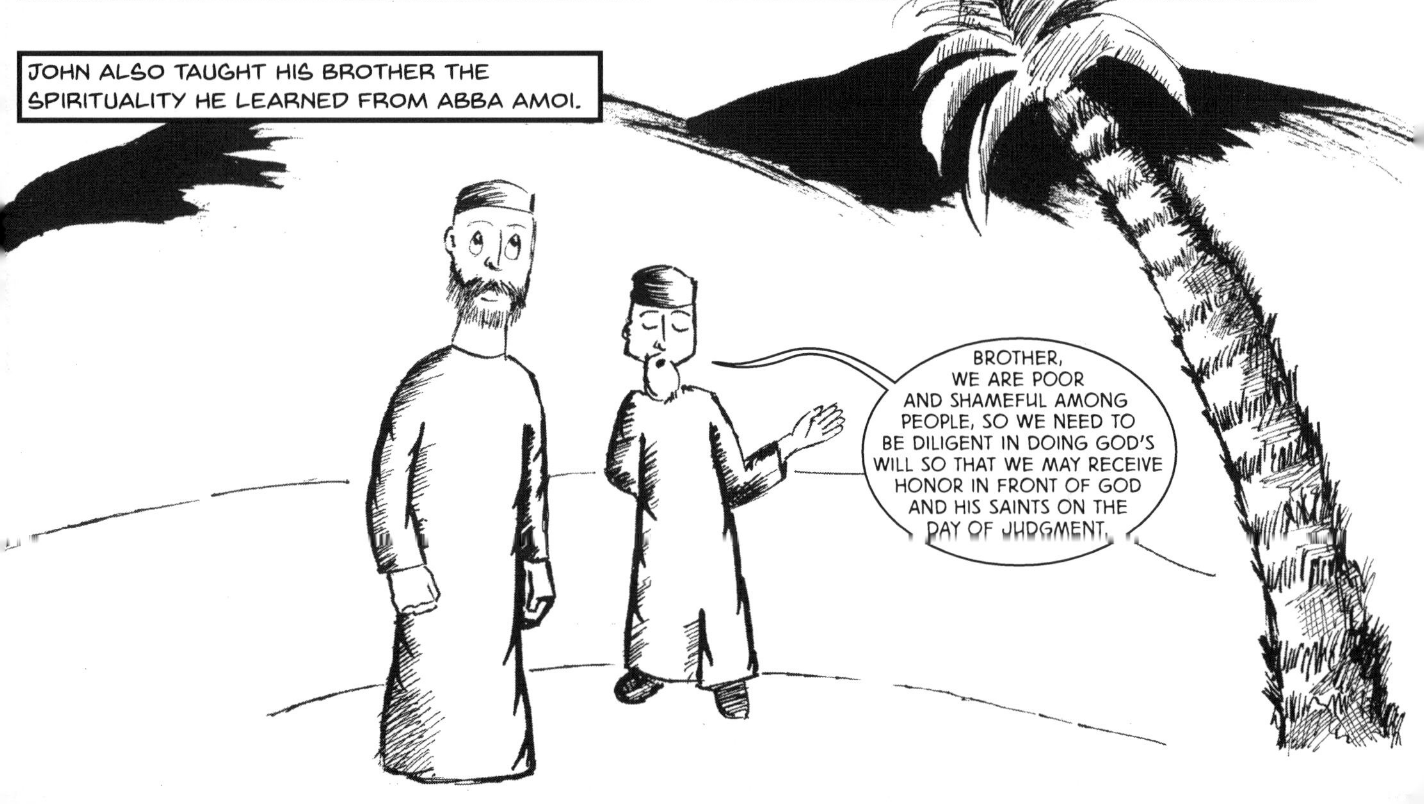
JOHN ALSO TAUGHT HIS BROTHER THE SPIRITUALITY HE LEARNED FROM ABBA AMOI.
BROTHER, WE ARE POOR AND SHAMEFUL AMONG PEOPLE, SO WE NEED TO BE DILIGENT IN DOING GOD'S WILL SO THAT WE MAY RECEIVE HONOR IN FRONT OF GOD AND HIS SAINTS ON THE DAY OF JUDGMENT.

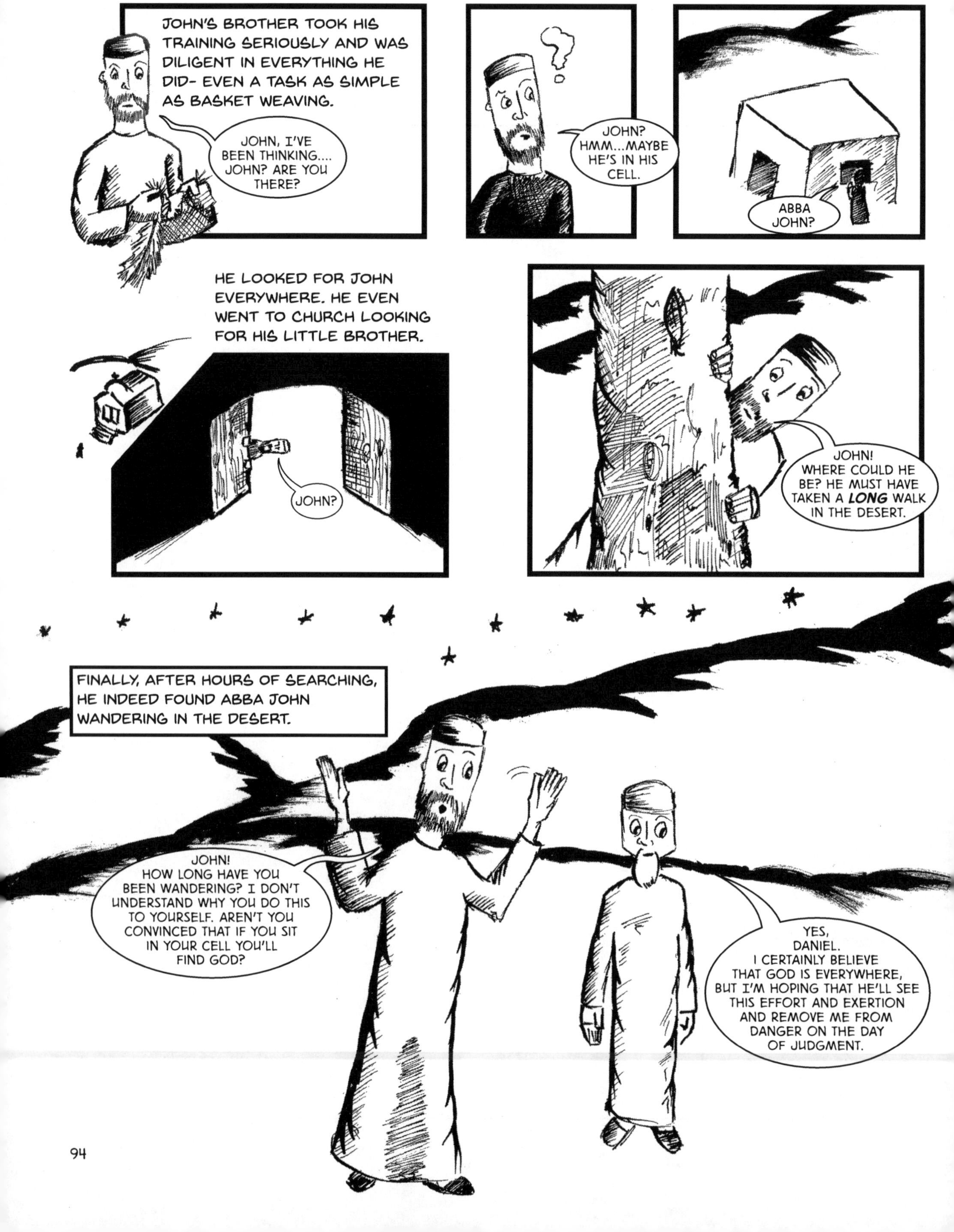
JOHN'S BROTHER TOOK HIS TRAINING SERIOUSLY AND WAS DILIGENT IN EVERYTHING HE DID- EVEN A TASK AS SIMPLE AS BASKET WEAVING.
JOHN, I'VE BEEN THINKING.... JOHN? ARE YOU THERE?
JOHN? HMM...MAYBE HE'S IN HIS CELL.
ABBA JOHN?
HE LOOKED FOR JOHN EVERYWHERE. HE EVEN WENT TO CHURCH LOOKING FOR HIS LITTLE BROTHER.
JOHN?
JOHN! WHERE COULD HE BE? HE MUST HAVE TAKEN A LONG WALK IN THE DESERT.
FINALLY, AFTER HOURS OF SEARCHING, HE INDEED FOUND ABBA JOHN WANDERING IN THE DESERT.
JOHN! HOW LONG HAVE YOU BEEN WANDERING? I DON'T UNDERSTAND WHY YOU DO THIS TO YOURSELF. AREN'T YOU CONVINCED THAT IF YOU SIT IN YOUR CELL YOU'LL FIND GOD?
YES, DANIEL. I CERTAINLY BELIEVE THAT GOD IS EVERYWHERE, BUT I'M HOPING THAT HE'LL SEE THIS EFFORT AND EXERTION AND REMOVE ME FROM DANGER ON THE DAY OF JUDGMENT.

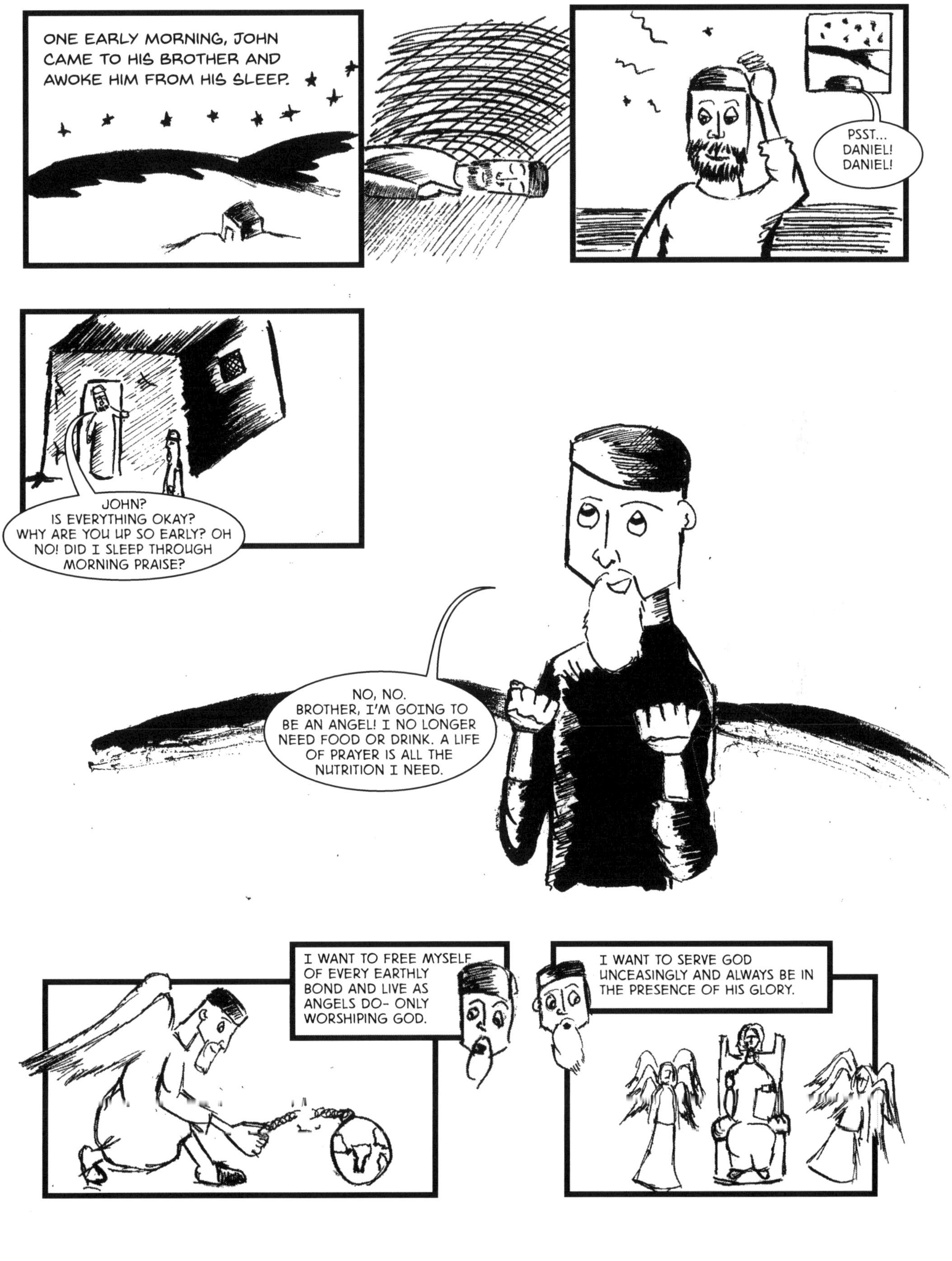
ONE EARLY MORNING, JOHN CAME TO HIS BROTHER AND AWOKE HIM FROM HIS SLEEP.
PSST... DANIEL! DANIEL!
JOHN? IS EVERYTHING OKAY? WHY ARE YOU UP SO EARLY? OH NO! DID I SLEEP THROUGH MORNING PRAISE?
NO, NO. BROTHER, I'M GOING TO BE AN ANGEL! I NO LONGER NEED FOOD OR DRINK. A LIFE OF PRAYER IS ALL THE NUTRITION I NEED.
I WANT TO FREE MYSELF OF EVERY EARTHLY BOND AND LIVE AS ANGELS DO- ONLY WORSHIPING GOD.
I WANT TO SERVE GOD UNCEASINGLY AND ALWAYS BE IN THE PRESENCE OF HIS GLORY.

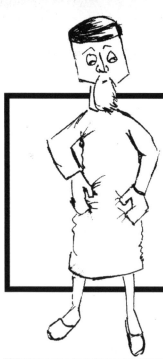

DESPITE HIS BROTHER'S WARNINGS, JOHN LEFT THE MONASTIC SETTLEMENT, TOOK OFF HIS TUNIC, AND WALKED FAR INTO THE DESERT.

HE PRAYED EARNESTLY AND DIDN'T STOP FOR FOOD OR DRINK- ONLY SLEEPING WHEN HE ABSOLUTELY HAS TO.

JOHN IGNORED HIS HUNGER AND THIRST AND INSTEAD FOCUSED ON PRAYER, SAYING, "THE LORD IS MY SHEPHERD; I SHALL NOT WANT."

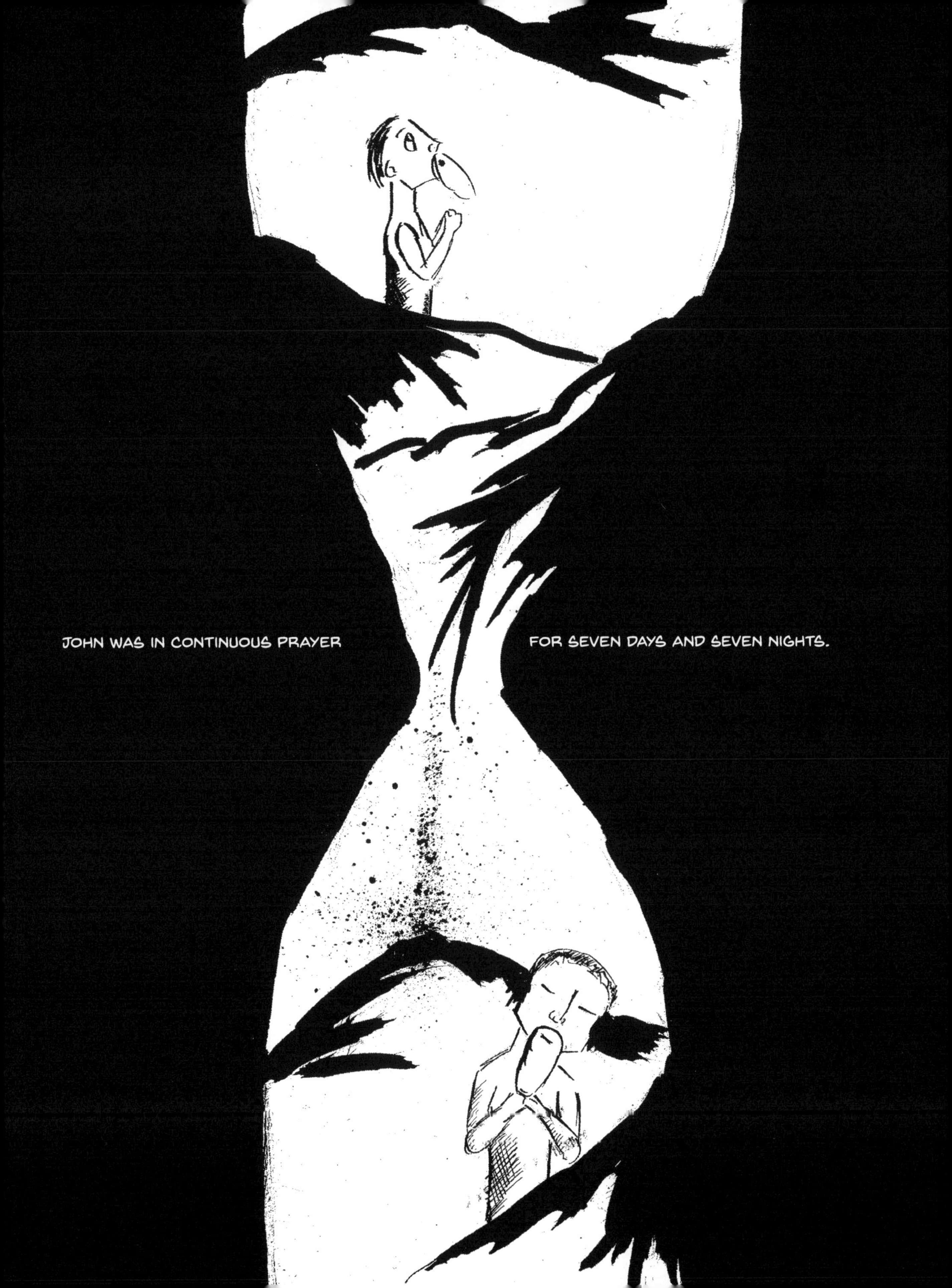
JOHN WAS IN CONTINUOUS PRAYER
FOR SEVEN DAYS AND SEVEN NIGHTS.

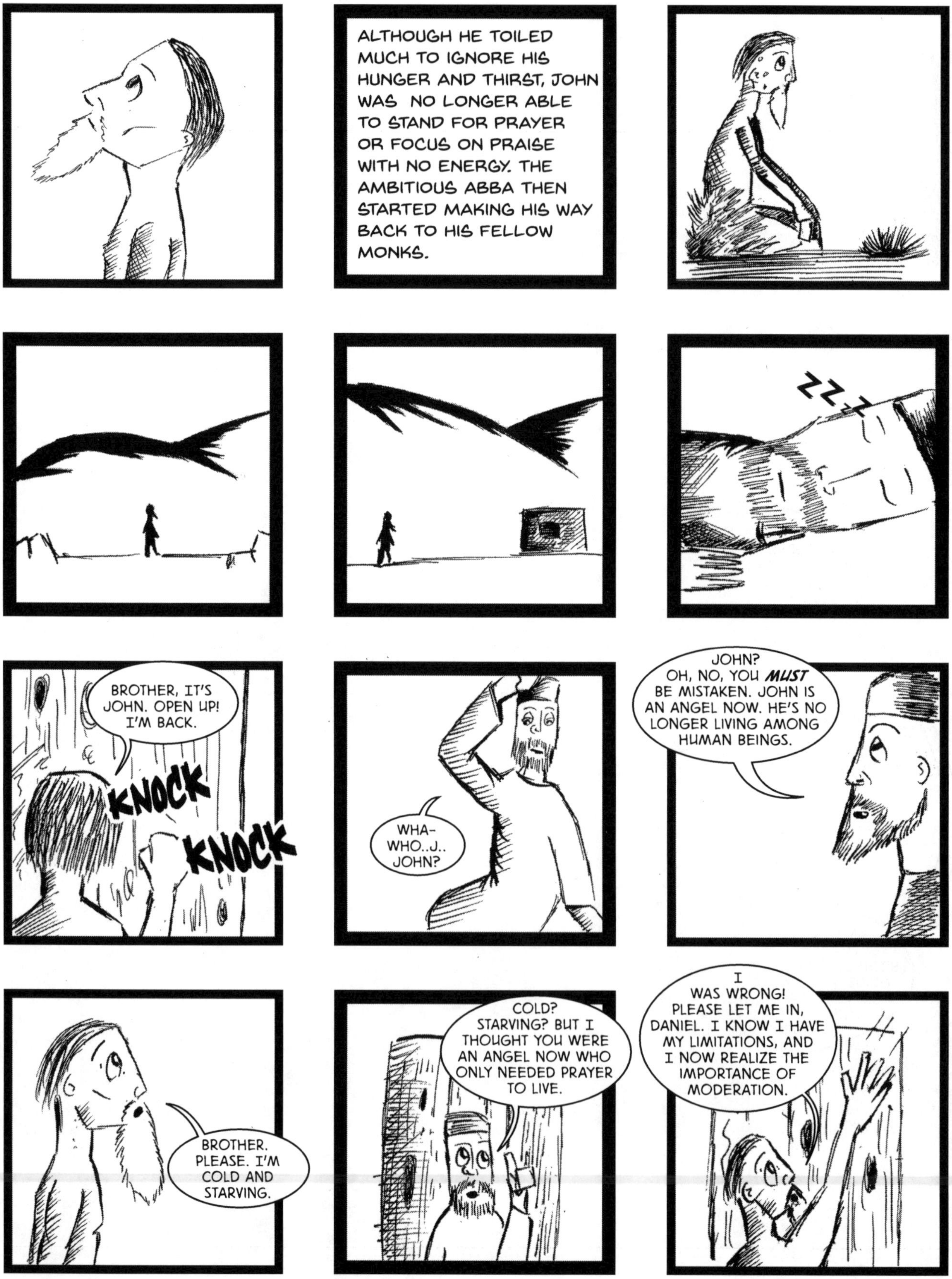

ALTHOUGH HE TOILED MUCH TO IGNORE HIS HUNGER AND THIRST, JOHN WAS NO LONGER ABLE TO STAND FOR PRAYER OR FOCUS ON PRAISE WITH NO ENERGY. THE AMBITIOUS ABBA THEN STARTED MAKING HIS WAY BACK TO HIS FELLOW MONKS.
ZZ..Z
BROTHER, IT'S JOHN. OPEN UP! I'M BACK.
KNOCK
KNOCK
WHA-WHO..J.. JOHN?
JOHN? OH, NO, YOU *MUST* BE MISTAKEN. JOHN IS AN ANGEL NOW. HE'S NO LONGER LIVING AMONG HUMAN BEINGS.
BROTHER. PLEASE. I'M COLD AND STARVING.
COLD? STARVING? BUT I THOUGHT YOU WERE AN ANGEL NOW WHO ONLY NEEDED PRAYER TO LIVE.
I WAS WRONG! PLEASE LET ME IN, DANIEL. I KNOW I HAVE MY LIMITATIONS, AND I NOW REALIZE THE IMPORTANCE OF MODERATION.

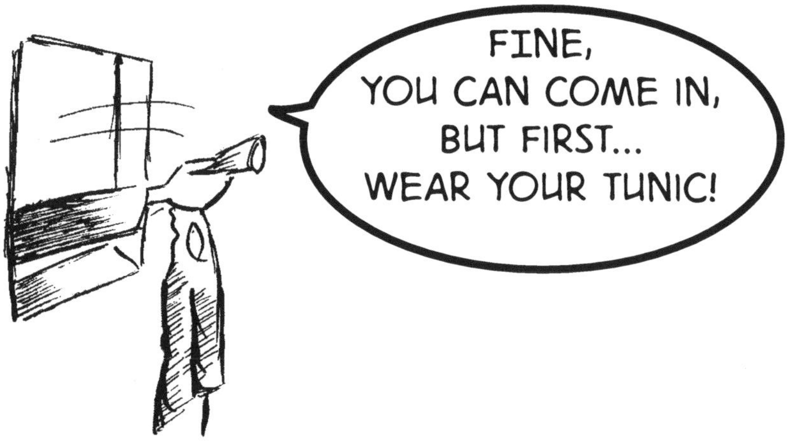
FINE, YOU CAN COME IN, BUT FIRST... WEAR YOUR TUNIC!

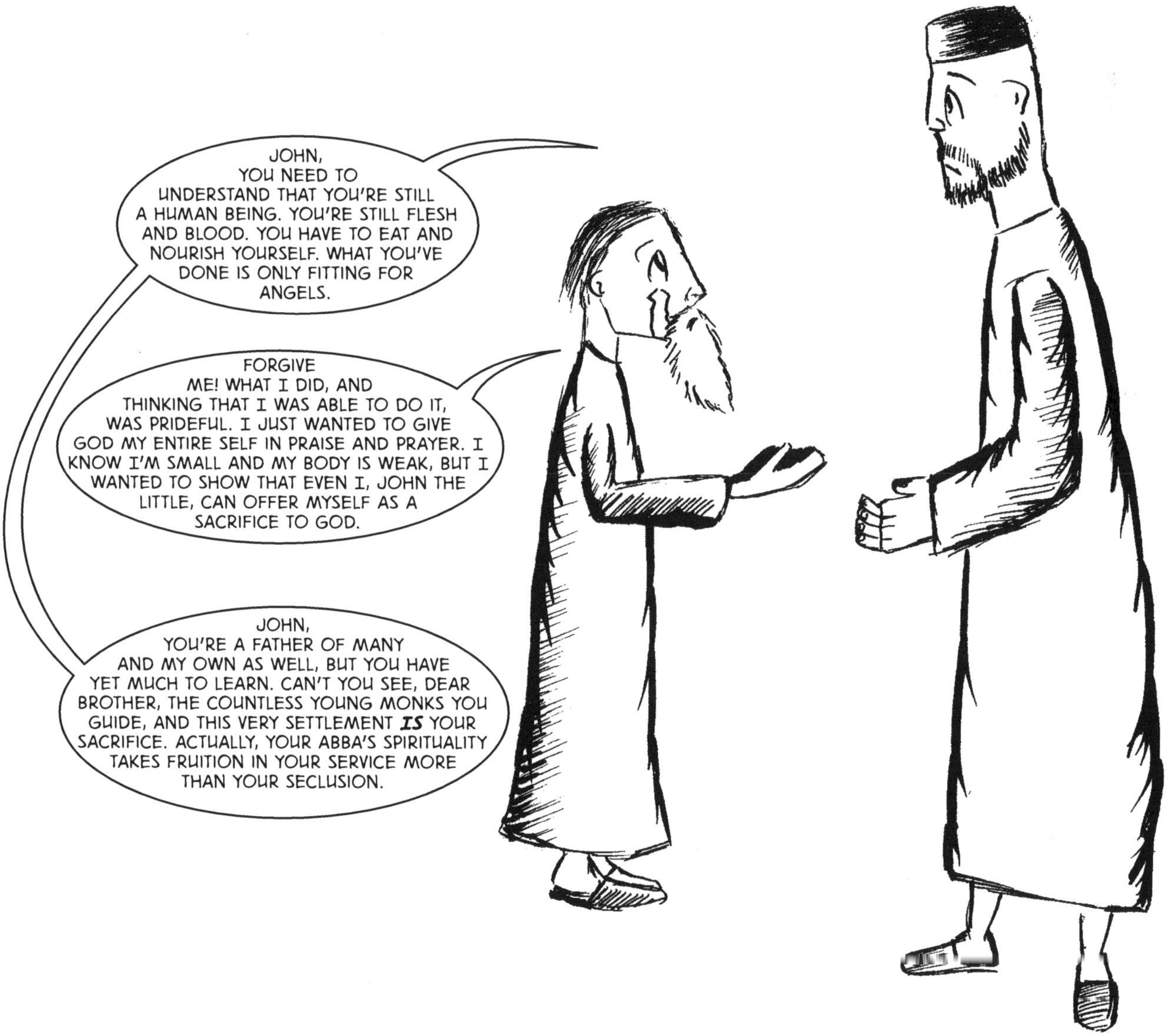
JOHN, YOU NEED TO UNDERSTAND THAT YOU'RE STILL A HUMAN BEING. YOU'RE STILL FLESH AND BLOOD. YOU HAVE TO EAT AND NOURISH YOURSELF. WHAT YOU'VE DONE IS ONLY FITTING FOR ANGELS.
FORGIVE ME! WHAT I DID, AND THINKING THAT I WAS ABLE TO DO IT, WAS PRIDEFUL. I JUST WANTED TO GIVE GOD MY ENTIRE SELF IN PRAISE AND PRAYER. I KNOW I'M SMALL AND MY BODY IS WEAK, BUT I WANTED TO SHOW THAT EVEN I, JOHN THE LITTLE, CAN OFFER MYSELF AS A SACRIFICE TO GOD.
JOHN, YOU'RE A FATHER OF MANY AND MY OWN AS WELL, BUT YOU HAVE YET MUCH TO LEARN. CAN'T YOU SEE, DEAR BROTHER, THE COUNTLESS YOUNG MONKS YOU GUIDE, AND THIS VERY SETTLEMENT ***IS*** YOUR SACRIFICE. ACTUALLY, YOUR ABBA'S SPIRITUALITY TAKES FRUITION IN YOUR SERVICE MORE THAN YOUR SECLUSION.

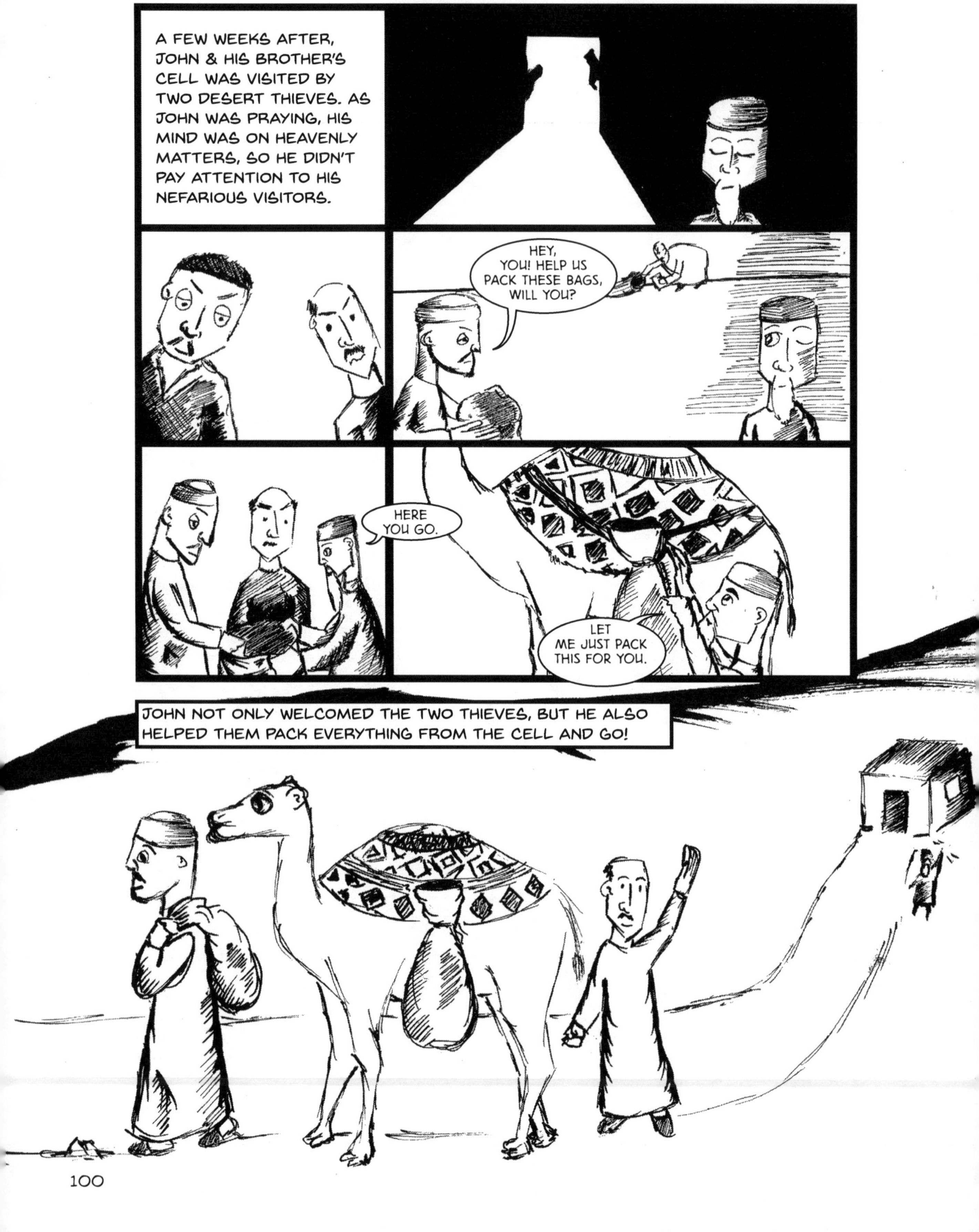
A FEW WEEKS AFTER, JOHN & HIS BROTHER'S CELL WAS VISITED BY TWO DESERT THIEVES. AS JOHN WAS PRAYING, HIS MIND WAS ON HEAVENLY MATTERS, SO HE DIDN'T PAY ATTENTION TO HIS NEFARIOUS VISITORS.
HEY, YOU! HELP US PACK THESE BAGS, WILL YOU?
HERE YOU GO.
LET ME JUST PACK THIS FOR YOU.
JOHN NOT ONLY WELCOMED THE TWO THIEVES, BUT HE ALSO HELPED THEM PACK EVERYTHING FROM THE CELL AND GO!

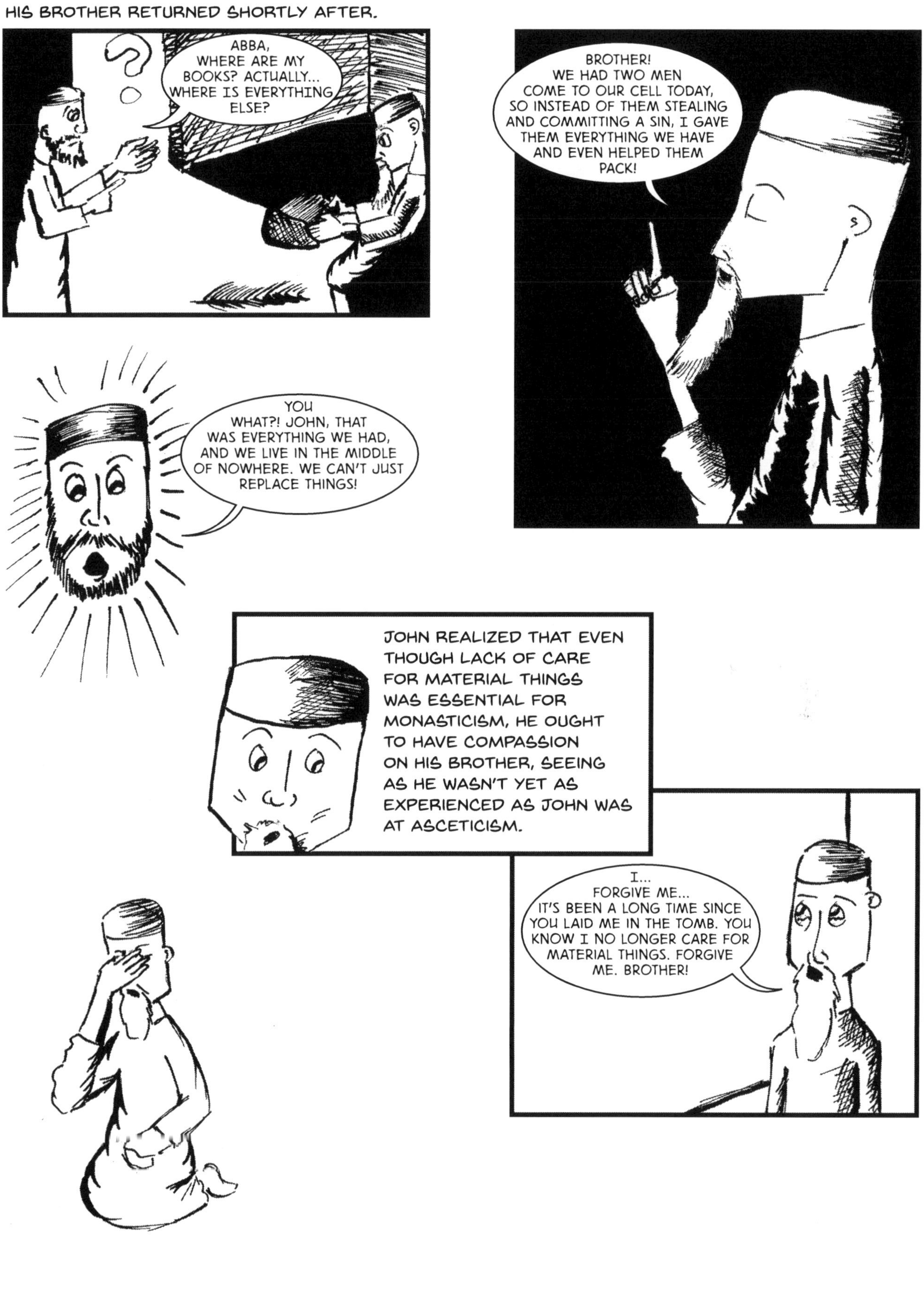
HIS BROTHER RETURNED SHORTLY AFTER.
ABBA, WHERE ARE MY BOOKS? ACTUALLY... WHERE IS EVERYTHING ELSE?
BROTHER! WE HAD TWO MEN COME TO OUR CELL TODAY, SO INSTEAD OF THEM STEALING AND COMMITTING A SIN, I GAVE THEM EVERYTHING WE HAVE AND EVEN HELPED THEM PACK!
YOU WHAT?! JOHN, THAT WAS EVERYTHING WE HAD, AND WE LIVE IN THE MIDDLE OF NOWHERE. WE CAN'T JUST REPLACE THINGS!
JOHN REALIZED THAT EVEN THOUGH LACK OF CARE FOR MATERIAL THINGS WAS ESSENTIAL FOR MONASTICISM, HE OUGHT TO HAVE COMPASSION ON HIS BROTHER, SEEING AS HE WASN'T YET AS EXPERIENCED AS JOHN WAS AT ASCETICISM.
I... FORGIVE ME... IT'S BEEN A LONG TIME SINCE YOU LAID ME IN THE TOMB. YOU KNOW I NO LONGER CARE FOR MATERIAL THINGS. FORGIVE ME. BROTHER!

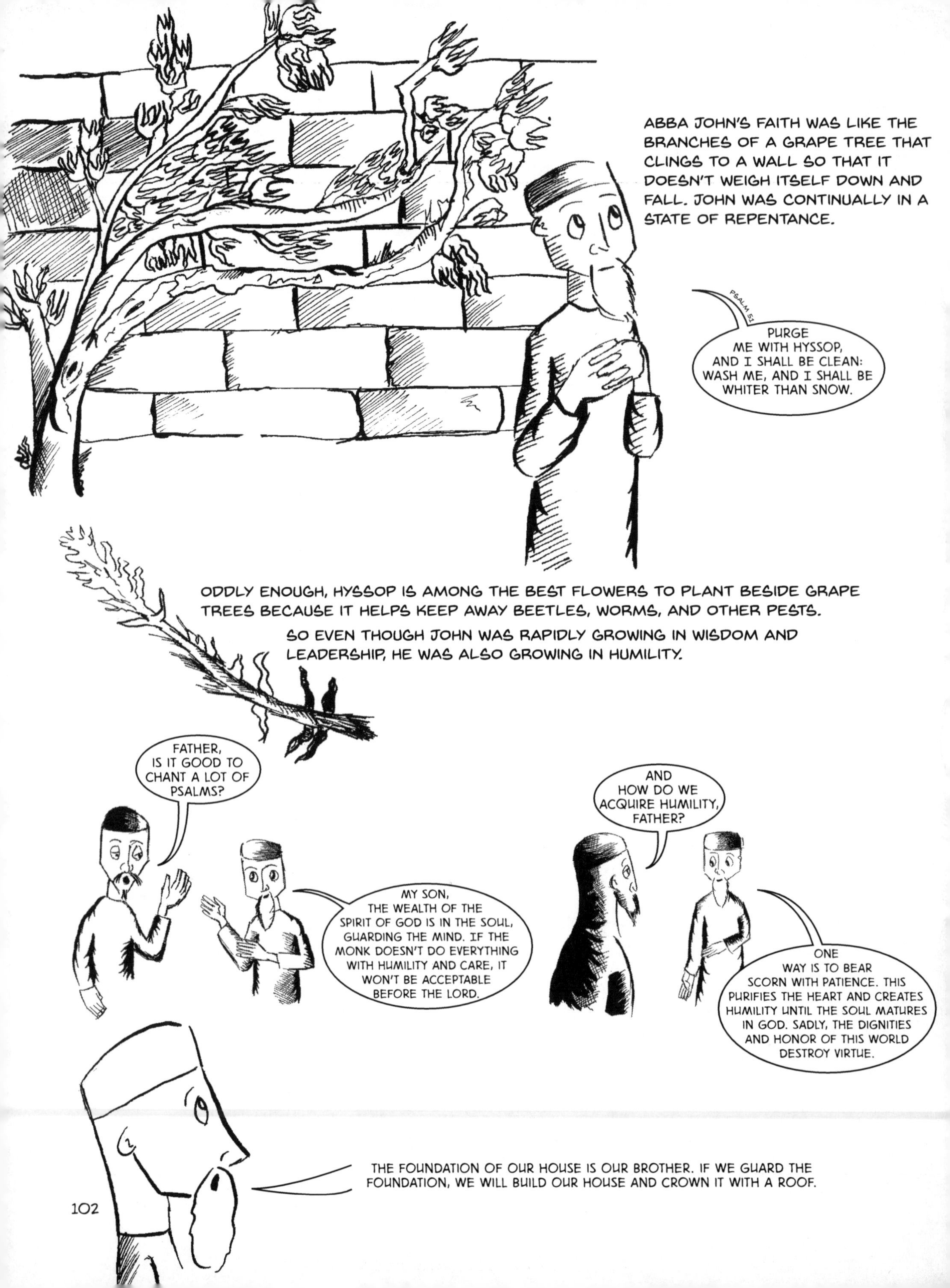
ABBA JOHN'S FAITH WAS LIKE THE BRANCHES OF A GRAPE TREE THAT CLINGS TO A WALL SO THAT IT DOESN'T WEIGH ITSELF DOWN AND FALL. JOHN WAS CONTINUALLY IN A STATE OF REPENTANCE.
PSALM 51
PURGE ME WITH HYSSOP, AND I SHALL BE CLEAN: WASH ME, AND I SHALL BE WHITER THAN SNOW.
ODDLY ENOUGH, HYSSOP IS AMONG THE BEST FLOWERS TO PLANT BESIDE GRAPE TREES BECAUSE IT HELPS KEEP AWAY BEETLES, WORMS, AND OTHER PESTS.
SO EVEN THOUGH JOHN WAS RAPIDLY GROWING IN WISDOM AND LEADERSHIP, HE WAS ALSO GROWING IN HUMILITY.
FATHER, IS IT GOOD TO CHANT A LOT OF PSALMS?
MY SON, THE WEALTH OF THE SPIRIT OF GOD IS IN THE SOUL, GUARDING THE MIND. IF THE MONK DOESN'T DO EVERYTHING WITH HUMILITY AND CARE, IT WON'T BE ACCEPTABLE BEFORE THE LORD.
AND HOW DO WE ACQUIRE HUMILITY, FATHER?
ONE WAY IS TO BEAR SCORN WITH PATIENCE. THIS PURIFIES THE HEART AND CREATES HUMILITY UNTIL THE SOUL MATURES IN GOD. SADLY, THE DIGNITIES AND HONOR OF THIS WORLD DESTROY VIRTUE.
THE FOUNDATION OF OUR HOUSE IS OUR BROTHER. IF WE GUARD THE FOUNDATION, WE WILL BUILD OUR HOUSE AND CROWN IT WITH A ROOF.

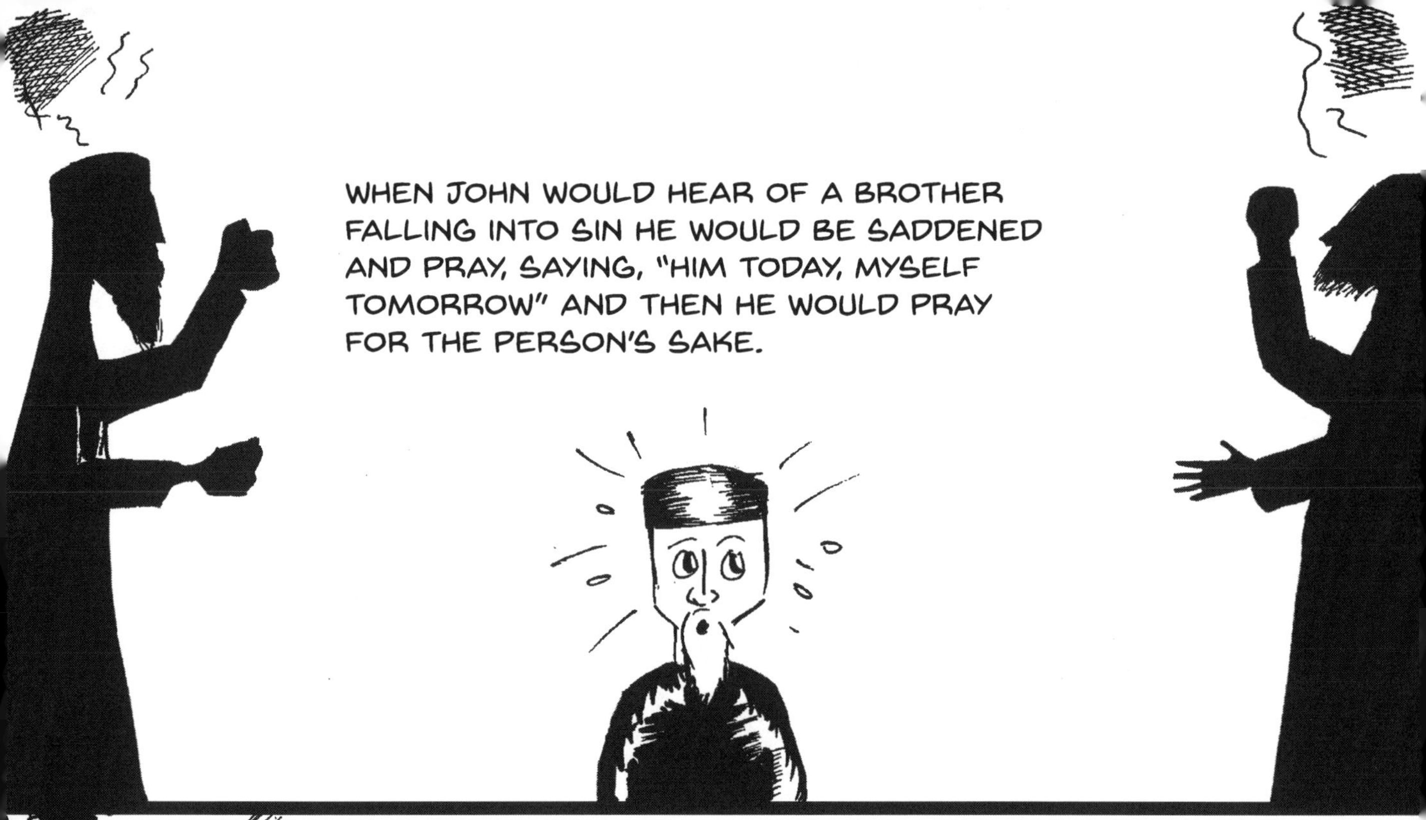
WHEN JOHN WOULD HEAR OF A BROTHER FALLING INTO SIN HE WOULD BE SADDENED AND PRAY, SAYING, "HIM TODAY, MYSELF TOMORROW" AND THEN HE WOULD PRAY FOR THE PERSON'S SAKE.

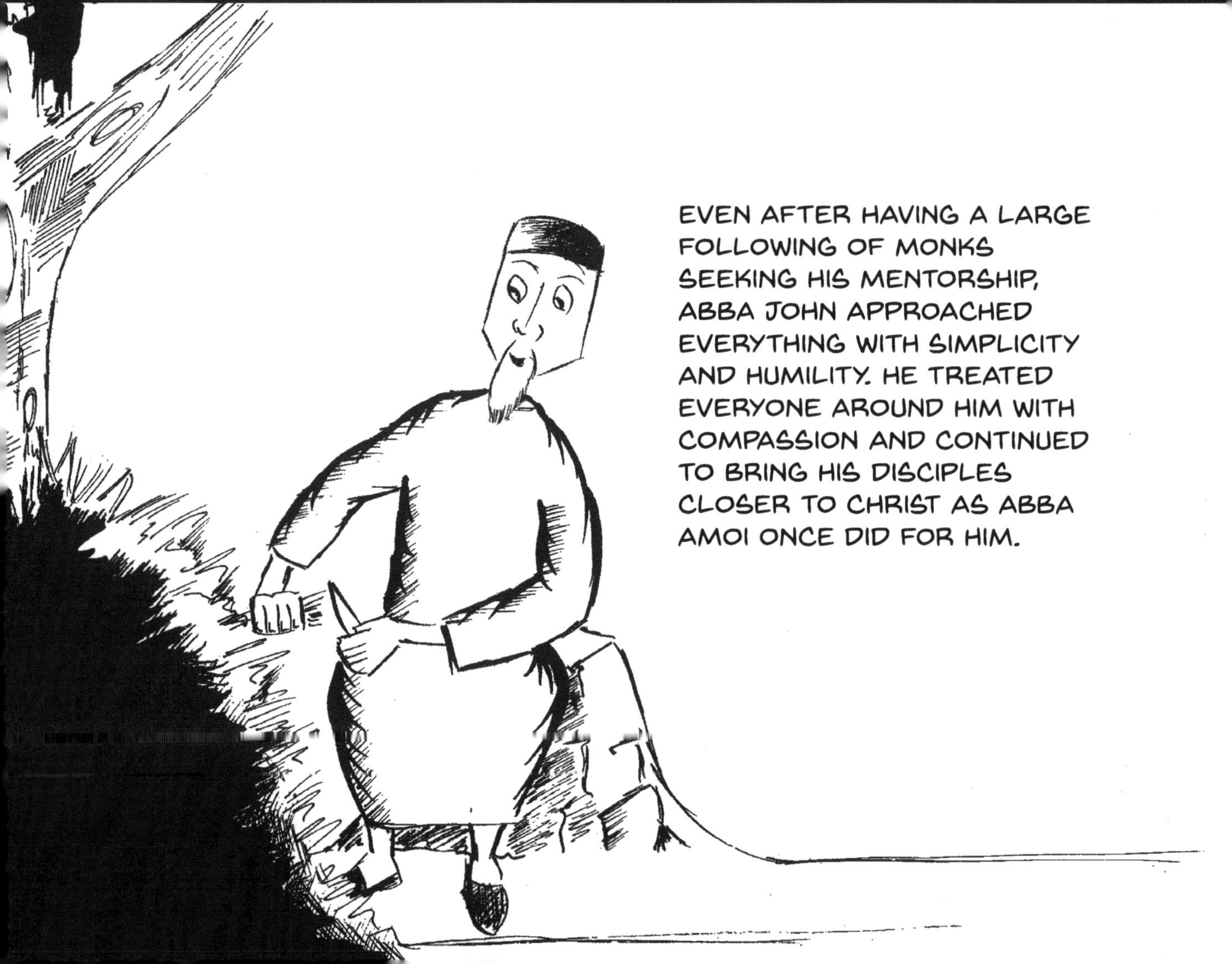
EVEN AFTER HAVING A LARGE FOLLOWING OF MONKS SEEKING HIS MENTORSHIP, ABBA JOHN APPROACHED EVERYTHING WITH SIMPLICITY AND HUMILITY. HE TREATED EVERYONE AROUND HIM WITH COMPASSION AND CONTINUED TO BRING HIS DISCIPLES CLOSER TO CHRIST AS ABBA AMOI ONCE DID FOR HIM.

# Chapter Four

# Fruits

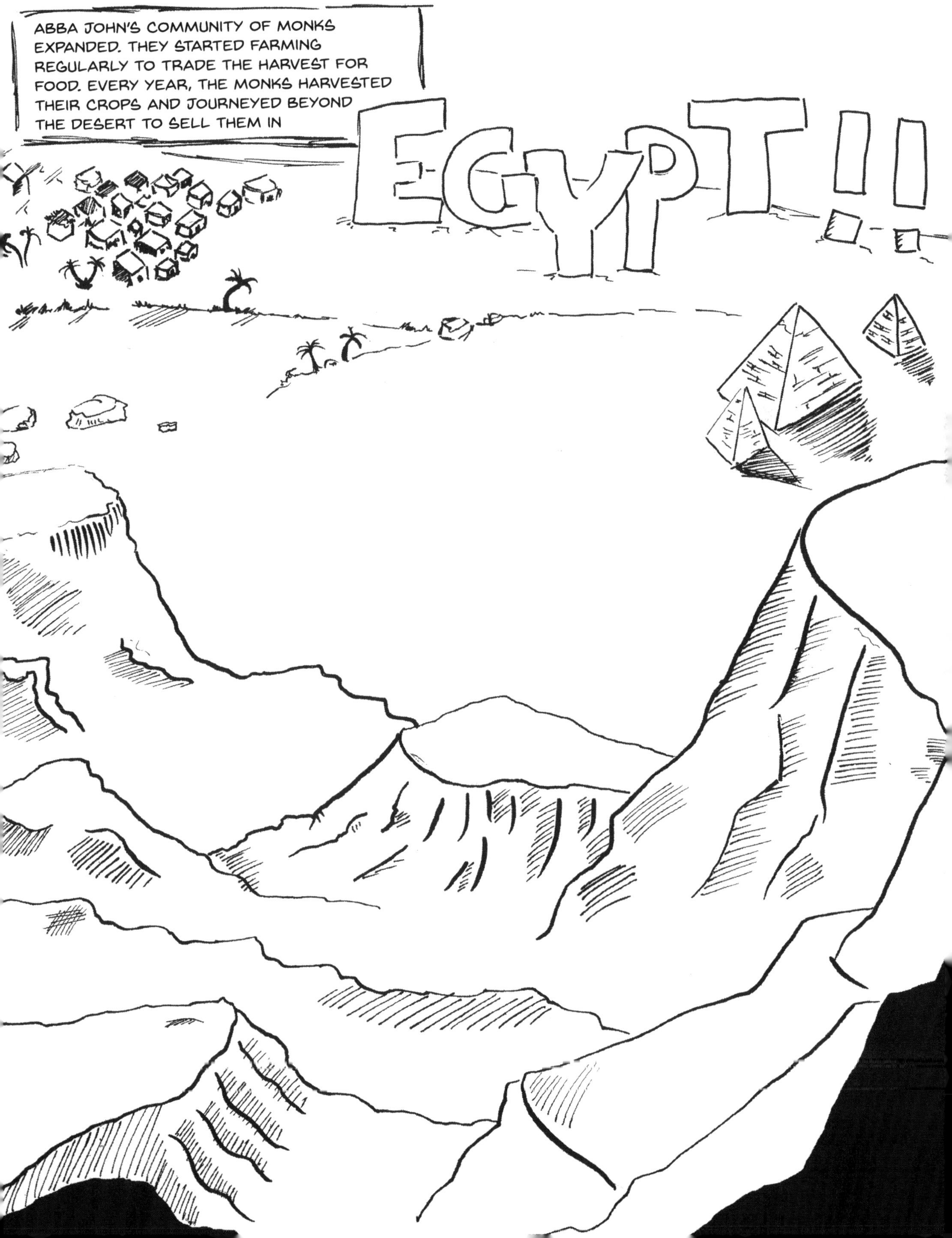
ABBA JOHN'S COMMUNITY OF MONKS EXPANDED. THEY STARTED FARMING REGULARLY TO TRADE THE HARVEST FOR FOOD. EVERY YEAR, THE MONKS HARVESTED THEIR CROPS AND JOURNEYED BEYOND THE DESERT TO SELL THEM IN
EGYPT!!

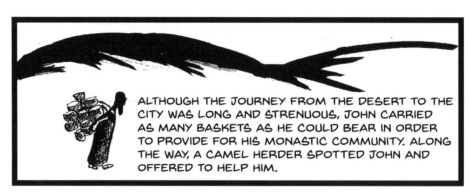

ALTHOUGH THE JOURNEY FROM THE DESERT TO THE CITY WAS LONG AND STRENUOUS, JOHN CARRIED AS MANY BASKETS AS HE COULD BEAR IN ORDER TO PROVIDE FOR HIS MONASTIC COMMUNITY. ALONG THE WAY, A CAMEL HERDER SPOTTED JOHN AND OFFERED TO HELP HIM.

THE DESERT OF SCETIS IS NO PLACE FOR AN ELDERLY MAN LIKE YOU! COME, LET ME LOAD YOUR BASKETS ON MY CAMEL AND WALK WITH ME.

JOHN ACCEPTED THE CAMEL HERDER'S OFFER, BUT WHEN THEY STARTED WALKING, THE MAN STARTED SINGING WORLDLY SONGS AND UTTERING FOUL WORDS.

I UNDERSTAND WHY YOU'RE LEAVING THE DESERT AND GOING TO EGYPT, OLD MAN.

THE WOMEN IN EGYPT ARE A BEAUTY TO BEHOLD! I KNOW THIS GIRL WHO...

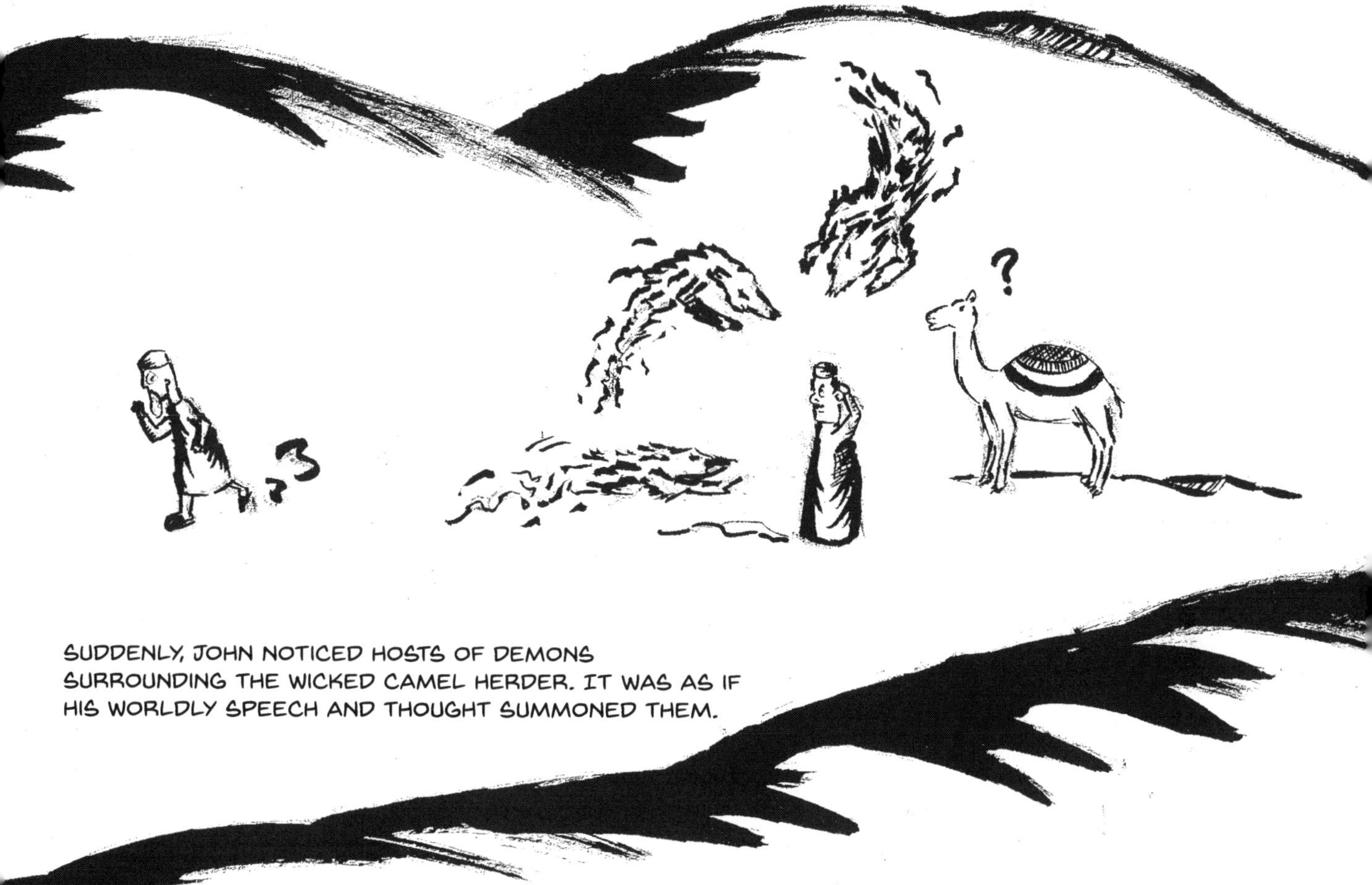

SUDDENLY, JOHN NOTICED HOSTS OF DEMONS SURROUNDING THE WICKED CAMEL HERDER. IT WAS AS IF HIS WORLDLY SPEECH AND THOUGHT SUMMONED THEM.

ABBA JOHN IMMEDIATELY ABANDONED THE BASKETS. HE TURNED AROUND AND RAN IN THE OPPOSITE DIRECTION WHILE CHANTING THE PSALMS AND WORDS OF THE BIBLE IN ORDER TO FREE HIS MIND OF THE WORDS HE JUST HEARD.

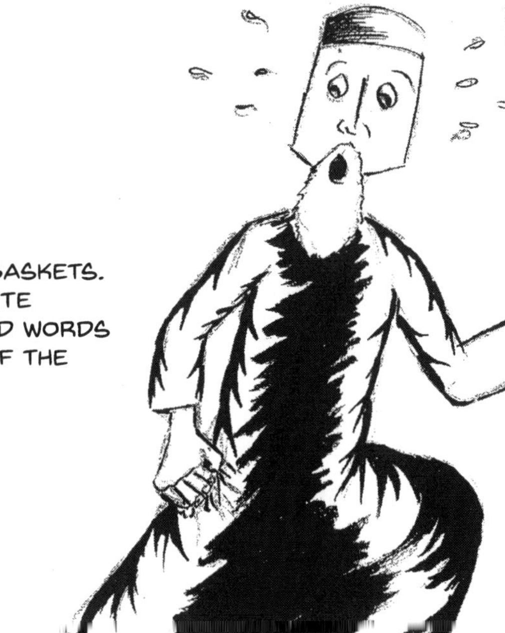

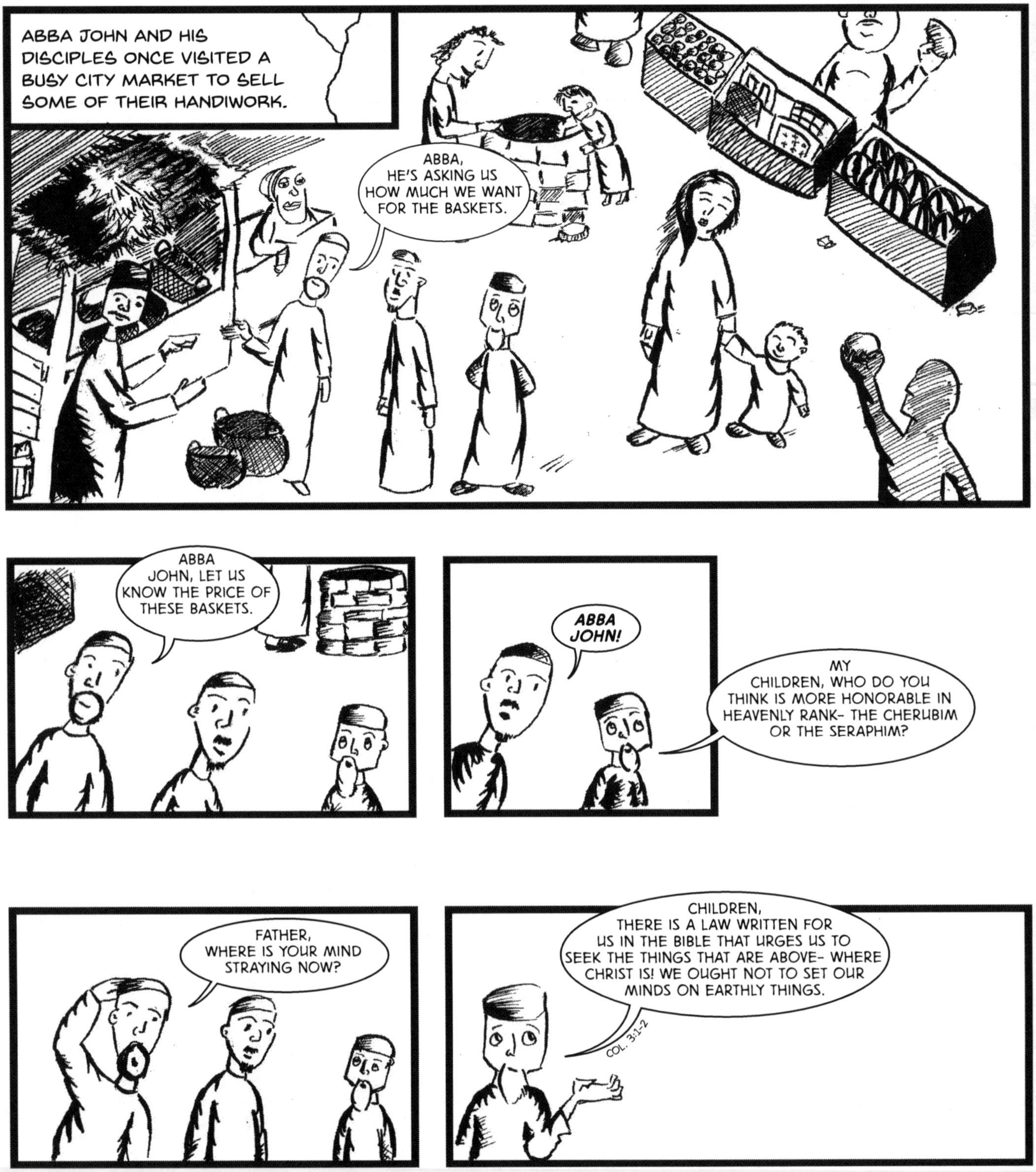
ABBA JOHN AND HIS DISCIPLES ONCE VISITED A BUSY CITY MARKET TO SELL SOME OF THEIR HANDIWORK.
ABBA, HE'S ASKING US HOW MUCH WE WANT FOR THE BASKETS.
ABBA JOHN, LET US KNOW THE PRICE OF THESE BASKETS.
ABBA JOHN!
MY CHILDREN, WHO DO YOU THINK IS MORE HONORABLE IN HEAVENLY RANK- THE CHERUBIM OR THE SERAPHIM?
FATHER, WHERE IS YOUR MIND STRAYING NOW?
CHILDREN, THERE IS A LAW WRITTEN FOR US IN THE BIBLE THAT URGES US TO SEEK THE THINGS THAT ARE ABOVE- WHERE CHRIST IS! WE OUGHT NOT TO SET OUR MINDS ON EARTHLY THINGS.
COL. 3:1-2

IF YOU ASK ANYONE WHO KNEW HIM, THEY WOULD TELL YOU ABBA JOHN'S CITIZENSHIP WAS IN THE HEAVENLY JERUSALEM, NOT ON EARTH.

ONE TIME, ABBA JOHN SOAKED TWO BASKETS' WORTH OF PLAITING IN WATER, HOPING TO LATER WEAVE THEM INTO TWO BASKETS. JOHN BEGAN TO WORK, AND, AS USUAL, BEGAN TO PRAY AND REFLECT ON THINGS THAT ARE FROM ABOVE.

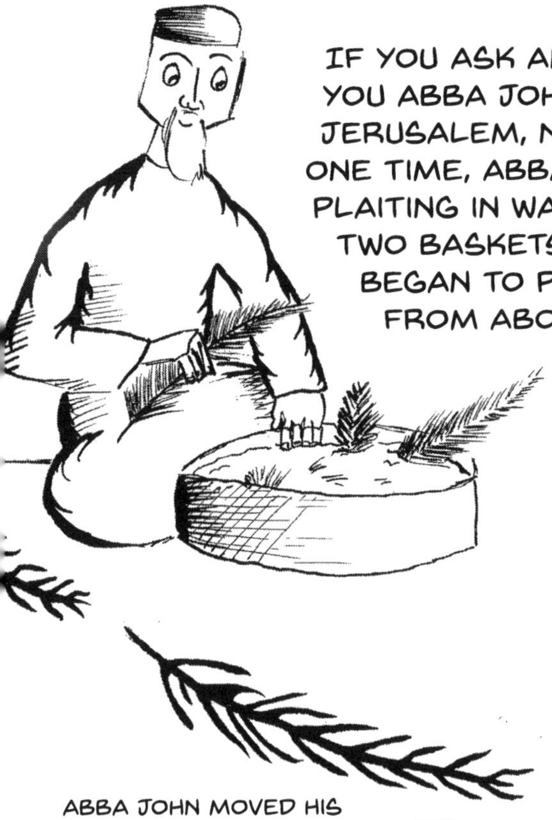

"OUR CITIZENSHIP IS IN HEAVEN. WE EAGERLY WAIT FOR THE SAVIOR, THE LORD JESUS CHRIST, WHO WILL TRANSFORM OUR LOWLY BODIES THAT THEY MAY BE CONFORMED TO HIS GLORIOUS BODY."

ABBA JOHN MOVED HIS FINGERS WITH SKILLFUL PRECISION - NOT ONLY WEAVING THE PALM FRONDS BUT ALSO WEAVING PRAYERS AND THOUGHTS OF GOODNESS AS HE WORKED.

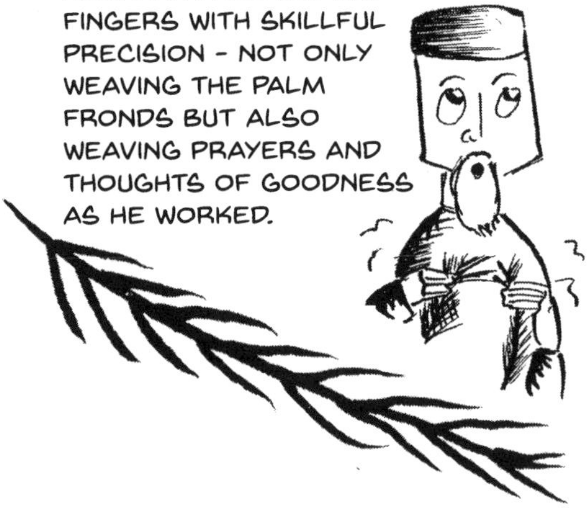

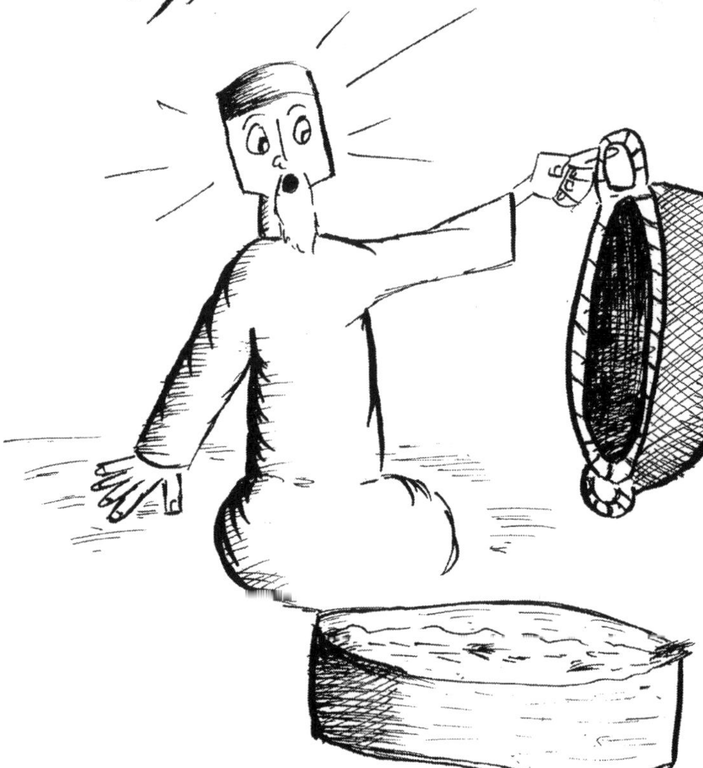

HOWEVER, JOHN SOON BEGAN TO WEAVE ALL THE PALMS HE SOAKED INTO ONE SINGLE BASKET. HE ONCE AGAIN PAID NO MIND TO EARTHLY MATTERS AS HE FOCUSED ON HEAVENLY ONES- AND ONLY REALIZED IT WAS SO AFTER HE FINISHED WEAVING THE NOW-OVERSIZED BASKET!

ANOTHER TIME, A BROTHER CAME TO ABBA JOHN'S CELL ASKING FOR FINISHED BASKETS TO SELL.

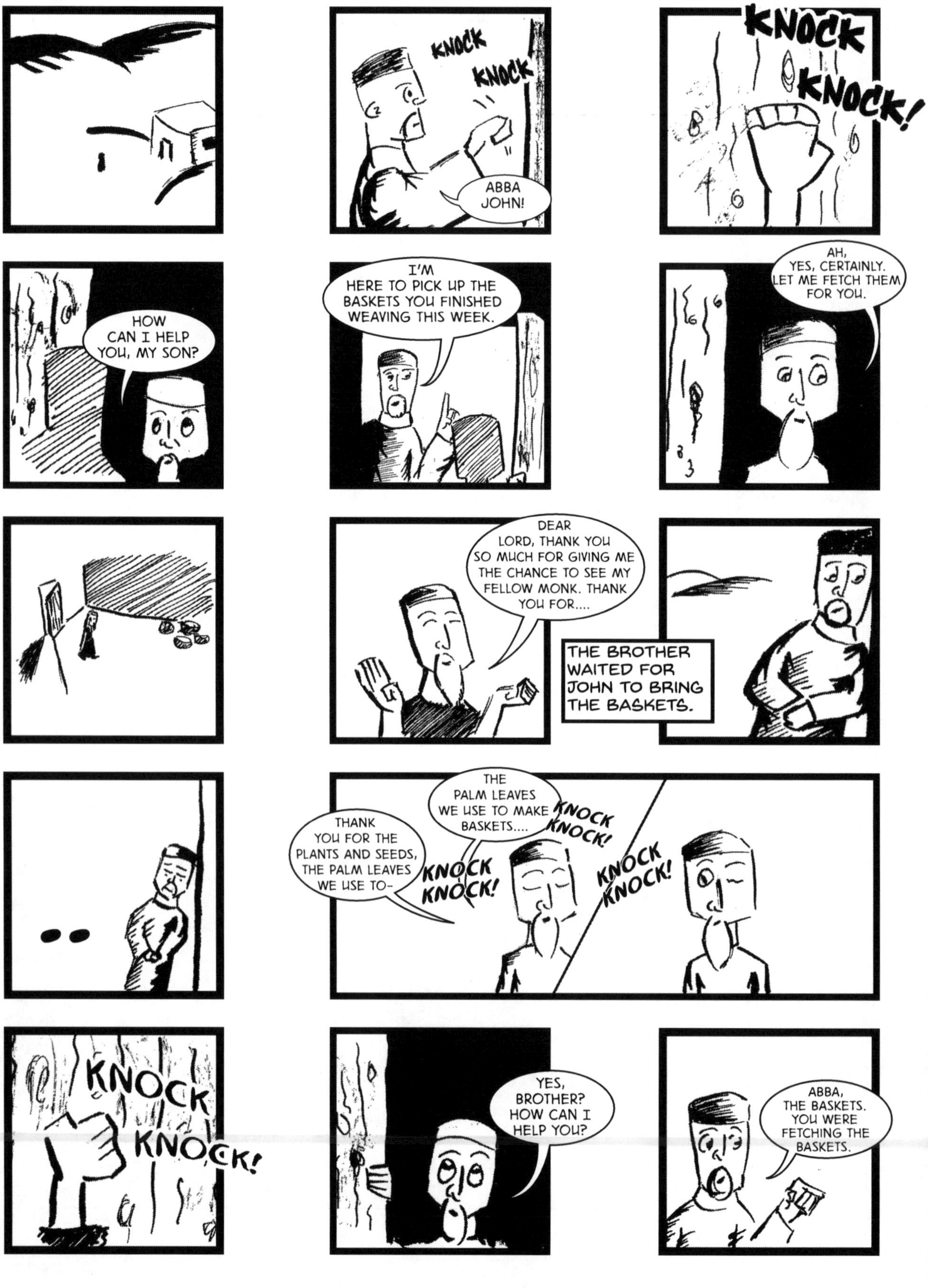

KNOCK
KNOCK
ABBA JOHN!
KNOCK
KNOCK!
HOW CAN I HELP YOU, MY SON?
I'M HERE TO PICK UP THE BASKETS YOU FINISHED WEAVING THIS WEEK.
AH, YES, CERTAINLY. LET ME FETCH THEM FOR YOU.
DEAR LORD, THANK YOU SO MUCH FOR GIVING ME THE CHANCE TO SEE MY FELLOW MONK. THANK YOU FOR....
THE BROTHER WAITED FOR JOHN TO BRING THE BASKETS.
THANK YOU FOR THE PLANTS AND SEEDS, THE PALM LEAVES WE USE TO-
KNOCK KNOCK!
THE PALM LEAVES WE USE TO MAKE BASKETS....
KNOCK KNOCK!
KNOCK KNOCK!
KNOCK
KNOCK!
YES, BROTHER? HOW CAN I HELP YOU?
ABBA, THE BASKETS. YOU WERE FETCHING THE BASKETS.

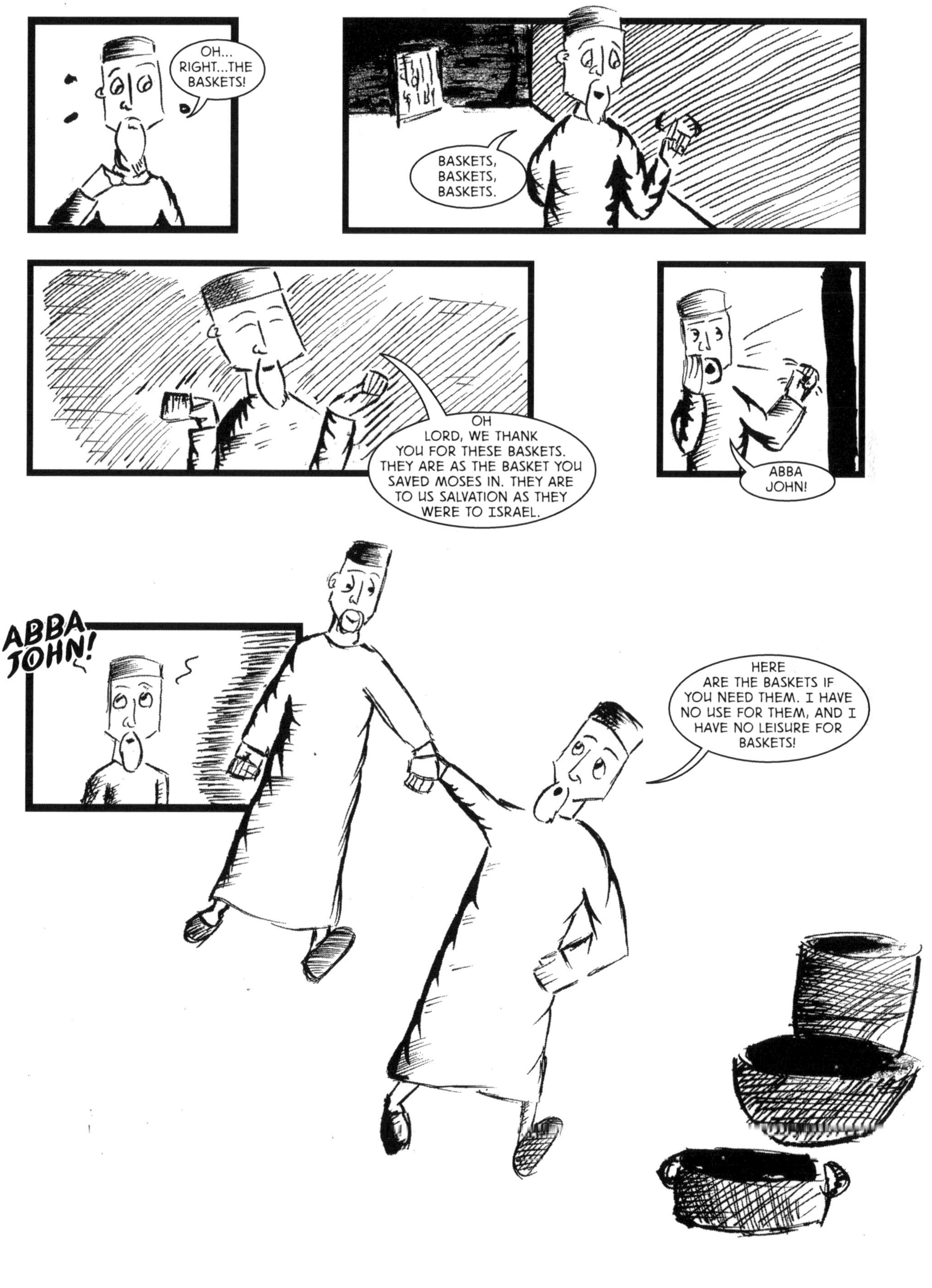
OH... RIGHT...THE BASKETS!
BASKETS, BASKETS, BASKETS.
OH LORD, WE THANK YOU FOR THESE BASKETS. THEY ARE AS THE BASKET YOU SAVED MOSES IN. THEY ARE TO US SALVATION AS THEY WERE TO ISRAEL.
ABBA JOHN!
ABBA JOHN!
HERE ARE THE BASKETS IF YOU NEED THEM. I HAVE NO USE FOR THEM, AND I HAVE NO LEISURE FOR BASKETS!

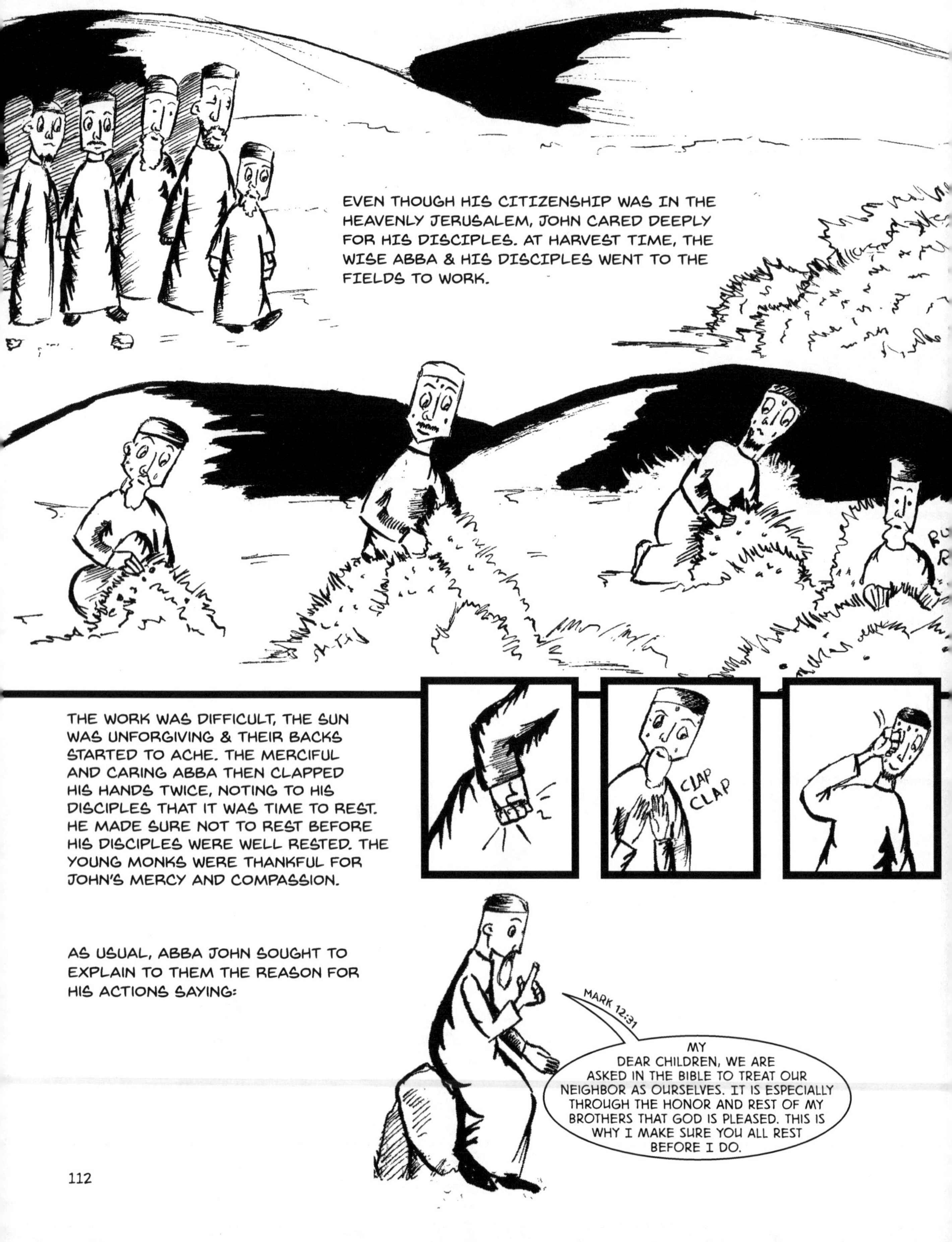
EVEN THOUGH HIS CITIZENSHIP WAS IN THE HEAVENLY JERUSALEM, JOHN CARED DEEPLY FOR HIS DISCIPLES. AT HARVEST TIME, THE WISE ABBA & HIS DISCIPLES WENT TO THE FIELDS TO WORK.
THE WORK WAS DIFFICULT, THE SUN WAS UNFORGIVING & THEIR BACKS STARTED TO ACHE. THE MERCIFUL AND CARING ABBA THEN CLAPPED HIS HANDS TWICE, NOTING TO HIS DISCIPLES THAT IT WAS TIME TO REST. HE MADE SURE NOT TO REST BEFORE HIS DISCIPLES WERE WELL RESTED. THE YOUNG MONKS WERE THANKFUL FOR JOHN'S MERCY AND COMPASSION.
CLAP CLAP
AS USUAL, ABBA JOHN SOUGHT TO EXPLAIN TO THEM THE REASON FOR HIS ACTIONS SAYING:
MARK 12:31
MY DEAR CHILDREN, WE ARE ASKED IN THE BIBLE TO TREAT OUR NEIGHBOR AS OURSELVES. IT IS ESPECIALLY THROUGH THE HONOR AND REST OF MY BROTHERS THAT GOD IS PLEASED. THIS IS WHY I MAKE SURE YOU ALL REST BEFORE I DO.

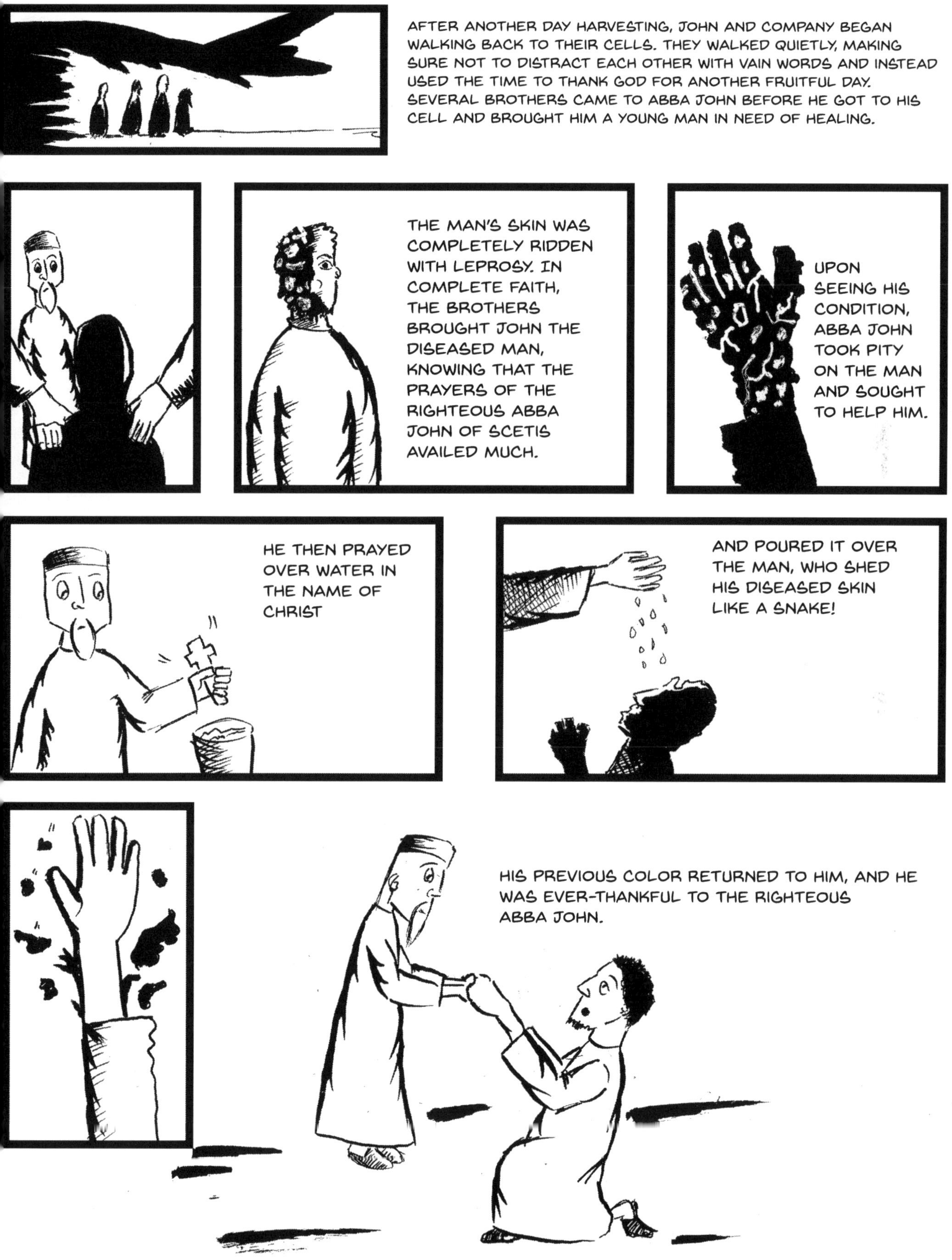
AFTER ANOTHER DAY HARVESTING, JOHN AND COMPANY BEGAN WALKING BACK TO THEIR CELLS. THEY WALKED QUIETLY, MAKING SURE NOT TO DISTRACT EACH OTHER WITH VAIN WORDS AND INSTEAD USED THE TIME TO THANK GOD FOR ANOTHER FRUITFUL DAY. SEVERAL BROTHERS CAME TO ABBA JOHN BEFORE HE GOT TO HIS CELL AND BROUGHT HIM A YOUNG MAN IN NEED OF HEALING.
THE MAN'S SKIN WAS COMPLETELY RIDDEN WITH LEPROSY. IN COMPLETE FAITH, THE BROTHERS BROUGHT JOHN THE DISEASED MAN, KNOWING THAT THE PRAYERS OF THE RIGHTEOUS ABBA JOHN OF SCETIS AVAILED MUCH.
UPON SEEING HIS CONDITION, ABBA JOHN TOOK PITY ON THE MAN AND SOUGHT TO HELP HIM.
HE THEN PRAYED OVER WATER IN THE NAME OF CHRIST
AND POURED IT OVER THE MAN, WHO SHED HIS DISEASED SKIN LIKE A SNAKE!
HIS PREVIOUS COLOR RETURNED TO HIM, AND HE WAS EVER-THANKFUL TO THE RIGHTEOUS ABBA JOHN.

IN A SIMILAR FASHION, ABBA JOHN WAS ONCE WALKING BACK FROM A DAY AT HARVEST WHEN HE CAME ACROSS A WOMAN BEING FLAYED BY A DEMON. THE WOMAN WAS SHRIEKING IN AGONY, SO ABBA JOHN TOOK COMPASSION ON HER AND STOPPED TO PRAY OVER HER.

WHAT DO YOU WANT WITH ME, YOU SHORT LITTLE MONK! I LEFT YOU THE DESERT, AND NOW YOU COME BOTHER ME HERE TOO! LEAVE ME ALONE!

THE DEMON LEFT THE WOMAN IN FRUSTRATION, AND SHE WAS COMPLETELY CURED. THE YOUNGER MONKS WHO BEHELD THIS MARVELED AT THIS MIRACLE THAT TOOK PLACE THROUGH ABBA JOHN, AND THEY GLORIFIED GOD.

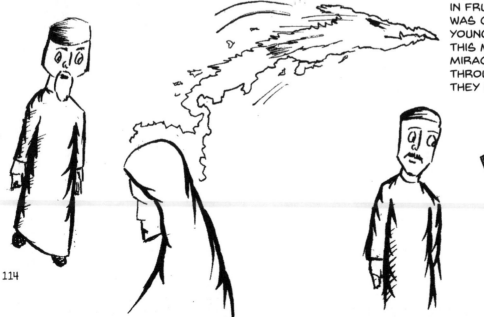

A WHILE AFTER DANIEL PASSED AWAY, LEAVING HIS LITTLE BROTHER JOHN IN SADNESS. JOHN WAS THANKFUL THAT HE GOT TO SPEND TIME WITH HIS BROTHER EVEN AFTER MONASTICISM AND THAT HE GOT TO SEE HIM BECOME A MONK. THE RIGHTEOUS JOHN GLORIFIED GOD AND MADE SURE TO REMEMBER THE NUMEROUS LESSONS HIS BROTHER DANIEL TAUGHT HIM. FELLOW MONKS WERE MOVED AS WELL BECAUSE DANIEL WASN'T ONLY AN OLDER BROTHER TO JOHN BUT TO THE ENTIRE COMMUNITY OF MONKS.

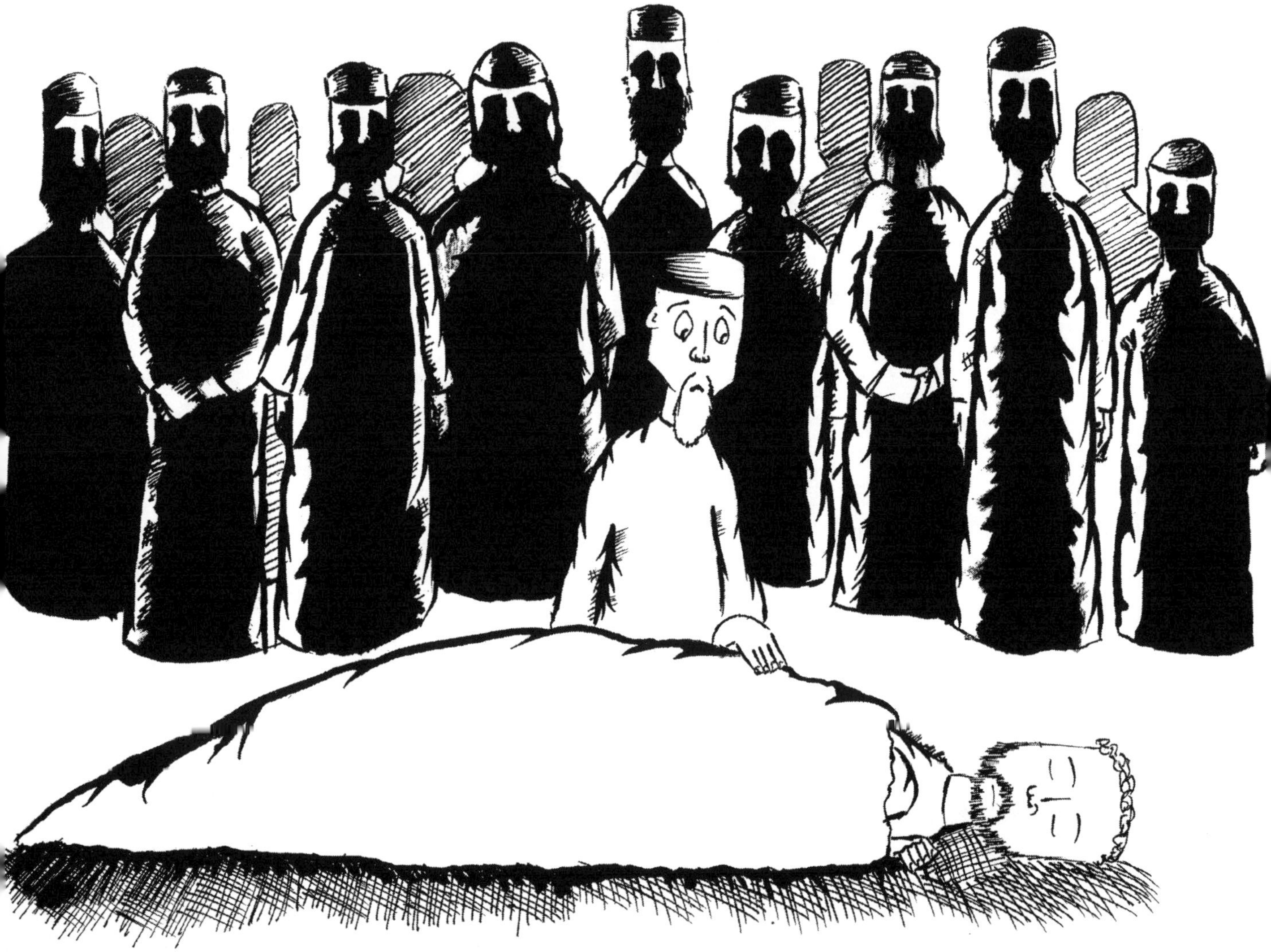

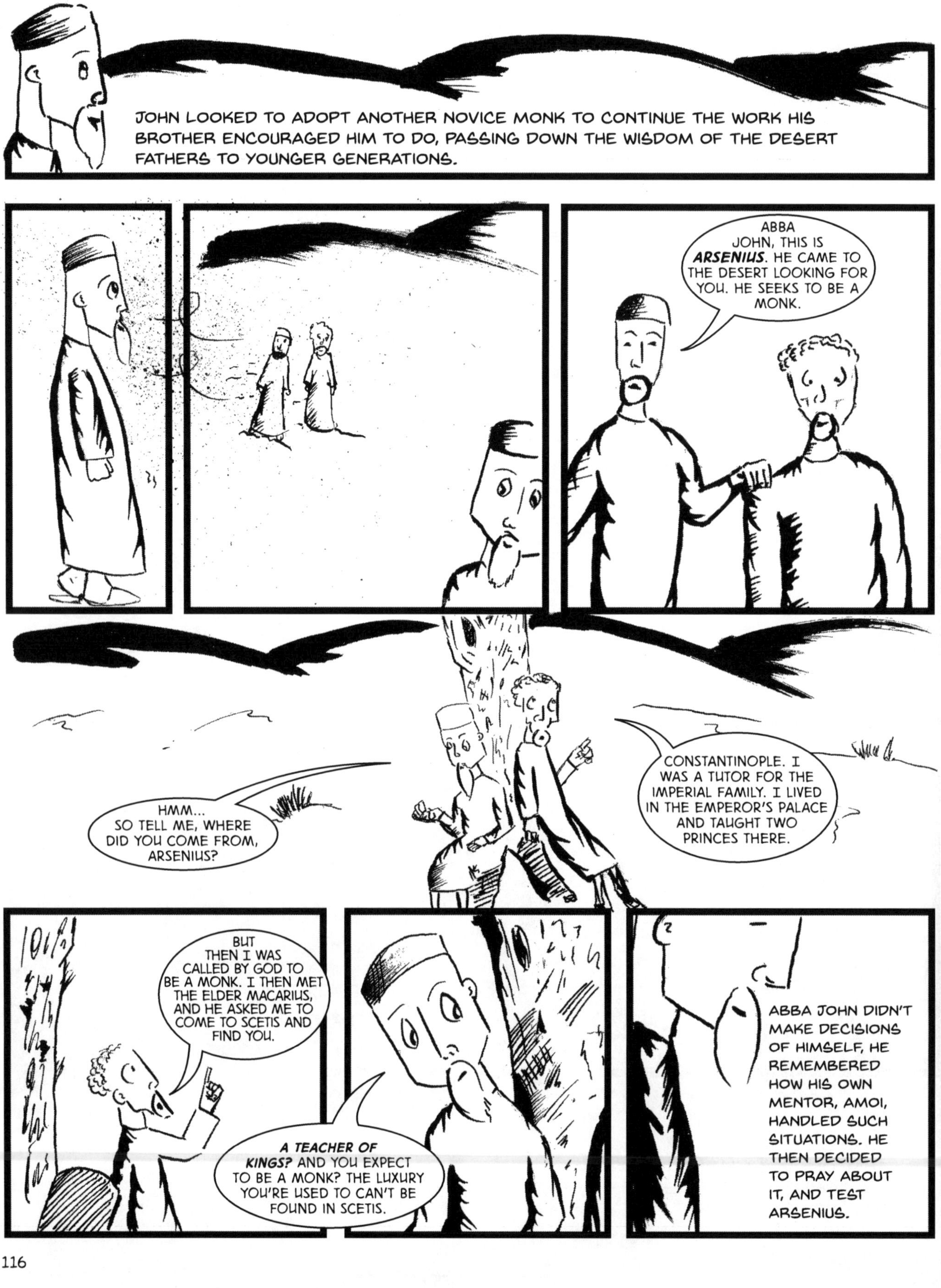

JOHN LOOKED TO ADOPT ANOTHER NOVICE MONK TO CONTINUE THE WORK HIS BROTHER ENCOURAGED HIM TO DO, PASSING DOWN THE WISDOM OF THE DESERT FATHERS TO YOUNGER GENERATIONS.
ABBA JOHN, THIS IS ARSENIUS. HE CAME TO THE DESERT LOOKING FOR YOU. HE SEEKS TO BE A MONK.
HMM... SO TELL ME, WHERE DID YOU COME FROM, ARSENIUS?
CONSTANTINOPLE. I WAS A TUTOR FOR THE IMPERIAL FAMILY. I LIVED IN THE EMPEROR'S PALACE AND TAUGHT TWO PRINCES THERE.
BUT THEN I WAS CALLED BY GOD TO BE A MONK. I THEN MET THE ELDER MACARIUS, AND HE ASKED ME TO COME TO SCETIS AND FIND YOU.
A TEACHER OF KINGS? AND YOU EXPECT TO BE A MONK? THE LUXURY YOU'RE USED TO CAN'T BE FOUND IN SCETIS.
ABBA JOHN DIDN'T MAKE DECISIONS OF HIMSELF, HE REMEMBERED HOW HIS OWN MENTOR, AMOI, HANDLED SUCH SITUATIONS. HE THEN DECIDED TO PRAY ABOUT IT, AND TEST ARSENIUS.

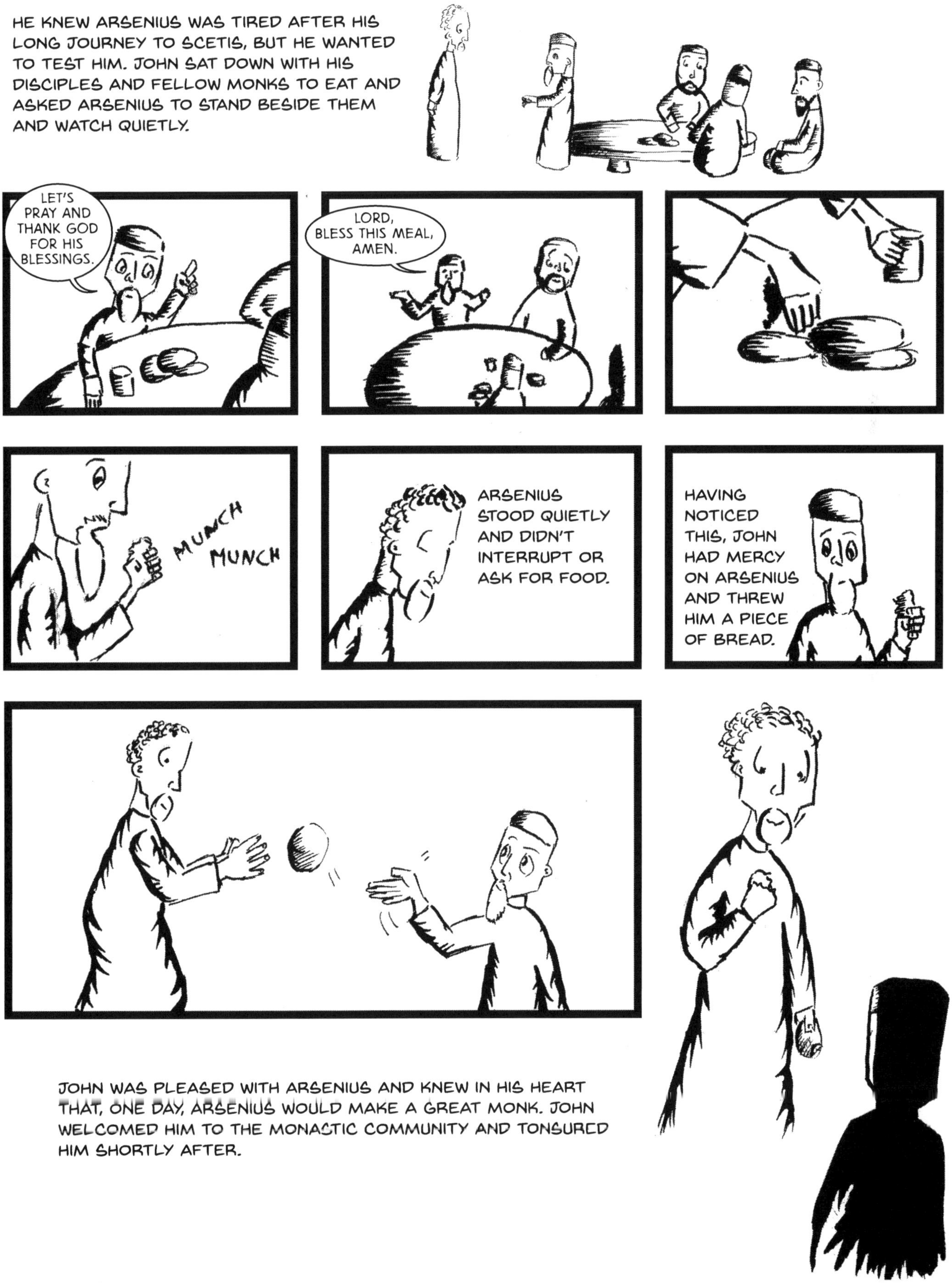
HE KNEW ARSENIUS WAS TIRED AFTER HIS LONG JOURNEY TO SCETIS, BUT HE WANTED TO TEST HIM. JOHN SAT DOWN WITH HIS DISCIPLES AND FELLOW MONKS TO EAT AND ASKED ARSENIUS TO STAND BESIDE THEM AND WATCH QUIETLY.
LET'S PRAY AND THANK GOD FOR HIS BLESSINGS.
LORD, BLESS THIS MEAL, AMEN.
MUNCH MUNCH
ARSENIUS STOOD QUIETLY AND DIDN'T INTERRUPT OR ASK FOR FOOD.
HAVING NOTICED THIS, JOHN HAD MERCY ON ARSENIUS AND THREW HIM A PIECE OF BREAD.
JOHN WAS PLEASED WITH ARSENIUS AND KNEW IN HIS HEART THAT, ONE DAY, ARSENIUS WOULD MAKE A GREAT MONK. JOHN WELCOMED HIM TO THE MONACTIC COMMUNITY AND TONSURED HIM SHORTLY AFTER.

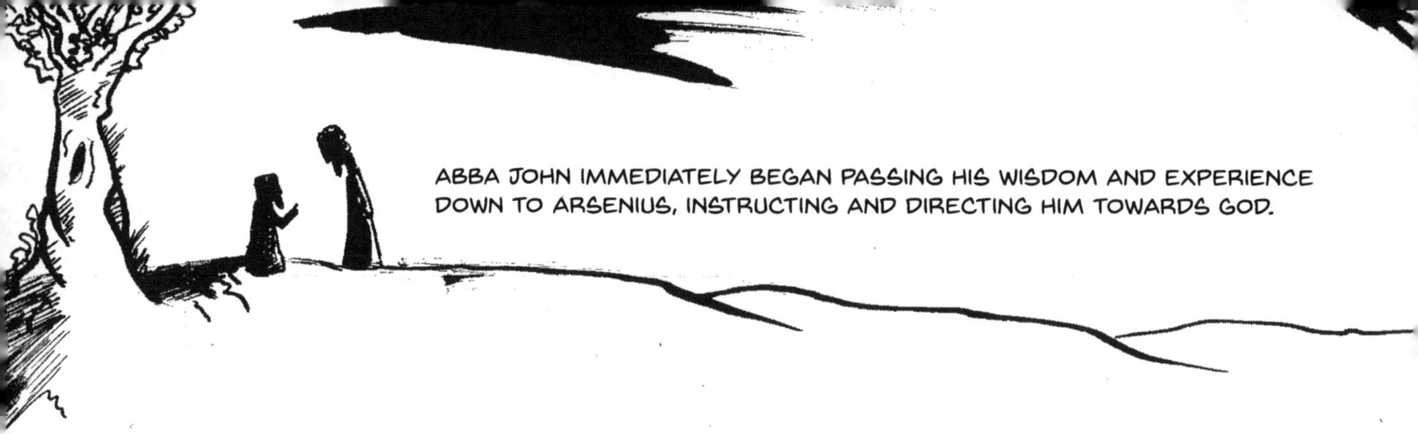
ABBA JOHN IMMEDIATELY BEGAN PASSING HIS WISDOM AND EXPERIENCE DOWN TO ARSENIUS, INSTRUCTING AND DIRECTING HIM TOWARDS GOD.

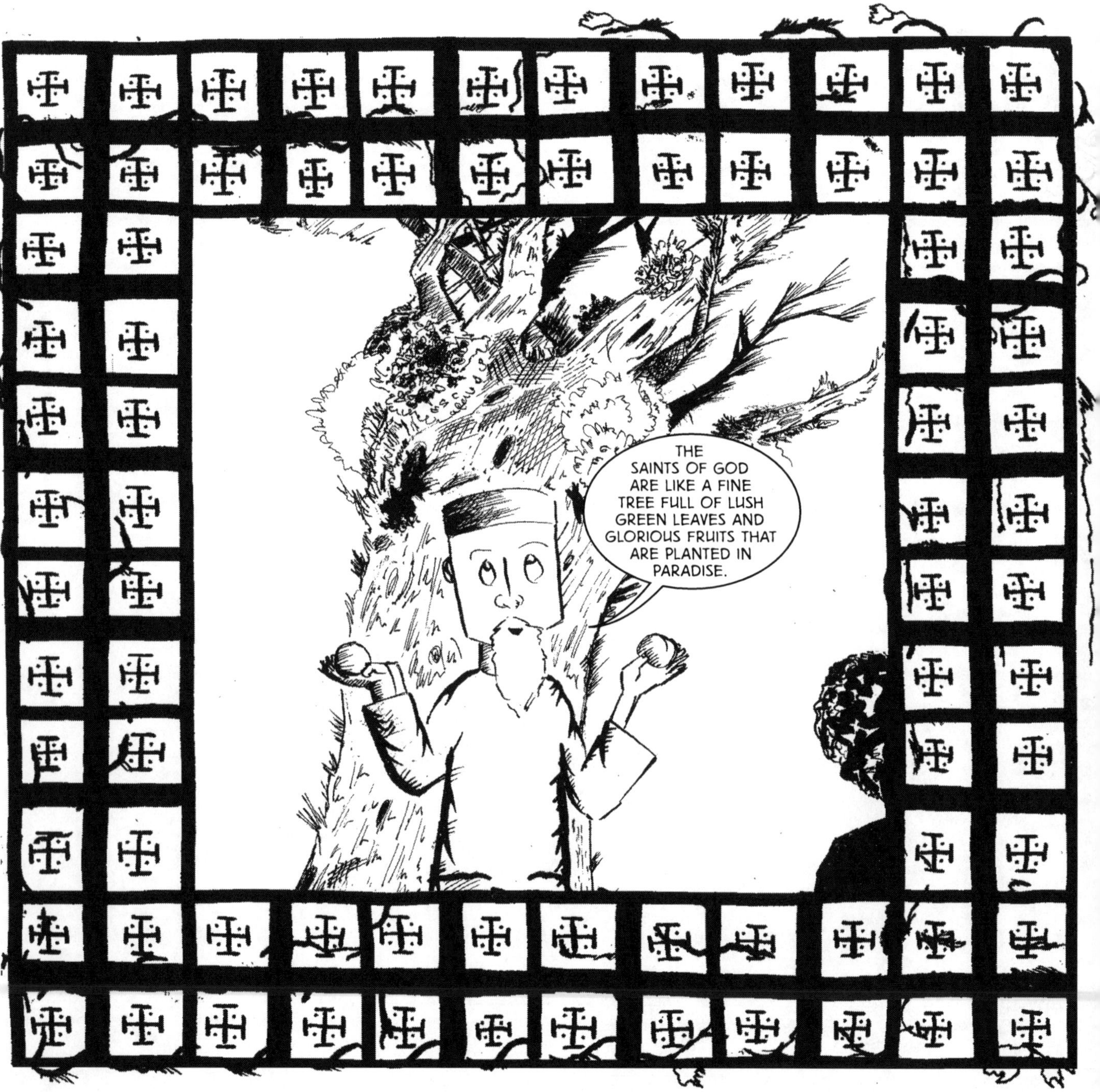
THE SAINTS OF GOD ARE LIKE A FINE TREE FULL OF LUSH GREEN LEAVES AND GLORIOUS FRUITS THAT ARE PLANTED IN PARADISE.

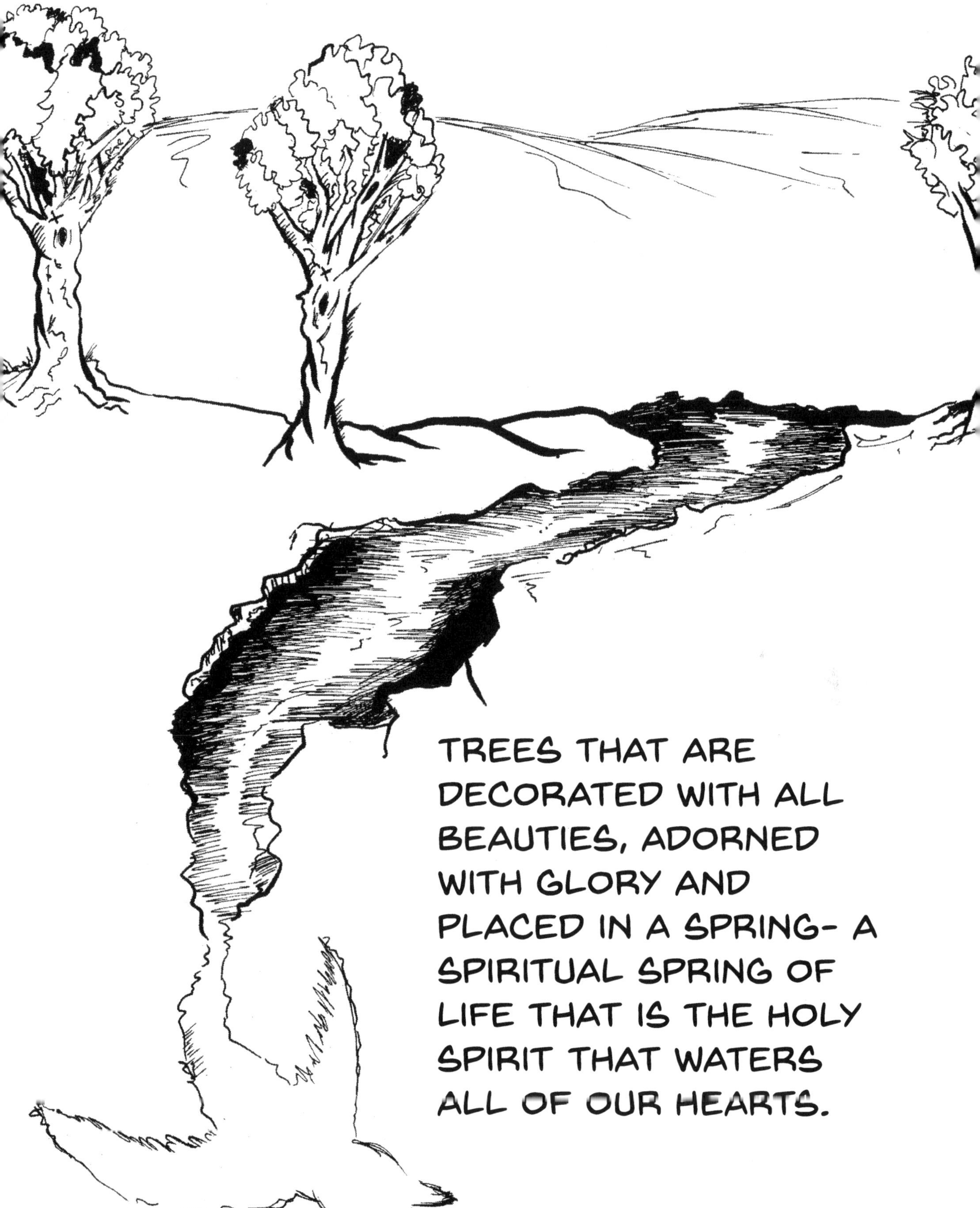

TREES THAT ARE DECORATED WITH ALL BEAUTIES, ADORNED WITH GLORY AND PLACED IN A SPRING- A SPIRITUAL SPRING OF LIFE THAT IS THE HOLY SPIRIT THAT WATERS ALL OF OUR HEARTS.

LIKEWISE, IF A KERNEL OF WHEAT HAS TO DIE IN ORDER TO GIVE FRUIT, AND CHRIST HAD TO GIVE HIS LIFE ON THE CROSS IN ORDER TO GIVE US LIFE, THE SAINTS TOO HAVE TO PRESENT THEIR LIVES IN SACRIFICE IN ORDER TO BEAR FRUIT.

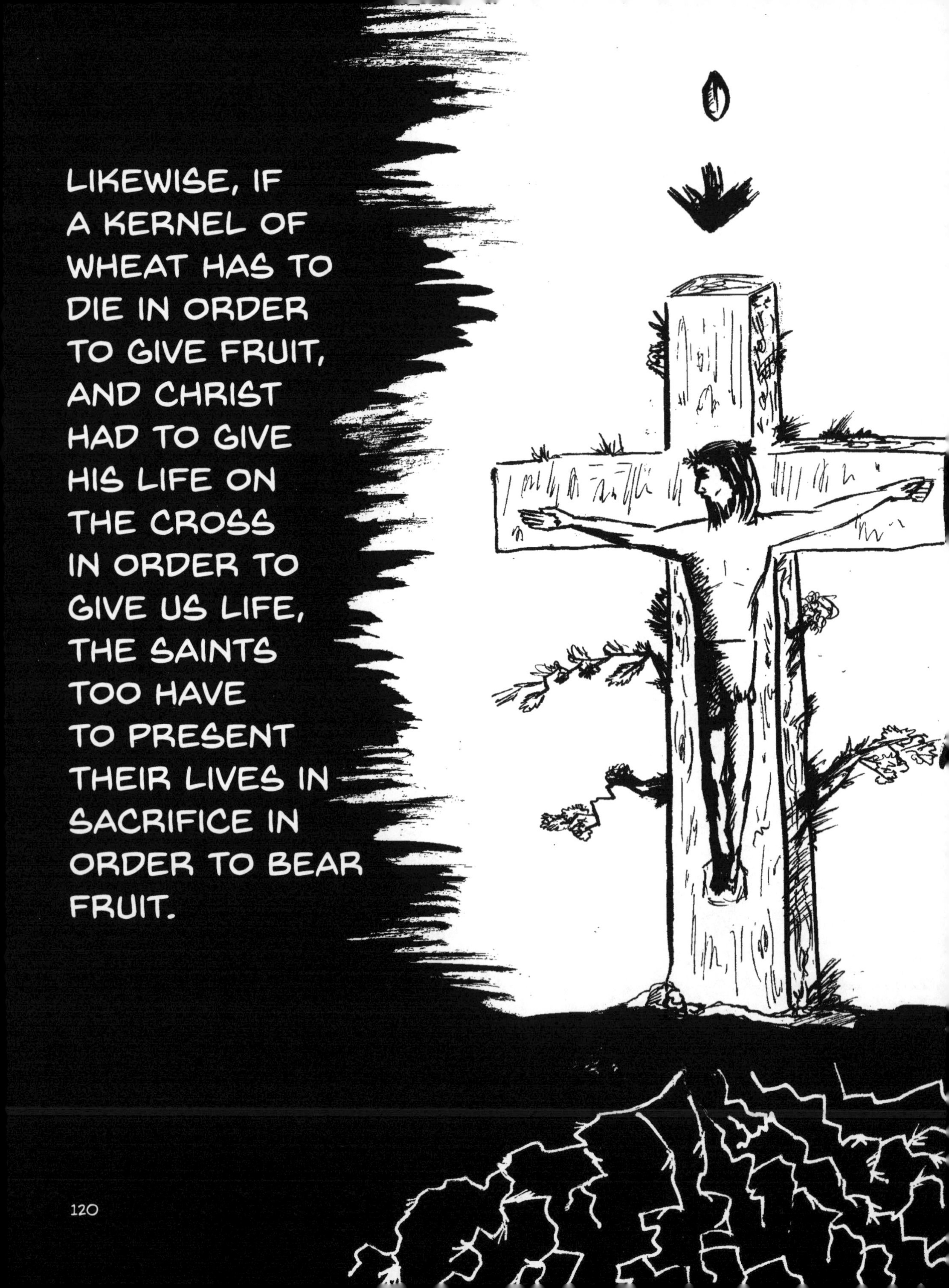

ABBA JOHN PRACTICED WHAT HE PREACHED. JUST AS A CRAFTSMAN CAN TALK FOR HOURS ABOUT HIS CRAFT, ABBA JOHN LOST TRACK OF TIME SPEAKING ABOUT CHRIST. WHENEVER A BROTHER VISITED JOHN AT DUSK, THE TWO WOULD TALK ABOUT HEAVENLY MATTERS UNTIL IT WAS NIGHT TIME. AT THAT POINT, ABBA JOHN WOULD PREPARE THE BROTHER A MEAL BEFORE HE SENT HIM ON HIS WAY.

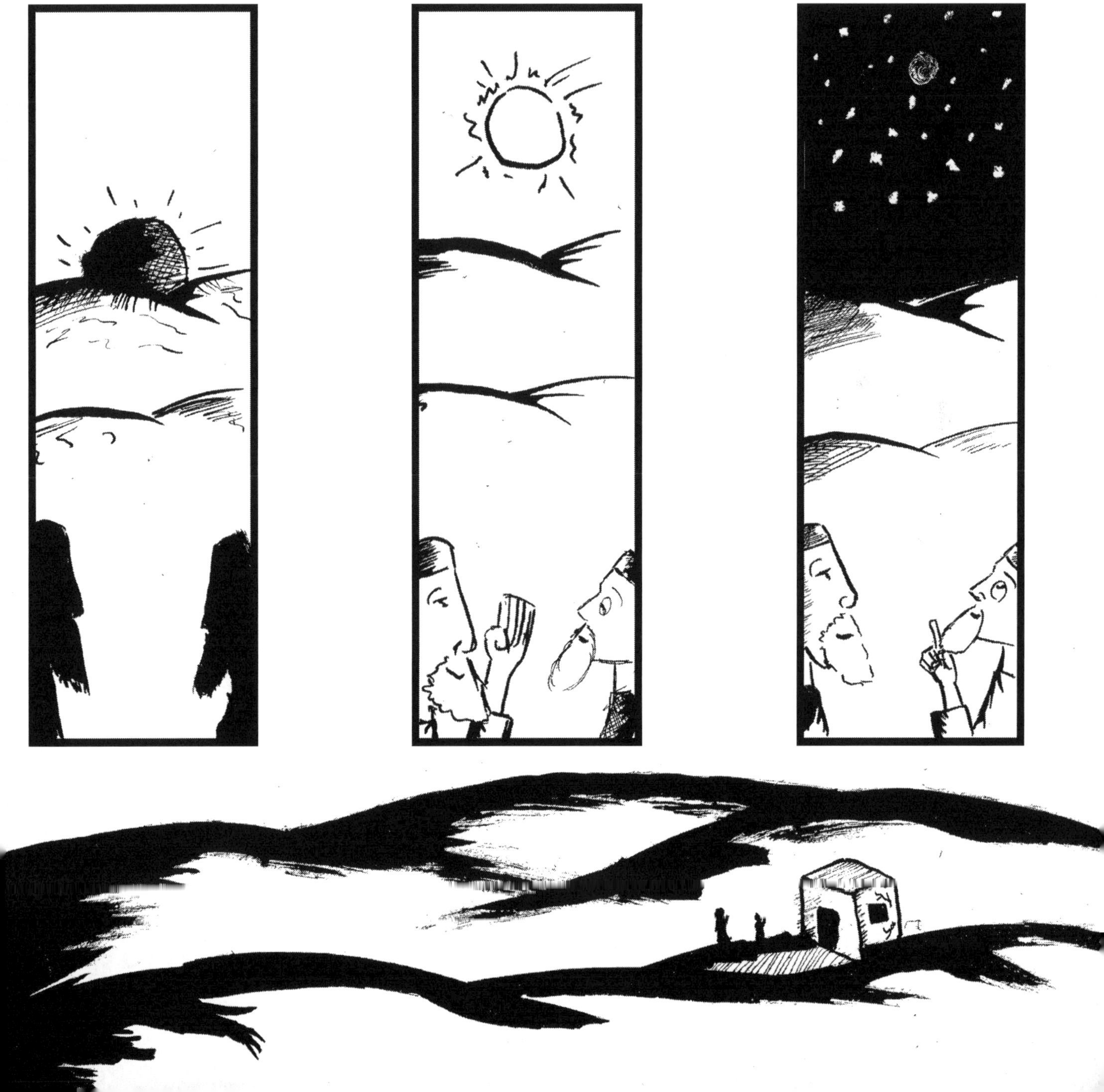

LIKE SO, JOHN CONTINUED GROWING IN ASCETICISM, TEACHING HIS DISCIPLES, AND MAKING MIRACLES IN THE NAME OF CHRIST.

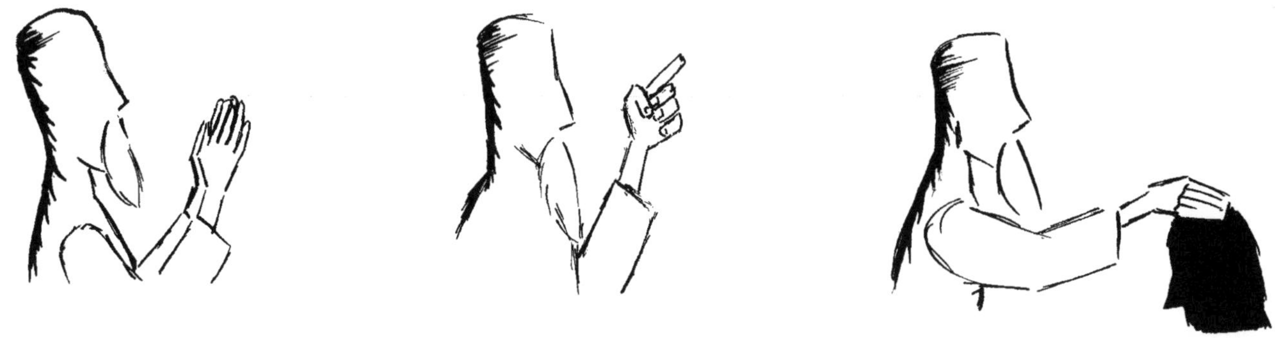

POPE THEOPHILUS OF ALEXANDRIA LEARNED OF SAINT JOHN'S HOLINESS AND SOUGHT TO ORDAIN HIM AS A PRIEST SO THAT HIS FRUITS COULD MULTIPLY. HE ORDAINED ABBA JOHN AND GAVE HIM THE TITLE "THE HEGUMEN OF SCETIS" - AS IN THE LEADER AND CHIEF OF SCETIS!

AS HE WAS GETTING ORDAINED, EVERYONE PRESENT HEARD A LOUD VOICE EXCLAIM:

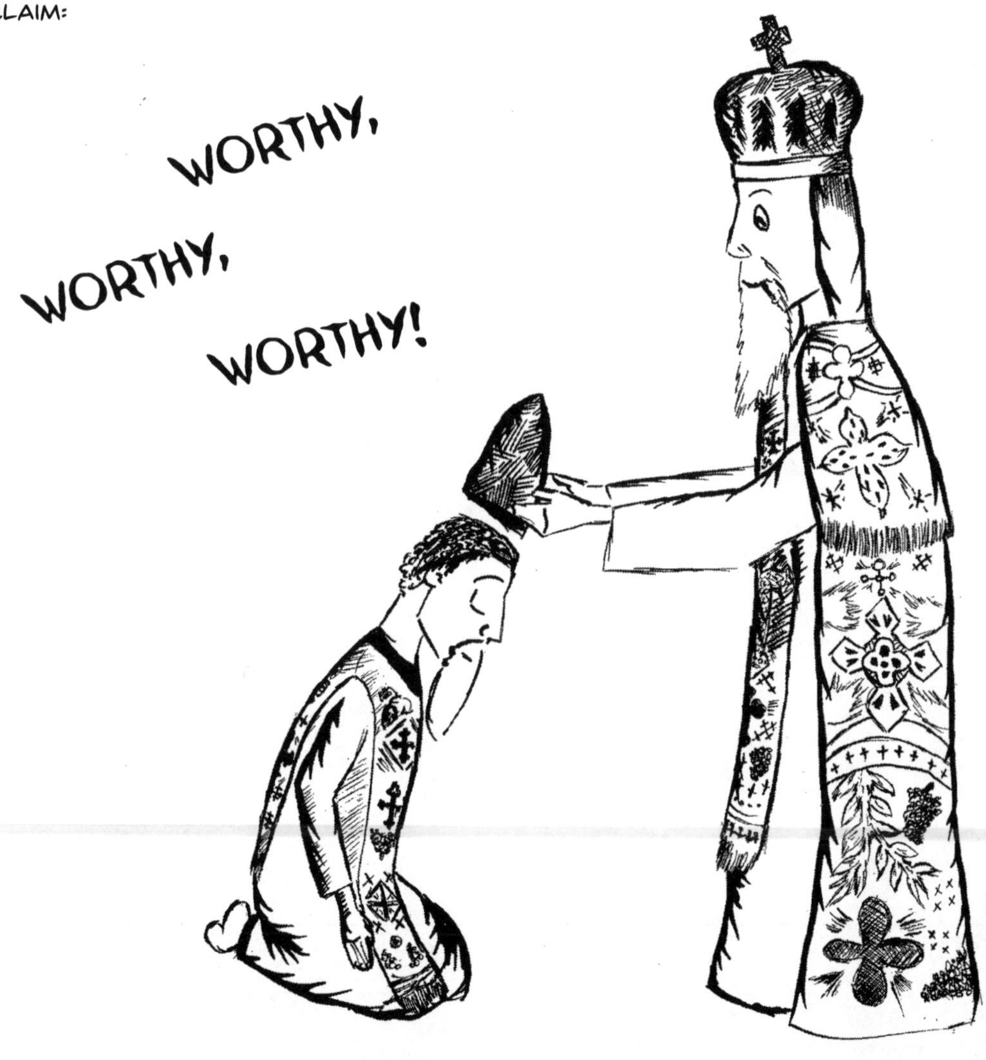
WORTHY,
WORTHY,
WORTHY!

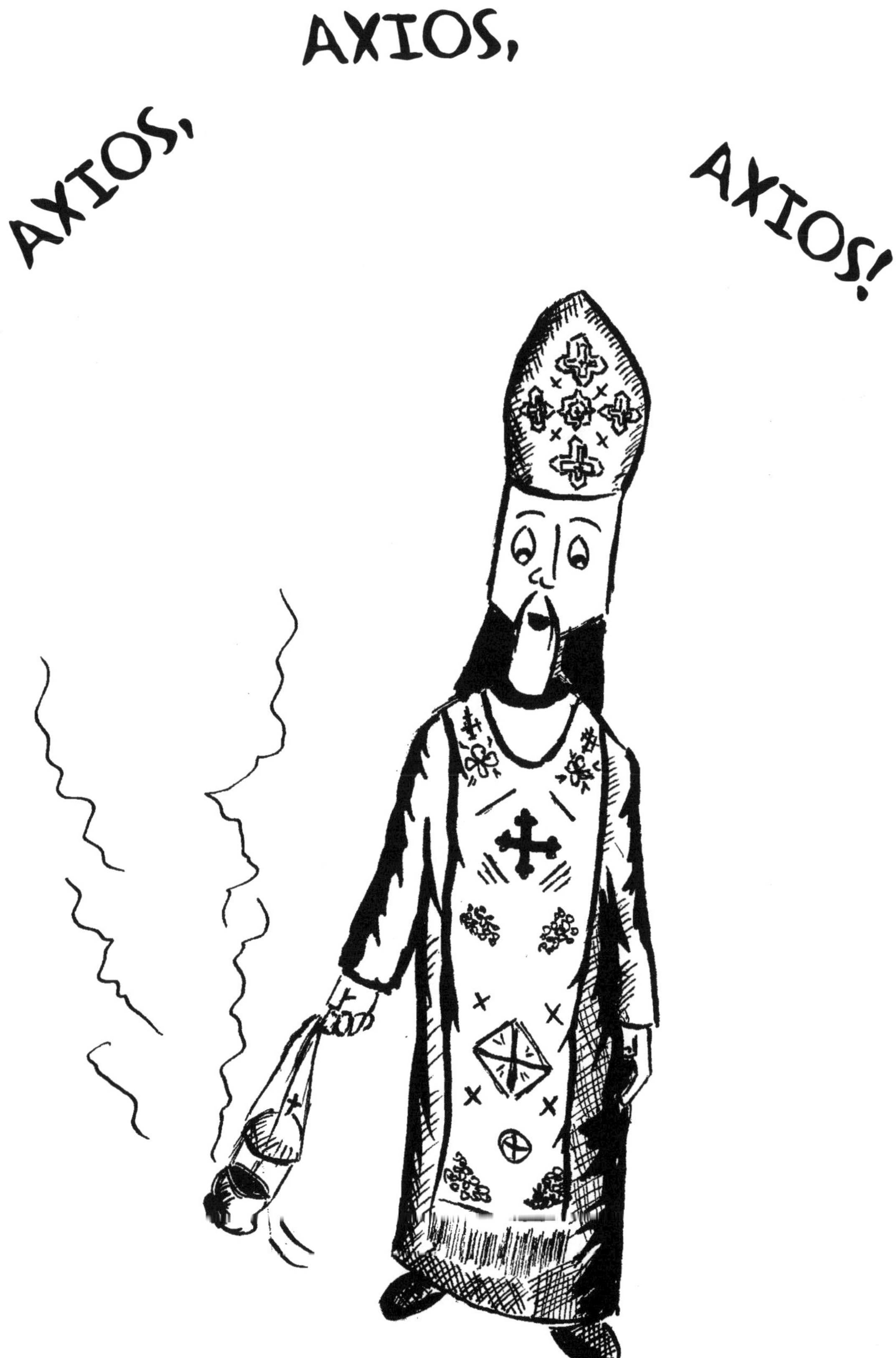
AXIOS,
AXIOS,
AXIOS!

# Chapter Five

# Forests

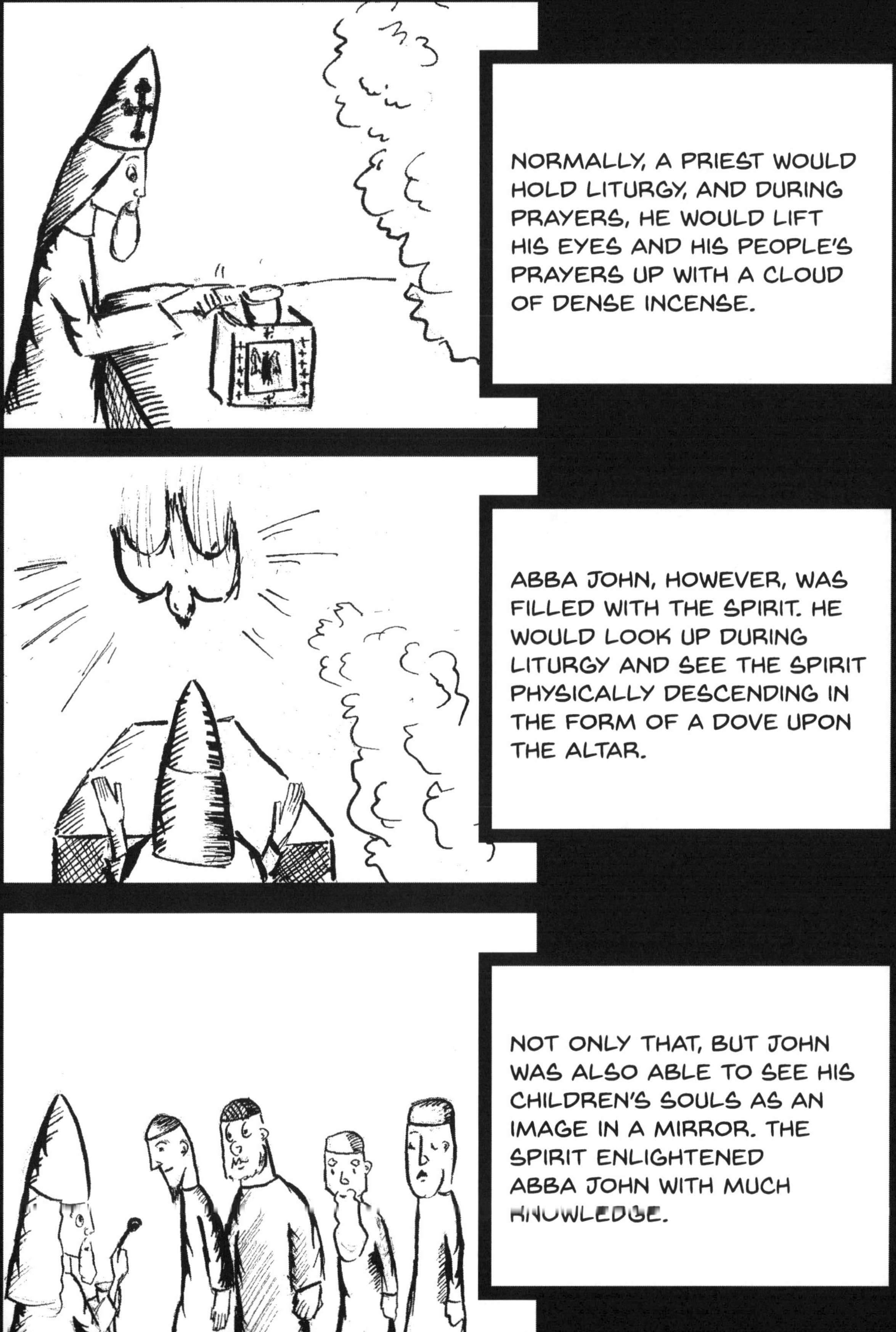
NORMALLY, A PRIEST WOULD HOLD LITURGY, AND DURING PRAYERS, HE WOULD LIFT HIS EYES AND HIS PEOPLE'S PRAYERS UP WITH A CLOUD OF DENSE INCENSE.
ABBA JOHN, HOWEVER, WAS FILLED WITH THE SPIRIT. HE WOULD LOOK UP DURING LITURGY AND SEE THE SPIRIT PHYSICALLY DESCENDING IN THE FORM OF A DOVE UPON THE ALTAR.
NOT ONLY THAT, BUT JOHN WAS ALSO ABLE TO SEE HIS CHILDREN'S SOULS AS AN IMAGE IN A MIRROR. THE SPIRIT ENLIGHTENED ABBA JOHN WITH MUCH KNOWLEDGE.

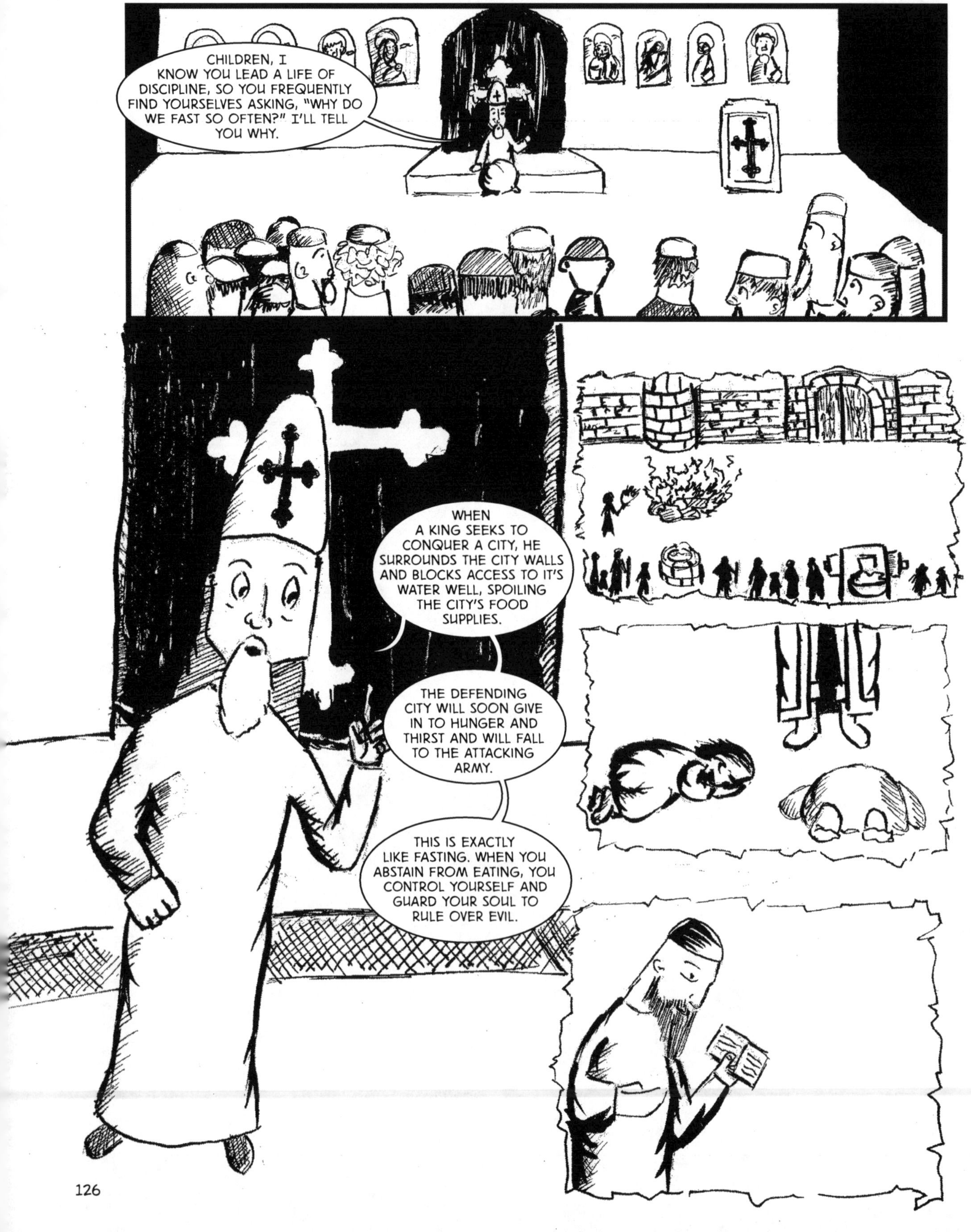
CHILDREN, I KNOW YOU LEAD A LIFE OF DISCIPLINE, SO YOU FREQUENTLY FIND YOURSELVES ASKING, "WHY DO WE FAST SO OFTEN?" I'LL TELL YOU WHY.
WHEN A KING SEEKS TO CONQUER A CITY, HE SURROUNDS THE CITY WALLS AND BLOCKS ACCESS TO IT'S WATER WELL, SPOILING THE CITY'S FOOD SUPPLIES.
THE DEFENDING CITY WILL SOON GIVE IN TO HUNGER AND THIRST AND WILL FALL TO THE ATTACKING ARMY.
THIS IS EXACTLY LIKE FASTING. WHEN YOU ABSTAIN FROM EATING, YOU CONTROL YOURSELF AND GUARD YOUR SOUL TO RULE OVER EVIL.

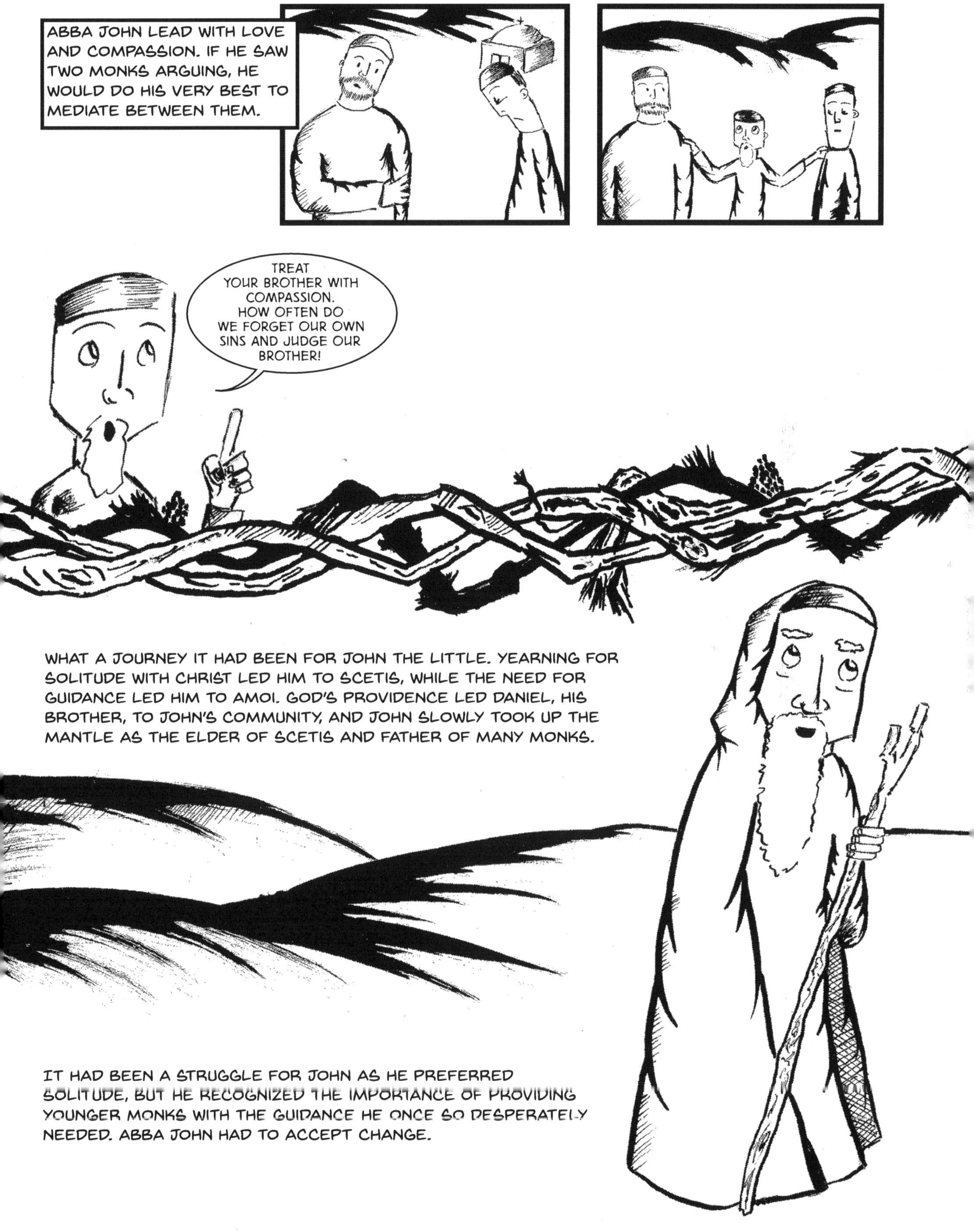
ABBA JOHN LEAD WITH LOVE AND COMPASSION. IF HE SAW TWO MONKS ARGUING, HE WOULD DO HIS VERY BEST TO MEDIATE BETWEEN THEM.
TREAT YOUR BROTHER WITH COMPASSION. HOW OFTEN DO WE FORGET OUR OWN SINS AND JUDGE OUR BROTHER!
WHAT A JOURNEY IT HAD BEEN FOR JOHN THE LITTLE. YEARNING FOR SOLITUDE WITH CHRIST LED HIM TO SCETIS, WHILE THE NEED FOR GUIDANCE LED HIM TO AMOI. GOD'S PROVIDENCE LED DANIEL, HIS BROTHER, TO JOHN'S COMMUNITY, AND JOHN SLOWLY TOOK UP THE MANTLE AS THE ELDER OF SCETIS AND FATHER OF MANY MONKS.
IT HAD BEEN A STRUGGLE FOR JOHN AS HE PREFERRED SOLITUDE, BUT HE RECOGNIZED THE IMPORTANCE OF PROVIDING YOUNGER MONKS WITH THE GUIDANCE HE ONCE SO DESPERATELY NEEDED. ABBA JOHN HAD TO ACCEPT CHANGE.

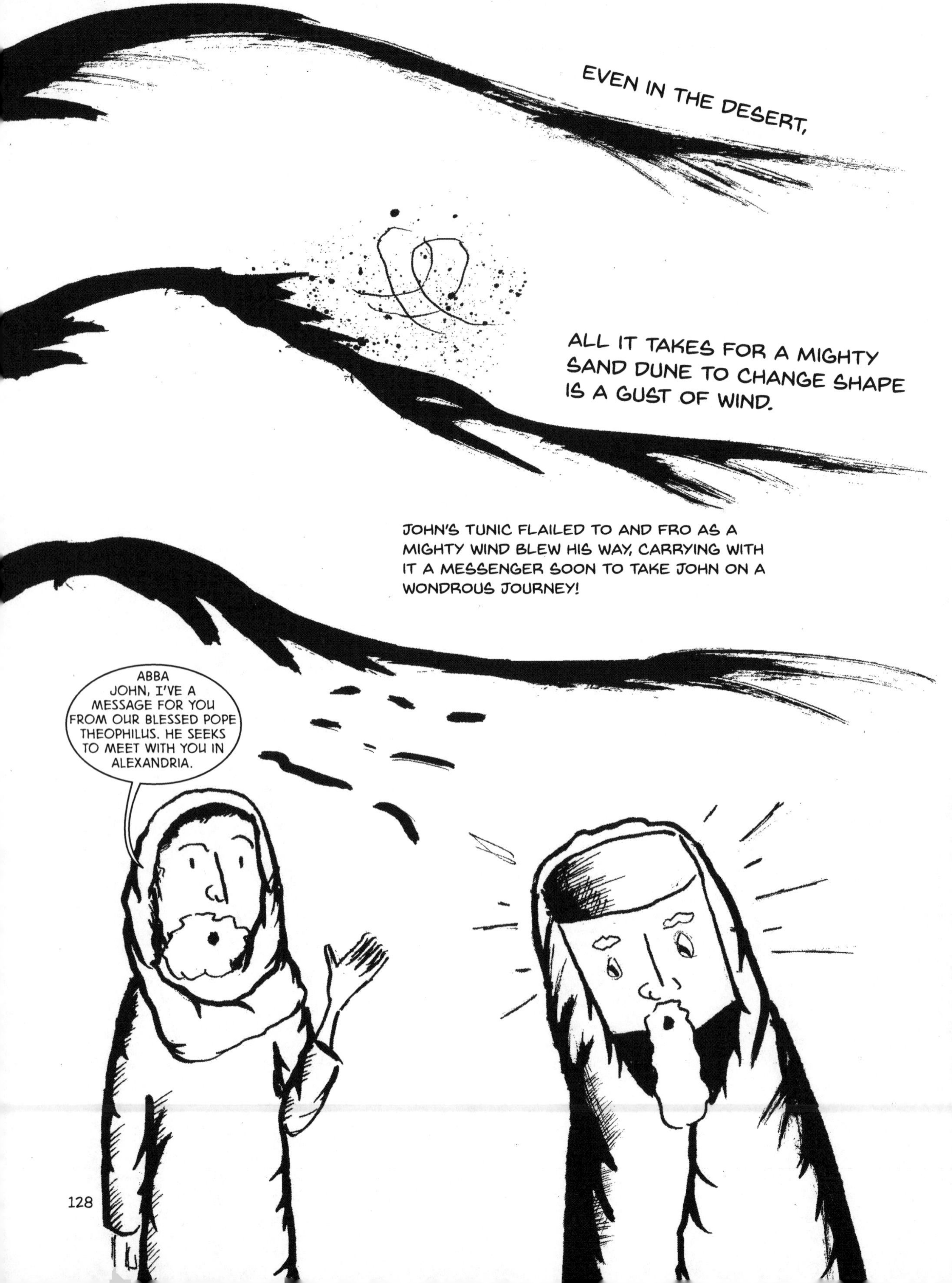
EVEN IN THE DESERT,
ALL IT TAKES FOR A MIGHTY SAND DUNE TO CHANGE SHAPE IS A GUST OF WIND.
JOHN'S TUNIC FLAILED TO AND FRO AS A MIGHTY WIND BLEW HIS WAY, CARRYING WITH IT A MESSENGER SOON TO TAKE JOHN ON A WONDROUS JOURNEY!
ABBA JOHN, I'VE A MESSAGE FOR YOU FROM OUR BLESSED POPE THEOPHILUS. HE SEEKS TO MEET WITH YOU IN ALEXANDRIA.

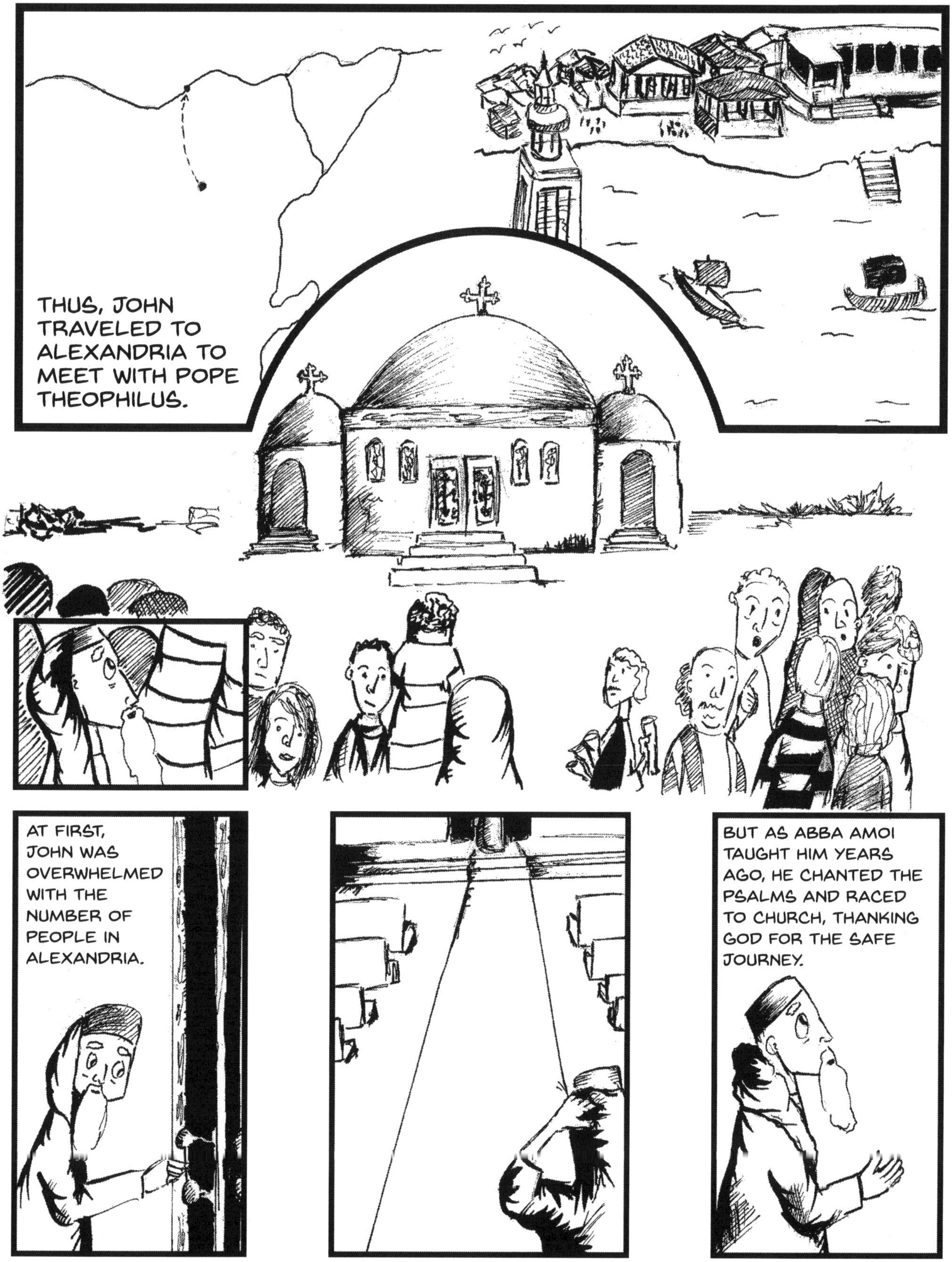
THUS, JOHN TRAVELED TO ALEXANDRIA TO MEET WITH POPE THEOPHILUS.
AT FIRST, JOHN WAS OVERWHELMED WITH THE NUMBER OF PEOPLE IN ALEXANDRIA.
BUT AS ABBA AMOI TAUGHT HIM YEARS AGO, HE CHANTED THE PSALMS AND RACED TO CHURCH, THANKING GOD FOR THE SAFE JOURNEY.

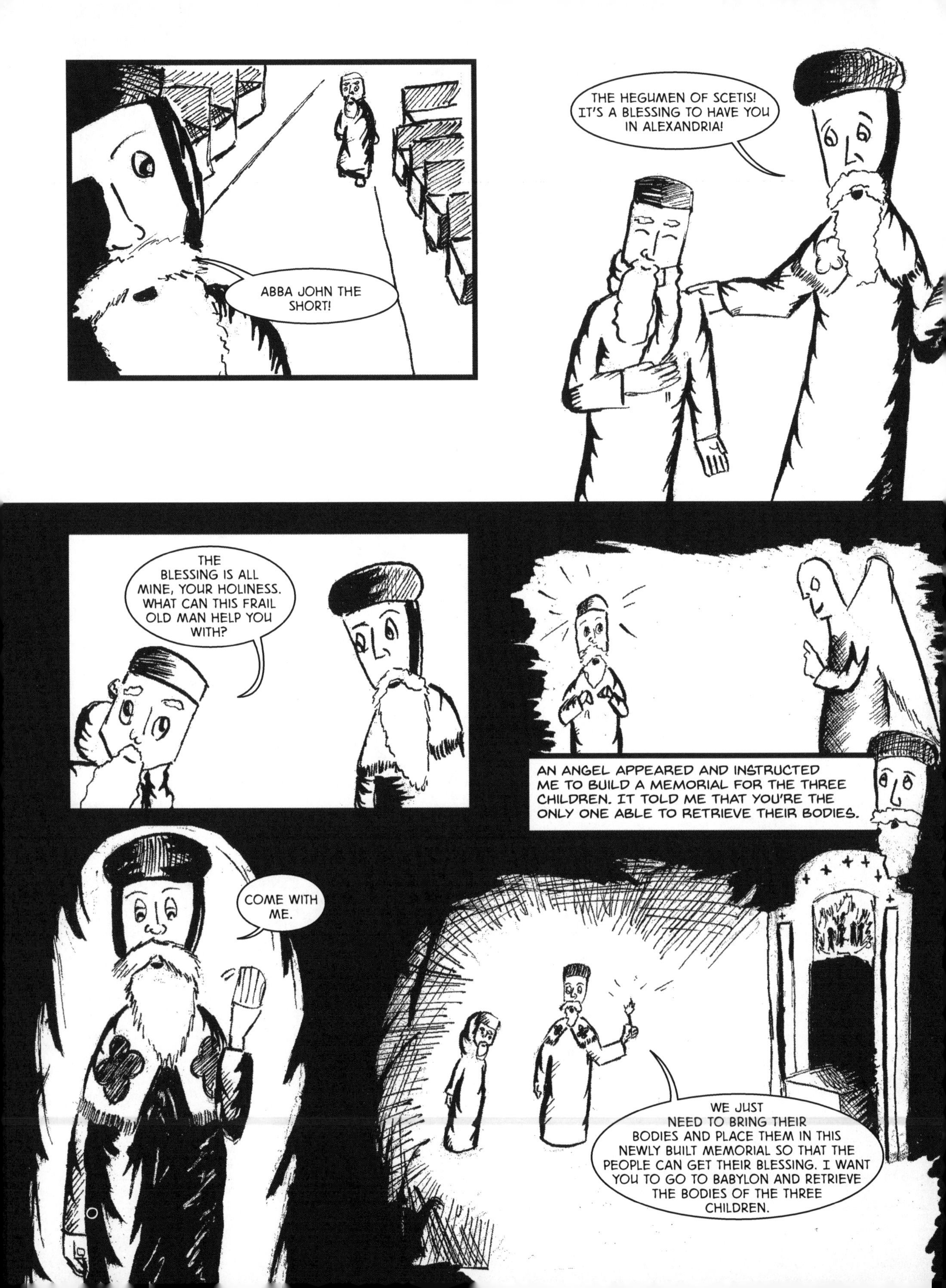
ABBA JOHN THE SHORT!
THE HEGUMEN OF SCETIS! IT'S A BLESSING TO HAVE YOU IN ALEXANDRIA!
THE BLESSING IS ALL MINE, YOUR HOLINESS. WHAT CAN THIS FRAIL OLD MAN HELP YOU WITH?
AN ANGEL APPEARED AND INSTRUCTED ME TO BUILD A MEMORIAL FOR THE THREE CHILDREN. IT TOLD ME THAT YOU'RE THE ONLY ONE ABLE TO RETRIEVE THEIR BODIES.
COME WITH ME.
WE JUST NEED TO BRING THEIR BODIES AND PLACE THEM IN THIS NEWLY BUILT MEMORIAL SO THAT THE PEOPLE CAN GET THEIR BLESSING. I WANT YOU TO GO TO BABYLON AND RETRIEVE THE BODIES OF THE THREE CHILDREN.

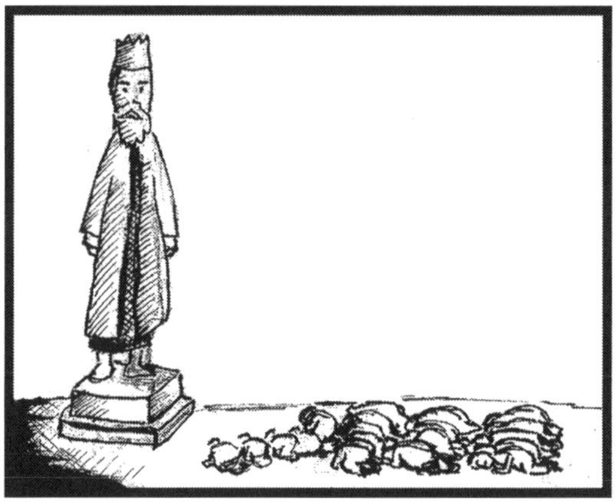

"YOU SEE, JOHN, THEIR STORY IS QUITE INSPIRING. AT A TIME WHEN EVERYONE WAS BOWING TO IDOLS,

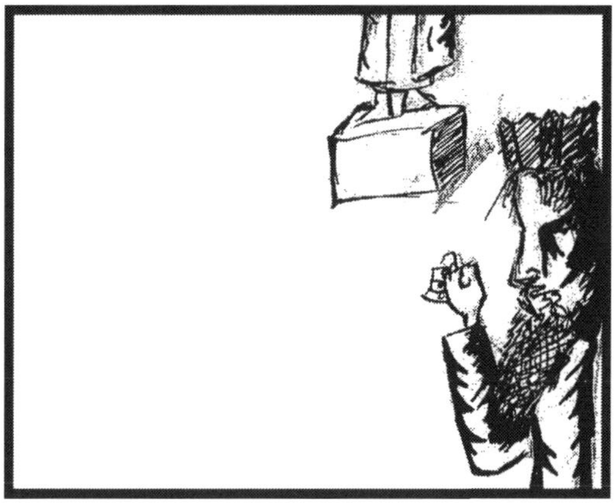

THEY STOOD FIRM. HOW INSPIRING IT IS TO REFLECT ON THEIR STRONG FAITH IN DIFFICULT SITUATIONS.

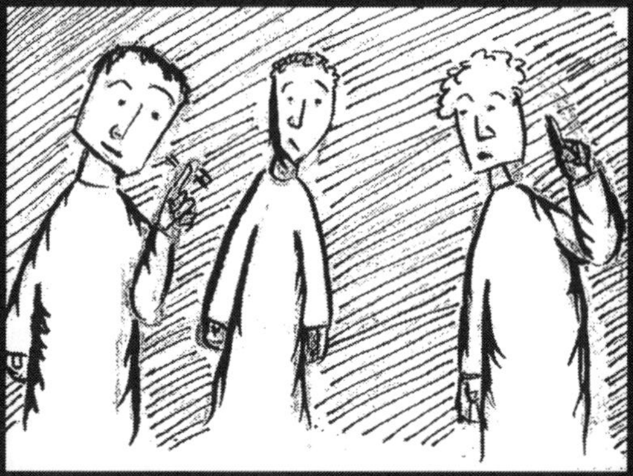

AND TO REMEMBER THE WAY THEY REFUSED TO BOW DOWN TO IDOLS,

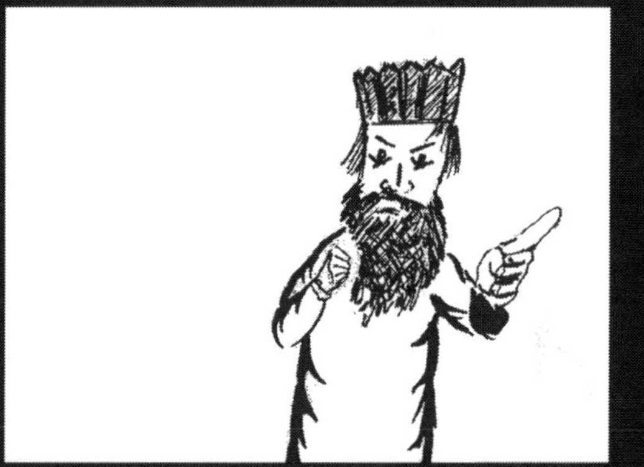

NOT TO MENTION THEIR RESILIENCE IN THE FACE OF TERRIBLE PUNISHMENT,

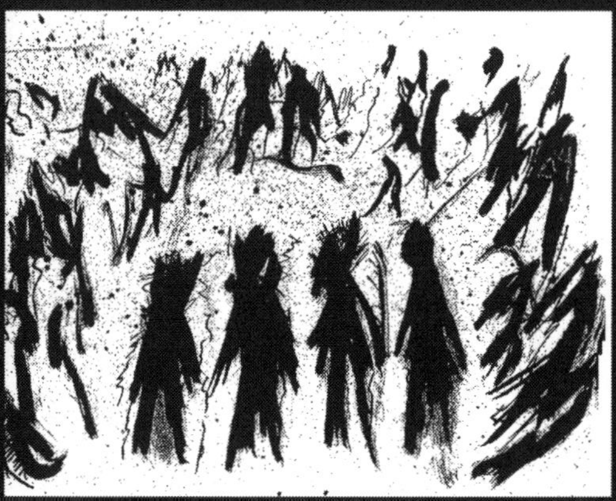

AND OF COURSE HOW CALMING IT IS TO REMEMBER CHRIST DWELLING IN THEIR MIDST AT TIMES OF TROUBLE."

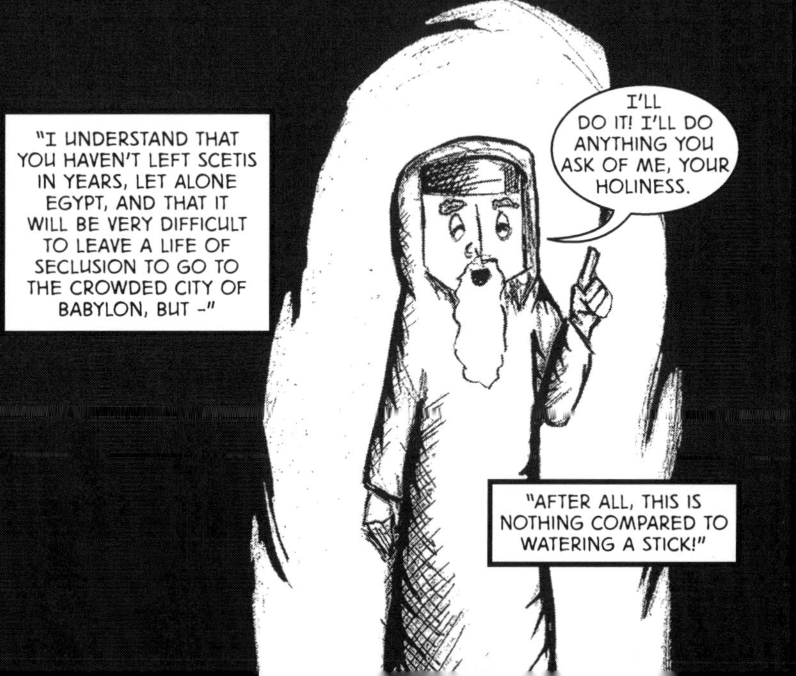
"I UNDERSTAND THAT YOU HAVEN'T LEFT SCETIS IN YEARS, LET ALONE EGYPT, AND THAT IT WILL BE VERY DIFFICULT TO LEAVE A LIFE OF SECLUSION TO GO TO THE CROWDED CITY OF BABYLON, BUT –"
I'LL DO IT! I'LL DO ANYTHING YOU ASK OF ME, YOUR HOLINESS.
"AFTER ALL, THIS IS NOTHING COMPARED TO WATERING A STICK!"

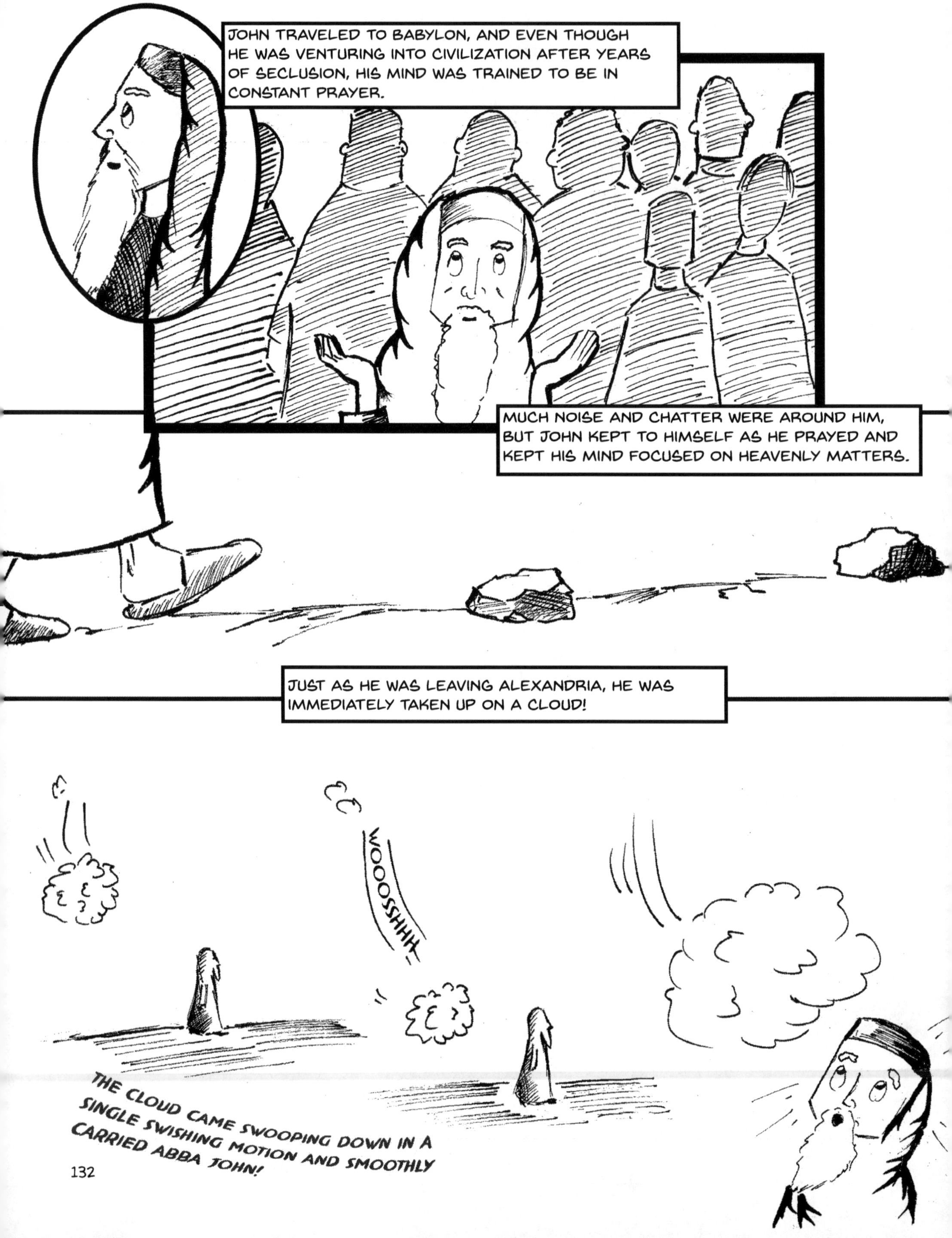

JOHN TRAVELED TO BABYLON, AND EVEN THOUGH HE WAS VENTURING INTO CIVILIZATION AFTER YEARS OF SECLUSION, HIS MIND WAS TRAINED TO BE IN CONSTANT PRAYER.
MUCH NOISE AND CHATTER WERE AROUND HIM, BUT JOHN KEPT TO HIMSELF AS HE PRAYED AND KEPT HIS MIND FOCUSED ON HEAVENLY MATTERS.
JUST AS HE WAS LEAVING ALEXANDRIA, HE WAS IMMEDIATELY TAKEN UP ON A CLOUD!
WOOOSSHHH
THE CLOUD CAME SWOOPING DOWN IN A SINGLE SWISHING MOTION AND SMOOTHLY CARRIED ABBA JOHN!

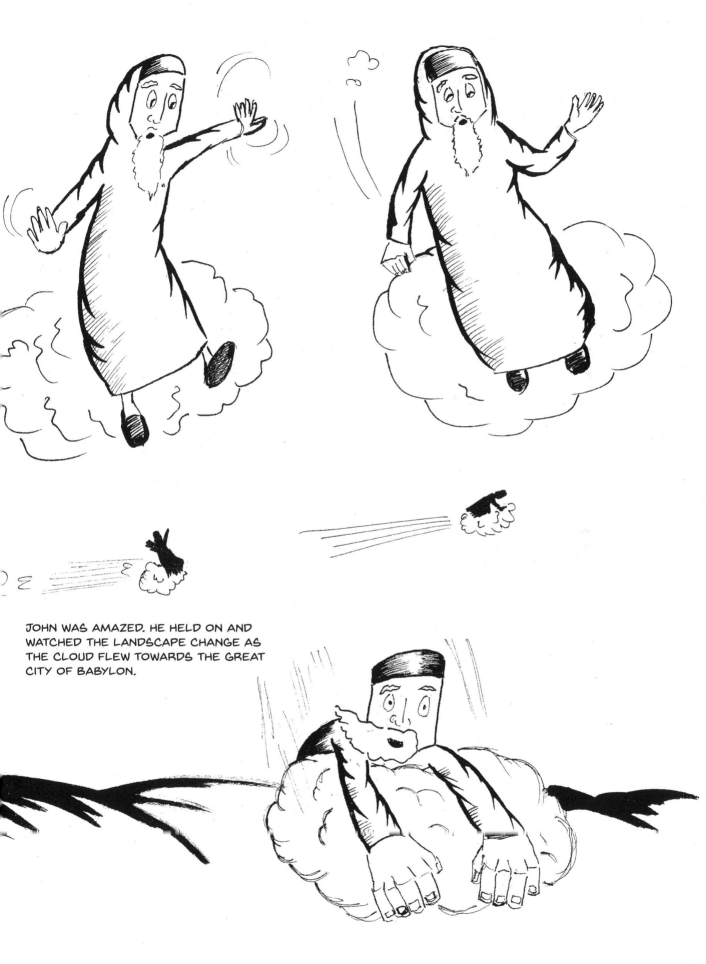

JOHN WAS AMAZED. HE HELD ON AND WATCHED THE LANDSCAPE CHANGE AS THE CLOUD FLEW TOWARDS THE GREAT CITY OF BABYLON.

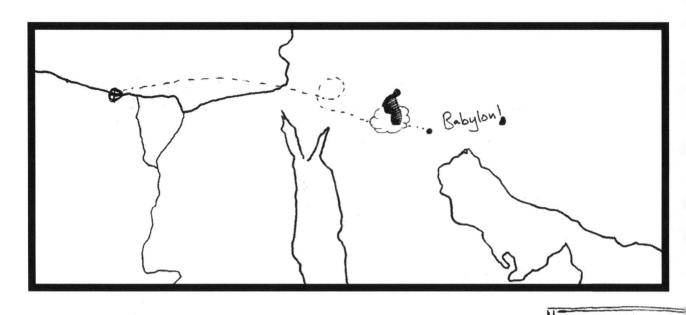

Babylon!

THE CLOUD TOWERED OVER BABYLON AS IT CARRIED JOHN TO THE PLACE WHERE THE THREE CHILDREN WERE BURIED.

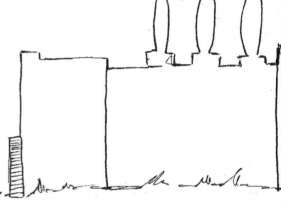

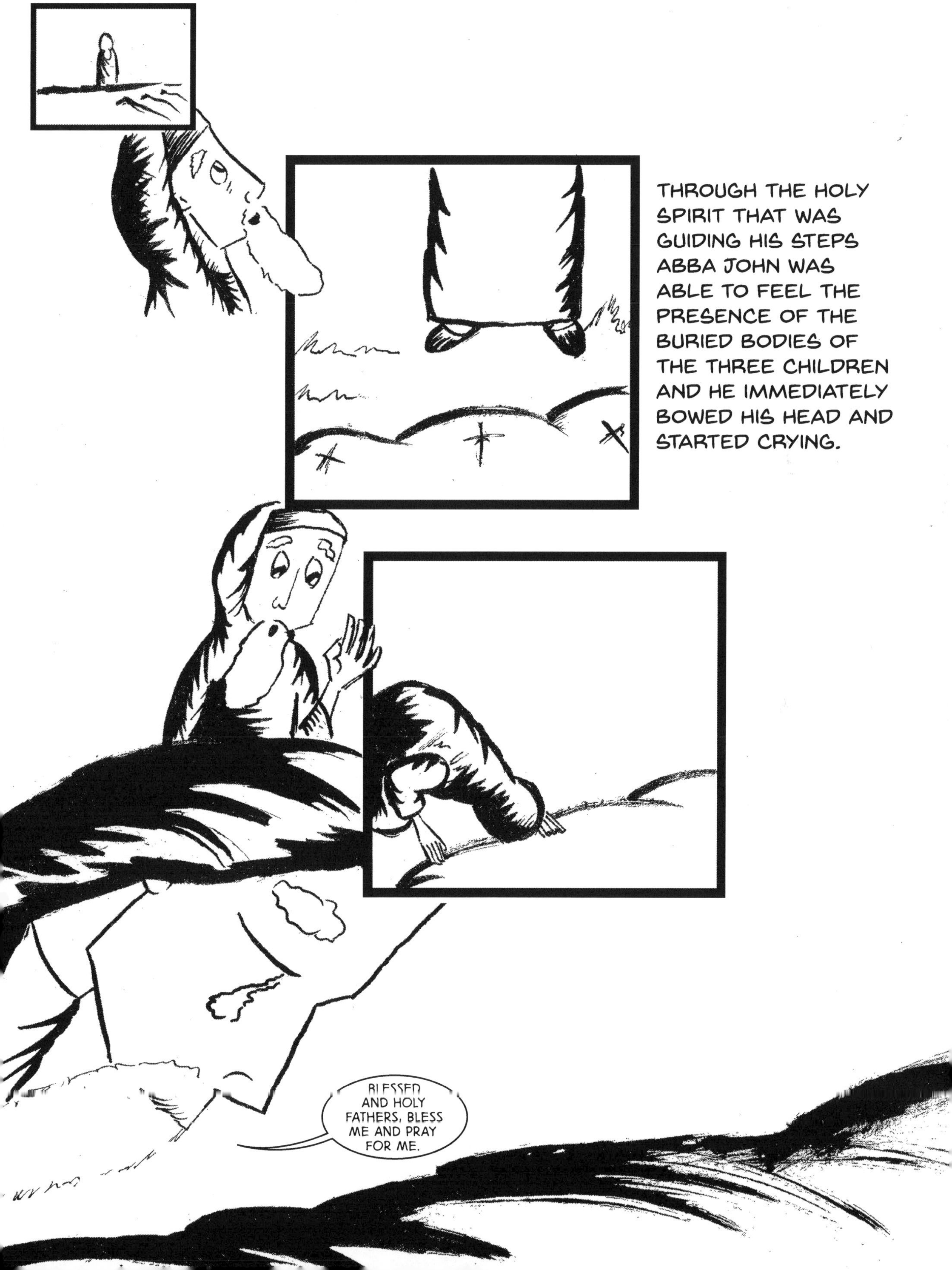
THROUGH THE HOLY SPIRIT THAT WAS GUIDING HIS STEPS ABBA JOHN WAS ABLE TO FEEL THE PRESENCE OF THE BURIED BODIES OF THE THREE CHILDREN AND HE IMMEDIATELY BOWED HIS HEAD AND STARTED CRYING.
BLESSED AND HOLY FATHERS, BLESS ME AND PRAY FOR ME.

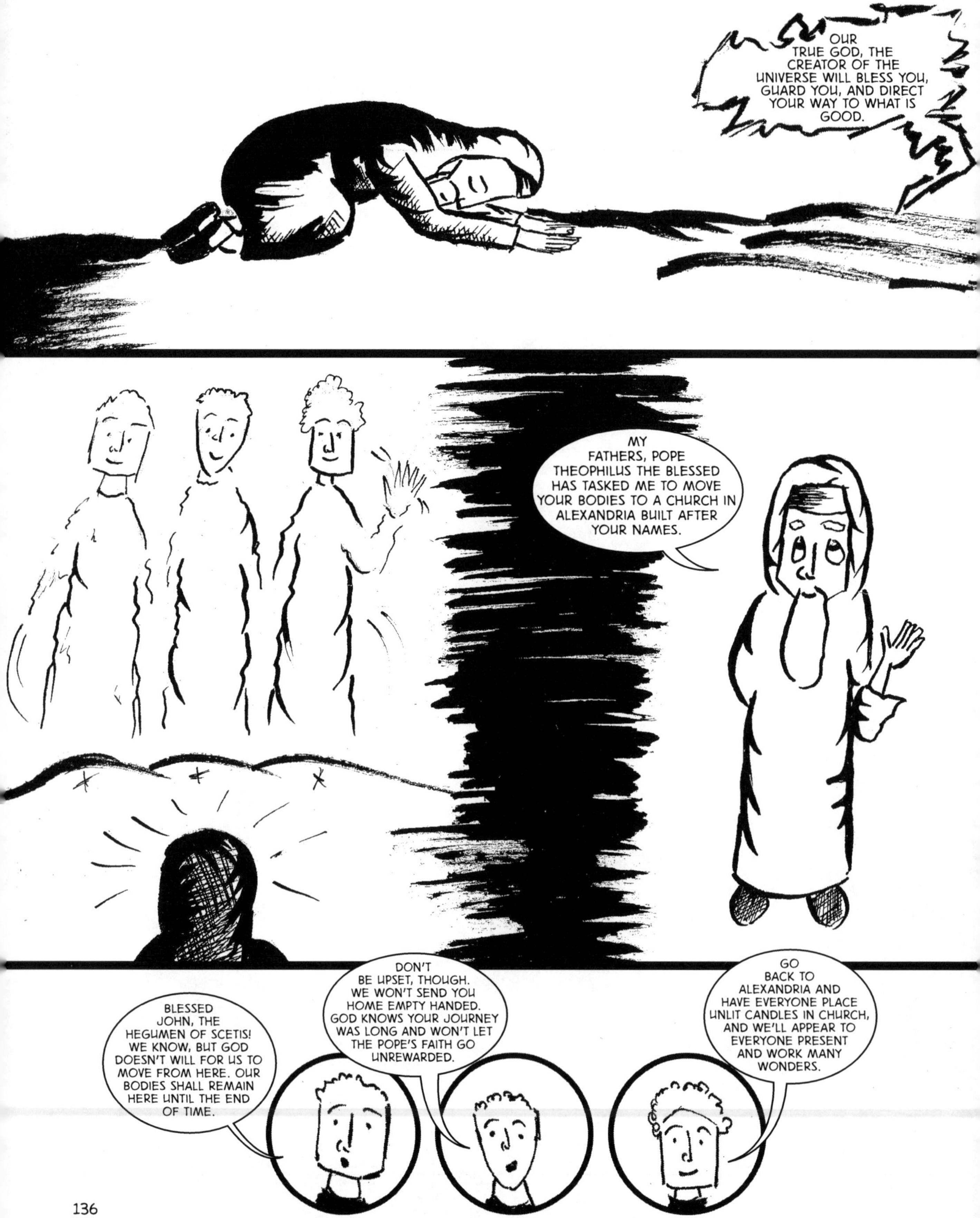
OUR TRUE GOD, THE CREATOR OF THE UNIVERSE WILL BLESS YOU, GUARD YOU, AND DIRECT YOUR WAY TO WHAT IS GOOD.
MY FATHERS, POPE THEOPHILUS THE BLESSED HAS TASKED ME TO MOVE YOUR BODIES TO A CHURCH IN ALEXANDRIA BUILT AFTER YOUR NAMES.
BLESSED JOHN, THE HEGUMEN OF SCETIS! WE KNOW, BUT GOD DOESN'T WILL FOR US TO MOVE FROM HERE. OUR BODIES SHALL REMAIN HERE UNTIL THE END OF TIME.
DON'T BE UPSET, THOUGH. WE WON'T SEND YOU HOME EMPTY HANDED. GOD KNOWS YOUR JOURNEY WAS LONG AND WON'T LET THE POPE'S FAITH GO UNREWARDED.
GO BACK TO ALEXANDRIA AND HAVE EVERYONE PLACE UNLIT CANDLES IN CHURCH, AND WE'LL APPEAR TO EVERYONE PRESENT AND WORK MANY WONDERS.

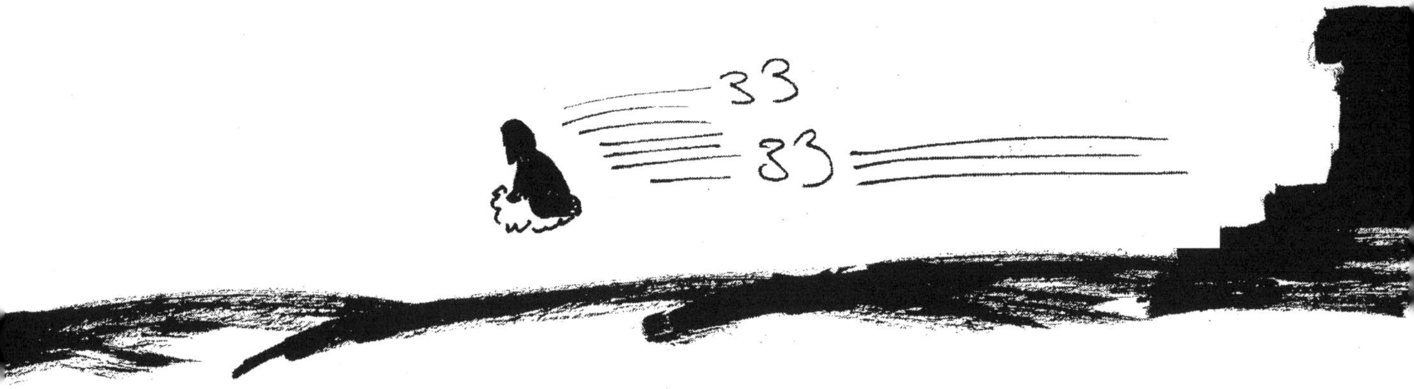

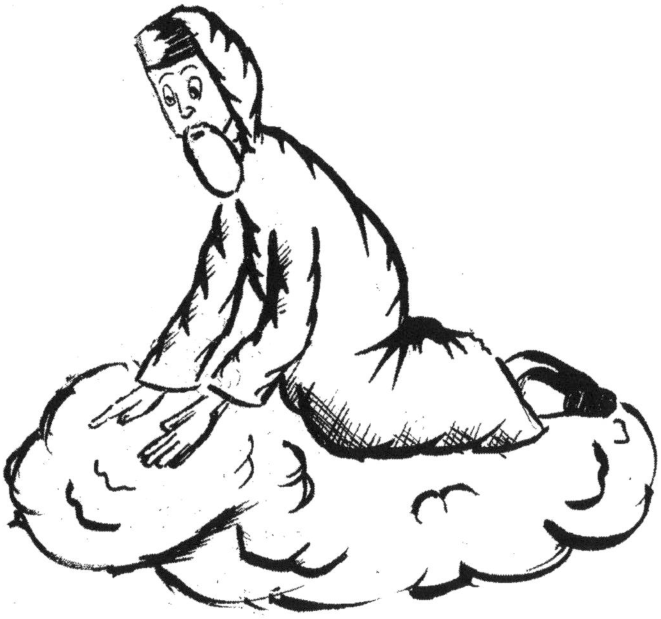

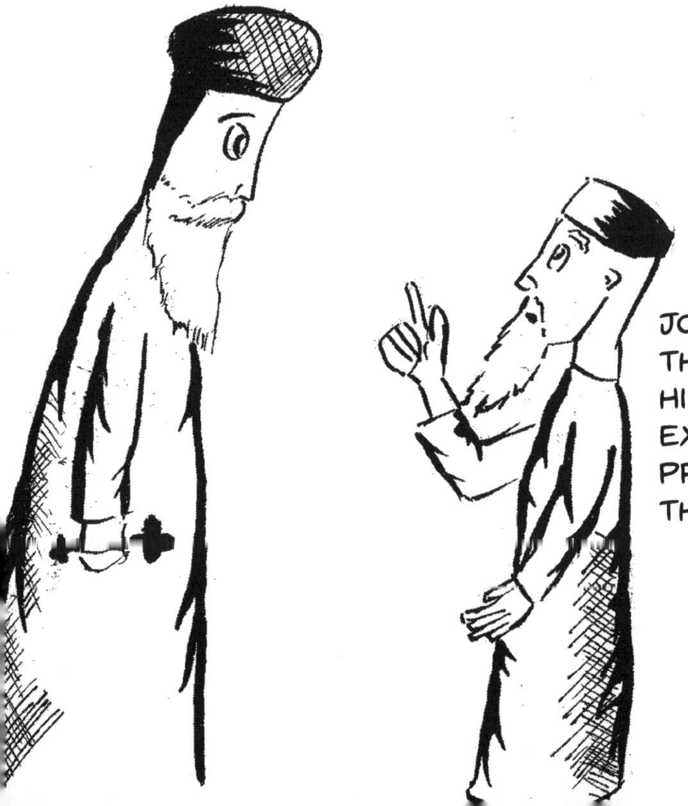

JOHN TOLD POPE THEOPHILUS WHAT THE THREE CHILDREN HAD TOLD HIM, AND THUS THE BLESSED POPE EXCITEDLY GATHERED THE BISHOPS, PRIESTS, AND THE CONGREGATION FOR THIS JOYOUS OCCASION.

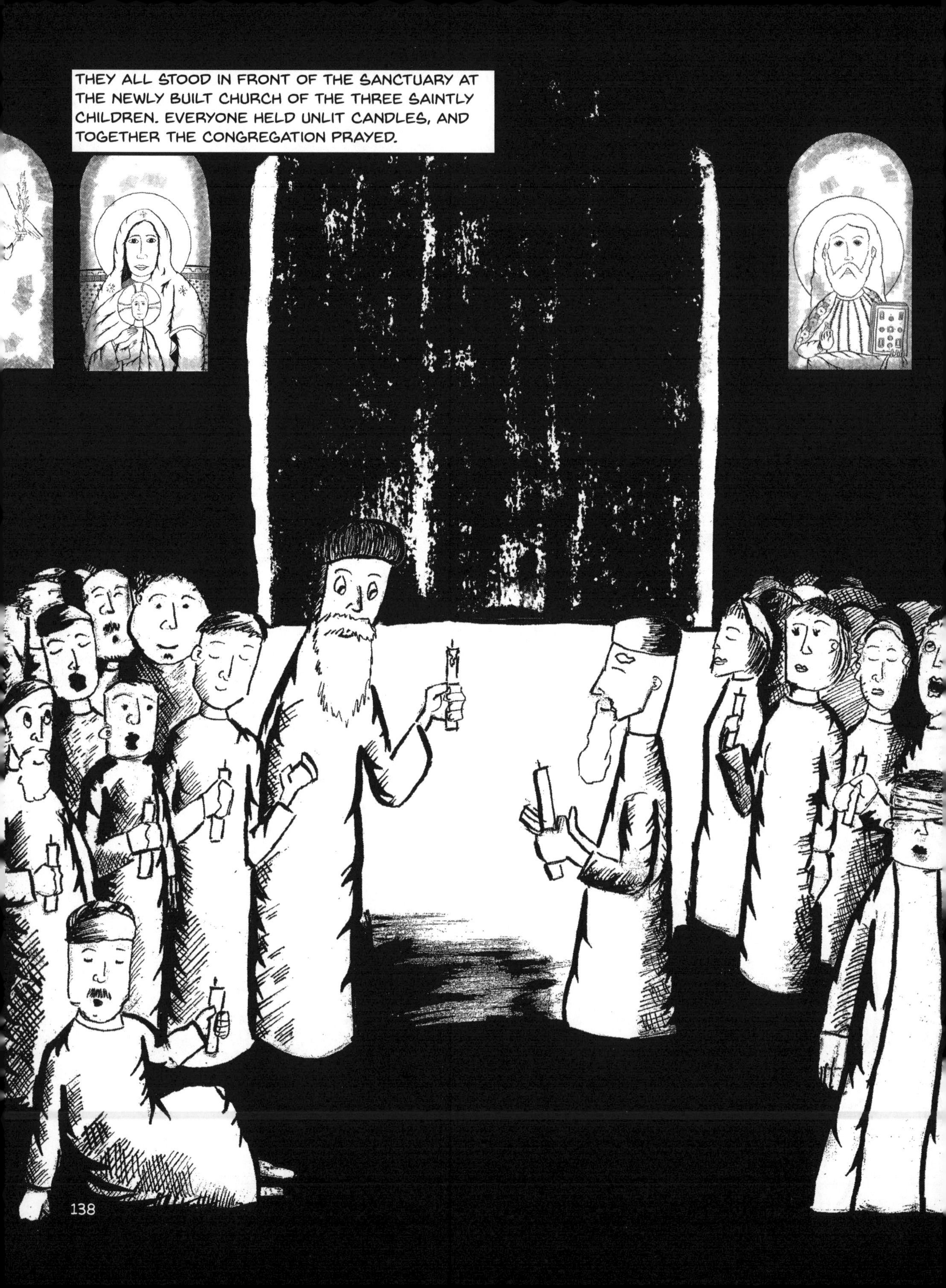
THEY ALL STOOD IN FRONT OF THE SANCTUARY AT THE NEWLY BUILT CHURCH OF THE THREE SAINTLY CHILDREN. EVERYONE HELD UNLIT CANDLES, AND TOGETHER THE CONGREGATION PRAYED.

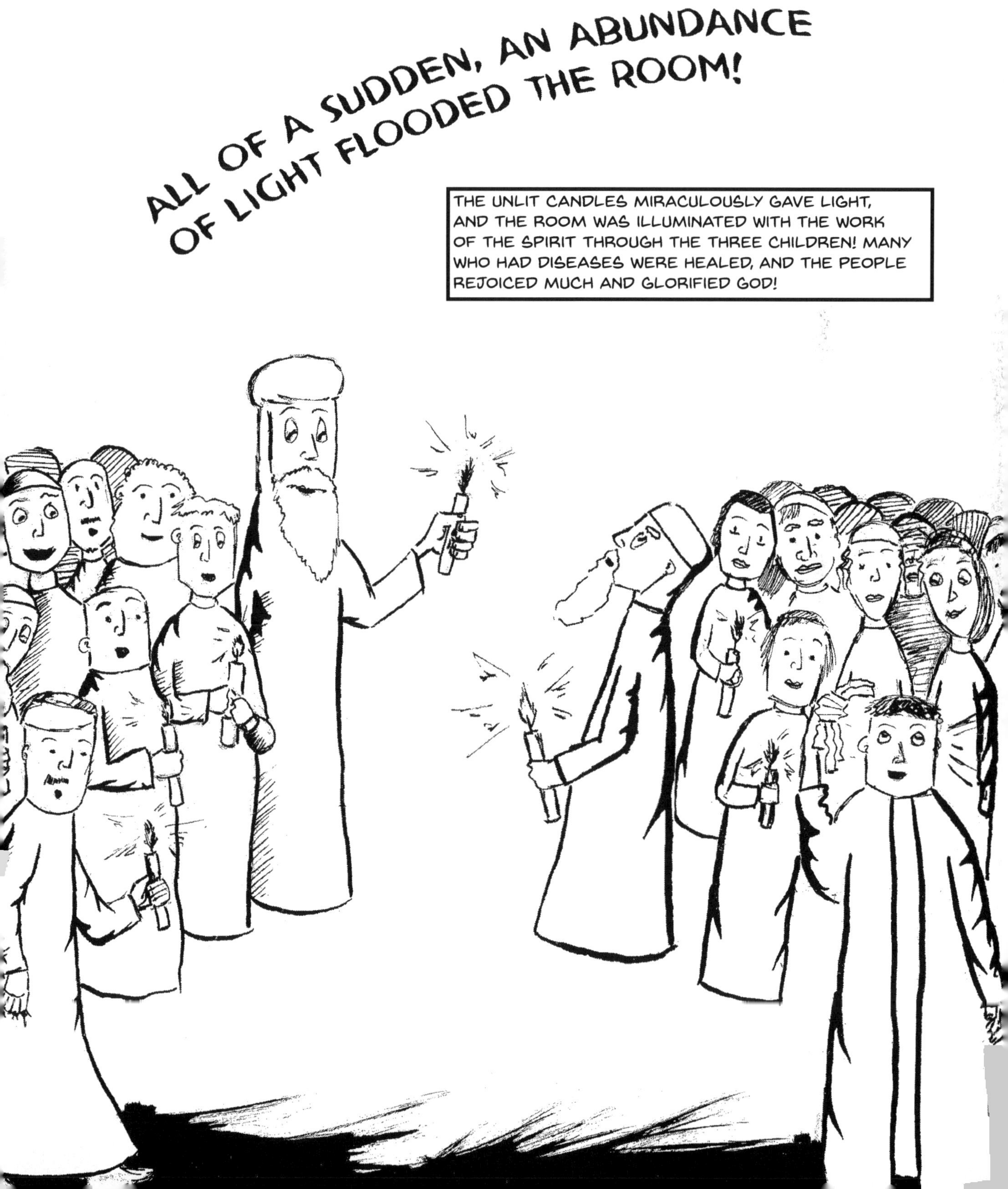
ALL OF A SUDDEN, AN ABUNDANCE OF LIGHT FLOODED THE ROOM!
THE UNLIT CANDLES MIRACULOUSLY GAVE LIGHT, AND THE ROOM WAS ILLUMINATED WITH THE WORK OF THE SPIRIT THROUGH THE THREE CHILDREN! MANY WHO HAD DISEASES WERE HEALED, AND THE PEOPLE REJOICED MUCH AND GLORIFIED GOD!

FOLLOWING THIS WONDROUS MIRACLE, THE CONGREGATION GATHERED TOGETHER IN JOY AND SANG PRAISES TO THE THREE SAINTLY CHILDREN. POPE THEOPHILUS CONSECRATED THE NEW ALTAR UNDER THEIR NAME AND COVERED IT WITH HOLY OIL.

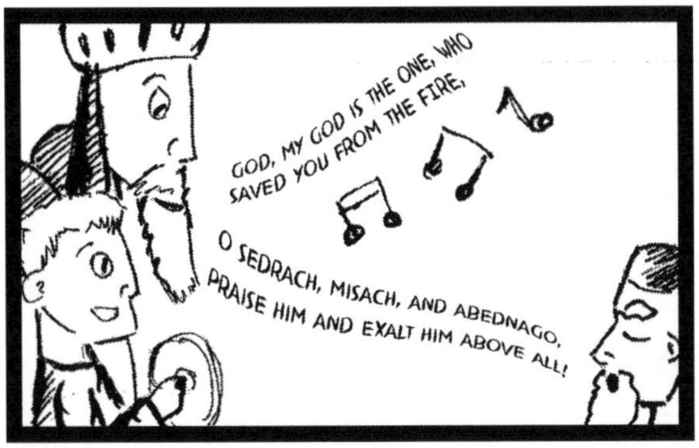
GOD, MY GOD IS THE ONE, WHO SAVED YOU FROM THE FIRE,
O SEDRACH, MISACH, AND ABEDNAGO, PRAISE HIM AND EXALT HIM ABOVE ALL!

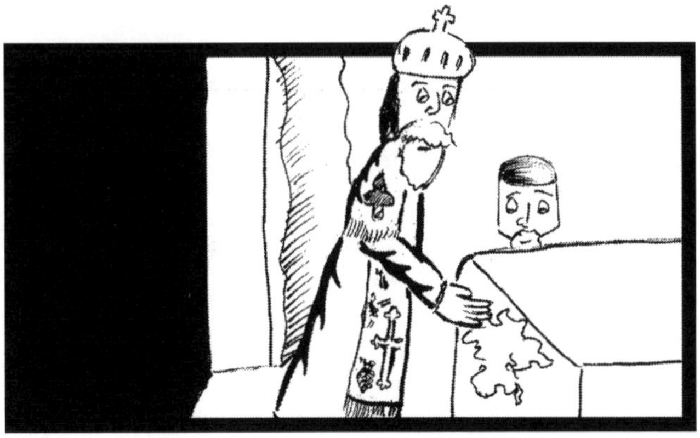

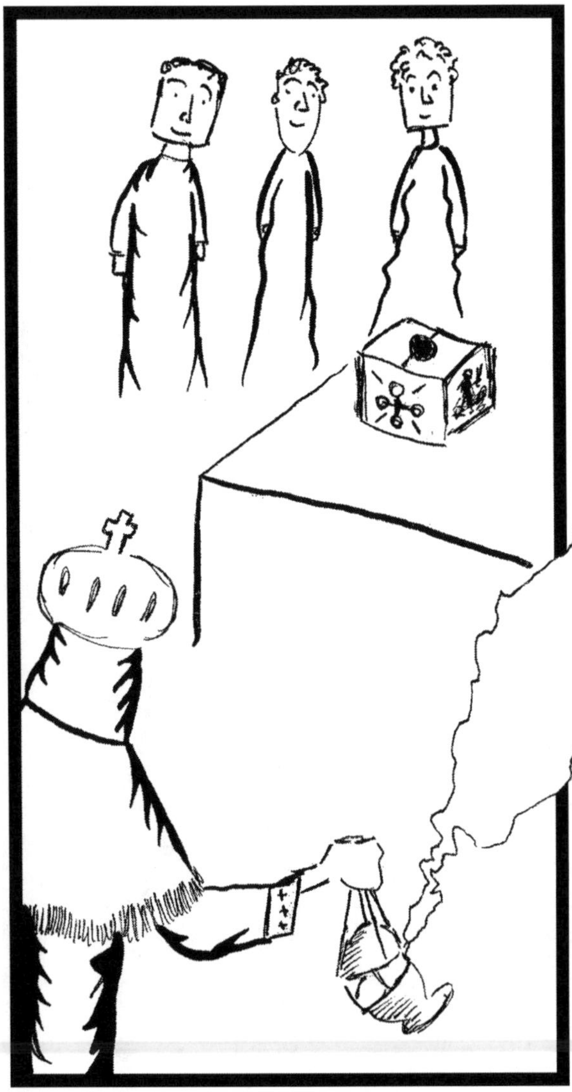

WHILE PRAYING THE FIRST LITURGY ON THE ALTAR, ABBA JOHN AND POPE THEOPHILUS LOOKED UP IN AWE AS THE THREE SAINTLY CHILDREN APPEARED TO THEM. OTHER BELIEVERS SAW THEM AS WELL.

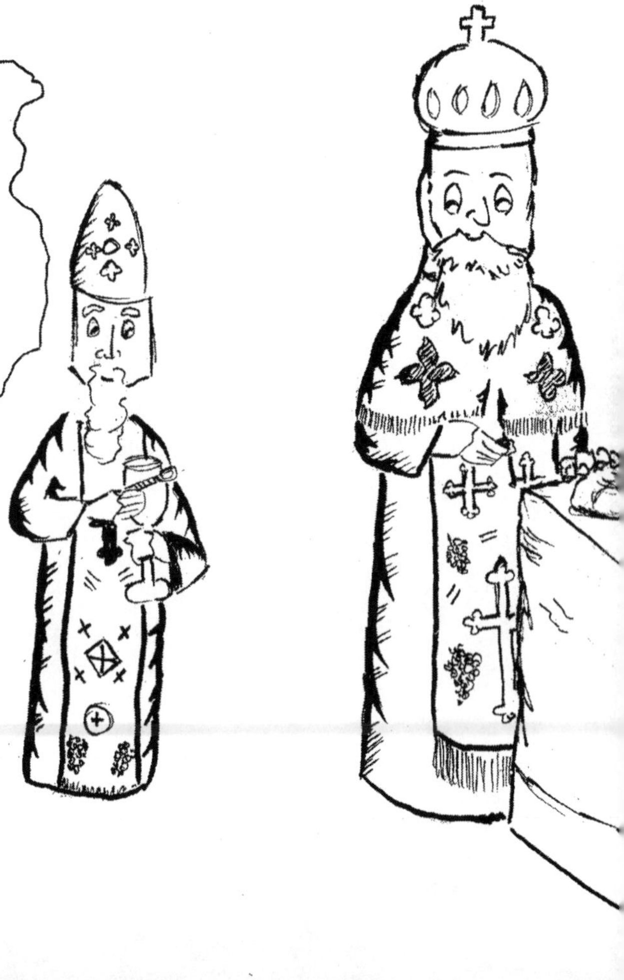

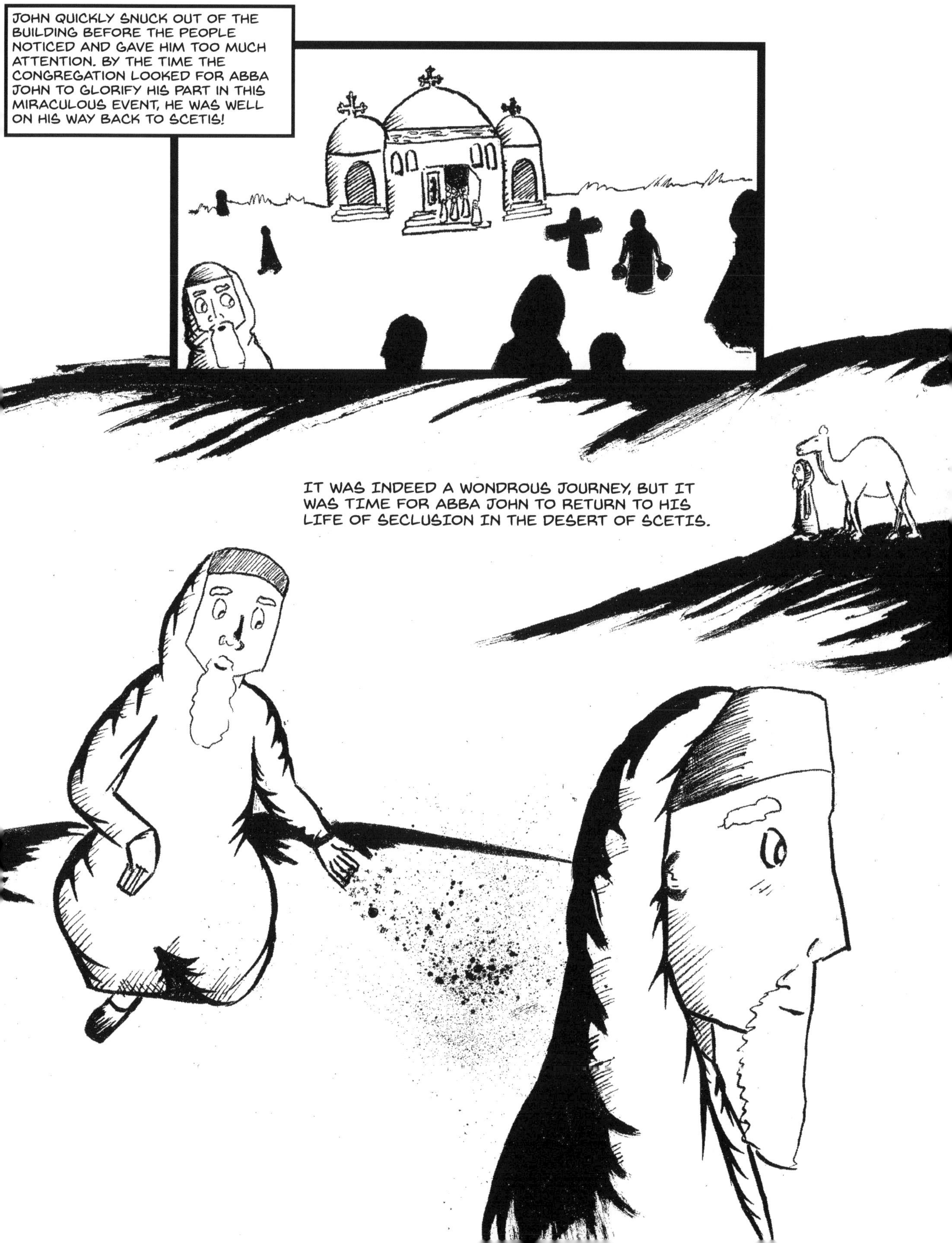
JOHN QUICKLY SNUCK OUT OF THE BUILDING BEFORE THE PEOPLE NOTICED AND GAVE HIM TOO MUCH ATTENTION. BY THE TIME THE CONGREGATION LOOKED FOR ABBA JOHN TO GLORIFY HIS PART IN THIS MIRACULOUS EVENT, HE WAS WELL ON HIS WAY BACK TO SCETIS!
IT WAS INDEED A WONDROUS JOURNEY, BUT IT WAS TIME FOR ABBA JOHN TO RETURN TO HIS LIFE OF SECLUSION IN THE DESERT OF SCETIS.

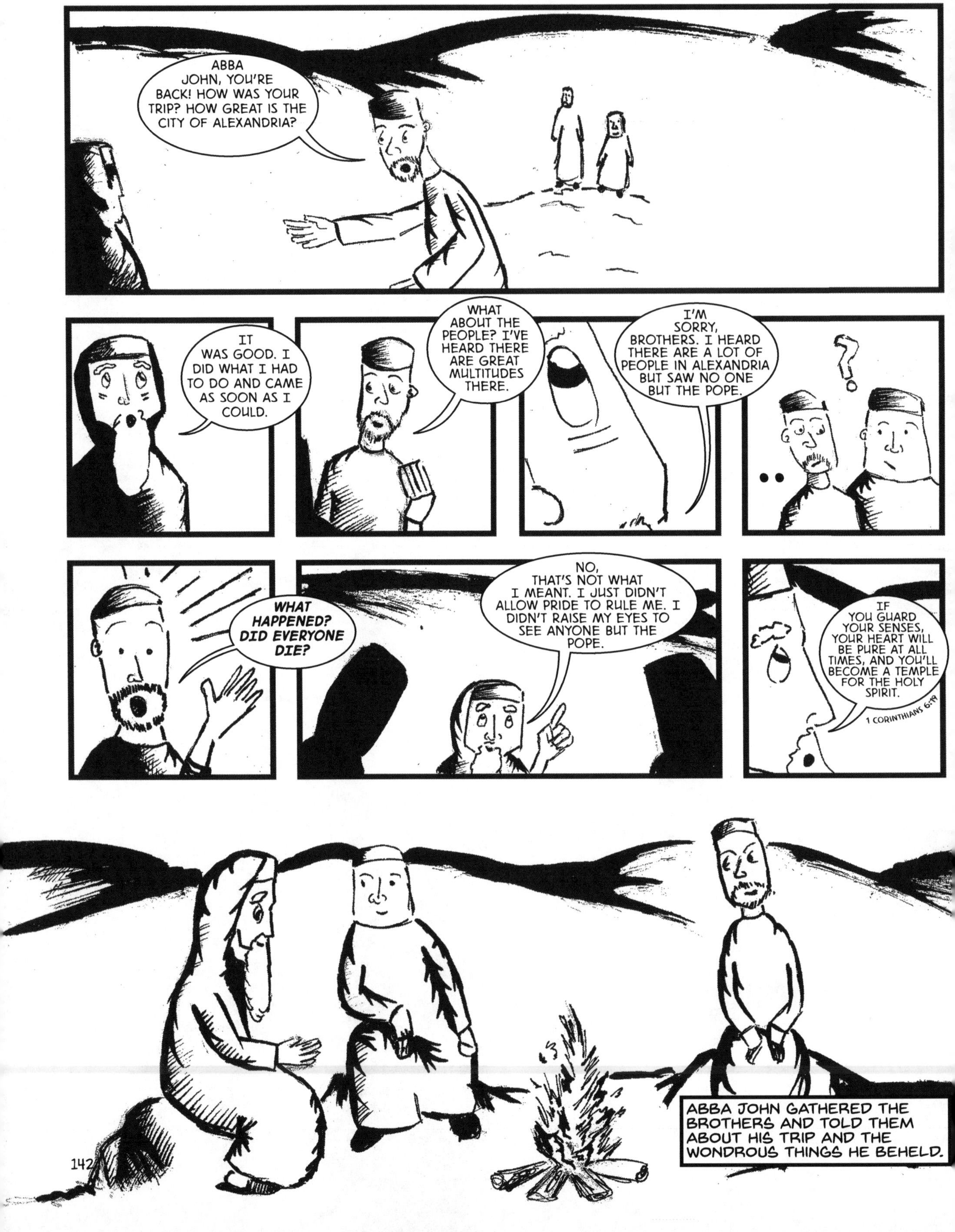
ABBA JOHN, YOU'RE BACK! HOW WAS YOUR TRIP? HOW GREAT IS THE CITY OF ALEXANDRIA?
IT WAS GOOD. I DID WHAT I HAD TO DO AND CAME AS SOON AS I COULD.
WHAT ABOUT THE PEOPLE? I'VE HEARD THERE ARE GREAT MULTITUDES THERE.
I'M SORRY, BROTHERS. I HEARD THERE ARE A LOT OF PEOPLE IN ALEXANDRIA BUT SAW NO ONE BUT THE POPE.
?
..
WHAT HAPPENED? DID EVERYONE DIE?
NO, THAT'S NOT WHAT I MEANT. I JUST DIDN'T ALLOW PRIDE TO RULE ME. I DIDN'T RAISE MY EYES TO SEE ANYONE BUT THE POPE.
IF YOU GUARD YOUR SENSES, YOUR HEART WILL BE PURE AT ALL TIMES, AND YOU'LL BECOME A TEMPLE FOR THE HOLY SPIRIT.
1 CORINTHIANS 6:19
ABBA JOHN GATHERED THE BROTHERS AND TOLD THEM ABOUT HIS TRIP AND THE WONDROUS THINGS HE BEHELD.

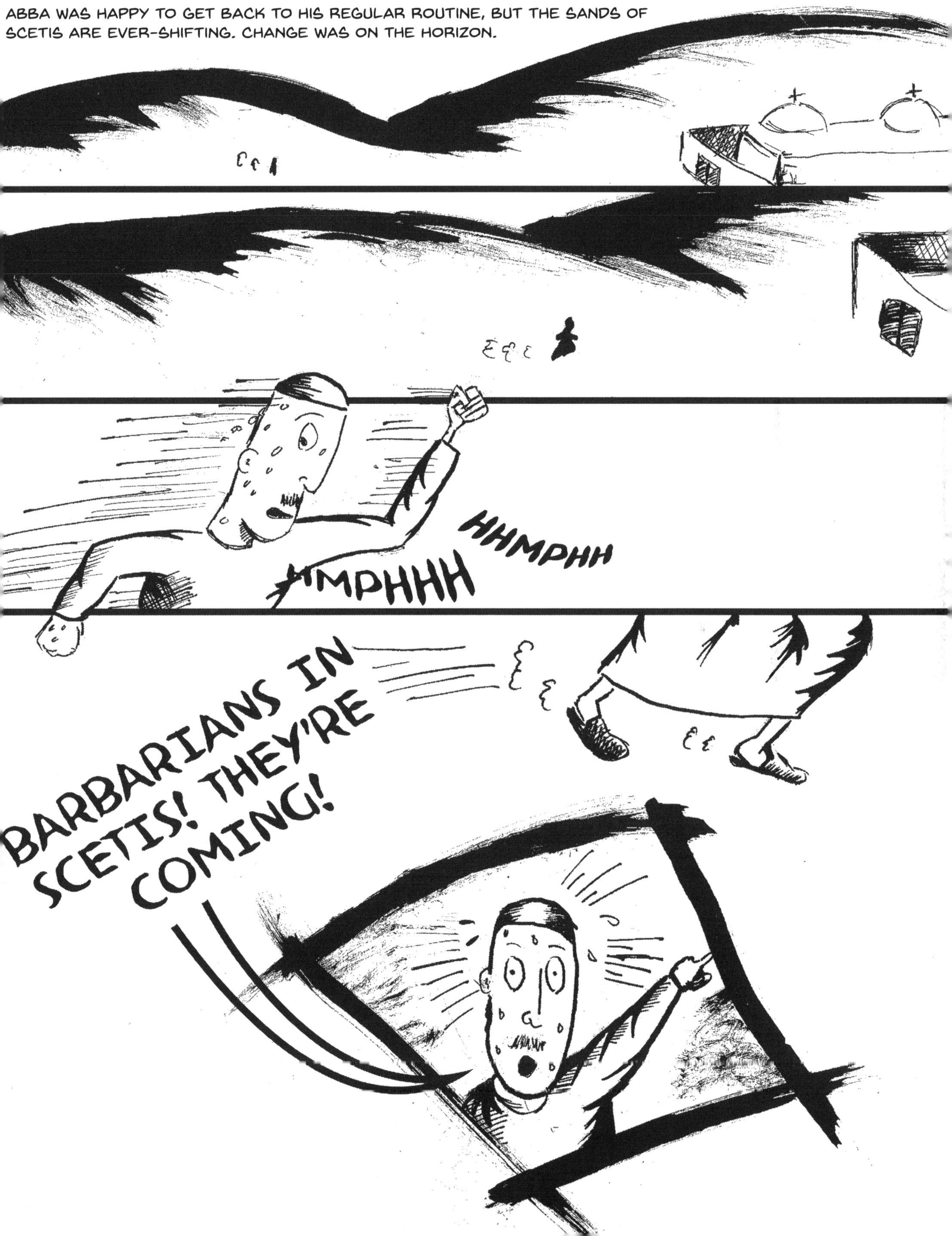
ABBA WAS HAPPY TO GET BACK TO HIS REGULAR ROUTINE, BUT THE SANDS OF SCETIS ARE EVER-SHIFTING. CHANGE WAS ON THE HORIZON.
HHMPHH
HMPHHH
BARBARIANS IN SCETIS! THEY'RE COMING!

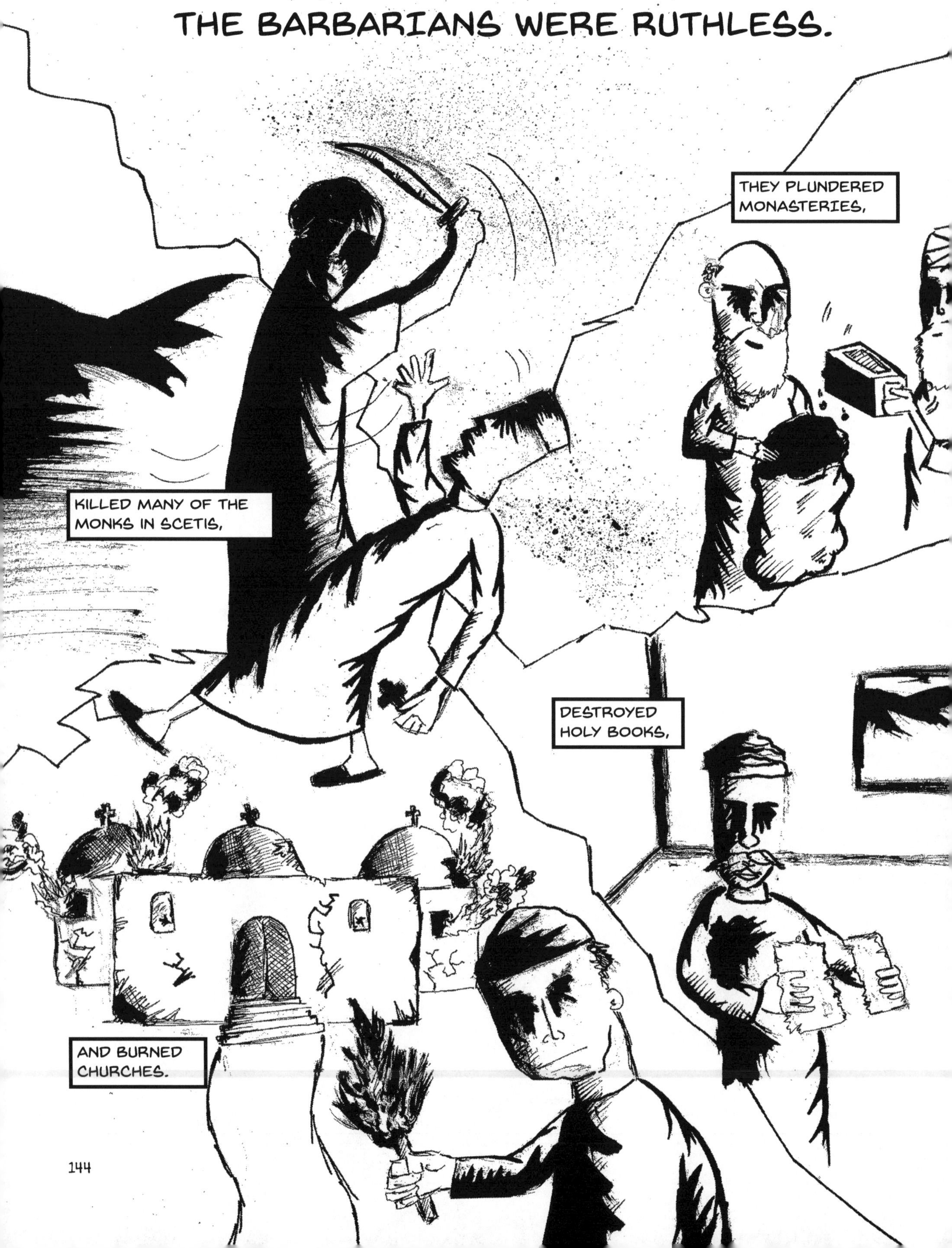
THE BARBARIANS WERE RUTHLESS.
KILLED MANY OF THE MONKS IN SCETIS,
THEY PLUNDERED MONASTERIES,
DESTROYED HOLY BOOKS,
AND BURNED CHURCHES.

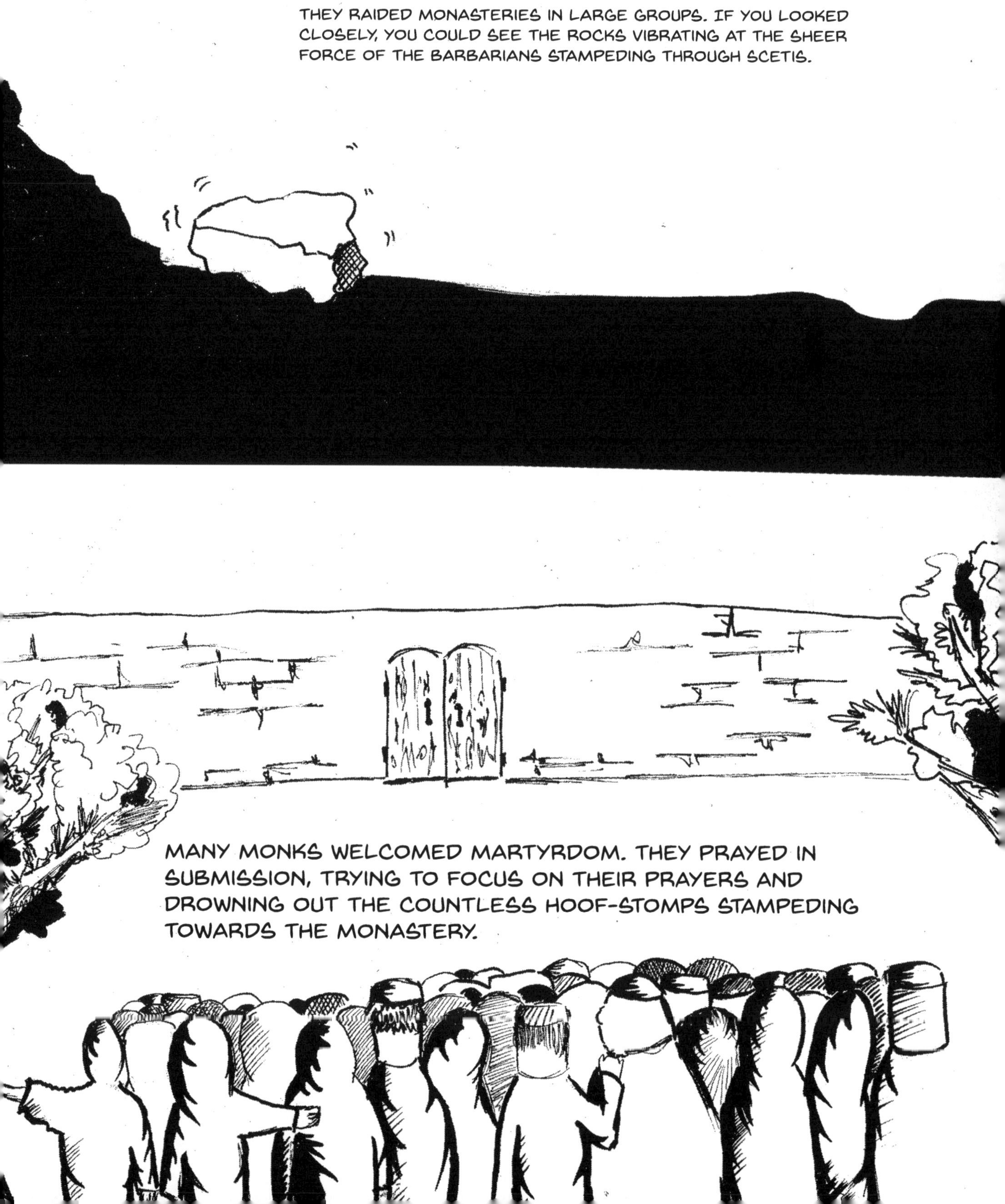
THEY RAIDED MONASTERIES IN LARGE GROUPS. IF YOU LOOKED CLOSELY, YOU COULD SEE THE ROCKS VIBRATING AT THE SHEER FORCE OF THE BARBARIANS STAMPEDING THROUGH SCETIS.
MANY MONKS WELCOMED MARTYRDOM. THEY PRAYED IN SUBMISSION, TRYING TO FOCUS ON THEIR PRAYERS AND DROWNING OUT THE COUNTLESS HOOF-STOMPS STAMPEDING TOWARDS THE MONASTERY.

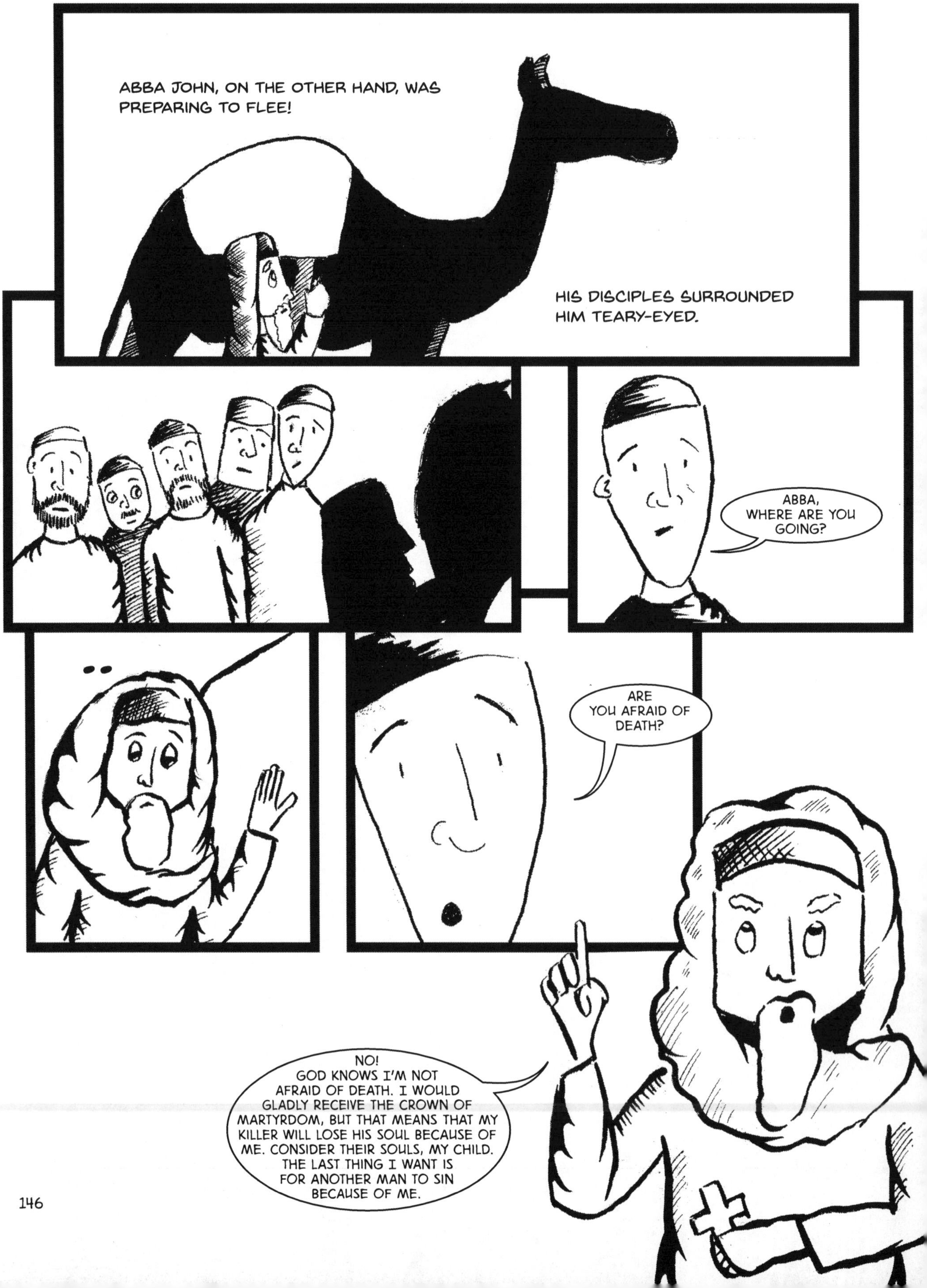
ABBA JOHN, ON THE OTHER HAND, WAS PREPARING TO FLEE!
HIS DISCIPLES SURROUNDED HIM TEARY-EYED.
ABBA, WHERE ARE YOU GOING?
..
ARE YOU AFRAID OF DEATH?
NO! GOD KNOWS I'M NOT AFRAID OF DEATH. I WOULD GLADLY RECEIVE THE CROWN OF MARTYRDOM, BUT THAT MEANS THAT MY KILLER WILL LOSE HIS SOUL BECAUSE OF ME. CONSIDER THEIR SOULS, MY CHILD. THE LAST THING I WANT IS FOR ANOTHER MAN TO SIN BECAUSE OF ME.

THE YOUNG MONKS THEN RELUCTANTLY HELPED ABBA JOHN THE SHORT GET ON A CAMEL.

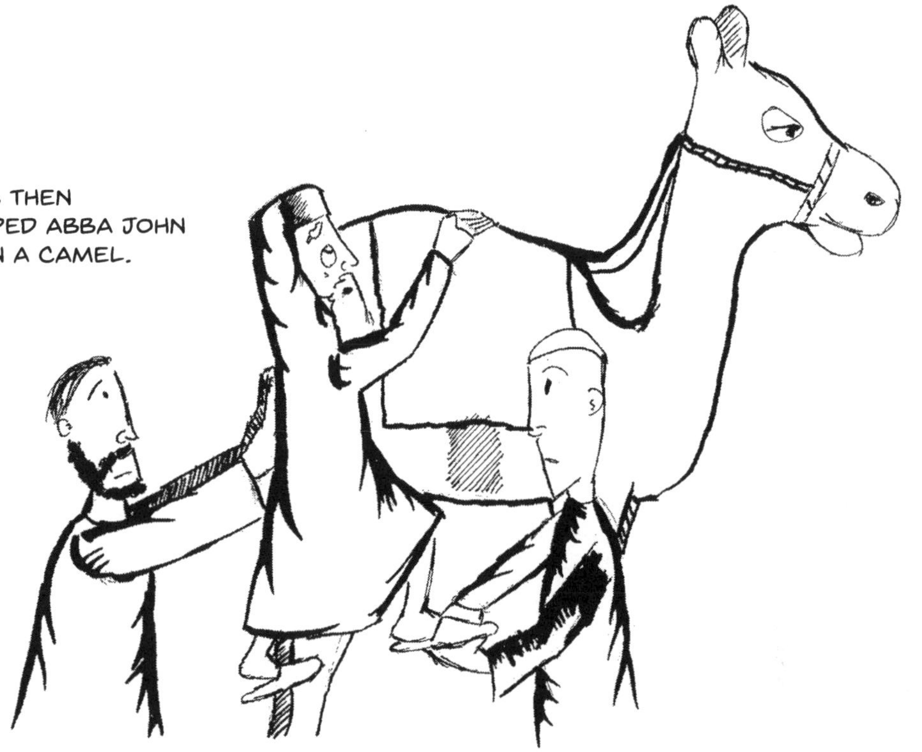

HE LOOKED AT THEM ONE MORE TIME AND SAID,

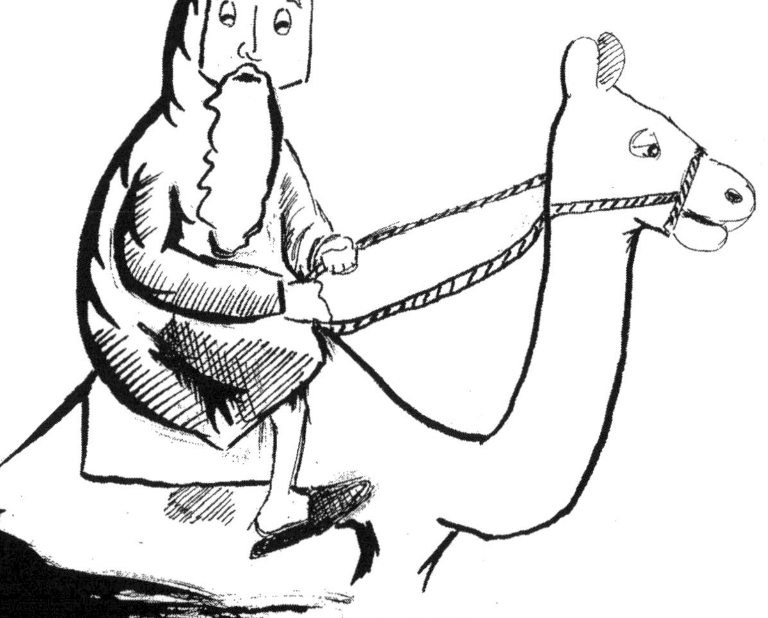

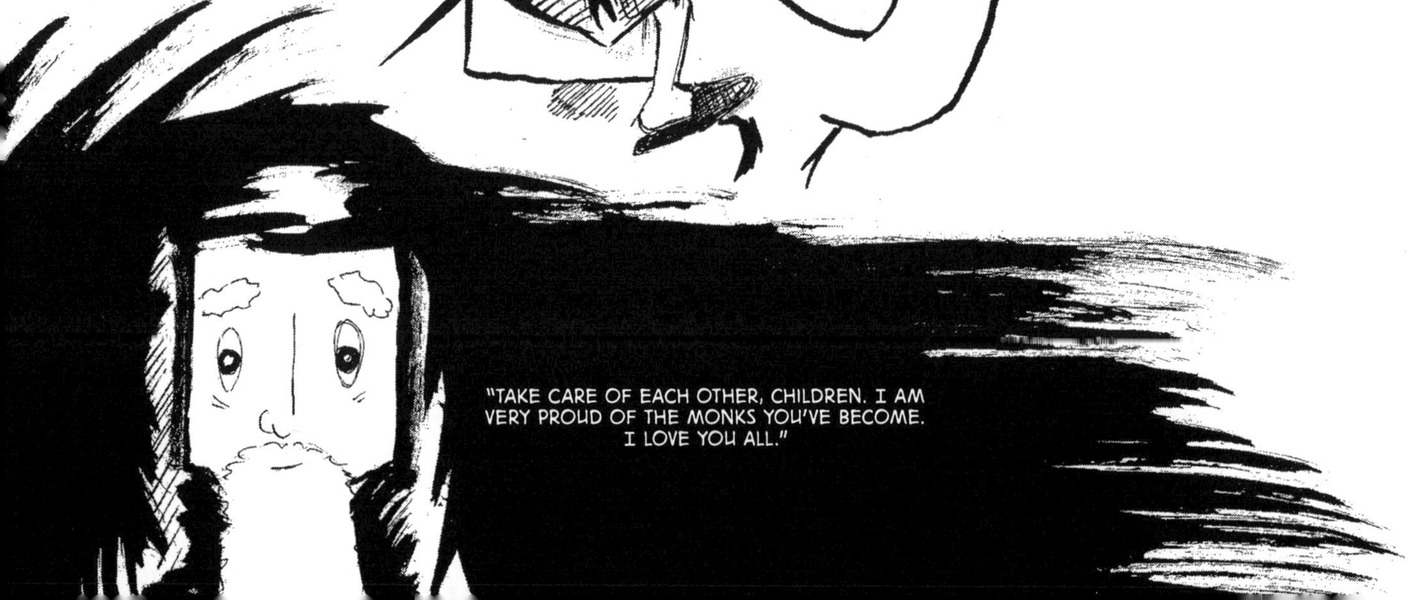
"TAKE CARE OF EACH OTHER, CHILDREN. I AM VERY PROUD OF THE MONKS YOU'VE BECOME. I LOVE YOU ALL."

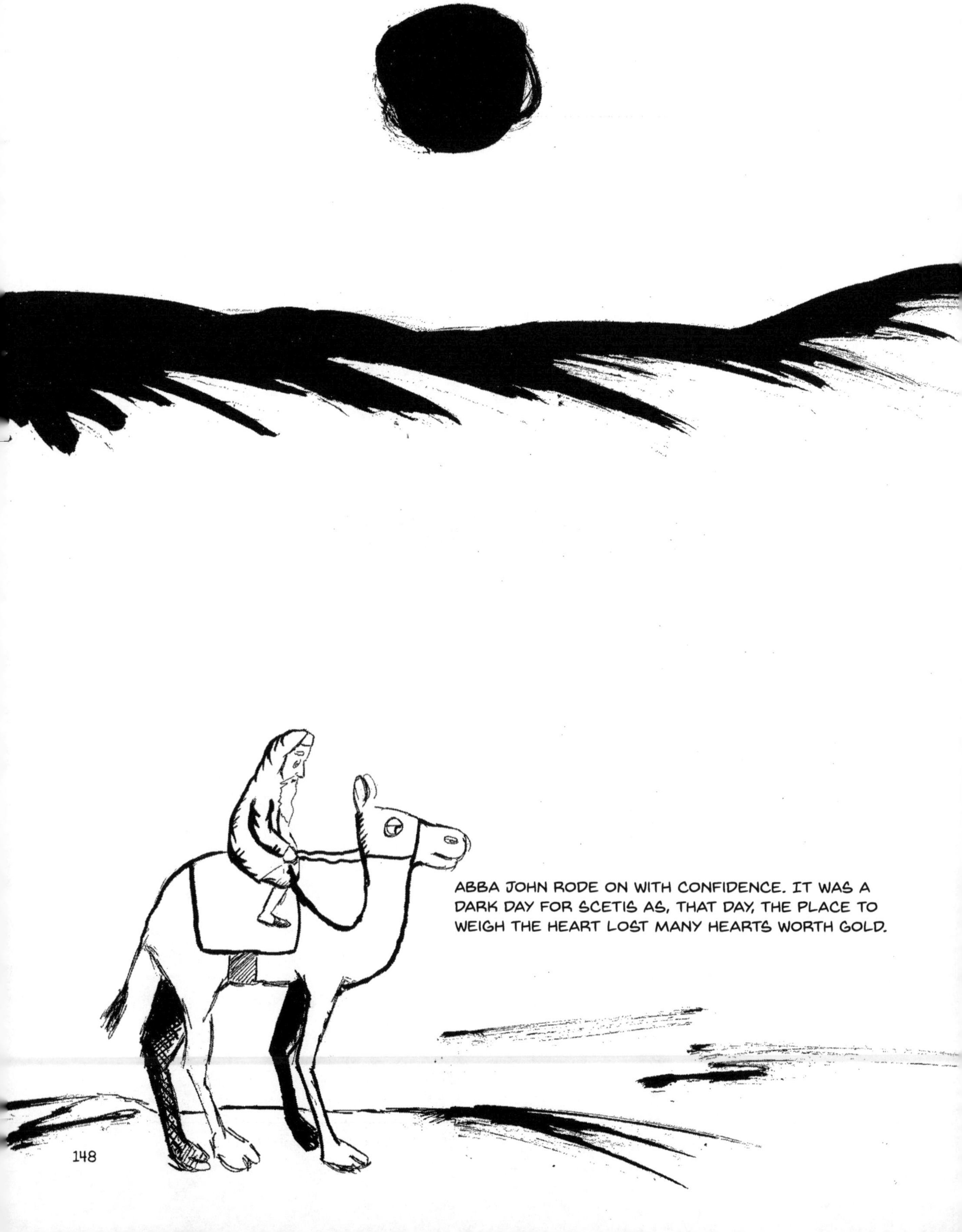
ABBA JOHN RODE ON WITH CONFIDENCE. IT WAS A DARK DAY FOR SCETIS AS, THAT DAY, THE PLACE TO WEIGH THE HEART LOST MANY HEARTS WORTH GOLD.

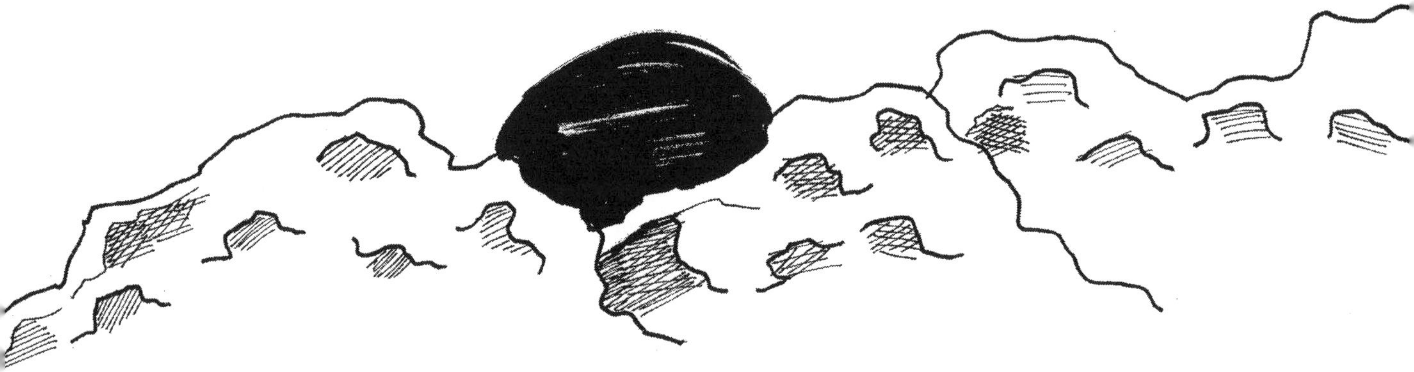

JOHN JOURNEYED TO THE EAST-MOST DESERT IN THE LAND OF EGYPT

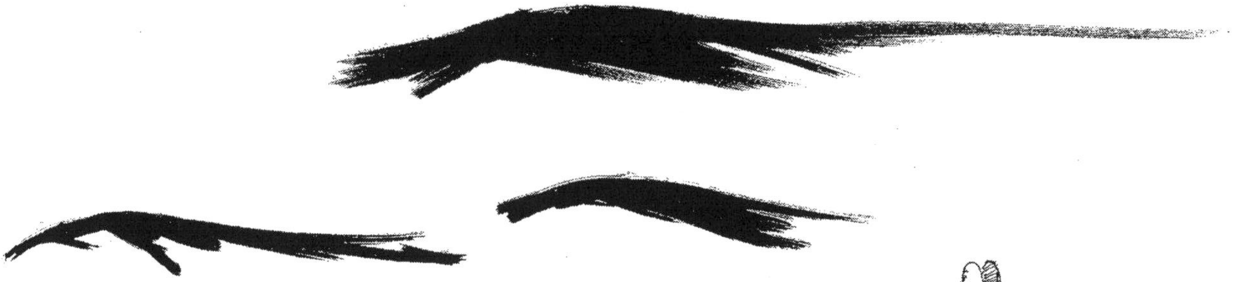

IT WAS A VERY DIFFERENT PLACE GIVEN THAT JOHN HAD SPENT SO MANY YEARS IN SCETIS. THE BLUE AND RED HUES DRAPED OVER THE MOUNTAINS THAT TOWERED ABOVE ABBA JOHN'S SHORT FRAME, AND THEY STOOD OUT IN COMPARISON TO THE LITTLE HILLS OF SCETIS.

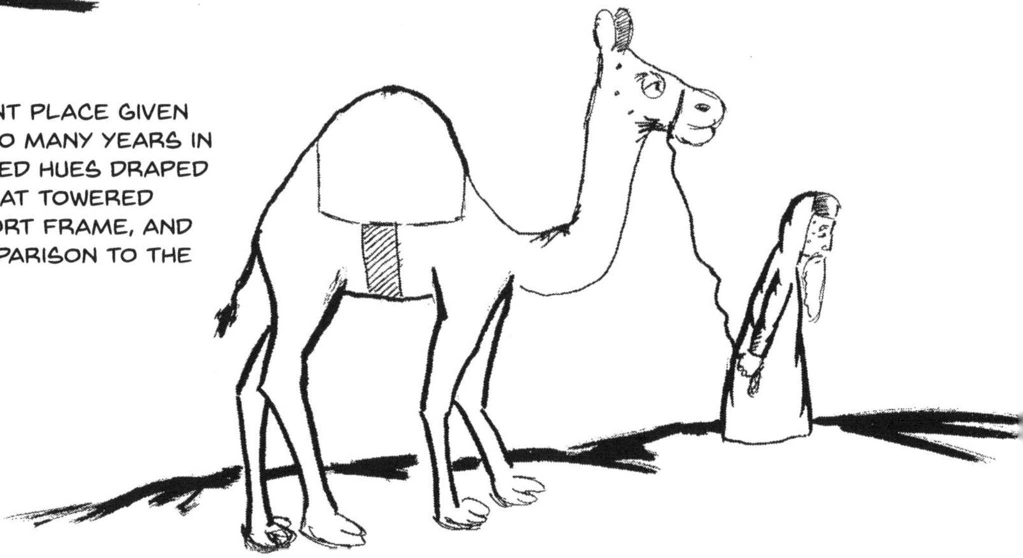

EVEN THE SAND WAS DIFFERENT. THE NATRON SALT GAVE THE SAND IN SCETIS ITS DISTINCT WHITE COLOR, UNLIKE THE YELLOWISH SAND OF THE RED SEA MOUNTAINSCAPE.

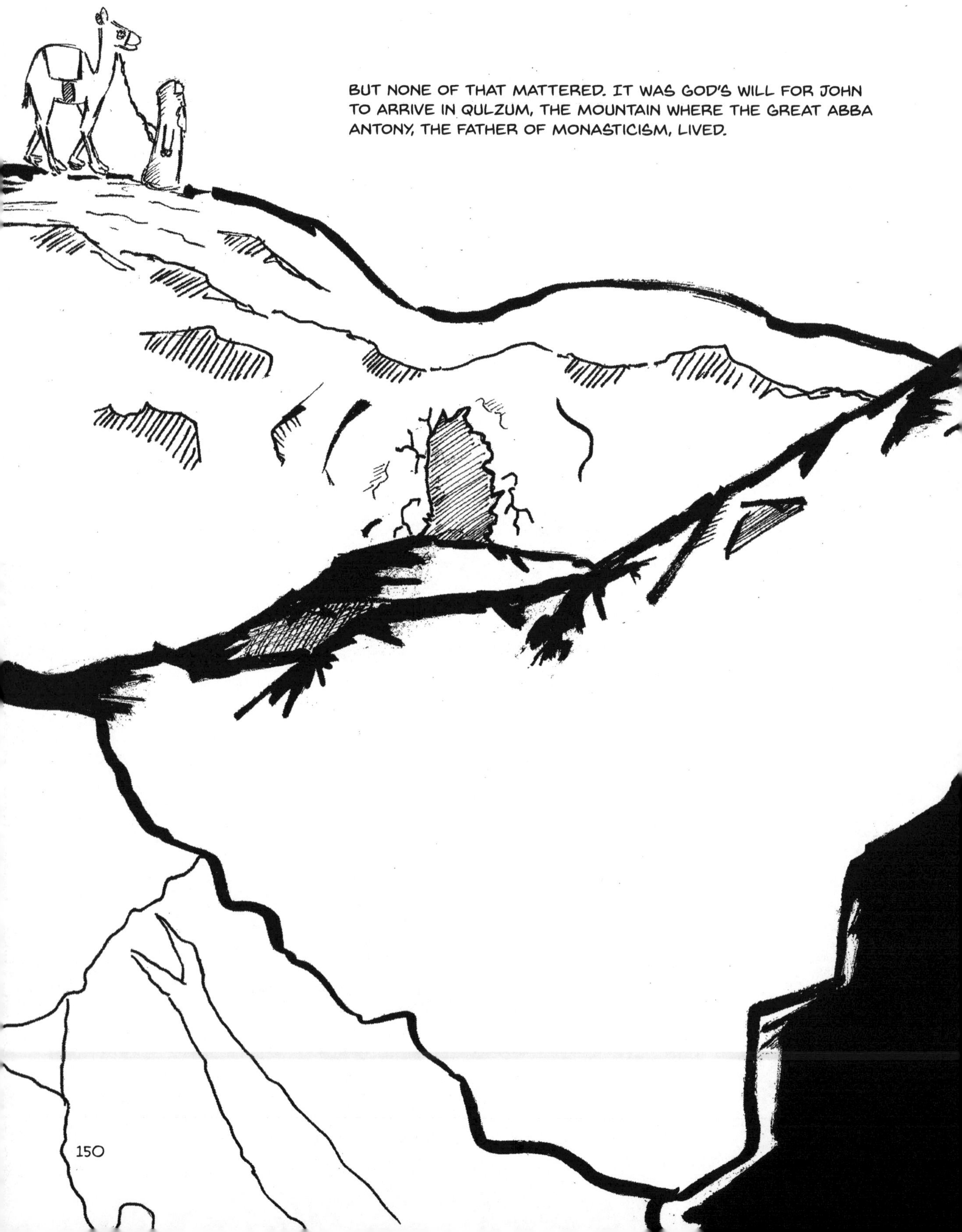
BUT NONE OF THAT MATTERED. IT WAS GOD'S WILL FOR JOHN TO ARRIVE IN QULZUM, THE MOUNTAIN WHERE THE GREAT ABBA ANTONY, THE FATHER OF MONASTICISM, LIVED.

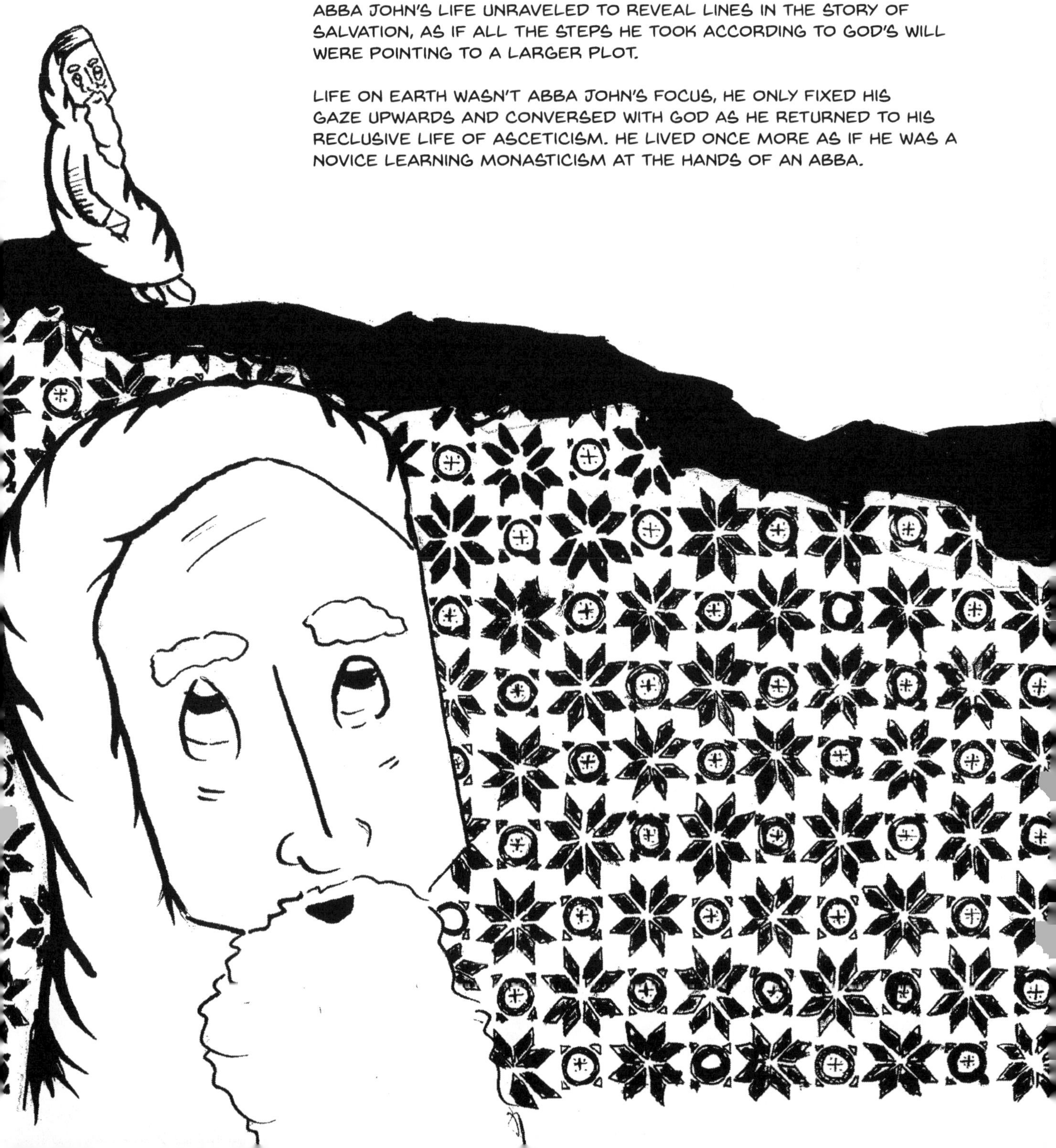
ABBA JOHN'S LIFE UNRAVELED TO REVEAL LINES IN THE STORY OF SALVATION, AS IF ALL THE STEPS HE TOOK ACCORDING TO GOD'S WILL WERE POINTING TO A LARGER PLOT.
LIFE ON EARTH WASN'T ABBA JOHN'S FOCUS, HE ONLY FIXED HIS GAZE UPWARDS AND CONVERSED WITH GOD AS HE RETURNED TO HIS RECLUSIVE LIFE OF ASCETICISM. HE LIVED ONCE MORE AS IF HE WAS A NOVICE LEARNING MONASTICISM AT THE HANDS OF AN ABBA.

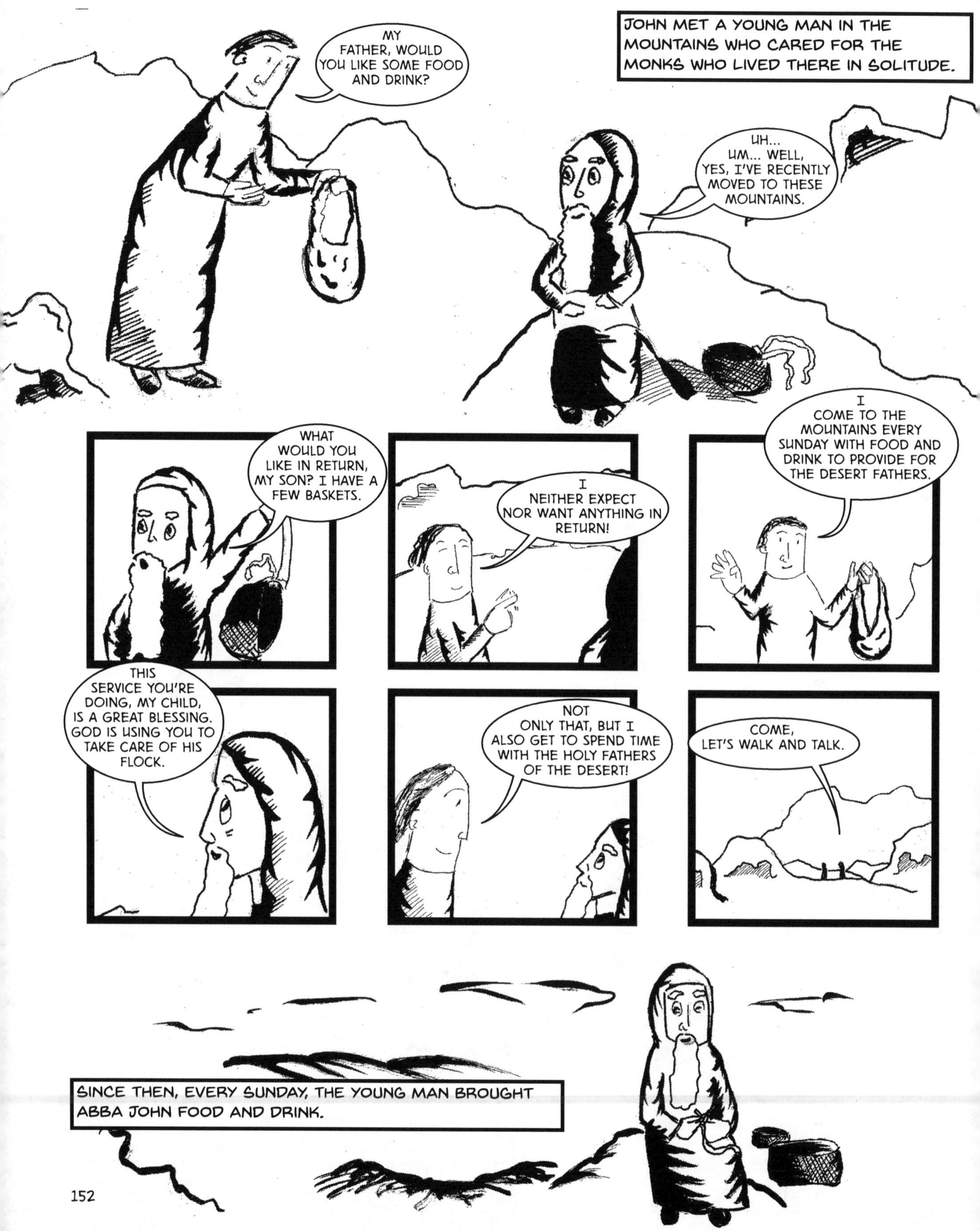
JOHN MET A YOUNG MAN IN THE MOUNTAINS WHO CARED FOR THE MONKS WHO LIVED THERE IN SOLITUDE.
MY FATHER, WOULD YOU LIKE SOME FOOD AND DRINK?
UH... UM... WELL, YES, I'VE RECENTLY MOVED TO THESE MOUNTAINS.
WHAT WOULD YOU LIKE IN RETURN, MY SON? I HAVE A FEW BASKETS.
I NEITHER EXPECT NOR WANT ANYTHING IN RETURN!
I COME TO THE MOUNTAINS EVERY SUNDAY WITH FOOD AND DRINK TO PROVIDE FOR THE DESERT FATHERS.
THIS SERVICE YOU'RE DOING, MY CHILD, IS A GREAT BLESSING. GOD IS USING YOU TO TAKE CARE OF HIS FLOCK.
NOT ONLY THAT, BUT I ALSO GET TO SPEND TIME WITH THE HOLY FATHERS OF THE DESERT!
COME, LET'S WALK AND TALK.
SINCE THEN, EVERY SUNDAY, THE YOUNG MAN BROUGHT ABBA JOHN FOOD AND DRINK.

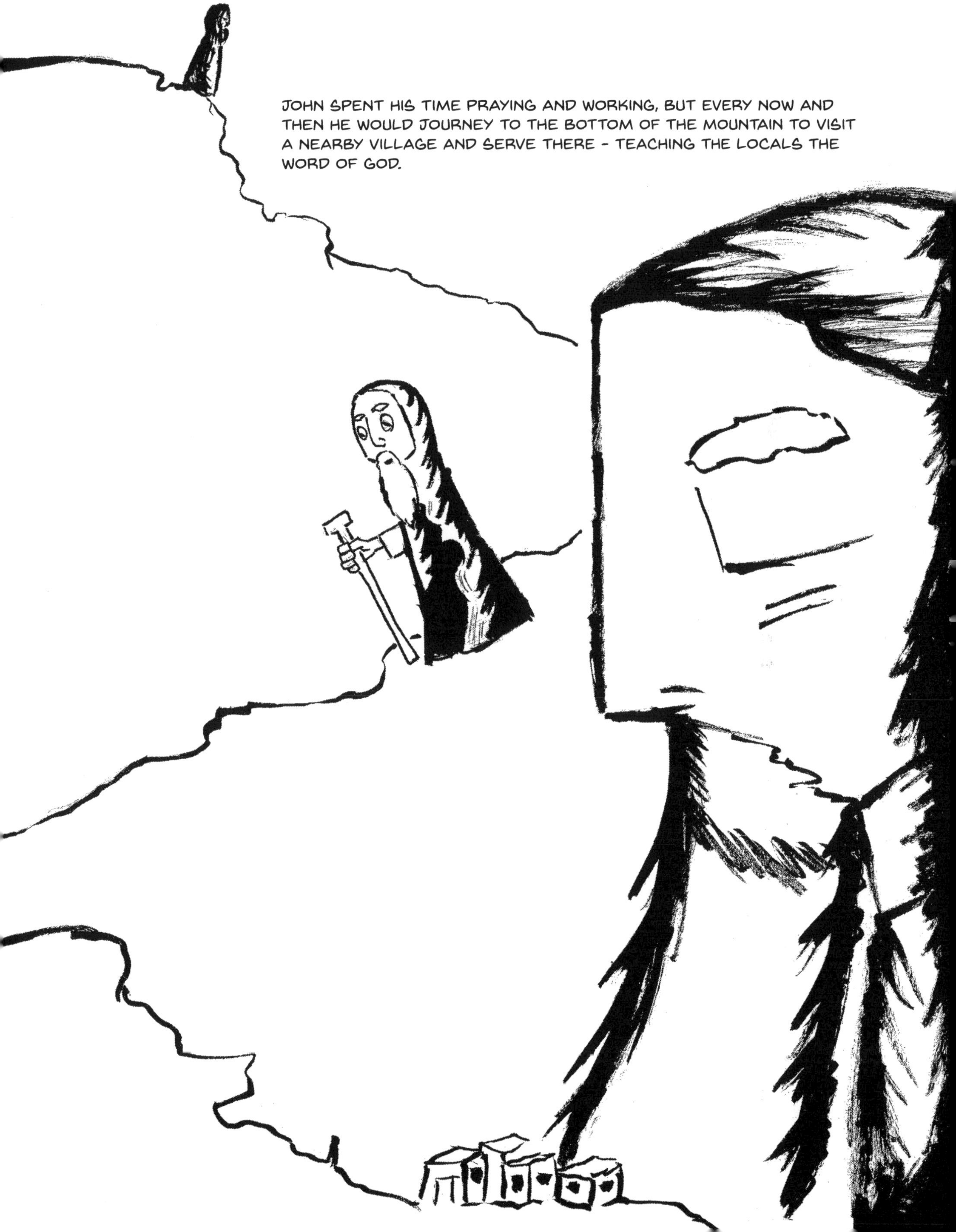
JOHN SPENT HIS TIME PRAYING AND WORKING, BUT EVERY NOW AND THEN HE WOULD JOURNEY TO THE BOTTOM OF THE MOUNTAIN TO VISIT A NEARBY VILLAGE AND SERVE THERE - TEACHING THE LOCALS THE WORD OF GOD.

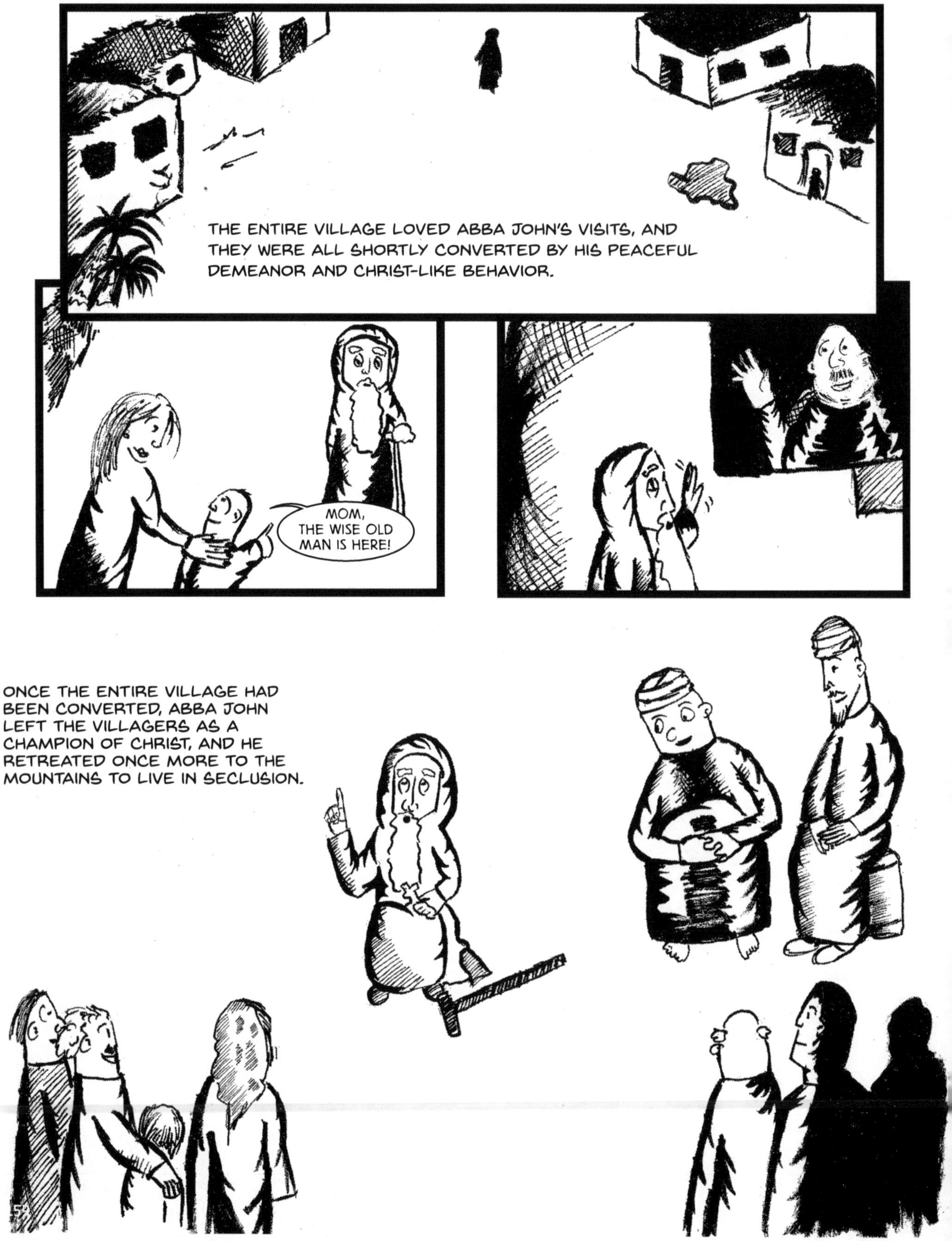
THE ENTIRE VILLAGE LOVED ABBA JOHN'S VISITS, AND THEY WERE ALL SHORTLY CONVERTED BY HIS PEACEFUL DEMEANOR AND CHRIST-LIKE BEHAVIOR.
MOM, THE WISE OLD MAN IS HERE!
ONCE THE ENTIRE VILLAGE HAD BEEN CONVERTED, ABBA JOHN LEFT THE VILLAGERS AS A CHAMPION OF CHRIST, AND HE RETREATED ONCE MORE TO THE MOUNTAINS TO LIVE IN SECLUSION.

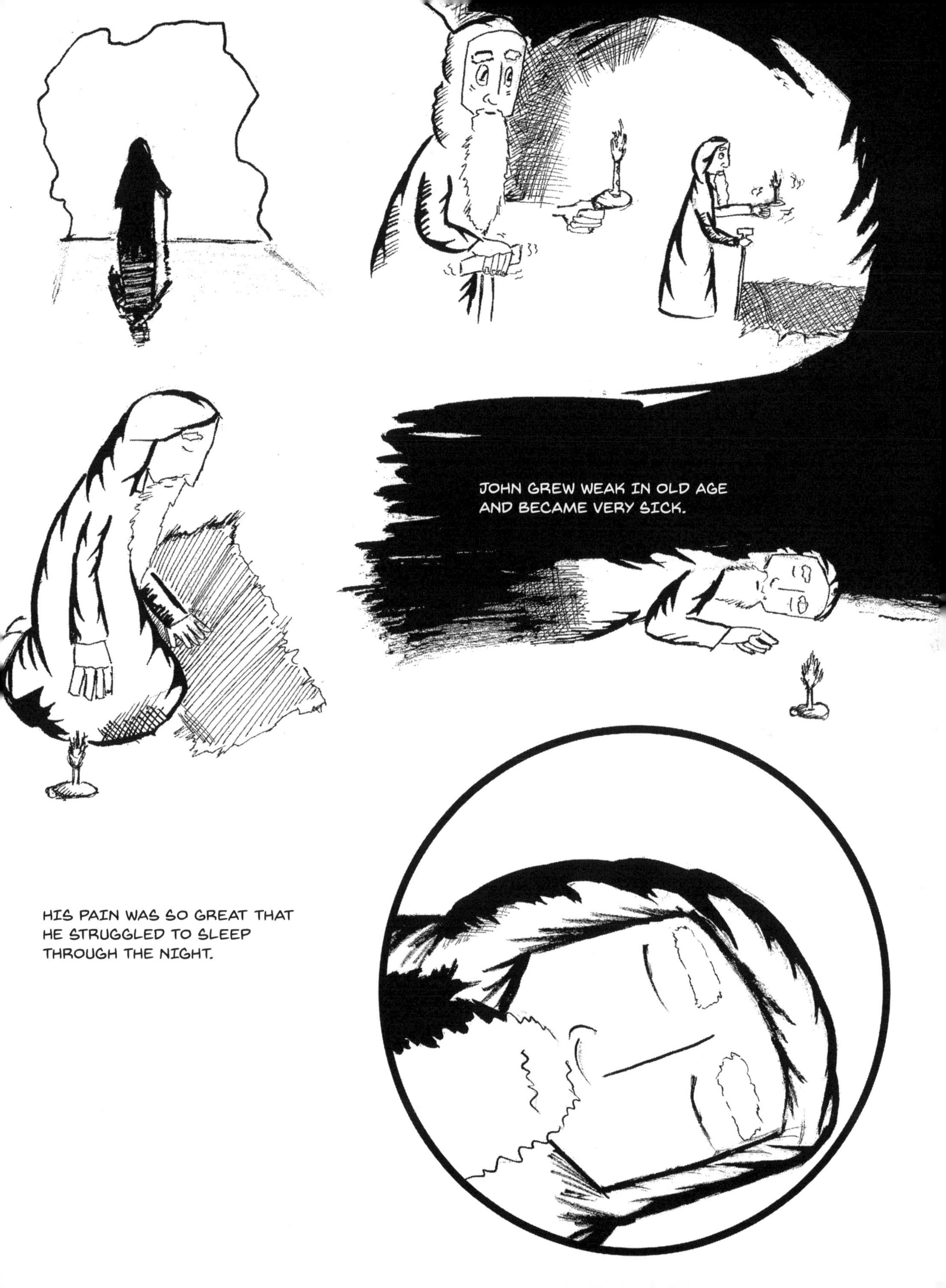
JOHN GREW WEAK IN OLD AGE AND BECAME VERY SICK.
HIS PAIN WAS SO GREAT THAT HE STRUGGLED TO SLEEP THROUGH THE NIGHT.

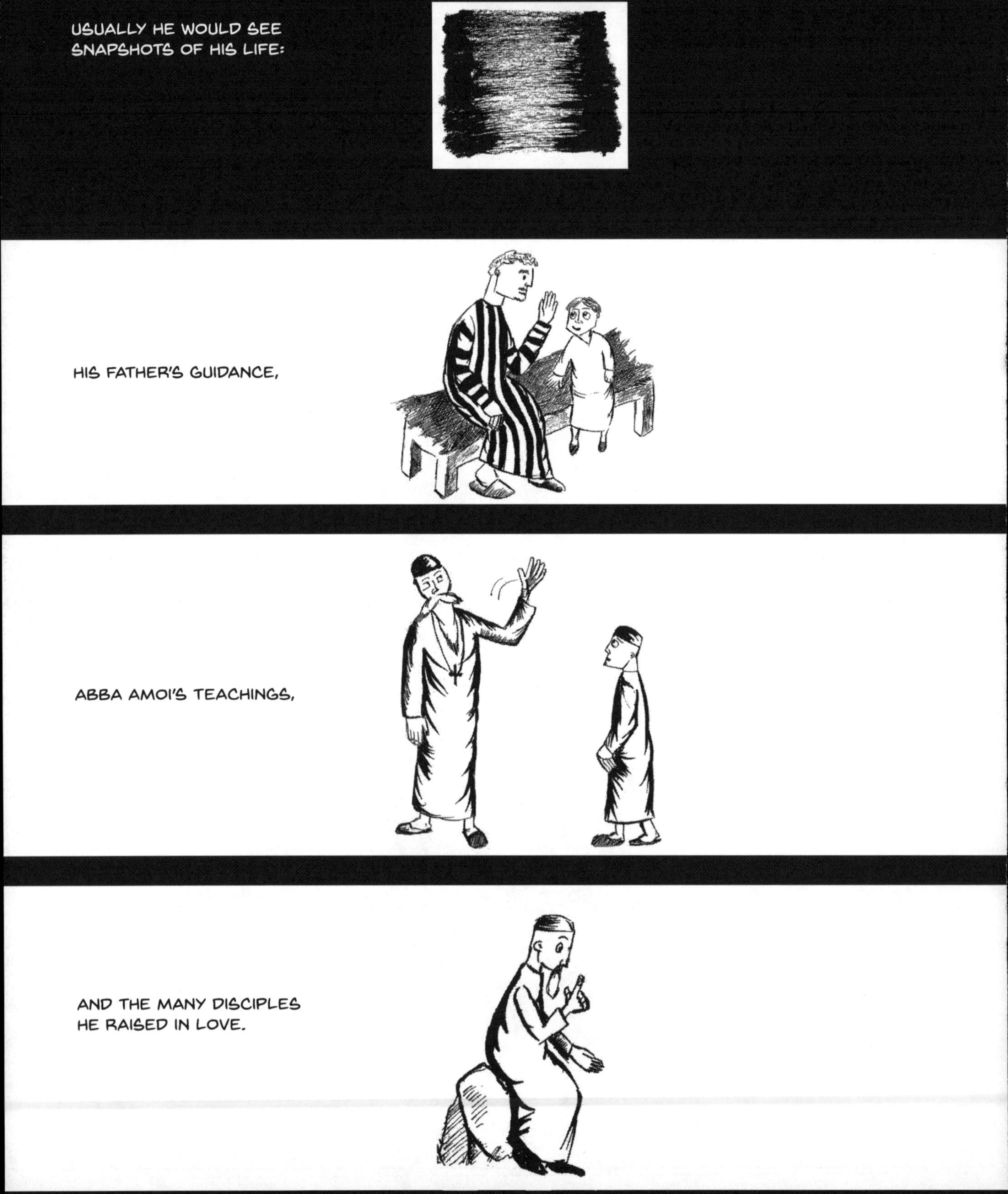
USUALLY HE WOULD SEE SNAPSHOTS OF HIS LIFE:
HIS FATHER'S GUIDANCE,
ABBA AMOI'S TEACHINGS,
AND THE MANY DISCIPLES HE RAISED IN LOVE.

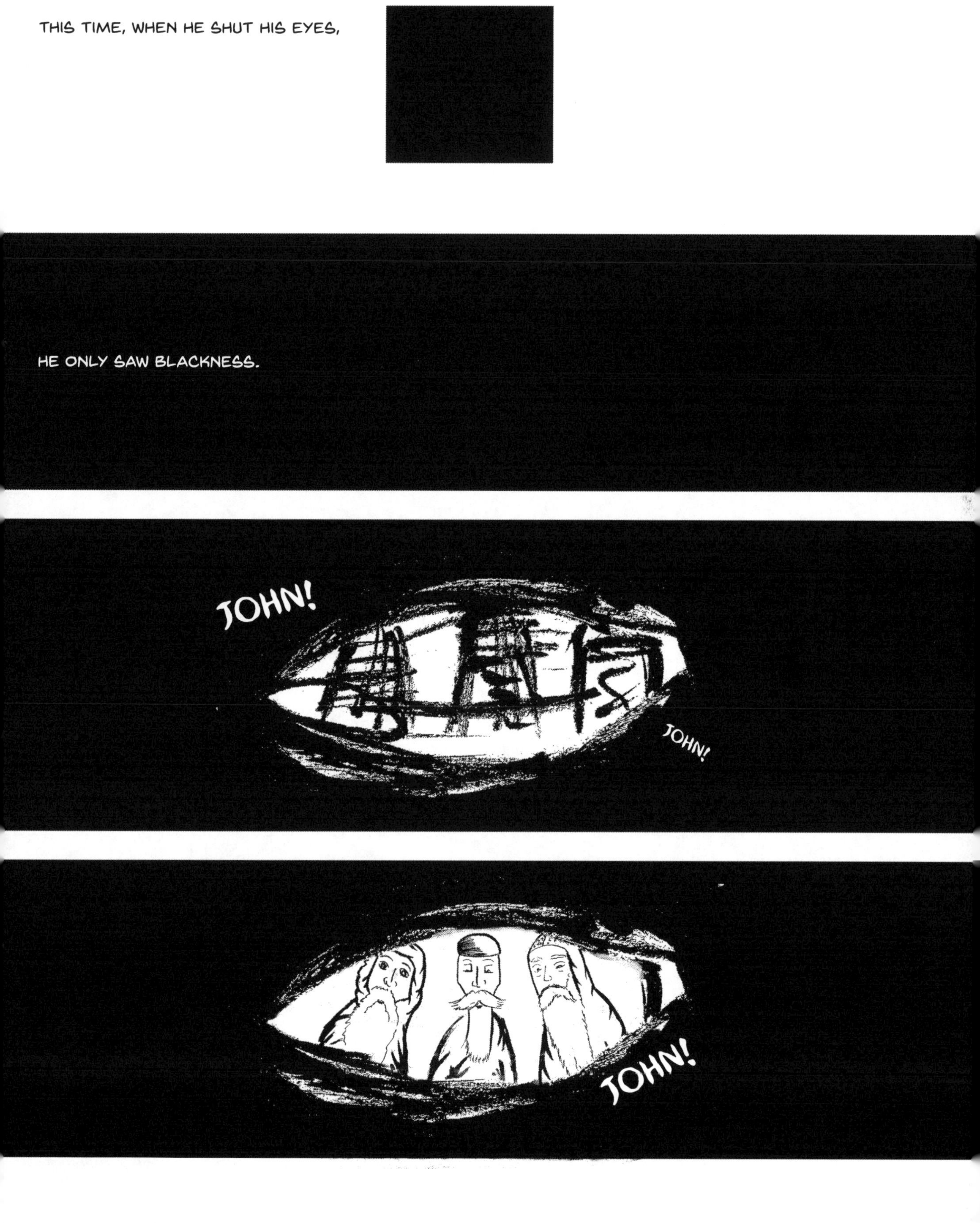
THIS TIME, WHEN HE SHUT HIS EYES,
HE ONLY SAW BLACKNESS.
JOHN!
JOHN!
JOHN!

JOHN OPENED HIS EYES, AND THREE FIGURES SLOWLY CAME INTO FOCUS. HIS SENSES RACED TO MAKE SENSE OF HIS SURROUNDINGS. HE SMELLED A SWEET AROMA LIKE THAT OF INCENSE, AND HEARD A VOICE HE HADN'T HEARD IN YEARS. TO JOHN'S SURPRISE, ABBA AMOI WAS STANDING RIGHT IN FRONT OF HIM, ALONG WITH THE GREAT DESERT FATHERS MACARIUS AND THE FATHER OF MONASTICISM ANTONY THE GREAT!

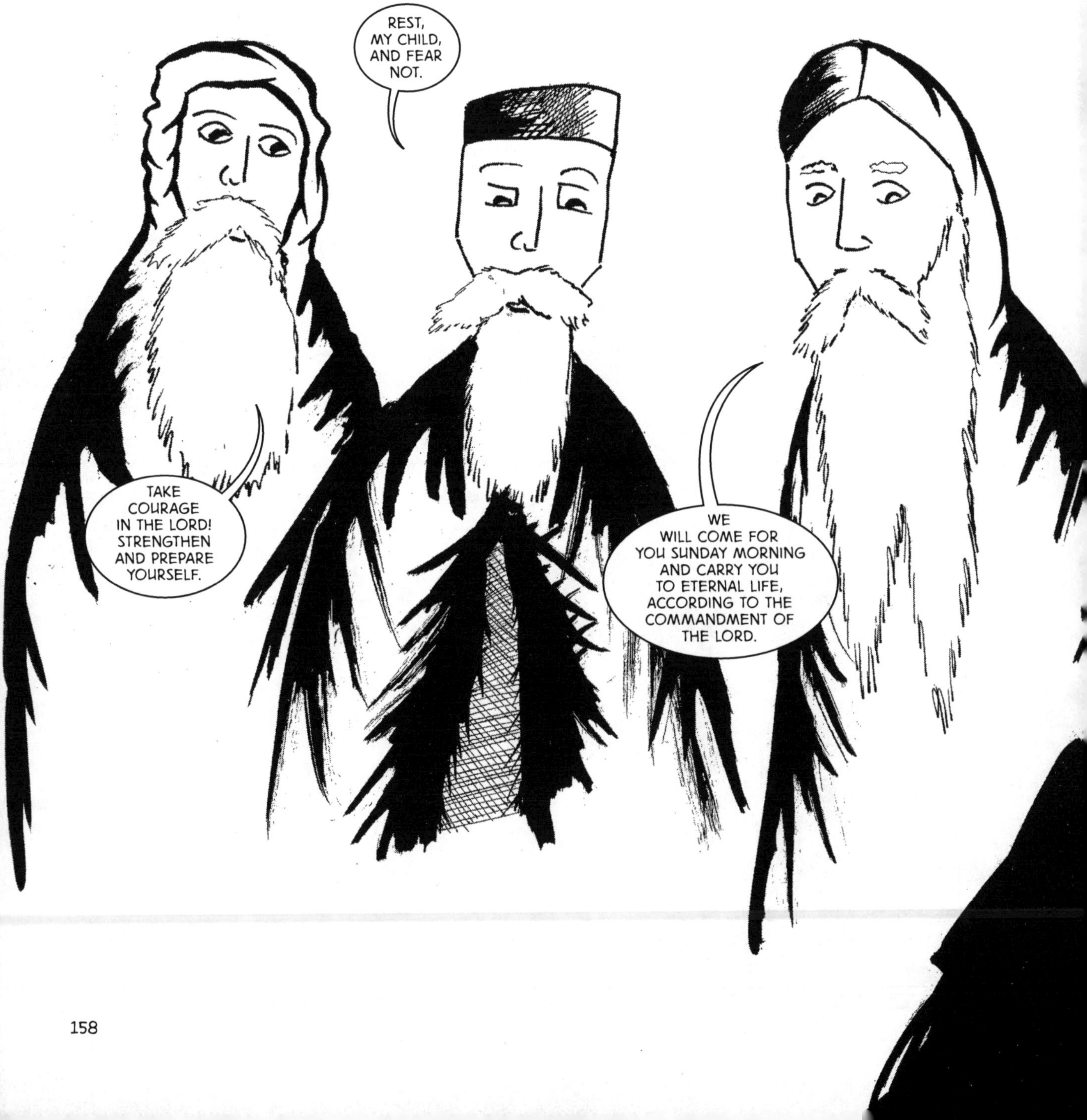
REST, MY CHILD, AND FEAR NOT.
TAKE COURAGE IN THE LORD! STRENGTHEN AND PREPARE YOURSELF.
WE WILL COME FOR YOU SUNDAY MORNING AND CARRY YOU TO ETERNAL LIFE, ACCORDING TO THE COMMANDMENT OF THE LORD.

AFTER THEY SAID THIS, THEY DISAPPEARED FROM HIS SIGHT. ON FRIDAY, JOHN SENT HIS GOD-LOVING SERVANT TO THE CITY. HE DID THIS SO THAT NO ONE IS PRESENT WHEN HE DIES.

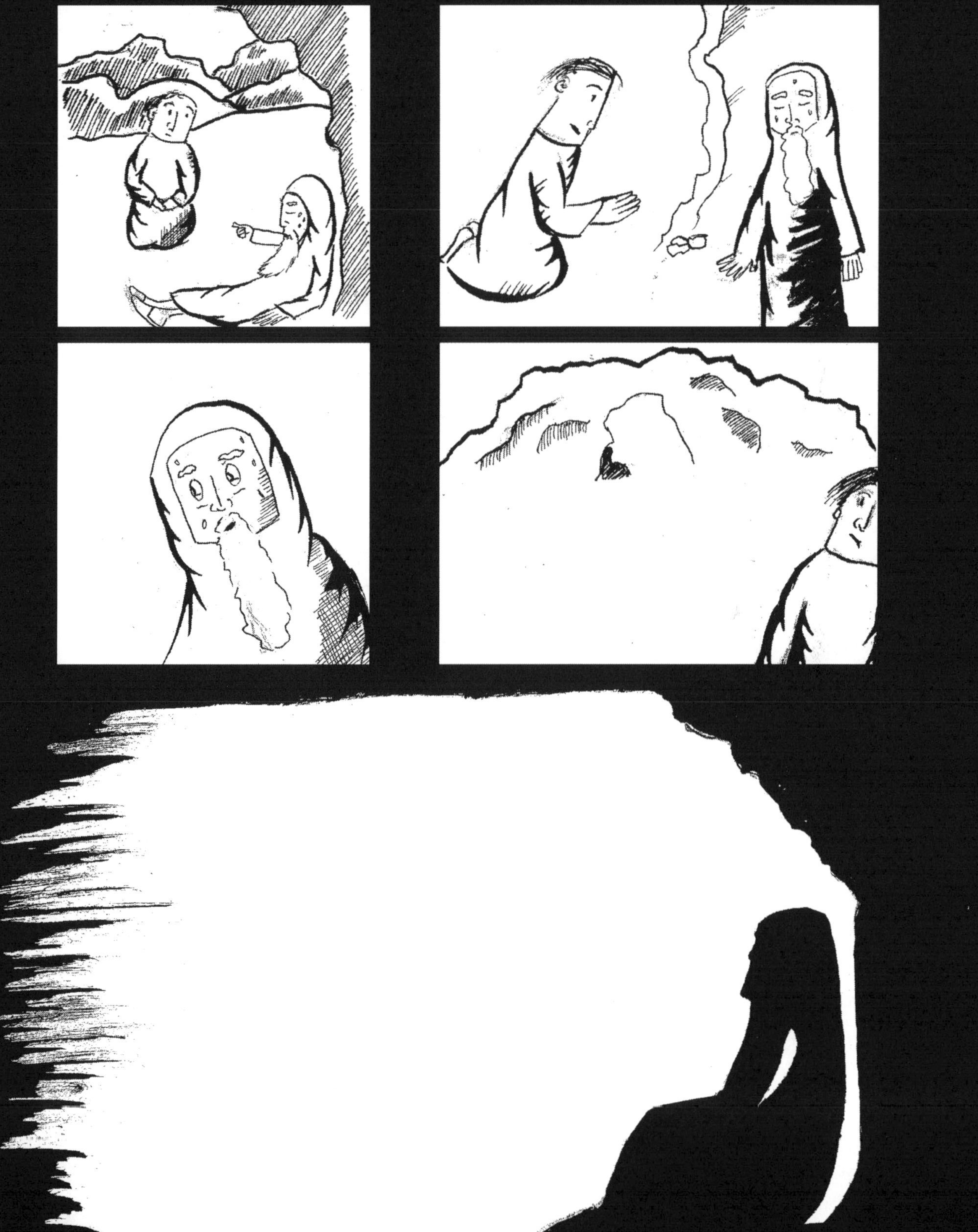

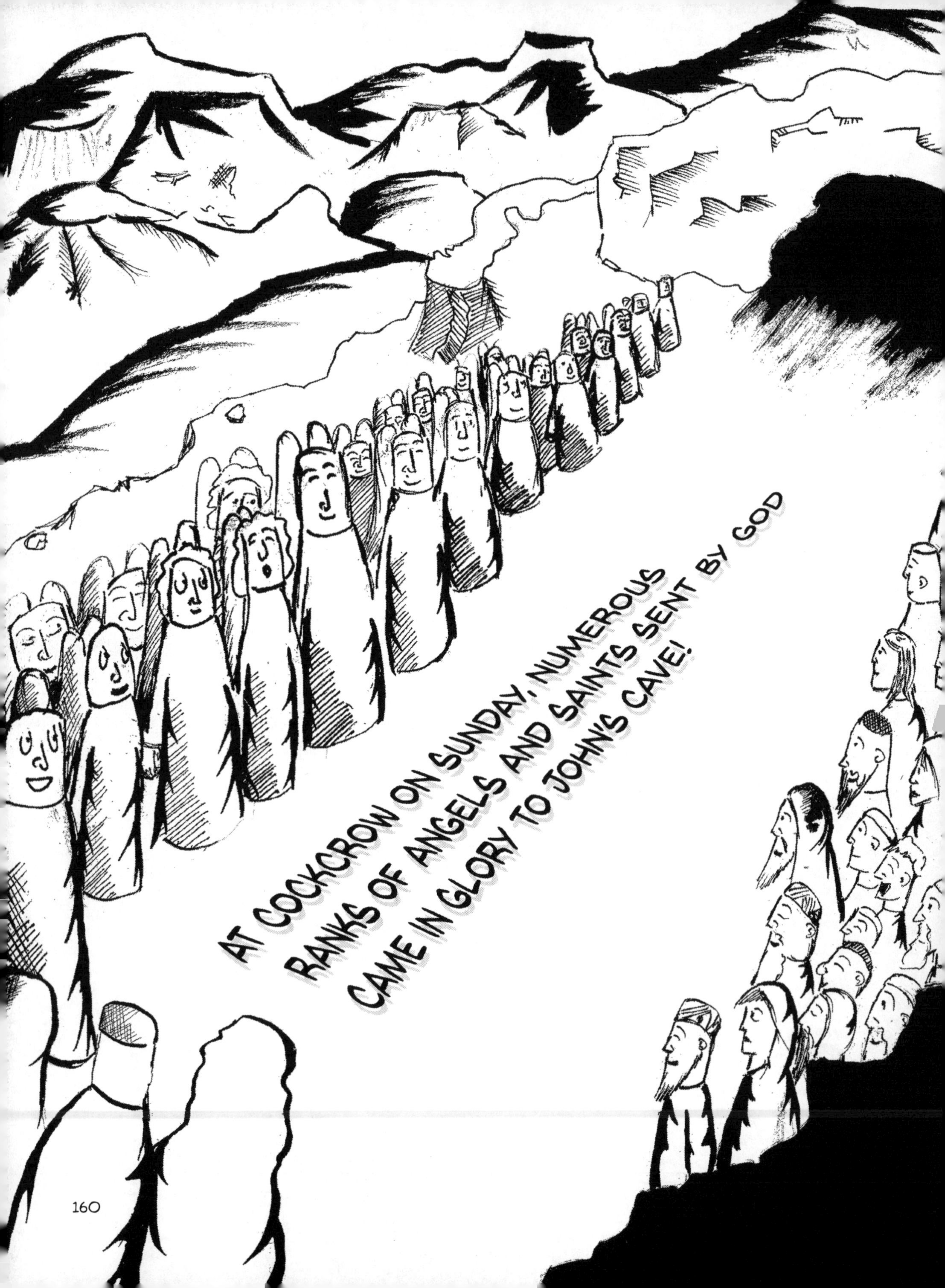
AT COCKCROW ON SUNDAY, NUMEROUS
RANKS OF ANGELS AND SAINTS SENT BY GOD
CAME IN GLORY TO JOHN'S CAVE!

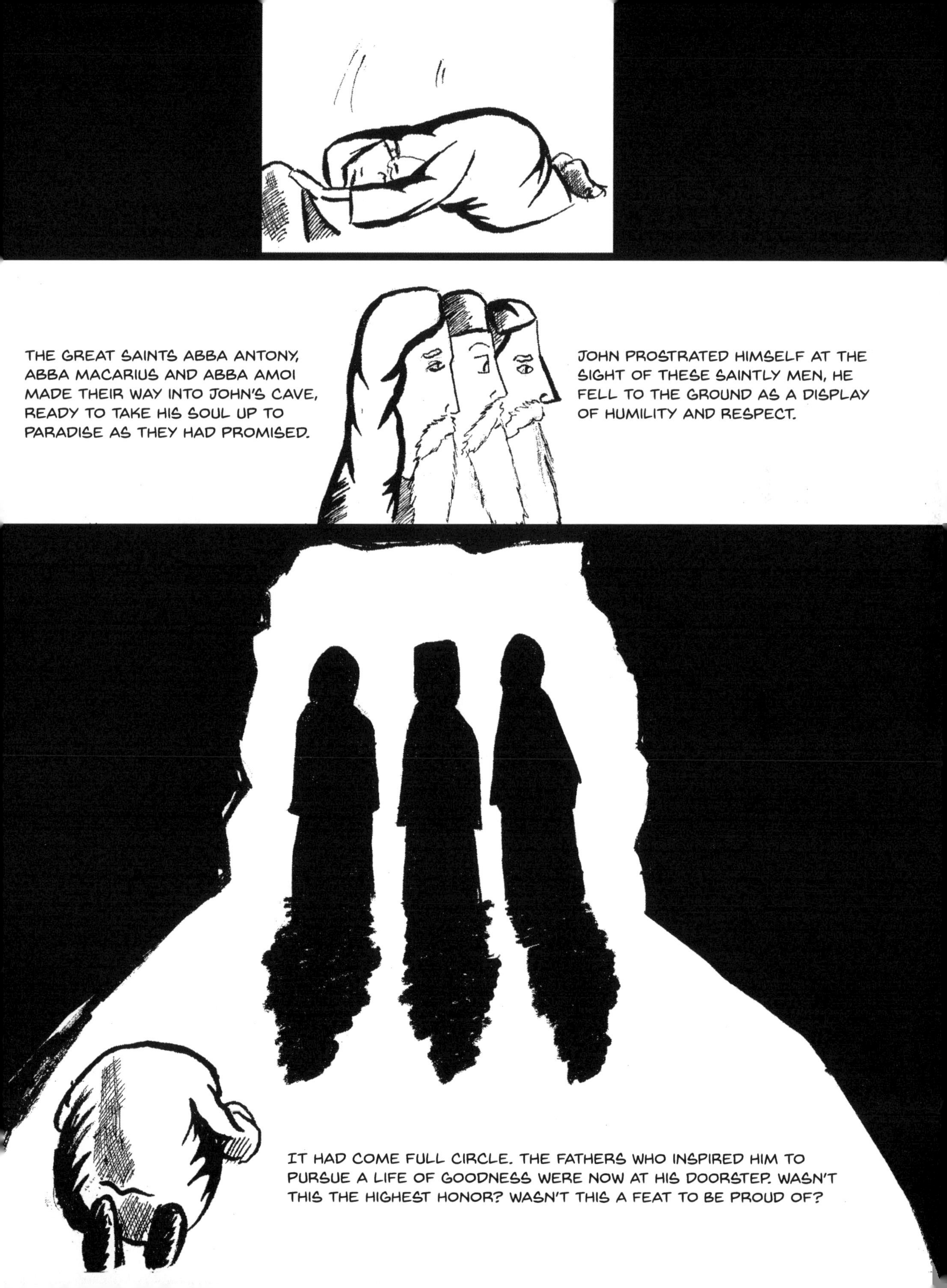
THE GREAT SAINTS ABBA ANTONY, ABBA MACARIUS AND ABBA AMOI MADE THEIR WAY INTO JOHN'S CAVE, READY TO TAKE HIS SOUL UP TO PARADISE AS THEY HAD PROMISED.
JOHN PROSTRATED HIMSELF AT THE SIGHT OF THESE SAINTLY MEN, HE FELL TO THE GROUND AS A DISPLAY OF HUMILITY AND RESPECT.
IT HAD COME FULL CIRCLE. THE FATHERS WHO INSPIRED HIM TO PURSUE A LIFE OF GOODNESS WERE NOW AT HIS DOORSTEP. WASN'T THIS THE HIGHEST HONOR? WASN'T THIS A FEAT TO BE PROUD OF?

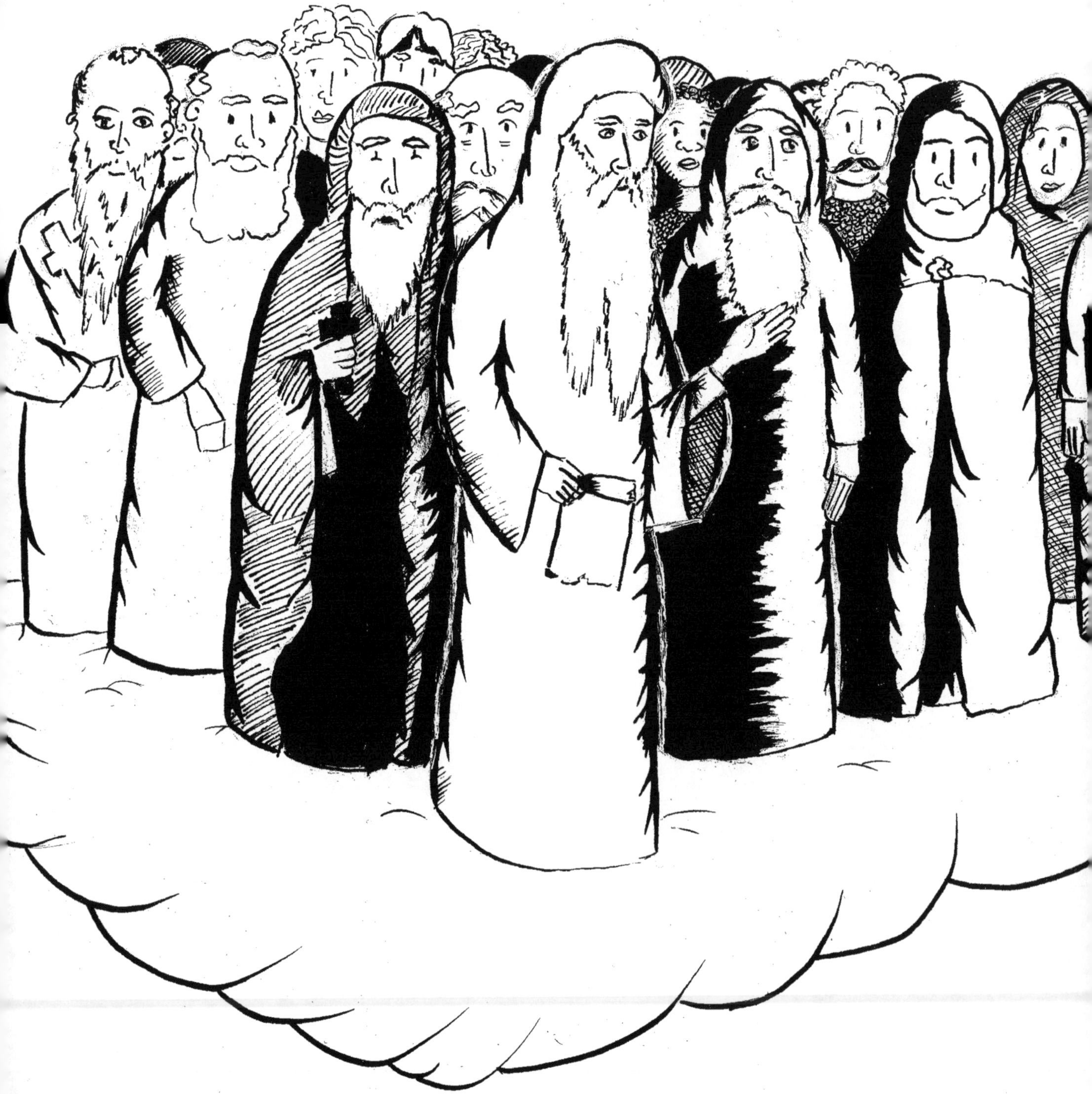

PERHAPS LITTLE JOHN WOULD HAVE BOASTED OF THIS, BUT
JOHN THE LITTLE DOESN'T KNOW PRIDE. LIKE A FRUITFUL
KERNEL OF WHEAT BOWS ITS HEAD AS IT MATURES, ABBA
JOHN SHOWED HUMILITY TO HIS VERY LAST SECOND.

WITH THIS, THE SAINTLY FATHER JOHN THE SHORT GAVE UP
THE SPIRIT.

THE YOUNG SERVANT, NOW BACK FROM THE CITY, WAS CLIMBING UP TO ABBA JOHN'S CAVE WHEN HE LOOKED UP AND SAW THE HOST OF SAINTS AND ANGELS.

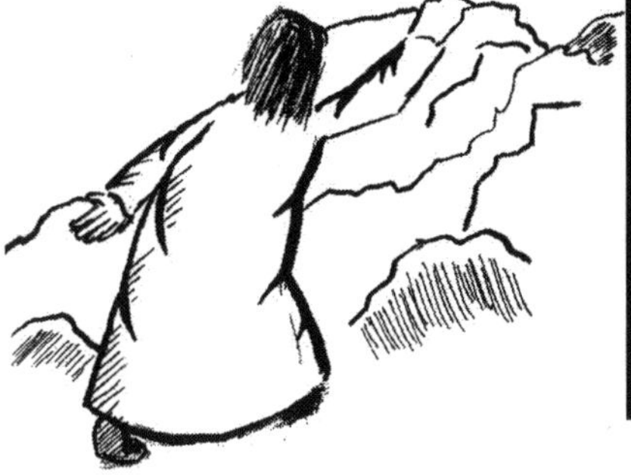

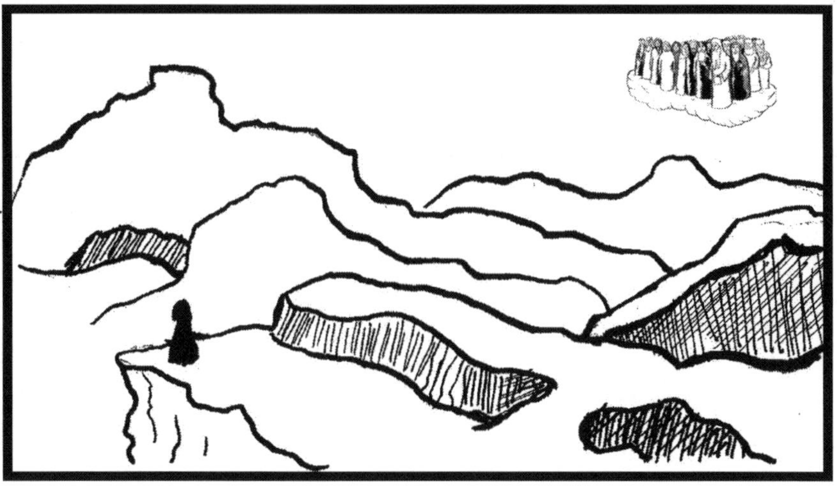

AN ANGEL OF THE LORD APPEARED TO THE YOUNG MAN AND HELPED HIM UNDERSTAND WHAT HE WAS BEHOLDING.

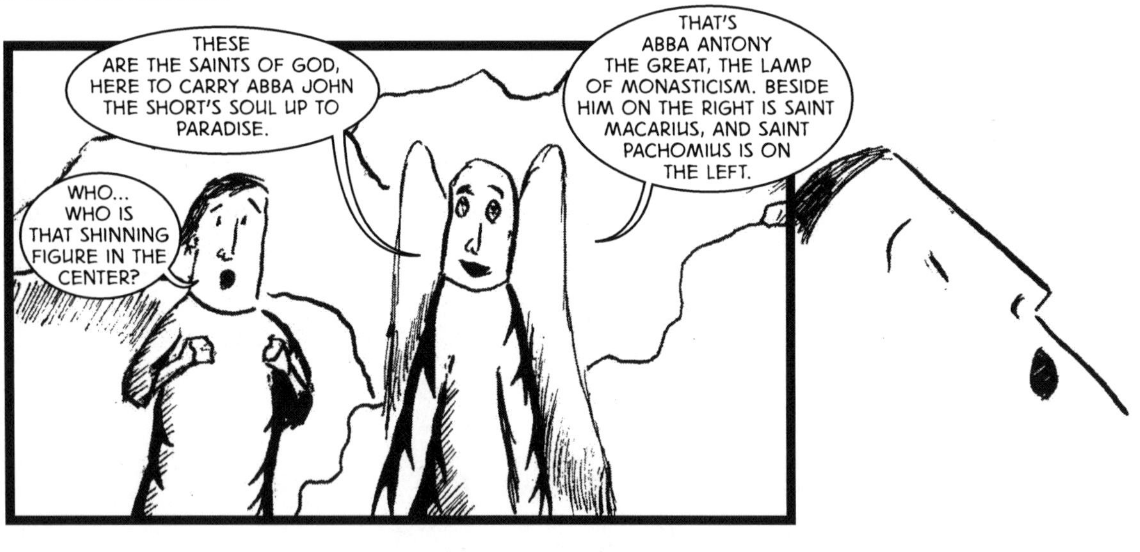
THESE ARE THE SAINTS OF GOD, HERE TO CARRY ABBA JOHN THE SHORT'S SOUL UP TO PARADISE.
WHO... WHO IS THAT SHINNING FIGURE IN THE CENTER?
THAT'S ABBA ANTONY THE GREAT, THE LAMP OF MONASTICISM. BESIDE HIM ON THE RIGHT IS SAINT MACARIUS, AND SAINT PACHOMIUS IS ON THE LEFT.

THE ANGEL CONTINUED LISTING THE SAINTS BY NAME, AND THE YOUNG MAN LISTENED IN BEWILDERMENT. ALL OF A SUDDEN, SADNESS GRIPPED HIM. HE WAS SO OVERWHELMED BY THE MAGNIFICENCE OF THIS VISION THAT HE OVERLOOKED WHAT IT MEANT.

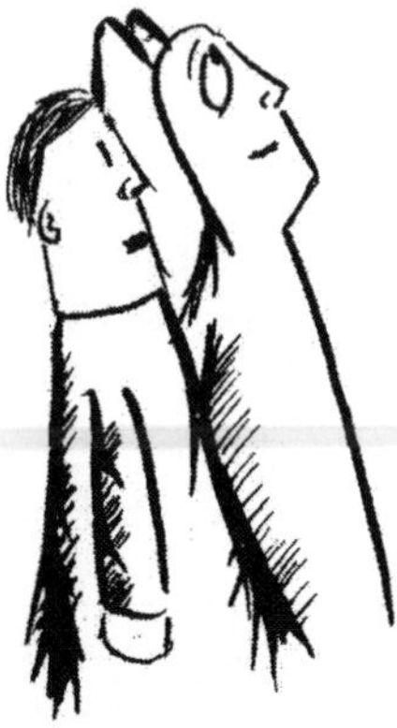

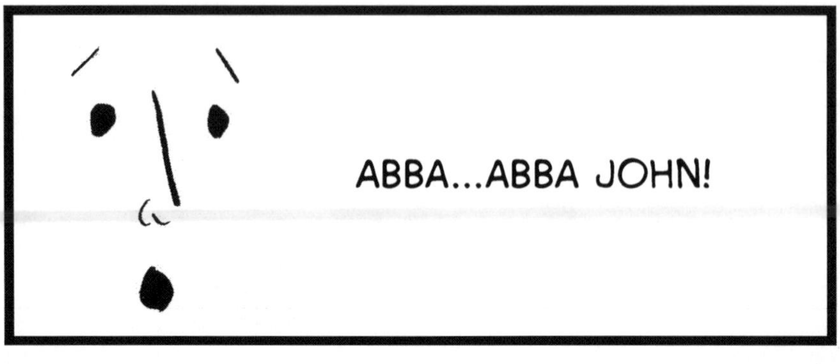
ABBA...ABBA JOHN!

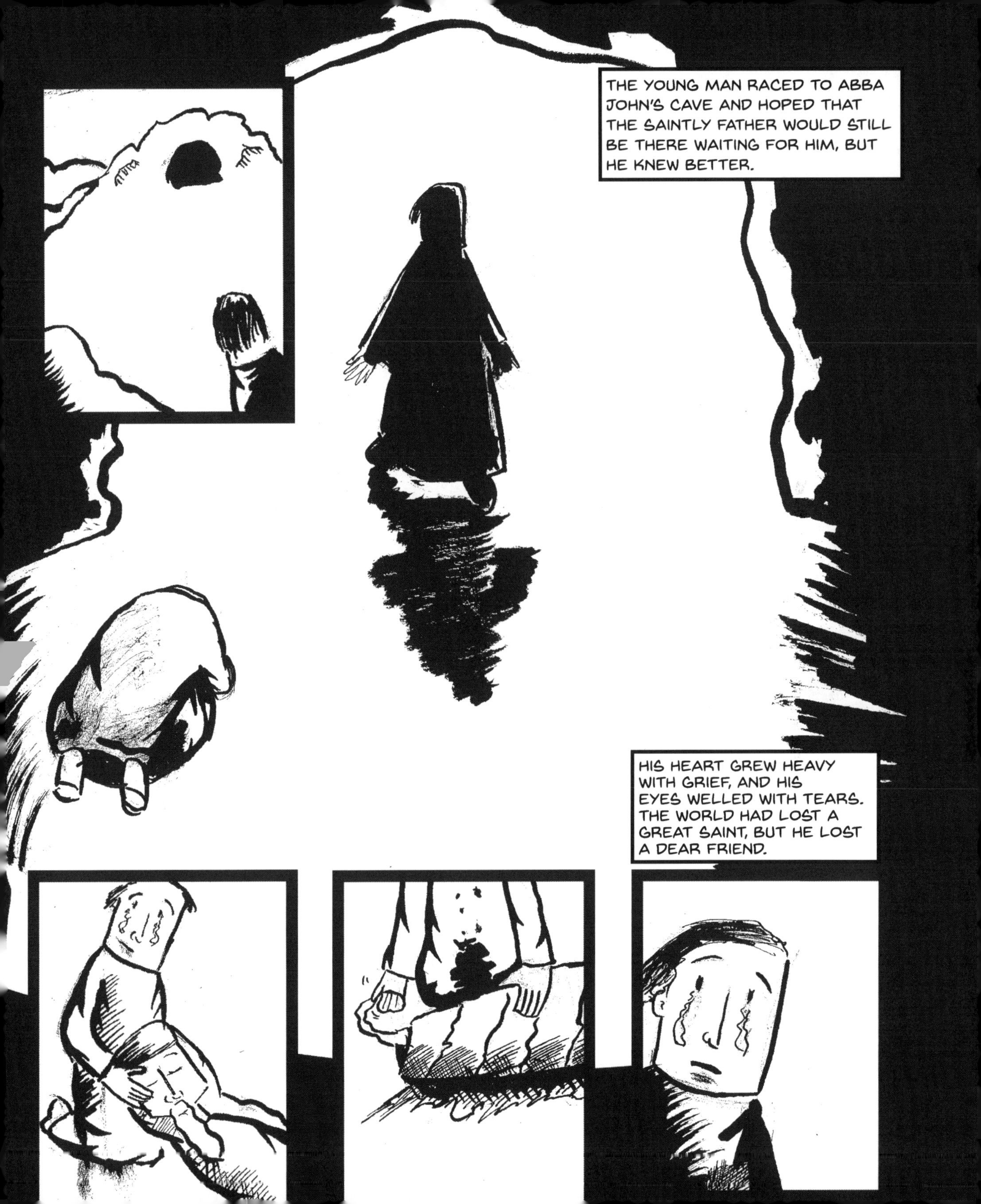
THE YOUNG MAN RACED TO ABBA JOHN'S CAVE AND HOPED THAT THE SAINTLY FATHER WOULD STILL BE THERE WAITING FOR HIM, BUT HE KNEW BETTER.
HIS HEART GREW HEAVY WITH GRIEF, AND HIS EYES WELLED WITH TEARS. THE WORLD HAD LOST A GREAT SAINT, BUT HE LOST A DEAR FRIEND.

THE DISCIPLE GENTLY WRAPPED ABBA JOHN'S BODY IN FABRIC AND FETCHED MEN FROM THE VILLAGE TO BRING ABBA JOHN'S BODY DOWN. WHEN THE CITY HEARD, IT MOURNED GREATLY FOR THE DEATH OF THE WISE ELDER, AND EVERYONE CAME TO RECEIVE HIM.

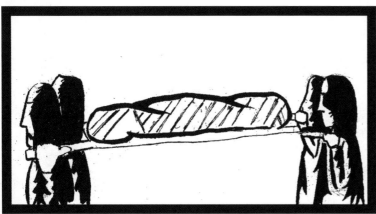

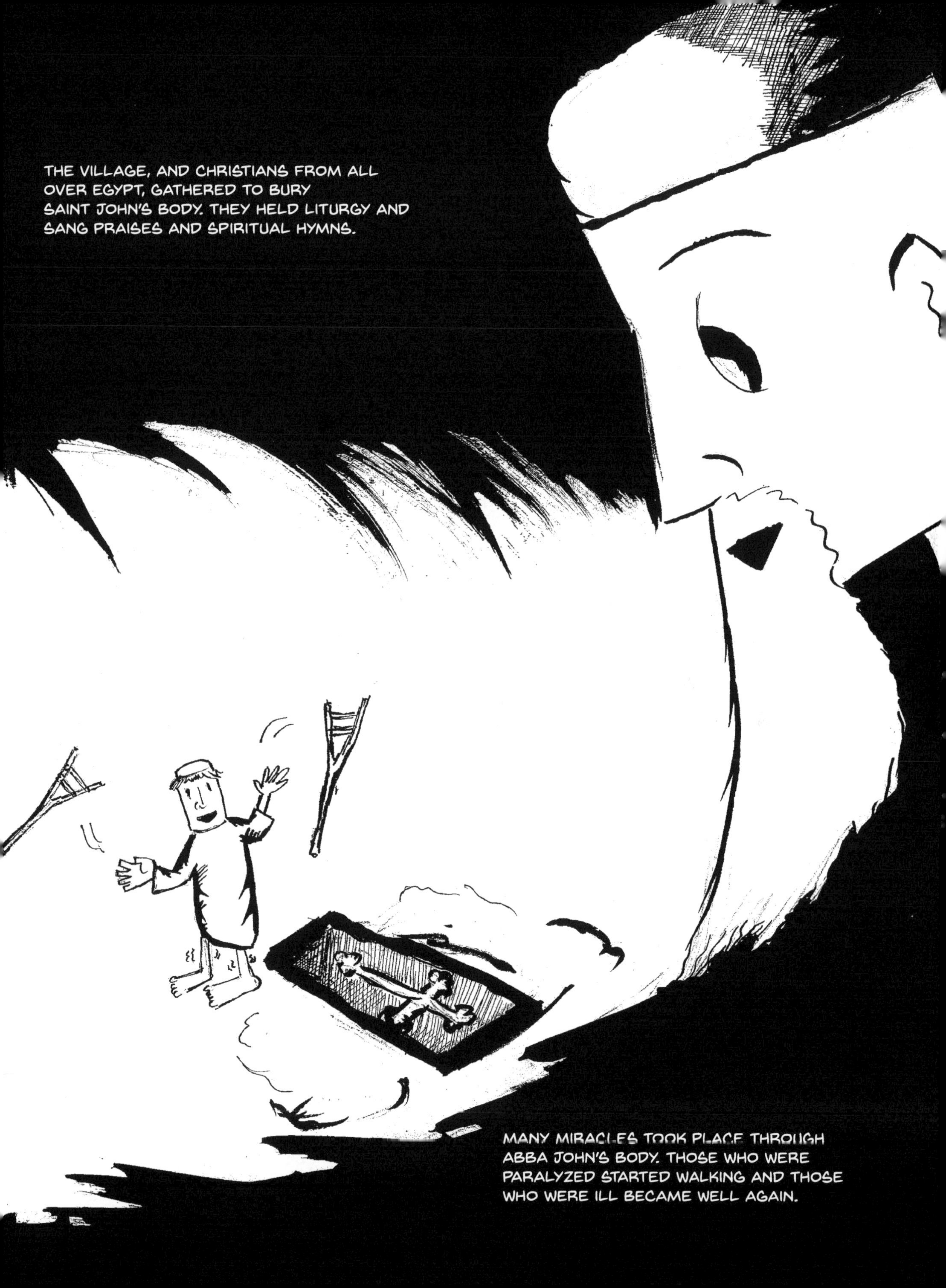
THE VILLAGE, AND CHRISTIANS FROM ALL OVER EGYPT, GATHERED TO BURY SAINT JOHN'S BODY. THEY HELD LITURGY AND SANG PRAISES AND SPIRITUAL HYMNS.
MANY MIRACLES TOOK PLACE THROUGH ABBA JOHN'S BODY. THOSE WHO WERE PARALYZED STARTED WALKING AND THOSE WHO WERE ILL BECAME WELL AGAIN.

# Epilogue

THE SAINTS OF GOD ARE LIKE TREES. THEIR LIVES START WITH SEEDS SOWN BY CHRIST THAT GROW WITH GUIDANCE AND ATTENTION TO ETERNAL LIFE INTO BEAUTIFUL TREES, THAT THEN FORM A GARDEN OF GOODNESS. EACH ONE IS VERY MUCH ALIVE AND CONTINUALLY GIVES FRUIT.

SAINT JOHN'S MONASTERY WAS ONLY SECOND TO THE MONASTERY OF SAINT MACARIUS IN SIZE AND LEADERSHIP, SERVING AS A BEACON TO CHRISTIANITY AND A LIGHT FOR THE CHURCH TO FOLLOW THROUGH THE MIDDLE AGES.

SAINT PISHOY STARTED A MONASTERY THAT EXISTS TO THIS DAY. SAINT JOHN WROTE DOWN THE STORY OF SAINT PISHOY FOR US TO LEARN FROM.

ARSENIUS GREW TO BE A PROLIFIC CHURCH SAINT, ARSENIUS THE GREAT.

ABOUT A CENTURY LATER, THE LIFE OF SAINT JOHN WAS STILL ECHOING AS AN EXAMPLE OF GOODNESS AND WAS FINALLY WRITTEN DOWN BY BISHOP ZACHARIAS OF SAKHA.

IN THE 14TH CENTURY THE STORY WAS TRANSLATED BY EMILE C. AMELINEAU, A FRENCH ARCHAEOLOGIST.

LATER IN 2004, THE MANUSCRIPT WAS TRANSLATED INTO ENGLISH BY PROFESSOR TIM VIVIAN AND DEACON SEVERUS.

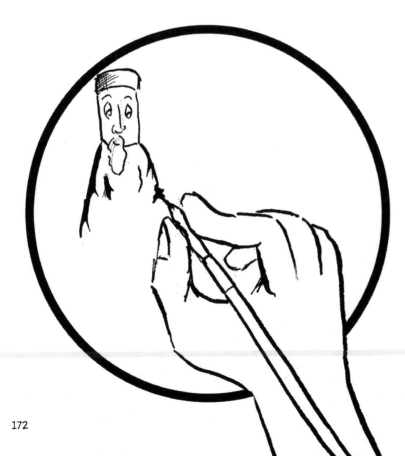

IN 2013, I READ THEIR BOOK AND WAS MOVED BY SAINT JOHN'S STORY TO WRITE AND ILLUSTRATE THIS GRAPHIC NOVEL.

THESE ARE JUST A FEW OF THE FRUITS OF SAINT JOHN THE SHORT'S LIFE.

NOW THAT YOU'VE READ HIS STORY AS WELL, THE TREE WILL ONLY KEEP BRINGING FORTH MORE FRUIT.

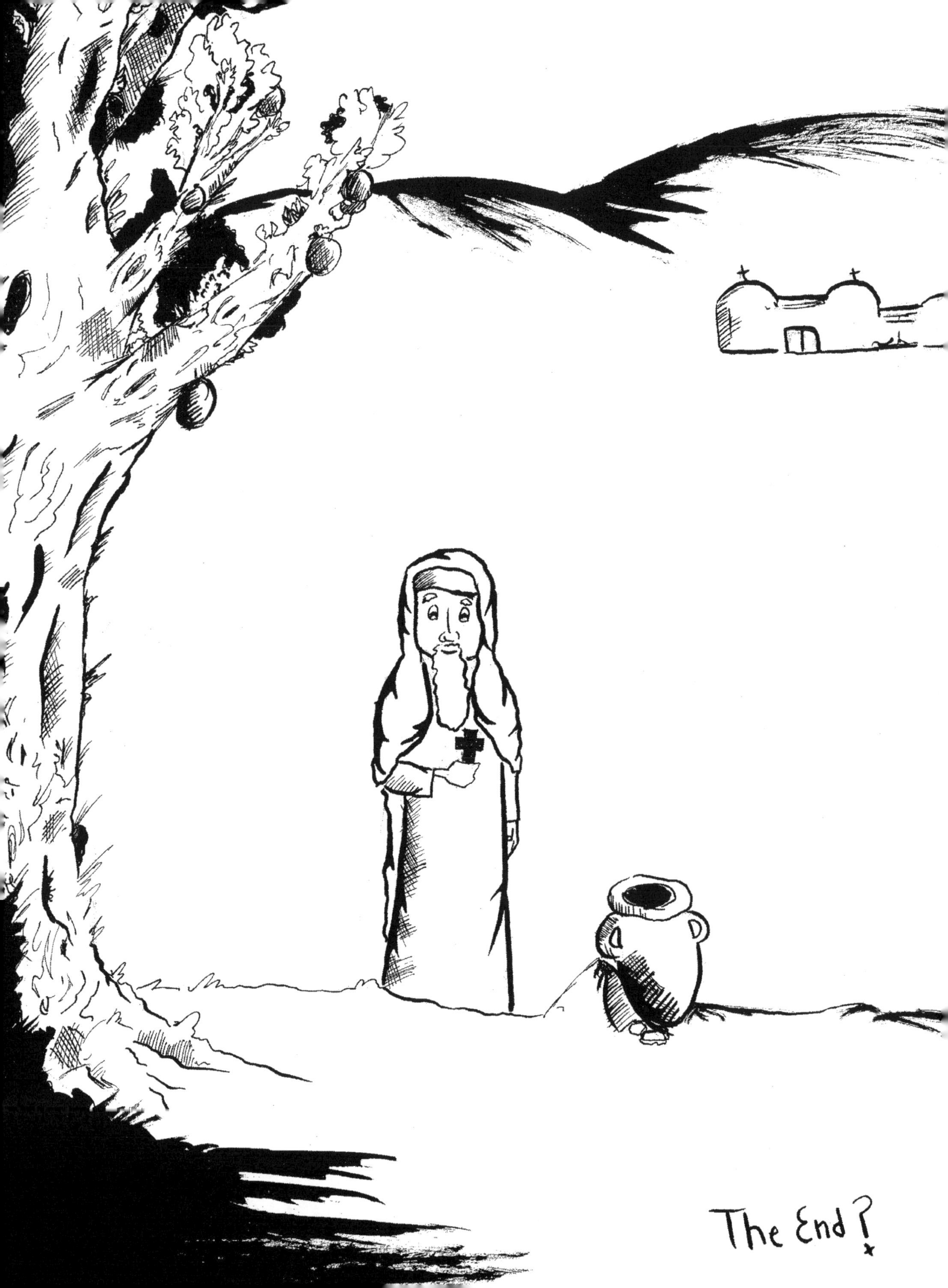
The End?

# REFERENCES

SAINT JOHN THE DWARF OF EGYPT, AND LEONIDAS PAPADOPULOS. SAINT PAISIOS THE GREAT. 1998.

VIVIAN, TIM, ET AL. THE HOLY WORKSHOP OF VIRTUE: THE LIFE OF JOHN THE LITTLE BY ZACHARIAS OF SAKHA. LITURGICAL. 2010.

YANNEY, RODOLPH. "SAINT JOHN THE SHORT." COPTIC CHURCH REVIEW, VOL. 5, NO. 3, FALL 1984, PP. 92-100.

# NOTES

### PAGE 6:
INSPIRED BY "CHRIST THE TRUE VINE", A 16TH CENTURY GREEK ICON. THE VISUAL IS BASED ON THE THEME OF JOHN CHAPTER 15. IT BREAKS OUT TO THE DESERT FATHERS AND MOTHERS TO EMPHASIZE THEIR CONNECTION TO CHRIST.

### PAGE 16:
THE STORY OF JOHN'S BROTHER ADVISING HIM AGAINST LEAVING TO BE A MONK IS THE SAME STORY ON PAGE 98. THE COPTIC MANUSCRIPT PLACES IT LATER IN JOHN'S LIFE, WHILE SCHOLARS PLACE IT EARLIER. I PUT IT IN BOTH PLACES AND USED THEM IN DIFFERENT WAYS: ONE TO HIGHLIGHT HIS GROWTH AND THAT HE WASN'T BORN READY FOR MONASTICISM, AND THE OTHER TO EMPHASIZE THAT EVEN WHEN HE'S AN ABBA HE WAS LEARNING AND GROWING.

### PAGE 15:
IF SAINT ANTONY WENT TO THE DESERT THE YEAR 300, SAINT ATHANASIUS BECAME PATRIARCH 328 AND SAINT JOHN BORN 339, THEN JOHN WOULD'VE LIKELY HEARD ABOUT SAINT ANTONY BY THE TIME HE WAS A YOUNG MAN. BASED ON A CHRONOLOGY OUTLINED IN "THE TREASURES OF COPTIC ART" BY GAWDAT GABRA AND MARIANNE EATON-KRAUSS.

### PAGE 15:
MONASTERY VISUAL IS BASED ON AN ILLUSTRATION FROM THE 1800S OF THE MONASTERY OF SAINT MACARIUS. IT CAN BE FOUND ON PAGE 84 IN "CHRISTIAN EGYPT" BY MASSIMO CAPUANI.

## PAGE 23:

THE DAILY LIFE OF MONKS IN SCETIS IS DETAILED IN AN ARTICLE BY RUDOLPH YANNEY ON SAINT JOHN THE SHORT IN "COPTIC CHURCH REVIEW".

## PAGE 29

ALTHOUGH ST. PACHOMIUS HAD CREATED WALLED MONASTIC COMMUNITIES IN UPPER EGYPT BY THE 4TH CENTURY, THEY DIDN'T MAKE IT TO SCETIS UNTIL THE 9TH CENTURY. MEANING THE MONASTERY JOHN TRAVELS TO SHOULD TECHNICALLY NOT BE THERE, BUT I FOUND HAVING A STRONG VISUAL PRESENCE OF A MONASTERY IS IMPORTANT TO THE NARRATIVE.

## PAGE 40

THE COPTIC LIFE OF SAINT JOHN DOESN'T TOUCH ON HIS TIME WITH SAINT PISHOY, BUT THE LIFE OF PISHOY WRITTEN BY SAINT JOHN THE SHORT HIMSELF DOES.

## PAGE 44

"EXCEPT THROUGH GREAT HUMILITY IN YOUR WHOLE HEART AND MIND AND SPIRIT AND SOUL AND BODY, YOU WILL NOT BE ABLE TO INHERIT THE KINGDOM OF GOD". QUOTE BY SAINT ANTONY IS FROM HIS SIXTH LETTER TO HIS DISCIPLES.

## PAGE 44

"GOD MY GOD IS THE ONE, WHO SAVED YOU FROM THE FIRE" IS A LINE FROM THE GREEK HYMN "O SING UNTO HIM" WRITTEN FOR THE THREE SAINTLY CHILDREN.

## PAGE 151

THE PATTERN BEHIND ABBA JOHN IS INSPIRED BY AN ANCIENT 6TH CENTURY COPTIC DESIGN FROM THE MONASTERY OF ST. APOLLO IN BAWIT. FOUND IN "THE TREASURES OF COPTIC ART" BY GAWDAT GABRA AND MARIANNE EATON-KRAUSS.

# SAYINGS OF ABBA JOHN

"I THINK IT IS BEST THAT A MAN SHOULD HAVE A LITTLE BIT OF ALL THE VIRTUES. THEREFORE, GET UP EARLY EVERY DAY AND ACQUIRE THE BEGINNING OF EVERY VIRTUE AND EVERY COMMANDMENT OF GOD. USE GREAT PATIENCE, WITH FEAR AND LONG-SUFFERING, IN THE LOVE OF GOD, WITH ALL THE FERVOR OF YOUR SOUL AND BODY. EXERCISE GREAT HUMILITY, BEAR WITH INTERIOR DISTRESS; BE VIGILANT AND PRAY OFTEN WITH REVERENCE, WITH PURITY OF SPEECH AND CONTROL OF YOUR EYES. WHEN YOU ARE DESPISED DO NOT GET ANGRY; BE AT PEACE, AND DO NOT RENDER EVIL FOR EVIL. DO NOT PAY ATTENTION TO THE FAULTS OF OTHERS, AND DO NOT TRY TO COMPARE YOURSELF WITH OTHERS, KNOWING YOU ARE LESS THAN EVERY CREATED THING. RENOUNCE EVERYTHING MATERIAL AND THAT WHICH IS OF THE FLESH. LIVE BY THE CROSS, IN WARFARE, IN POVERTY OF SPIRIT, IN VOLUNTARY SPIRITUAL ASCETICISM, IN FASTING, PENITENCE AND TEARS, IN DISCERNMENT, IN PURITY OF SOUL, TAKING HOLD OF THAT WHICH IS GOOD. DO YOUR WORK IN PEACE. PERSEVERE IN KEEPING VIGIL, IN HUNGER AND THIRST, IN COLD AND NAKEDNESS, AND IN SUFFERINGS."

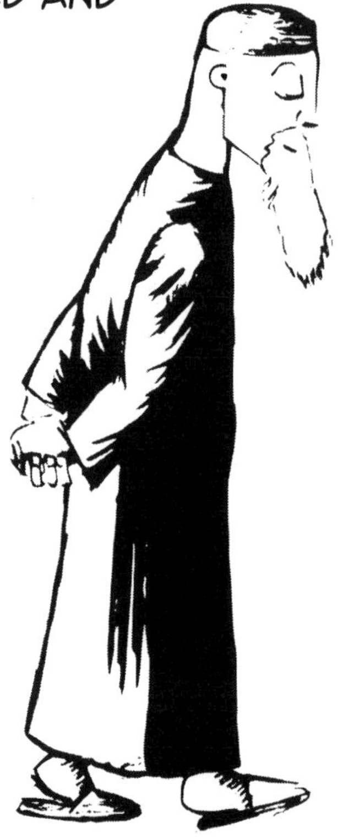

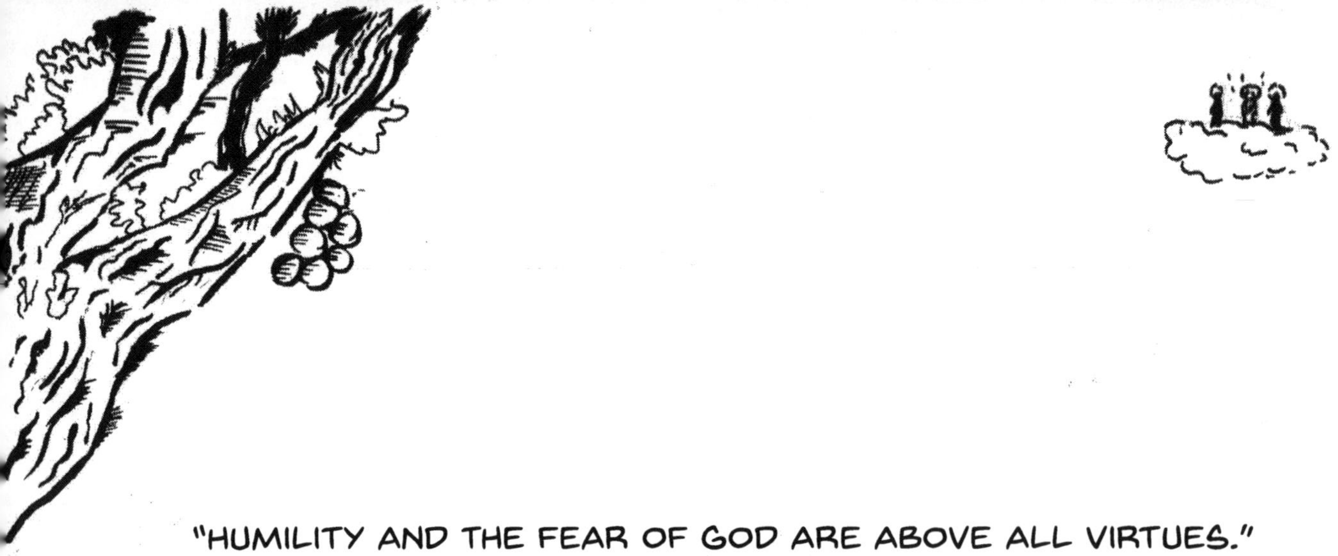

"HUMILITY AND THE FEAR OF GOD ARE ABOVE ALL VIRTUES."

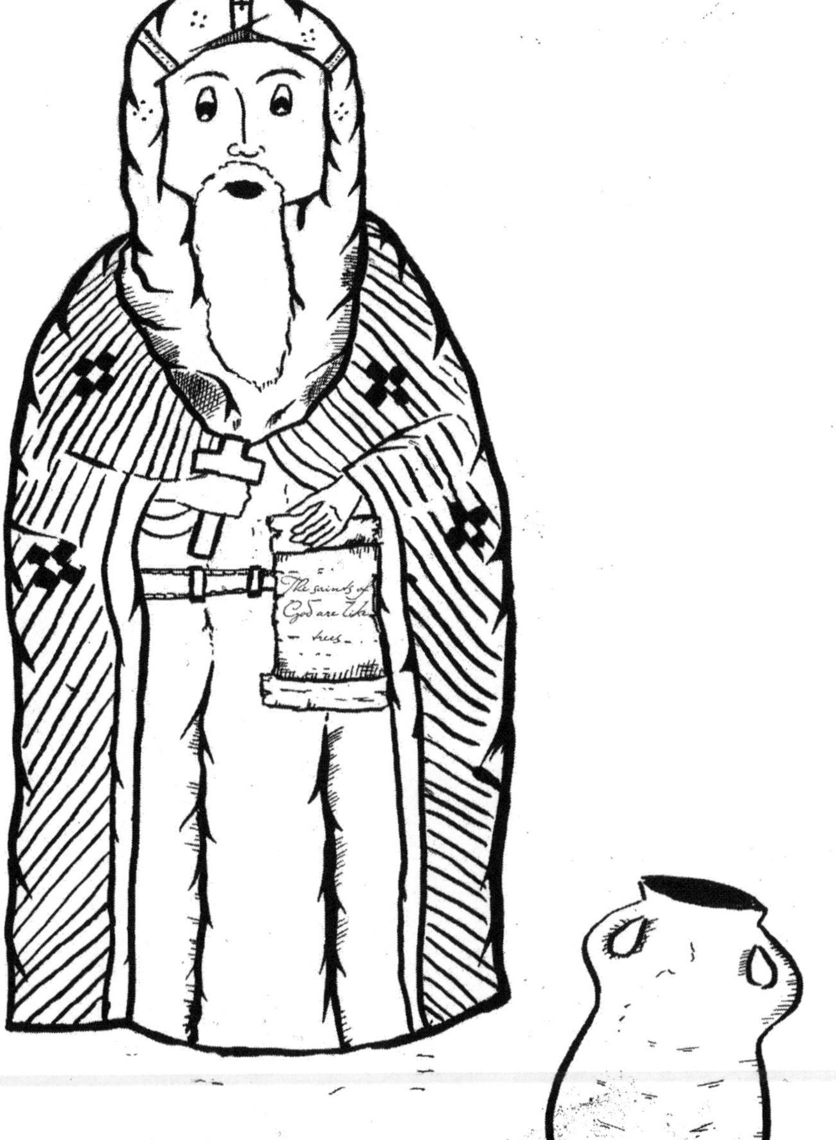
The saints of God are like trees

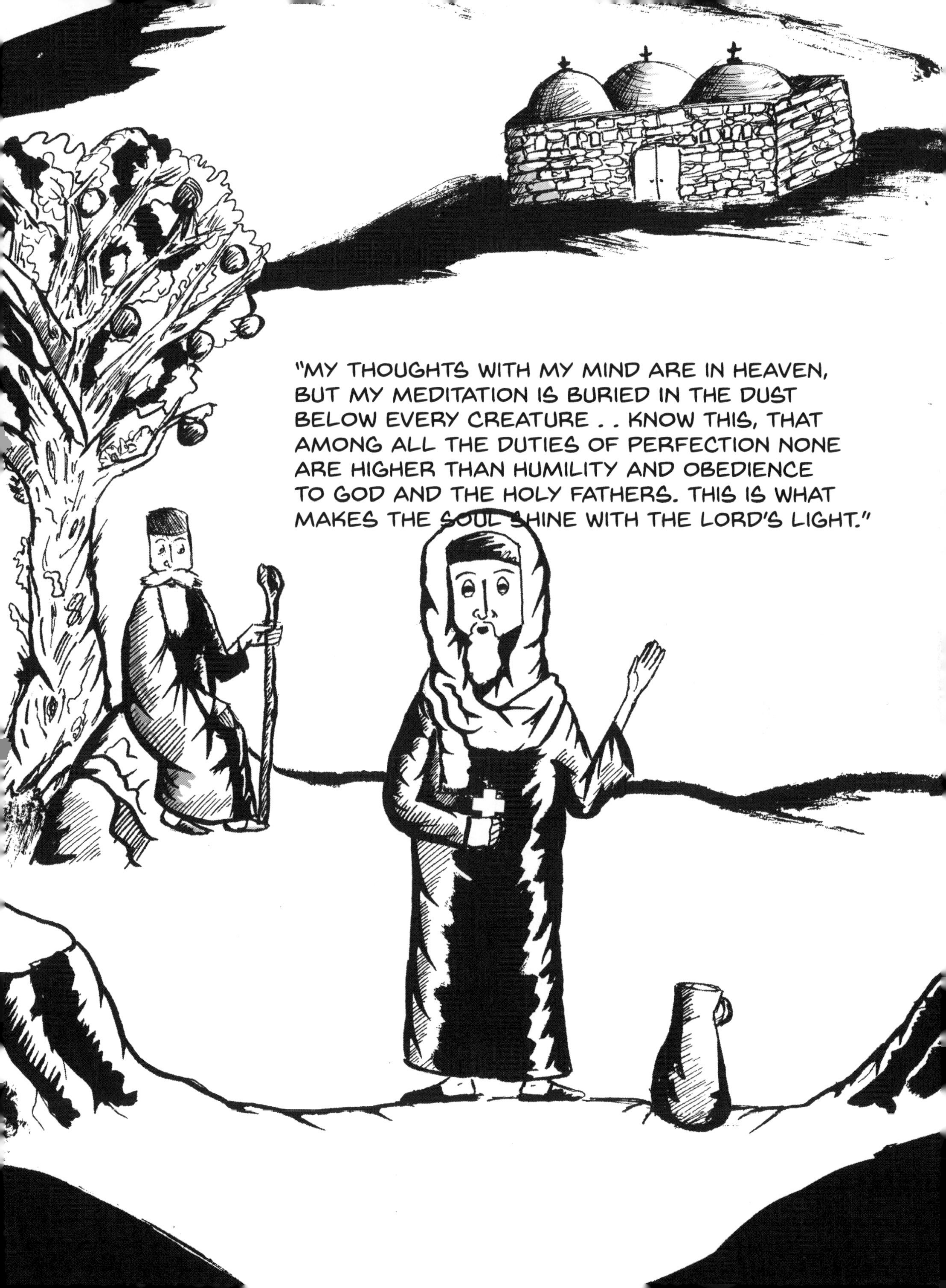
"MY THOUGHTS WITH MY MIND ARE IN HEAVEN, BUT MY MEDITATION IS BURIED IN THE DUST BELOW EVERY CREATURE . . KNOW THIS, THAT AMONG ALL THE DUTIES OF PERFECTION NONE ARE HIGHER THAN HUMILITY AND OBEDIENCE TO GOD AND THE HOLY FATHERS. THIS IS WHAT MAKES THE SOUL SHINE WITH THE LORD'S LIGHT."

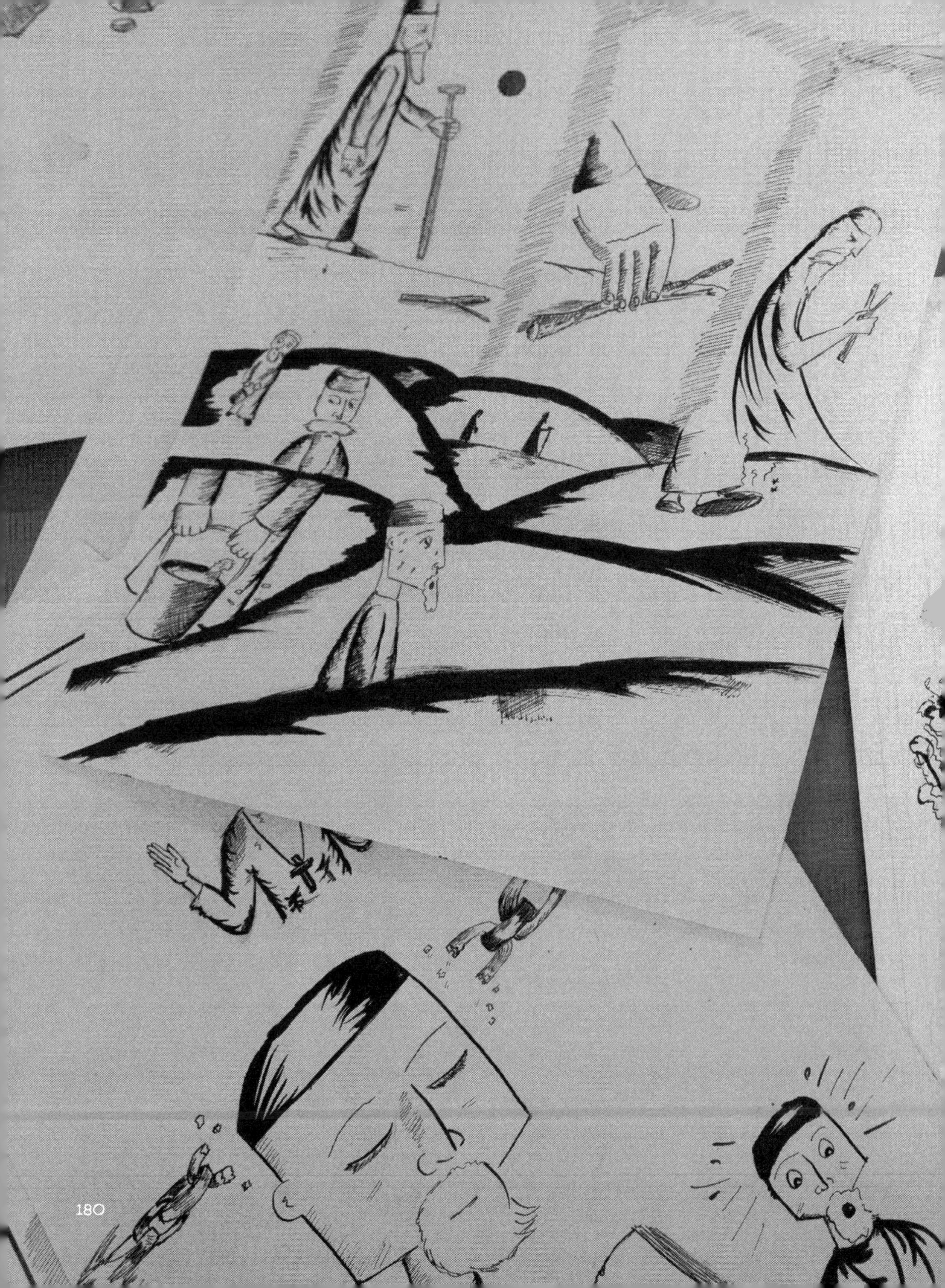

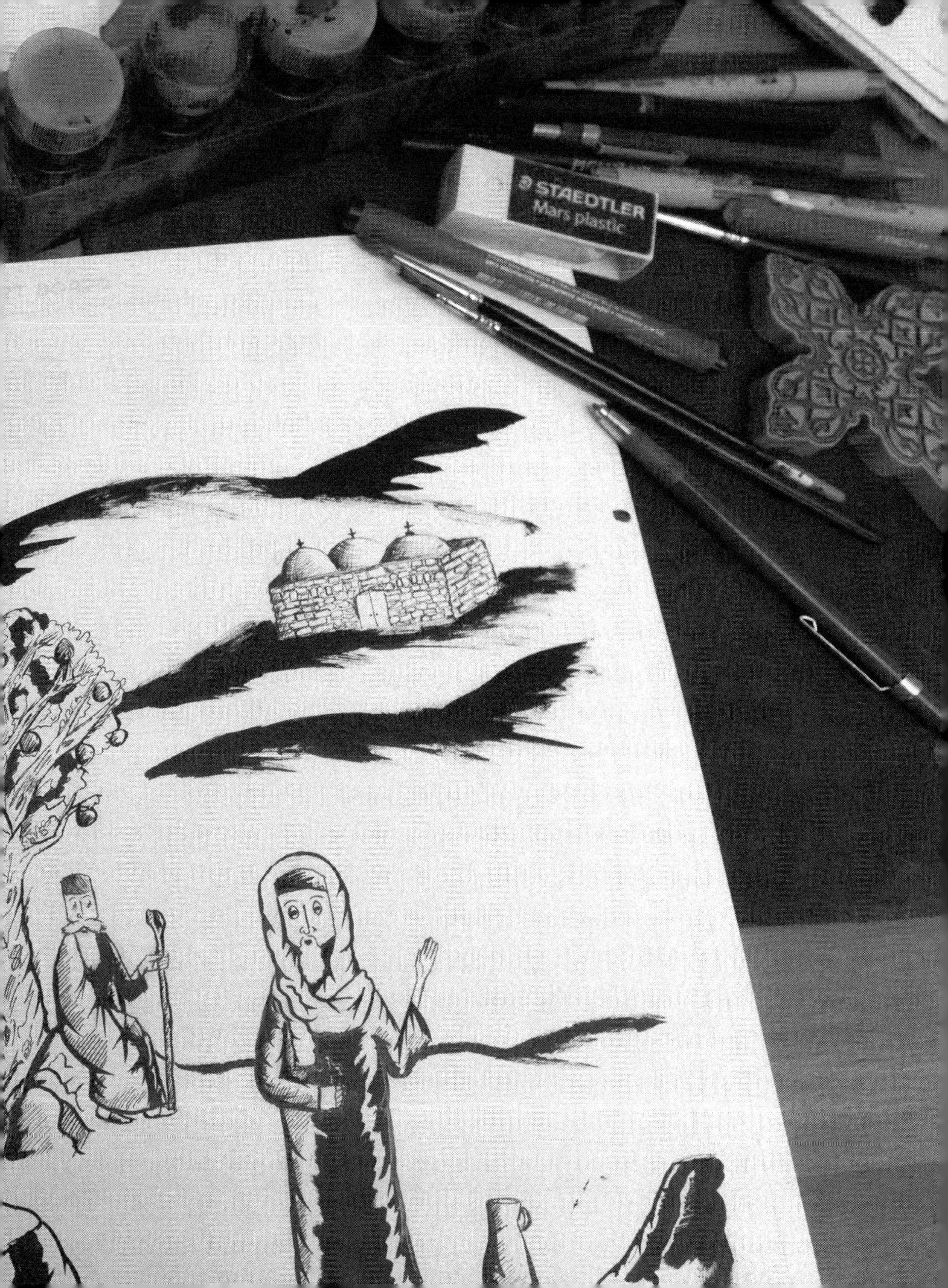
STAEDTLER
Mars plastic

# ABOUT THE AUTHOR

MICHAEL ELGAMAL IS A CANADIAN WRITER AND ARTIST. HE STARTED THE "CREATIVE ORTHODOX" BLOG TO TELL STORIES OF ANCIENT CHRISTIANITY. MICHAEL LIVES IN ONTARIO, CANADA WITH HIS WIFE MARGIE.

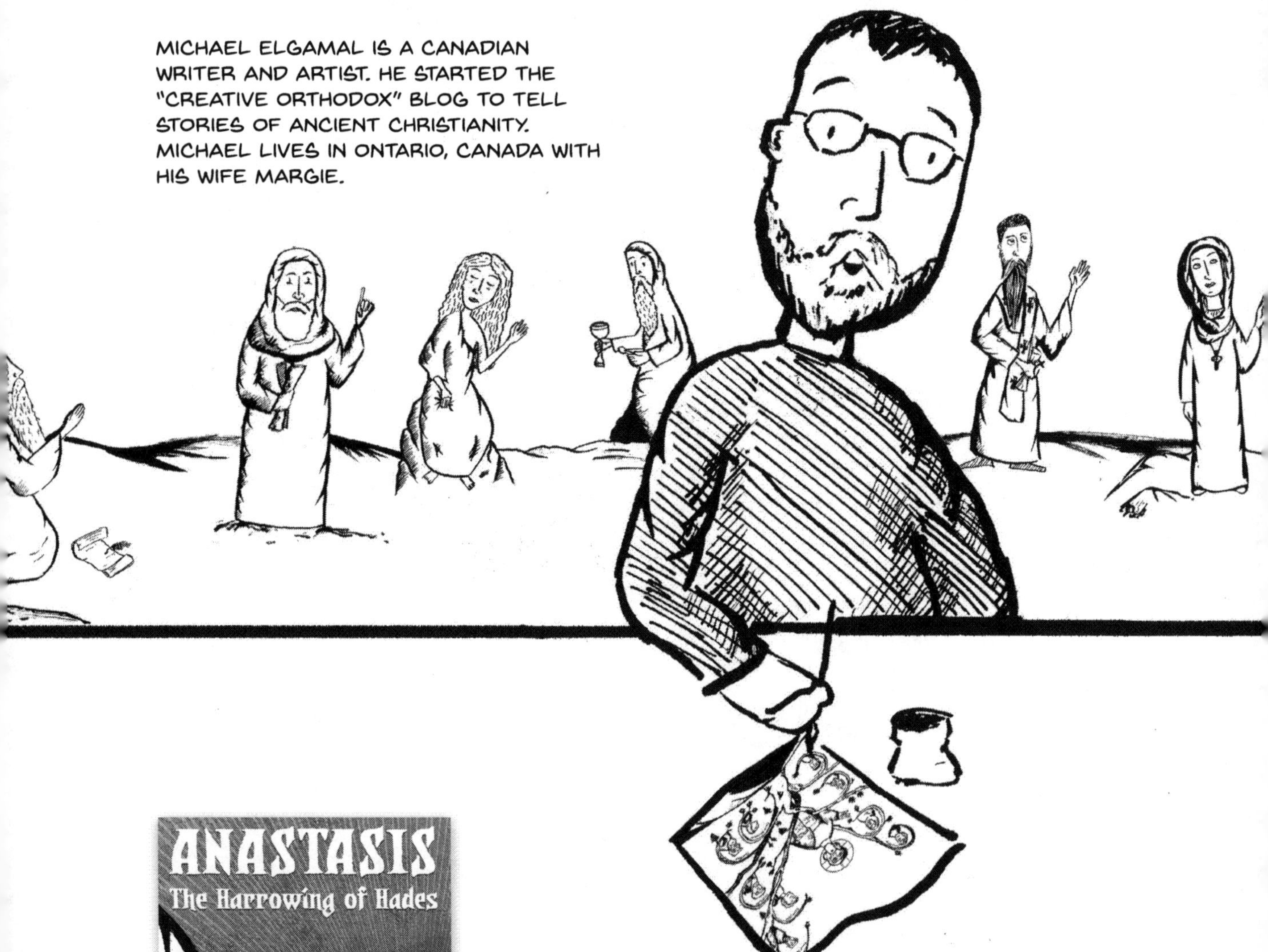

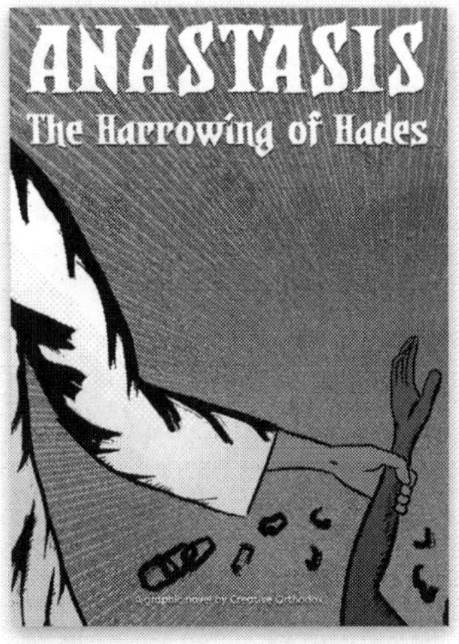
ANASTASIS
The Harrowing of Hades

***ALSO BY THE AUTHOR***

***"ANASTASIS: THE HARROWING OF HADES"***
A FULL-COLOUR GRAPHIC NOVEL THAT EXPLORES WHAT HAPPENED TO THE OLD TESTAMENT SOULS IN HADES, THE EMOTIONAL BUILD-UP TO CRUCIFIXION AND THE CONSEQUENCES OF CHRIST'S ENIGMATIC DESCENT INTO HELL.

BUY ANASTASIS TODAY!

Made in United States
Troutdale, OR
10/26/2023

14035189R00102